The Silent Church

NIHIL OBSTAT

JOHN M. A. FEARNS, S.T.D.
Censor Liborum

IMPRIMATUR

✠ FRANCIS CARDINAL SPELLMAN
Archbishop of New York

September 13, 1954

The Silent Church

Facts and Documents Concerning
Religious Persecution
Behind the Iron Curtain

by
Lino Gussoni
and
Aristede Brunello

VERITAS PUBLISHERS
Post-Office Box 234
New York

FIRST EDITION IN ENGLISH

475

*To all those who, regardless of creed,
have made the supreme sacrifice in
their testimony to Christ*

Contents

I   Soviet Russia, 1917–1952   15

   A.   First Period: Persecution in Russia Proper,
        1917–1931   17

        The Situation in 1917   17
        The Church Totally Destroyed   18

   B.   Second Period: Persecution in Former Polish
        Territories, 1939–1945   19

        Destruction of Dioceses of the Latin Rite   20
        Persecution of Catholic Ruthenians   22

   C.   Third Period: Persecution in the Baltic States   33

        The Situation in 1940   33
          a)   Lithuania   33
          b)   Latvia   35
          c)   Esthonia   36

        Suppression During the First Occupation
        (June 1940–June 1941)   36
          a)   Lithuania   37
          b)   Latvia   45
          c)   Esthonia   46

        The Church After the Second Occupation (1944)   47
          a)   Lithuania   47
          b)   Latvia and Esthonia   58

   D.   Fourth Period: Suppression of the Greek-Catholic
        Church in Annexed Areas   58

II   Poland, 1945–1952   63

        The Beginnings of the Struggle   64
        A More Serious Situation After the Elections of
        January 17, 1947   70

The Campaign Against the Hierarchy and the
Clergy   74
The Attack Against "Caritas" and Attempted
Coercion of the Episcopate   79
The Agreement of April 14, 1950   87
The Communication of the Episcopate and the
Meaning of the Agreement   91
The Government Violates the Agreement First   93
The Episcopate's Courageous Memorandum to
the President of the Republic   96
Recent Events   103
Conclusion   108

III   Roumania   109

    A. Suppression of the Catholic Church of the
        Byzantine Rite   109

        The Situation of the Roumanian (Uniate)
        Catholic Church Before 1948   109
        Precursors of the Persecution of Religion   111
        The Decree of August 4: The New Regulation
        of Religions   117
        The Protest of the Apostolic Nunciature   123
        The Decisions of the Assembly of Cluj   127
        The Motion of the Assembly of Alba-Julia
        (October 21, 1948)   132
        Arrest and Internment of All Bishops   134
        Definitive Suppression by Decree of the
        Presidium of the RPR   135

    B. Suppression of the Catholic Church of the
        Latin Rite   136

        Reduction of Dioceses From Six to Two   136
        Arrest and Internment of All Bishops   137
        Suppression of All Religious Orders (Decree
        29, July 29, 1949)   138
        Arrest and Trial of the Bishop Mons. Pacha
        (September 1951)   141

    C. Conclusion   143

IV   Hungary, 1945–1953   145

  A.   Persecution of the Church   145
      The Situation in 1945   145
      First Communist Contacts With the Church
      (October 1944–December 1945)   147
      The Government Brings the Struggle Out Into
      the Open (January–August 1946)   149

  B.   Suppression of All Religious Associations and All
     Cultural, Social and Welfare Organizations of
     the Catholic Church (Decree 7330 1946 M.E.)   157
      The Struggle Begins Against Associations and
      Organizations   158
      Dissolution of Associations and Organizations
      Decreed (Decree 7330/46 M.E.)   160
      Vain Protests of the Episcopate   161
      Suppression of "Caritas" and All Other Aid
      Organizations   162

  C.   Suppression of Educational and Secular Institu-
     tions (Decree Law XXXIII, 1948) and Abolition
     of Compulsory Religious Instruction (Decree,
     September 5, 1949)   164
      Vain Protests of the Episcopate   175
      Suppression of All Colleges and Other
      Educational Institutions   178

  D.   Suppression of the Press   178

  E.   Suppression of All Outer Manifestations of the
     Faith, Including Religious Feasts   184
      Suppression of Religious Broadcasts   184
      Suppression of Every Individual and
      Collective Right   185

  F.   Dissolution of All Religious Orders (Decree,
     June 7 and September 7, 1950)   187
      The First Skirmishes   187
      Religious Orders Dissolved by Decree   190
      New Deportation Measures   192

G. The Open Struggle Against the Episcopate   194

    Arrest and Trial of Cardinal Mindszenty   199

H. Conclusion   204

    A List of Priests and Monks Assassinated,
Jailed, Interned or Deported   204

    Balance Sheet of Church Losses, 1945–1951   207

v   Czechoslovakia   210

A. Beginnings of Communist Persecution
(1945–1948)   210

    The Situation in 1945–1947   210

    Episcopal Attitude Toward Events of
February 1948   216

    The "Te Deum" for Gottwald's Election as
President of the Republic (June 14, 1948)   220

    Beginning of Systematic Persecution   222

       a) Suppression of the Catholic Press   222

       b) Nationalization of Catholic Schools   223

       c) Suppression of Catholic Action   224

    The Memorandum of Mons. Beran (April 4,
1949)   226

B. Attempts to Form a National Catholic Church
(May 1949–January 1950)   231

    Isolation of Bishops and Invitation to Clergy
to Cut Itself Off From the Hierarchy   231

    Bishops' Protest Letter to the Ministry of
Public Instruction (May 17, 1949)   232

    Secret Circular of the Episcopate to the
Clergy (May 17, 1949)   235

    Circular of the Archbishop of Prague
(May 28, 1949)   237

    Government Proclaims New "Catholic Action"   239

    New Intervention of the Bishops
(June 15, 1949)   243

The Police Confiscate the Bishop's Letter and
Occupy the Prague Archbishopric   245
A New Grave Joint Letter of the Episcopate
(June 19, 1949)   249
Condemnation by the Holy Office and Failure
of the Communist Catholic Action   255

C. Internment of Mons. Beran and Arrest of Others   256
Archbishop Mons. Beran   256
Protest to the Attorney General (August 5,
1949)   259
Recall of the Chargé d'Affaires of the Holy See   263
Anti-religious Laws   265
Intervention of the Holy See   268
Breaking Off Diplomatic Relations With the
Holy See   270
Trials of Exponents of the Clergy   274
The First Big Trial Against Ten Priests
(April 31, 1950)   275

D. Attempts to Form a "National Church"
(April 1950–June 1952)   280
Arrest and "Concentration" of All Members
of Religious Orders   280
The Communist Press "Explains" the Arrests   282
Harsh Treatment of Monks   283
New Attempts to Form a "National Catholic
Church"   285
Nationalization of Seminaries and Theological
Schools Abolished   287
Trial of Bishop Mons. Zela and Eight Others
(November–December 1950)   289
Trials of Three Bishops and Many Priests and
Monks (January–February 1951)   290
Attempts to Establish a New Hierarchy   293
The Holy See Condemns the New Hierarchy   295
Recent Developments (June 1951–June 1952)   298

VI Albania, 1944–1952   303

    The Situation Before 1944   303
    Immediate Suppression of Newspapers and
    Associations   307
    Searches and Arrests in the Religious Houses
    (December 1944–February 1945)   308
    Persecution of Institutions and Agencies in
    Northern Albania (March–April 1945)   310
    Expulsion of Apostolic Delegate (May 24, 1945)   311
    Suppression of Schools, and Campaign Against
    Religious Orders (May–December 1945)   312
    Two Jesuits Sentenced to Death (January–
    February 1946)   313
    Expulsion of Italian Missionaries   314
    Extermination of Priests and Churches
    (March–December 1946)   315
    The Trial of Tirana (April 1947)   317
    Imprisonment of the Metropolitan of Durazzo
    and Execution of the Bishops of Sappa and
    Alessio (February–March 1948)   319
    Attempts to Create a National Catholic
    Church (June–August 1952)   321
    The New "Regulation" Approved (March 17,
    1952)   323
    Conclusion: Balance Sheet to December 1952   324

VII Bulgaria, 1945–1952   326

    The Situation in 1944   326
    The First Three Years of the Communist
    Regime (1944–1947)   328
    Suppression of Schools and Other Educational
    Institutions (1948)   329
    Closing the Apostolic Delegation   332
    The Final Phase of the Persecution   333

VIII Jugoslavia, 1944–1952   338

    The Church, Its Geographical and Statistical
    Distribution in Jugoslavia   338
    The Beginning of the Struggle   340
    Trial of Archbishop Mons. Stepinac and
    Three Bishops   349
    Communist Persecution After Stepinac's
    Sentencing   354
    The Last Stages of the Persecution (1951–1952)   360
    The Rupture of Diplomatic Relations With
    the Holy See   381

Sources and Bibliography   384

    a)   General View   384
    b)   Russia and the Baltic Countries   385
    c)   Poland   387
    d)   Roumania   387
    e)   Hungary   388
    f)   Czechoslovakia   389
    g)   Albania   390
    h)   Bulgaria   390
    i)   Jugoslavia   390

CHAPTER I

Soviet Russia, 1917–1952

Russia was the first country in which the Communist Government, hardly upon seizing power, unleashed its campaign of persecution against the Catholic Church. The phases of this monstrous struggle, among the most serious recorded in the history of mankind, can be divided into four distinct periods:

First period (1917–1931), during which the Russian Communist Government carried on a systematic decimation of the Catholic Church existing within the confines of pre-Soviet Russia, destroying within a time span of a little over 13 years 5 Dioceses, 681 parishes and 980 churches; in the process a total of 13 Bishops, 912 priests and approximately 1,600,000 of the faithful were arrested, scattered or deported.

Second period (1939–1941), during which the Russian Communist Government proceeded to exterminate the entire Catholic Church in the former Polish territories, annexed to Russia in 1939 following the Russo-German pact of September, 1939, in which were included 9 Archdioceses and Dioceses to which an approximate total of 8,437,000 Catholics, 5,340 priests, and 4,843 parishes belonged.

Third period (1939–1944), during which the Russian Communist Government undertook the systematic decimation of the Catholic Church in Lithuania, Esthonia and Latvia, driving between 12 and 14 Bishops from their Sees in the space of two years, arresting more than a thousand priests, and deporting more than a million of the faithful to Siberia or exterminating them on the spot.

Fourth period (1945–1952), during which the Russian Communist Government, which in the meantime had seized other territories formerly belonging to Hungary, Czechoslovakia and Poland, proceeded to carry out the total extermination of the last Catholic communities existing in these territories.

These included a total of about 600,000 faithful, 300 priests and several hundred churches, institutions, schools and other Catholic agencies.

In these four periods, which comprehensively embrace a time period of approximately thirty years, the Soviet Communist Government has destroyed or reduced practically to naught five entire ecclesiastical provinces having a complex of 24 Archdioceses and Dioceses; deported, dispersed or killed 27 Archbishops and Bishops; arrested, interned or executed 7000 priests; closed, confiscated or destroyed 8000 churches; requisitioned or incorporated 3000 religious houses and institutions; arrested, dispersed or exiled 10,000 monks and nuns; suppressed hundreds of colleges, shelters, schools, hospitals, and other Catholic welfare agencies; deported under unimaginable conditions to Siberia and elsewhere more than five million Catholics, and subjected the rest to the most terrible persecutions and vexations.

The documented proofs of this frightening work of destruction, carried out by the Russian Communist Government against the Catholic Church from 1917 to today, will be reported in the following pages and they will constitute the most serious act of accusation against a Government and regimes which prefer to designate themselves as "democratic."

A. FIRST PERIOD:
PERSECUTION IN RUSSIA PROPER, 1917–1931

THE SITUATION IN 1917

In 1917, when the Communists in Russia seized power, the Catholic Church constituted only a small minority, that is, about 3% of the total population. The overwhelming majority of the population, indeed about 80%, belonged to the Orthodox Church which was the only one officially recognized by the Czars and which was accorded special priveleges. The Catholic Church and the other religious minorities (Protestants, Jews, Moslems, etc.) were tolerated merely and in the Russian "Svod Zakanov," a collection of laws, they were listed as "foreign religious confessions."

Nevertheless, at the moment of Communist seizure of power in November 1917, the Catholic Church in Russia had developed to a point where it numbered in its fold a Catholic population of almost 1,600,000, living in the old and new territories definitively ceded to Russia by the Treaty of Riga in 1921. They were distributed in the following five large Dioceses:

1) *Archdiocese of Mohilev:* It included the northern territories of Russia, its principal seat was in Petersburg, and under its jurisdiction it numbered 300,000 faithful, 131 parishes, 226 churches, 324 priests, an Ecclesiastical Academy in Petersburg, and various other Catholic institutions.

2) *Diocese of Minsk:* This was an auxiliary of that of Mohilev and it included the territories of White Russia with about 200,000 faithful, 103 priests, 57 parishes and more than one hundred churches.

3) *Diocese of Lutskzytomir:* It covered the territories of Volinia with approximately 300,000 faithful, 127 parishes, 200 churches and 90 priests. It included the principal Catholic centers of Kiev, with 39,000 Catholics; *Zytomir,* with 20,000; *Zviahl* with 19,000, *Polonne* with 10,000, *Lutsk,* with 6000. In addition there was a convent at *Zaslow* with 11 monks and a famous sanctuary at *Berdycev.*

4) *Diocese of Kamieniec-Podolsk for the territories of Podolia:*
This was situated in the southern part of Russia between the
Bug and the Dniester rivers. It numbered about 320,000 faithful,
108 parishes, 116 churches, 90 priests and a certain number of
religious houses and institutions.

5) *Diocese of Tiraspol:* With its principal seat in *Saratov,* it
covered the territories in the region of the Volga, Georgia,
Crimea and the Caucasus. It numbered about 360,000 faithful,
125 parishes, 218 churches, and 179 priests. It also had a large
seminary in *Saratov* and a certain number of religious institutions
and houses. Among its most important Catholic centers were
Odessa, with 30,000 Catholics, *Cherson* with 15,000, *Sebastapol*
with 10,000, *Saratov* with 6000, and *Tiflis* with 15,000.

There were moreover, in the territory of the Latin Diocese,
about 38,000 Armenian Catholics, administered to by an Apostolic Administrator with his seat in Tiflis. They were distributed
among 56 parishes, assisted by about sixty priests, all of the
Armenian rite.

In addition to these large groups of Catholics existing in
Russia proper, there were in Asiatic Russia other groups whose
total number was about 150,000 Catholics. They were distributed
in 37 parishes with about forty priests, attached to the "Apostolic
Vicariate of Siberia," with its seat in *Vladivostok* and with centers in *Omsk, Tomsk, Irkutsk* and *Taszkient.*

THE CHURCH TOTALLY DESTROYED

Already in 1931, after hardly fourteen years of Communist
power in Russia, of all this vast complex of faithful, Dioceses and
Catholic institutions, there did not exist a single Diocese, a single
Bishop, a single Catholic parish. By 1934 the Communist persecution against the Catholic Church could be said to have been
concluded, with the following tragic balance sheet:

	1917	1934
Archdioceses and Dioceses	7	none (100% destroyed)
Bishops and Apostolic Administrators	21	none (all imprisoned, deported, or exiled)
Churches or Chapels	980	3 (1 in Moscow, St. Louis of the French; 1 in Leningrad; 1 in Odessa)
Parishes	681	none (100% destroyed)
Priests and Members of Religious Orders	912	10 (80% killed, deported or disappeared; 10% expelled or exiled; 9% in hiding)
Religious Institutions and Houses	200	none (100% detroyed)
Schools and Charitable Activities	300	none (100% detroyed)
Ecclesiastical Seminaries and Academies	4	none (100% detroyed)
Catholic Press and Publications	10	none (100% detroyed)

B. SECOND PERIOD:
PERSECUTION IN FORMER POLISH TERRITORIES,
1939–1945

In November 1939, as a consequence of the Russian-German agreements, a large part of eastern Poland fell into the hands of

the Russians. Having just finished the destruction of the Catholic
Church once existent within the borders of Russia proper, as has
been seen, the Russians immediately dedicated themselves to
the systematic annihilation of all the Dioceses and Catholic institutions which had flourished in the former Polish territories.

The work of annihilation begun in 1939 and suspended in
1941—as a result of the occupation of those territories by the
Germans—was again resumed in 1944, following the defeat of
the Germans and it was definitely completed in 1945.

It was in this relatively brief period that the Russian Communists succeeded in bringing about the disappearance of 5
Latin Dioceses, 3 Ruthenian Dioceses and an Armenian Diocese,
with a total of about 8,437,000 Catholics, 4,843 parishes and
5,340 priests.

The stages of this progressive annihilation are documented
by an entire series of legislative enactments, police measures,
arrests, threats, deportations, etc., as regards the Dioceses of the
Latin rite. For the Dioceses of the eastern rite the destruction
of the Catholic Hierarchy took place by means of a forced entry
en masse of Catholics into the "Orthodox Russian Church."

DESTRUCTION OF DIOCESES OF THE LATIN RITE

1) *Archdiocese of Vilno:* This was one of the most ancient
Polish Catholic Dioceses, established in 1386, at the time of the
conversion of Lithuanian pagans to the Catholic faith. In 1939,
almost all of its territory fell under Soviet domination and a part
of it was annexed to the "Belo-Russian Republic, another part to
the Lithuanian republic, while a small part remained on Polish
territory. The Archbishop, Mons. Romauld Jalbrzykowski, who
had administered the Archdiocese from 1926, was forced to retire
to that portion of the Diocese which remained in Polish territory,
transferring his seat to Bialystok, where he is still at present with
his auxiliary, Mons. Ladislus Suszynski. His other auxiliary,
Archbishop Mons. Miecislus Reinys, who had remained to administer the Diocese in the area annexed to the Russians, was
arrested by the Russians as early as May 1947, immediately following an interview he gave to the Soviet "Tass" Agency. He was

deported to Russia and since then there has been no further news of him.

The Archdiocese numbered about 600 churches, 442 parishes, 560 priests and 1,052,000 Catholics. There is almost no news whatsoever of the fate which has been theirs. It is known that many churches are closed in the city of Vilno and in the countryside; that a large part of the clergy, which remained with the faithful, has disappeared; that a part of the population has been deported to Siberia and that in their stead members of different Mongolian tribes have been imported from the Asian steppes. These are largely pagan "Shamanists."

Even the ancient and celebrated university of Vilno, established by the Catholic hierarchy, has disappeared and with it all the schools, seminaries, colleges, and Catholic welfare agencies and institutions.

2) *Diocese of Pinsk:* It underwent the same fate as that of Vilno under whose jurisdiction it functioned. Its Bishop, Mons. Casmir Bukraba, who had administered it since 1932, died in exile in 1947. The assistant Bishop, Mons. Charles Niemira is still in exile. As a consequence no Bishop has administered this Diocese since 1947. Recently the Holy See has appointed an Apostolic Administrator for that part of the Diocese which remained on Polish territory, Mons. Michael Krzyski, who resides in a village situated east of the Curzon-Ribbentrop-Molotov line, called Drohiczyn N/Bugiem in Bialystok.

The Diocese, which once numbered 302 churches, 133 parishes, 148 priests and 565,000 Catholics, has almost been reduced to naught. The majority of the clergy has disappeared, almost all of the churches are closed, and a substantial part of the faithful has been deported. And this is all that can be said about this Diocese which was the birthplace of Saint Andrew Bobola.

3) *The Latin Archdiocese of Leopoli:* This was one of the most ancient, founded as early as 1492 and then divided into two jurisdictions in 1540, one for the faithful of the Latin rite and the other for those who practiced the Eastern or the Ruthenian rites. It had 997 churches, 416 parishes, 795 priests and almost 1,000,000 faithful. The venerable Archbishop, Mons. Boleslao Twardowski, was forced to leave the Diocese as far back as 1940

and to retire into exile in Poland where he died on November 22, 1944. He was succeeded by his auxiliary, Mons. Eugene Baziak, who could never set foot in that part of the Diocese which remained on Russian soil. He is actually administering that small portion of the Diocese in Polish territory from his residence in Lubaczow, outside the metropolis.

Frightful deportations took place in the city of Leopoli in February 1941 when in two days 200 trains took almost 200,000 men, women and children away, scattering them on Asiatic plains. In 1951 there were still two churches open in the city and a few in the provinces. But surviving priests were rare.

4) *Diocese of Luck:* It also was among the most ancient, having been established in the 13th century. It numbered about 400,000 faithful, 270 churches, 183 parishes and 246 priests in 1940. Today, according to the Pontifical Yearbook of 1952, it has hardly 5 churches and 3 priests.

Its Bishop, Mons. Adolph Szelazek, who had administered it since 1918 and who was more than 75 years old in 1940, was arrested, tried and exiled despite his venerable age. He died in exile on February 10, 1950.

5) *The Diocese of Premyslia of the Latins:* It was literally split in two as a result of the German-Russian pact of 1939: the city of Przemysl, chief center of the Diocese remained on the Polish side of the Curzon-Ribbentrop-Molotov line, while the larger part of the Diocese was incorporated into the Ukrainian Republic of the USSR By remaining in their seat it was possible for the Bishop, Mons. Frances Barda and his auxiliary, Mons. Adalebert Tomaka, to save themselves. But of this immense Diocese which once numbered 1,200,000 faithful, 600 churches, 454 parishes, 645 priests and about 150 members of religious orders, there are now left only fifty parishes, about one hundred priests and a little more than 200,000 faithful. The remainder of it, fallen in Russian hands, has undergone the same fate of the other incorporated Catholic Dioceses and there is scant news about their survival.

PERSECUTION OF CATHOLIC RUTHENIANS

At the same time of their persecution of Catholics of the

Latin rite, the Russians prepared their plan for the annihilation also of the Catholics of eastern or Ruthenian rite.[1]

These, numbering about 4,000,000 had re-joined the Roman Church in 1595, albeit they preserved the rites and traditions peculiar to the Byzantine Church. Since then they had formed a strong and well-organized Catholic group known under the designation "The Ruthenian Church." The seat of Leopoli was the center of this Church where its Archbishop resided. He had two Bishops under his jurisdiction in Premyslia and in Stanislawow with a complex of about 3,000 parishes, 2,500 priests and in addition several Seminaries, colleges, schools, religious institutes and houses and a Theological Academy in Leopoli.

The head of this Church then was the venerable Mons. Andrew Szepticky, Archbishop of Galicia for more than 43 years, and considered by all as the soul of his people because of his strong religious and patriotic personality. The Russians did not dare take any steps against him immediately after the occupation of September 1939, so they could not apply in full their program of extermination against the Ruthenian Catholic Church.

Instead they struck against many members of the clergy, arresting several hundreds of those most averse to their ideology. They closed some churches, transforming them into schools, they confiscated considerable amounts of church properties and would have done even more if two years later, in September of 1941, as a result of the sweeping German advance, they had not been compelled to abandon the territory of Galicia and retire much further to the east.

The second Russian occupation started in July 1944 and their attitude, at least in the beginning, appeared to be completely different than that of 1939. The churches were open, the clergy could freely exercise its functions, soldiers and even officers were seen at religious services, and at the funeral of the venerable Archbishop, Mons. Szepticky, who died November 1, 1944,

---

[1] See J. Flak, "Le Martyr de l'Eglise grecque unite en Pologne occupée," Begrand, 1947; and the White Book on the persecution of Ukrainian Catholics published in Rome by a group of exiled priests in 1953 under the title "The First Enchained."

Krushev, the first secretary of the Central Committee of the
Communist Party was seen among the mourners.

Little by little, however, the attitude of the Soviets towards
the Catholic Church began to change. In fact immediately after
the death of the Archbishop the Ukrainian communist chieftains
had begun to compel the more prominent priests and laymen to
attend courses in "re-education" and since many refused to attend these courses, given by Communist propagandists, the first
threats and arrests began.

Convinced that by such a method that they would never
succeed in bending the Church to their will, namely to make of
it an instrument of the State as they already had done with the
dissident Russian Church, they unleashed, at the beginning of
April 1945, a real press and propaganda campaign which was
akin to an open declaration of war.

The attack was launched by the newspaper "Volna Ukraina"
which in its edition of April 8, 1945, published an article under
the heading, "With the Cross and with the Knife," signed by a
certain Rosowich, in which the Ruthenian clergy was accused of
maintaining an underground opposition against the Soviet regime,
with the support of the Vatican, and that this could no longer
be tolerated. The dead Archbishop Szepticky himself was denounced as the person responsible "for having put the influence
of the Church at the service of anti-Russian propaganda." And
the article concluded with an invitation to the Ruthenian Church
to unite with the new Russian Orthodox Church, "the living
expression of Soviet patriotism."

On the days of April 11 and 12, 1945, the NKVD unleased a
general offensive. *All* the Bishopric seats of the "united ones"
were invaded by the police who requisitioned them, and *all* the
Catholic bishops in the territory occupied by the Russians were
arrested and deported from their seats.

On April 29, 1945, it was the turn of all the superiors of the
religious orders, the vicar generals and the other more influential
priests. In fact when about 500 of them assembled in the Cathedral of St. George, following the arrest of all the Bishops, in
order to examine the situation of the Ruthenian Church, they

suddenly found themselves surrounded by agents of the NKVD who opened fire upon them, wounding many fatally and arresting the rest.

On May 4, 1945, even the Capitular Vicar of the Armenian Archdiocese of Leopoli, Mons. Dionisius Kajatanovitz, was arrested together with the entire Armenian clergy of the city, among whom were the Canon Victor Kwapinski, the Canon Casmir Romoskano, and the Deacon Stanislaus Dobrit.

Concurrently with these events, two Russian Orthodox Bishops, sent by the Patriarch of Moscow, took possession of the Cathedral of St. George in Leopoli and the entire city was filled with Russian Orthodox priests who took possession of the parishes whose titular heads had been arrested or killed.

From Moscow the Patriarch Alexis sent an appeal, printed in large type by all the local newspapers, in which the surviving Ruthenian Catholics were invited to leave the Church of Rome and to join the Orthodox Russian Church.

For the purposes of documentation several paragraphs of the "Appeal" are given here:

> . . . From the most remote times you are linked to Russia and its people, not only through the language, but also because of your traditions and your customs. Now Divine Providence has restored her ancient frontiers to Russia; you therefore are our very own!
>
> To what have the late Metropolitan Mons. Szepticky and his colleagues exhorted you? They have urged you to submit to the yoke of Hitler, to bow your heads to him . . .
>
> Break, break the ties that hold you to the Vatican. It leads you, in its usual ways, towards darkness and material ruin; at this moment it wants you to turn your backs on the entire world, to arm against the friends of liberty and peace . . .
>
> Hasten your return to the bosom of your mother, the Russian Orthodox Church.

The plan of the governing authorities was by now quite clear, namely, to compel the surviving faithful of the Ruthenian Church to enter *en masse* the Russian Orthodox Church which had already agreed to collaborate with the Communist regime.

But to achieve this fusion and to give it a legitimate appearance a "Quisling" was necessary who would lend himself to the game of the authorities by gathering a first group of adherents about himself no matter how small.

The "Quisling" was found in the person of the priest Gabriel Kostelnik, known as the former director of a clerical review. He was sent to Moscow where he made contact with the Russian Patriarch, Alexis. Upon returning to Leopoli he established an "Initiating Committee for the passage of Greek Catholics to Orthodoxy," according to the directives he had received in Moscow, and of which he nominated himself president. He found two other collaborators in two other apostate priests, John Melnik, of the Diocese of Przemysl, and Anthony Pelvetsky, of the Diocese of Stanislawow. On May 18, together with them, he wrote his first letter addressed to Khodchanko, the "Commissar of the People's Council of the Socialist Soviet Republic." For purpose of documentation, herewith are some excerpts from the letter:

. . . We have committed a grave error in under-valuing the Soviet reality and the true mission of Russia. Under the leadership of its first Marshal, the incomparable STALIN, the courageous and wondrous Soviet Army has covered itself with immortal glory. It has destroyed the Hitlerian armies and rescued Europe from the shameful Nazi domination and all Slav peoples from perdition . . .

Marshal STALIN will go down in immortal history as the man who united the Ukrainian lands. All western Ukrainians thank him most cordially because we could never pay our moral debt to the Soviet Government.

Now our Church finds itself disorganized and sunk in a state of anarchy, and all this has had repercussions on our religious life. Such a situation cannot continue . . .

And this is the reason why we, the undersigned, representatives of our three Dioceses have decided to wrest our Church from this state of anarchy, to confirm her in the

Orthodox faith, and we ask that our efforts be approved.

Our activity must be carried out in agreement with the public authorities, with the committee of action and with the authorities of the Russian Orthodox Church.

This is why we ask the approval of our "Initiating Committee for the passage of Greek Catholics to Orthodoxy" and that we be given permission to direct the activity of the Committee itself.

The reply was not long in coming. On the following June 18, Citizen Khodchanko, in the name of the Supreme Soviet of the USSR, answered as follows;

. . . In response to your letter of May 28, 1945, and in conformity with the instructions of the Soviet of People's Commissars of the USSR. I communicate to you the following:

1) The "Initiating Committee for the re-union of the Greek-Catholic Church to the Russian Orthodox Church is recognized officially as the sole ecclesiastical juridical organ, invested with the power to govern the Greek-Catholic Church of the western Ukraine and to promote its union with the Russian Orthodox Church.

2) The Committee of Action has full authority to direct this Church in accordance with the Office of the Soviets of Peoples Commissars for the affairs of the Russian Orthodox Church attached to the Soviet of Peoples Commissars of the USSR, and for special cases in the districts, with the offices of the local Soviet.

3) While proceeding with the registering of Greek-Catholic deaconships, parishes and convents, the Initiating Committee must send to the department of Orthodox Church Affairs of the Peoples Commissars of the USSR, a list of the deaconships, parishes and respectively of the deacons, parish priests and superiors of convents who refuse to submit to the Initiating Committee for the passage of the Greek Catholic Church to the Orthodox Church.

(*signed*) KHODCHANKO

Kiev, June 28, 1945

At the same time the same directors of the "Initiating Committee" launched an "Appeal to the Greek-Catholic Clergy" in which after re-summarizing, in a manner certainly contrary to history, the origins and vicissitudes of the Greek Catholic Church in Galicia, with implied accusations against Poland and the Holy See, they continued thus:

. . . Now we have been liberated thanks to the Russians and to their incomparable Marshall, Stalin, for which reasons the union is now an anochronism. The political unity of the Ukraine imperiously demands religious unity.

It is sad and painful that our Bishops have not taken the correct path in this new religious and political situation and that this historical moment has found them inferior to their tasks.

It is clear therefore that this cannot last for long! Therefore with this we are informing you that with the permission of the Government there has been established an "Initiating Committee for the re-union of the Greek Catholic Church with the Orthodox Russian Church, whose seat is in Leopoli.

Its aim is to lead our Church out of the chaos and anarchy in which it finds itself.

It is clear that our "Committee" rests and will always rest on the positions of an integral patriotism as concerns the socialist Ukrainian Republic and the USSR.

As indicated by its name our "Committee" will have to lead our Greek-Catholic Church to a re-union with the Orthodox Church of all the Russias.

Meanwhile those priests who share our ideas must become members of the Initiating Committee as quickly as possible and that is in their interest because the certificate which we will issue will be necessary to them.

(*signed*) G. KOSTELNIK

G. MELNIK

A. PELVETSKY

Leopoli, May 28, 1945

The Committee had little success. Only 42 out of 2700 Catholic priests hastened to give their support to the Committee, while the overwhelming majority resisted all pressures with dignity and decorum.

In fact on July 1 a group of these loyal priests courageously sent a vibrant letter of protest to Molotov himself, the Commissar of Foreign Affairs of the USSR. This letter began as follows:

... After the arrest of all of our Bishops and a large number of priests of the western Ukrainian Greek-Catholic Church, and following the ban imposed on us forbidding us to be directed by a member of the Catholic clergy, our Church finds itself in an abnormal situation.

This situation is made more complicated by the fact that there has been constituted in Leopoli a so-called "Initiation Committee for the re-union of the Greek Catholic Church to the Orthodox Russian Church."

This "Committee" is presided by Dr. Kostelnik and by the Drs. Melnik and Pelvetsky, and on May 28, 1945, it published an "Appeal" to the Greek-Catholic clergy.

We priests of the Catholic Church will not linger here to answer to the historical inaccuracies which the letter of Dr. Kostelnik contains. The facts which it deals with are known to all.

We desire simply to have our position known as regards the USSR, and to present our petition to the Government. We would above all ask the Government to bear in mind that we profess and have the intention of professing the purest patriotism towards the socialist Republic of the Ukraine and towards the USSR, and that we intend to fulfil our duty towards the State conscientiously. In no case shall we become involved in any political activity, but we shall dedicate ourselves entirely to the salvation of our souls and of those of our people.

This we believe is the work that we can most usefully carry out for the prosperity not only of the Church but also of the State.

It is clear that we cannot obey a voice which invites us to deny our faith: a situation like the present one can swiftly lead to one of those religious struggles which—as history demonstrates—brings grief not only to the Church, but to the entire Nation.

We cannot believe that the Government wishes to persecute us for our faith. We believe, rather, that all this activity being carried out with the view of conversion to Orthodoxy is to be considered as a mis-understanding, and in a certain sense, as an arbitrary gesture of subaltern functionaries.

This is the reason why in the name of justice, we ask for ourselves and for our people of Western Ukraine, the freedom of ecclesiastical administration, which we have enjoyed during the past centuries and to which, according to the articles (124 of the Constitution) of Soviet law we are entitled.

As was to be foreseen this letter of protest received no answer. Instead on the following September 21 the struggle against the Greek-Catholic Church extended even to that part of the territory which had remained under the Poles. After having requisitioned the Bishop's seat Russian police arrested that venerable Bishop, Mons. Johosefat Joseph Kocylowski, locking him up in the jails of Rzceszow. Freed from prison on January 24, 1946, he was allowed to return to his seat in Przemysl for about a month, but on May 14, 1946, he once again saw the seat requisitioned by a Russian colonel of the NKVD who was accompanied by a Polish major of the UB and by the Ukrainian, Tishenko, who invited him to transfer himself "voluntarily" to Russia. After he refused to go, he was forcibly seized on June 20, 1946, and deported to Russia where he died on November 17, 1947, as a result of the hardships endured.

On June 27, 1946, hardly one week later, his auxiliary Bishop, Mons. Gregory Lakota, was also arrested together with the Chancellor of the Curia, Nicholas Hryclok, the rector of the Seminary, John Kuzyc and the Canon, Roman Rezzytylo. They were all deported to Russia from where nothing more has been heard from them.

Meanwhile a trial had been rigged up even against the Ruthenian Catholic Bishops already arrested in April 1945 and it had been stretched into a tremendous act of accusation which rang thus:

For traitorous and collaborationist activity on behalf of the German occupationists the following have been arrested by organs of the police: Slepoi, J. A., metropolitan of the Greek-Catholic Church; Czarnecki, N. A.; Budka N. M. and Chomyszyn, G., Bishop of Stanislawow, Latysewsky, G., auxiliary Bishop of Stanislawow, Kocilowskyi of Przemysl and Lakota, his auxiliary.

At the time of arrest documents were found in the possession of the said persons which revealed their criminal activity and complicity with the German-fascist occupiers and with the German espionage organs.

During the interrogation which took place the arrested confessed to being guilty of having carried out hostile activity against the USSR

The criminal activity of the accused on behalf of the German-fascist occupiers was confirmed by numerous examinations of witnesses and documentary data.

The trial of Slepoj, Kocilowsky, Chomyszyn, Budka and Latysewski, accused of crimes under articles 54–I and 54–U of the UK USSR has finished with the proceedings of inquiry and has been submitted for examination to the Military Tribunal.

The trial ended with the following sentences: (1) Mons. Slipy, 8 years of forced labor and deportation; (2) the 80-year old Bishop, Mons. Chomysyn to 10 years forced labor; (3) Monsignors Budka, Latysevskyi and Czarneckyi to 8 years each.

By thus eliminating all the Catholic Bishops the three apostate priests, who had taken over the leadership of the "Initiation Committee," organized a so-called "Sinod of the Ruthenian Church" in Leopoli.[2]

---

[2] The full proceedings of this Sinod were published in pamphlet form under the title "The Greek-Catholic Sinod held in Leopoli from March 8–10," Leopoli, 1946.

According to the report carried by the "Patriarchal Review of Moscow" (No. 4, 1946) 204 priests and 12 laymen participated in this Sinod. The Orthodox Russian Bishop, Maccarius of Leopoli, together with another Russian Bishop, Nestorius of Mukacev, are also supposed to have attended, as well as the ex-Catholic priests, Anthony Pelvetsky and Michael Melnik, who were consecrated Bishops several days before, on February 24 or 25, by the Russian Orthodox Metropolitan of Kiev. Although Kostelnik was the real chief of the apostasy he could not be consecrated Bishop because he was married.

During this Sinod the four Bishops present are supposed to have received "the abjuration of the Latin errors" on the part of the 204 Catholic priests. Telegrams of the accomplished rupture of the union with the Roman Church, signed at Brest-Litovsk in 1595, and of the consequent re-union of the Greek Catholic Church of the Ukraine with the Russian Orthodox Church, were supposed to have been sent to the Patriarch of Moscow, Alexis, to the oecumenical Patriarch of Constantinople, to Generalissimo Stalin, and to the Head of the Government of the Soviet Ukraine.

On the afternoon of March 9, the metroplitan Nicholas of Kiev, presided over the function in the name of the Patriarch of Moscow. He gave a speech on "the true and the false democracy" which, after an impassioned diatribe against the Vatican, concluded with these words:

> I hope with all my heart that the present celebration will be the beginning of the total liquidation of uniatism in our country. Then the Christians not only of all the Ukraine, but of our entire country, will form a single family . . . under the direction of a single Shepherd, the most Holy Patriarch of Moscow.

Following the Sinod, in the first days of April, a delegation from the Sinod itself, headed by the archpriest, Kostelnik, went to Moscow where it was received at the airport by a member of the "Soviet for Orthodox Church Affairs."

On April 5 the delegation was received by the Patriarch,

Alexis, and on April 7 it took part in a solemn religious function presided by the Patriarch himself who had at his side the two new Bishops Pelvetskyi and Melnik. They were then invited to a banquet at which even Karpov, head of the "Soviet for Orthodox Church Affairs" was present, and in the evening there was a grand reception in the quarters of the said "Soviet." The delegation took its leave from Mr. Karpov on April 9.

With this final act the drama of the Ruthenian Catholic Church of the Ukraine came to an end.

Beyond the Curzon-Ribbentrop-Moltov line, where in 1939 there were nine Catholic Dioceses (five Latin, three Ruthenian and one Armenian) with a complex of 8,457,000 faithful, 4,843 parishes, 5,347 priests, nine Seminaries with 800 students, more than one hundred Catholic high schools, 400 religious houses with more than 4,000 members and thousands of elementary schools, shelters, etc., by 1946, these had already been reduced by 80%. And today (1952) even on the basis of the fragmentary news that trickles through it is certain that now there exist only small groups scattered here and there, a rare church, and but few priests who have succeeded in avoiding deportations. All the rest no longer exists.

C. THIRD PERIOD:
PERSECUTION IN THE BALTIC STATES

THE SITUATION IN 1940

When on June 15, 1940, as a result of the Russian-German agreements of September 28, 1939, Soviet troops crossed the Lithuanian frontier and successively occupied Lithuania (June 15, 1940), Latvia (June 17, 1940) and Esthonia (June 17, 1940), the situation of the Catholic Church in each of the three states was as follows:

a) Lithuania

With the annexation of the greater part of the Archdiocese of Wilno to Lithuania carried out by the Soviets in September

1939, the Catholic population of Lithuania had risen to 2,875,000 faithful who represented about 85% of the population.

The national territory, from the hierarchic point of view, presented a division into six ecclesiastical administrative areas which were distributed as follows:

1) *Kaunas:* The metropolitan seat of all Lithuania which had a total of 560,000 Catholics in a population of 640,000, 239 churches, 120 parishes, 322 priests, and 43 religious houses with about 420 members. Its metropolitan Archbishop was Mons. Joseph Skvireckas, appointed in 1926. In April 1940, a few months before the Soviet occupation, Mons. Vincent Brizgys had been appointed as his auxiliary Bishop.

2. *Kaiserdorys:* This Diocese was under the jurisdiction of Kaunas. It numbered about 221,000 Catholics in a population of 229,000, and it had 80 churches, 66 parishes, 112 priests, 10 religious houses, 30 Catholic schools, etc. At the time of the Soviet occupation, Mons. Joseph Kukta was its Bishop.

3) *Panevezys:* This was another Diocese under the jurisdiction of Kaunas, the most populated, after the metropolis, with 420,000 faithful out of a population of 450,000. At the beginning of the Soviet occupation there was a total of 130 churches and chapels, 128 parishes, 254 priests, 12 religious houses and a hundred members of religious orders. Mons. Casimir Paltarokas was its Bishop, nominated in 1926 like the others.

4) *Telsiai:* This was the third Diocese in order of importance in Lithuania with 385,000 faithful out of a population of 401,000. It had more than 143 churches, 135 parishes, 288 priests, 12 religious houses and a certain number of schools and charitable institutions. Mons. Justin Staugaitis was its Bishop, and his auxiliary was Monsignor Vincent Borisevicius, appointed in February 1940 a few months before the Soviet occupation.

5) *Vilkavilskis:* This was the last Diocese under the jurisdiction of Kaunas with 350,000 Catholics among the 365,000 inhabitants. It had 120 churches, 101 parishes, 231 priests, and 20 religious houses with about 120 members. Mons. Anthony Karosas was its Bishop who, because of his advanced age (he was 85 in

1940) was assisted by a coadjutor in the person of Mons. Miecilaus Reinys who, however, in July 1940 was transferred to Vilno to administer, as vicar general, that part of the Diocese which had been assigned to Lithuania. A new coadjutor was appointed for Vilkaviskis, Mons. Vincent Padolskis.

6) *Vilno:* It was one of the largest Archdioceses, formerly Lithuanian but assigned to Poland in 1921 as a result of the treaty of Riga. It was again restored to Lithuania in 1939 following the Russian-German pact. It counted more than 1,000,000 Catholics, with 697 churches, 442 parishes, about 600 priests, and more than a hundred religious houses, with schools, colleges and a celebrated Catholic university in Vilno itself. Almost all of its territory had been assigned to Lithuania, including the Archbishopric city seat. The Archbishop Mons. Romauldo Jalbrzyhowski, together with his auxiliary, Mons. Casimir Nicholas Michalkiewicz (who died soon after) retired to Bialystok while, as has been said above, Mons. Miecislaus Reinys, who was elevated at the same time to the dignity of Archbishop, became vicar general of that part of the Diocese which was now in Lithuanian territory.

In Lithuania at the time of the Soviet occupation in June 1940 there were then the following:

a) 1 Metropolitan, 1 titular Archbishop, 4 Residential Bishops, 3 Auxiliary Bishops, and a Prelate who administered the Prelature of Klaipeda which included the Free City of Memel.

b) 2,875,000 Catholics out of a population of about 3,300,000.

c) 1,182 churches or chapels.

d) 911 parishes.

e) 1,482 priests.

f) A thousand members of religious orders, monks and nuns, who worked in many monasteries, schools, shelters, etc.

g) 4 seminaries with about 850 students and a Theological Faculty annexed to the University of Kaunas.

b) Latvia

In contrast to Lithuania where, as has been seen, the overwhelming majority of the population was Catholic at the time of the Soviet occupation, the majority (85%) in Latvia was Protestant, with the Catholic Church coming soon after with about 30%. The remainder were Orthodox, Jews or atheists.

The Catholic ecclesiastical organization in Latvia in 1940 included two Dioceses for the entire Latvian territory:

1) Riga: The Archbishopric seat and metropolitan with about 490,000 Catholics, 140 churches, 110 parishes, and 115 priests. The Archbishop-Metropolitan was Mons. Anthony Springovics who had Mons. Joseph Rancans as his auxiliary.

2) Liepajaff The Bishopric seat, under the jurisdiction of Riga, with about 90,000 Catholics, 50 churches, 40 parishes, 54 priests. Its Bishop was Mons. Anthony Urbss, appointed in 1938.

There were in all, therefore, about 600,000 Catholics, 160 churches, 150 parishes, 169 priests and a certain number of houses and religious institutions, among which a flourishing seminary in Riga.

c) Esthonia

The percentage of Catholics was even lower in Esthonia. Even here the majority was formed of Lutheran Protestants, who came after the Orthodox, the Catholics coming last with about 50,000 faithful in a country of about 1,000,000 inhabitants.

The only Catholic organization for all Esthonia was an "Apostolic Administration," established in 1924, detaching it from the Archdiocese of Riga, with its seat in Tallin. Mons. Edward Profittlich, with the title of Archbishop, was its titular head up to the moment of the Soviet occupation of Esthonia in 1940.

SUPPRESSION DURING THE FIRST OCCUPATION
(JUNE 1940—JUNE 1941)

Upon concluding its so-called pact of mutual assistance with the Baltic Republics on October 10, 1939, Russia had the following paragraph included:

ARTICLE 7.—The application of this treaty will in no wise be detrimental to the sovereign rights of the contracting parties and especially will it not be detrimental to their political institutions, their economic and social systems, their military organization, nor in general that which constitutes the principle of non-intervention in internal affairs.

A few days later Molotov, the Soviet Commissar for Foreign Affairs, commenting on the above-mentioned pact before the Supreme Council of the USSR declared:

The pacts concluded with the Baltic States in no manner involve any interference by the Soviet Union in the internal affairs of Esthonia, Latvia or Lithuania as certain interested foreign circles would like it to be believed . . . These pacts are rooted in a mutual respect for the political, social and economic system of each of the contracting parties . . . We promise a scrupulous and loyal execution of the pacts signed by us on the basis of reciprocity, and we declare that the insensate "cancans" about a Sovietization of the Baltic States are useless to our common enemies and to all the bands of anti-soviet provacateurs.

But these, alas, were only words pronounced only for the purpose of hiding from the eyes of the majority the real plan which the directors of the Kremlin had in readiness at the moment of the signing of the pact known as "mutual assistance." Indeed the aim of this plan was not only the temporary occupation of the above-mentioned countries, justified for reasons of war, but rather the complete Sovietization of these countries and the destruction of the Catholic Church.

Here follow in brief the successive stages of application of this plan of destruction, insofar as it concerns the Catholic Church, in each of these three countries.

a) Lithuania

After the Russian troops had crossed the Lithuanian border on June 15, 1940, Dekansov, the Vice-Commissar of Soviet Foreign Affairs established himself in Kaunas. He appointed the Moscow agent, J. Paleckis, head of the new Lithuanian government formed only of Social-Communist elements, while the President of the Republic, A. Smetona, with a few other members of the old government, was compelled to flee abroad.

On June 25, only ten days after the occupation, the new government, among its first acts, decreed the separation of Church and State.

On the following day, June 26, the Apostolic Nuntius, Mons. Centoz, was called to the Ministry of Foreign Affairs where he was formally informed of the denunciation of the Concordat with the Holy See, stipulated in 1927, and he himself was invited to leave Lithuanian territory in the shortest possible time.

On June 28 the abolition of religious instruction in the schools was decreed, the missions of chaplains were suppressed in the army, in hospitals, in asylums and in prisons. Moreover, the activity of the Faculty of Theology of the University of Kaunas was suspended, all private schools administered by members of religious orders were abolished and the teaching personnel of these schools was dismissed. Nuns who wished to keep their right to teach had to make new applications.

On the first of July 1940 the Parliament was dismissed, new elections were ordered and the entire government apparatus renewed after a tremendous purge.

On the night between July 11 and 12, 1940, in application of the secret plan already hatched in Moscow, the first group of Catholic priests, who were considered capable of informing or directing public opinion, was arrested, together with democratic party leaders, newspaper editors and high functionaries. In all, both in the city and in the country, about 2000 persons were arrested. Nothing more has been known about them nor has it been possible to know just what happened to them.

In the face of such acts the Catholic Episcopate protested and on July 24 the Bishop Coadjutor of Kaunas, Mons. Brizgys, referred directly to Venclova, the "People's Commissar for National Education," with a "Memorandum" on the situation of the schools in Lithuania.

The Government replied on July 25 with a decree nationalizing all church properties, confiscating all real estate belonging to the clergy, including Bishopric residences, offices, printing plants, etc., and by requisitioning and destroying all books, religious prints and objects. Thus, for example, a considerable part of the library of the Marianite Fathers in Mariempole was destroyed as were other collections of books, including rare and valuable ones, preserved in convents or religious houses.

On August 25 and September 4, the Archbishop Metropolite of Kaunas, Mons. J. Skvireckas, sent a personal letter to Paleckis and Gedvilas, respectively President of the Republic and President of the Council, in order to protest against the above-mentioned decrees and to request that the political prisoners be freed.

On October 2, 1940, almost as a reply to the protests of the Archbishop, the People's Vice-Commissar of Internal Affairs of the Soviet Socialist Republic of Lithuania, Mr. Gladkow, sent this "most urgent" circular to all district chiefs of the State Police:

Most urgent—absolutely secret

TO COMRADE PALEVIXIUS ALYTUS AND ALL THE DISTRICT CHIEFS OF THE SECTION FOR THE SECURITY OF THE STATE:

Data in possession of the NKVD reveal that Lithuanian priests, former directors of various Catholic organizations, as well as members who are particularly active in these organizations, are carrying out secret activities, and conducting themselves in a hostile manner towards the USSR.

This is their method:

1) In sermons, be they public or private, the priests express nationalistic ideas with which they create an anti-soviet mentality among the faithful.

2) For the same purpose they utilize their relations with the youth in schools (university and high school students, pupils of primary and secondary schools). From writings which have fallen into our hands we learn that, according to the instructions of the Bishop von Brizgys, some priests have been authorized to carry out an illegal activity among youth in order to educate them in a nationalist spirit, inculcating in them a hatred for the Communist system. The

priests carry out such an activity in almost all regions of Lithuania and above all in the churches on Sunday, in special courses, at youth gatherings and even in houses where groups of 10 to 12 young people meet. The influence which priests exercise on believing parents, so that these inculcate Catholic principles in their children, is not sufficiently appreciated.

3) The same anti-Communist activity is carried on inside associations of autonomous Catholic groups (Apostolate of Prayer, Third Order, etc.) which constitute political instruments in the hands of the clergy.

In order to stop this anti-soviet activity of the priests I order the following:

1) Make a complete list of all the priests in your district.

2) This list must include even the lists of directors of Catholic organizations and associations.

3) A campaign must be launched immediately by means of agents who must be recruited among the members of the parishes and among persons of the Bishopric Curie in your district.

4) At all costs priests and employees of churches (sextons, organists) who are in close contact with offices of Catholic associations and groups must be kept under close watch. Try even to make them function as agents and to furnish information. Explain to them that they must sow discord in Catholic organizations.

5) Look for priests and directors of associations who have relations with the Germans. The character of these relations must be explained.

6) In all districts in which there are monasteries a list of all members of the orders must be compiled. By means of suitable persons a net of agents and informers must be organized in the religious communities.

7) In the selection of agents and informers unpleasant surprises must be avoided. Proceed with great care, and if

necessary, make use of spies. Bear in mind the fact that at the present time a part of the clergy finds itself in a critical situation from a material point of view and this has shaken the foundations of its ideological position.

8) A documentation of every anti-soviet and anti-revolutionary activity must be established. The material gathered must be transmitted to the NKVD of the Soviet Socialist Republic of Lithuania.

9) Each Chief must send me, before October 10, a report on the hostile activity of the clergy.

10) Before October 15 a memorandum must be delivered to the Commissariat of the People (Security of the State, Sec. 2) on the dispositions taken by the priests with notes on the source of information and with indications of the measures foreseen for future activity.

Peoples' Commissar of Internal Affairs
(*signed*) GLADKOW

October 2, 1940

The circular immediately had its effect and every priest saw himself trailed day in day out wherever he went, while other spies were seen at the doors of churches, in uniform or in civilian clothes, taking down the names of all those who went in. The secretary of the Archbishop of Kaunas, D. Usorius, for example, had a spy assigned to him who followed him everywhere and, who, when he lost him from sight for a moment tried to trace him by telephone.

The result of this continual spying was the seizure and arrest of many priests who heard themselves accused of the strangest things. It has been estimated that towards the middle of November, after hardly five months of Soviet occupation, 10% of the Lithuanian priests had already been eliminated. Of these the names of 9 are known who were exiled to Siberia and of another 15 who were tortured or massacred. A quite similar fate was in store even for the greater part of the lay directors of Catholic Action.

On December 12, 1940, comrade Guzevicius, People's Commissar of Internal Affairs of the Soviet Socialist Republic of Lithuania, sent a circular to all the heads of the NKVD of the Soviet Socialist Republic of Lithuania ordering that Christmas Day be considered as a working day throughout the country.

It is of interest to report the complete text of the circular:

On the 25 and 26 of December, Catholics celebrate the holidays which they call "Christmas Holidays." During these feasts (from midnight of the 24th to the 25th) masses are said in all churches and sermons are given. These two days are considered as big holidays by believers, that is to say as non-working days.

The nationalist counter-revolutionary element and the clergy above all will take advantage of these Christmas Holidays for their anti-Soviet activity and above all they will attempt the following:

a) Cause a suspension of work in factories and schools.

b) Propagandize against participation in the elections, making use of the pulpits to pronounce religious sermons, more or less disguised, or even snatches of propaganda directed towards individuals or groups of faithful who go to church, or to the sacristies or the parish houses.

c) Distribute and disseminate counter-revolutionary publications under a religious label, or other.

d) Provoke street demonstrations or foment agitations or rebellions.

For the purpose of preventing incidents of this kind, you must:

1) Order your net of informers to keep you posted on all the anti-soviet preparations of the clergy and circles close to it, arranging for frequent meetings with these informers between the days of December 20 and 27.

2) Take the necessary measures for the purpose of guaranteeing the normal continuation of work in factories as well as in schools.

3) During the nights of December 23, 24, 25 and 26, organize motorized patrols, adding to the guards in the cities. For this purpose use, in collaboration with the Secretary of the Party's District Committee, active elements of the party and communist youth, giving them appropriate instructions.

4) Make minutes of all incidents having a provacative character and send me a report immediately.

(*signed*) GUZEVICIUS

REQUISITIONS OF THE SEMINARIES.—On January 13, 1941, a Government order brusquely closed even the Seminary of Kaunas, the only one which had remained open. The other three, in Telsiai, Vilkaviskis and Vilno, had already been closed since the beginning of the occupation. In fact part of the offices of the Ministry of Justice had been installed in the Seminary of Wilno.

When the Bishops, Brizgys and Paltarokas went to make a protest to, Pozdniakov, formerly Soviet minister in Lithuania and at that time the all-powerful delegate of the Kremlin, asking him at least to restore the rooms of the Seminary of Theology, the Soviet minister quickly declared that they should entertain no illusions, as if to say, of what use is a Seminary for the preparation of future priests? When these are ready to be ordained, there will no longer be need of them, because by then there will be no more priests!

PROHIBITION OF THE TEACHING OF RELIGION.—In the early days of April 1941 a new disposition of the Ministry of the Interior prohibited all priests from teaching religion be it in the schools or outside.

For the purpose of documentation here is a copy of the subscription form with which every priest had to declare his knowledge of this disposition:

. . . I, the undersigned, minister of the cult . . . residing at . . . town of . . . district . . . confirm with this declaration that on . . . April, 1941 there was communicated to me the formal prohibition of teaching religion to pupils, be it to children of pre-scholastic age, be it to those in school and that includes assembly halls as well as in the homes of parents or my own dwelling, that is to say in no place whatsoever. As a consequence I have no right to speak to them about religious questions.

At the same time it was communicated to me that in the case of non-execution of this order, I would be cited before a court. . . .

SUPPRESSION OF ALL RELIGIOUS HOLIDAYS.—As had been done with Christmas, the same was tried with Sunday and with all the other religious holidays. On Easter, for example, of 1941 a campaign was started during the Lenten season announcing that Good Friday, Holy Saturday and even Easter Sunday were work days. Those who failed to appear for work on those days, in fidelity to an ancient custom, were severely punished.

An attempt was even made to wipe out the memory of Sunday by declaring it a working day, with Saturday as the day of rest.

DEPORTATIONS AND MASS EXECUTIONS.—But the Communists wrote their blackest page of their first occupation in June 1941.

This took place during the nights from June 14 to 21 when 34,620 Lithuanians were deported, according to a list compiled by the Lithuanian Red Cross. This was the carrying out of a secret plan elaborated in Moscow on January 21, 1941, by Serov, the Vice Commissar of Police of the USSR, a plan which fell into the hands of Lithuanians at the end of June 1941 when the Russians were forced to leave Lithuania.

Among the victims are to be found the names of the ex-President of the Lithuanian Republic, Alexsandras Stulginskis, ex-presidents of the Council, P. Dovydaitis and A. Merkys, ex-ministers A. Tamosaitis, S. Silingas, J. Urbsys, A. Endzulaitis, A. Zilinskas, and numerous priests and directors of Catholic associations.

It was later in the week from June 22 to 30, 1941, during their retreat from Lithuania, that the Russians massacred *en masse* all the inmates of the concentration camp of Parvieniskiai, and the greater part of those interned in the prisons of Kaunas and Wilno. A total of more than 10,000 persons.

In one single night in the forest of Rainiai (in the precincts of Telsiai) all the intellectuals of the locality (judges, lawyers, priests, etc.) were massacred, a total of 70 persons.

On the road from Minsk to Mohilev, in the forest of Cervena, more than 2,000 Lithuanians, coming from all the prisons of the country en route to deportation to Russia, were mowed down by the machine guns of the escort guard. Among the victims of this other massacre were, K. Bizauskas, vice-president of the Council and the ministers Rusteika, Caplikas and Giedraitis.

In conformity with the plan of Serov about 700,000 Lithuanians were supposed to have been deported from Lithuania alone and among these were included almost all the priests and directors of Catholic organizations. It was only the German advance which prevented the execution of the plan, but it was only a reprieve, because, as we shall see, upon their return in 1944, that number in a few months would be surpassed.

b) Latvia

The invasion of Latvia by Russian troops began on June 17, 1940, two days after the invasion of Lithuania and it continued until July 1, 1940 when the Russians were forced to leave the country by the Germans.

The history of the first Soviet occupation is also darkened by a series of deeds and mis-deeds which, as was the case with Lithuania, is a burdensome and a painful story to relate. The plan was the same: to Sovietize all of Latvia in the shortest time possible so as to prepare its annexation to the USSR.

A. Vishinsky, the Vice Commissar for Foreign Affairs of the USSR, sent especially by Moscow, was charged with the execution of this plan. And even here the first blow was struck against the Catholic Church.

From the very first days of the occupation 12 priests were deported or killed and more than 6,000 Catholics were deported to Siberia and never heard from again, according to the testimony of Mons. Rancans, auxiliary Bishop of Riga, who is at present a refugee in Germany.

Even here with a decree dated March 20, 1941, all church properties of all kinds were confiscated, including the sacred vessels necessary to the service. Buildings, religious houses, schools, etc. were seized and confiscated.

But the greatest barbarity was reached on the night of June 13-14 1941 when 1,355 Latvians were massacred, and 32,895 persons were deported, interned or disappeared, among whom there were 7,497 women, 4,196 children, 1,086 officers, 105 doctors, 99 engineers, 64 lawyers, 38 priests, 175 writers and artists, 490 professors, 366 students, etc. Never, in the course of its history, had the Latvian people experienced such a mass extermination.

In the common graves uncovered at Jugla, Baltzers and in other places around Riga, among the thousands of victims of the Bolshevik terror of the first occupation, there were also found many priests and monks on whose bodies could be seen traces of the torture to which they had been submitted before their massacre.

The Catholic Church of Latvia emerged from this first period of the Soviet occupation considerably decimated, but the rest was carried out by the Nazis from 1941 to 1944 and by the Communists after 1945.

c) Esthonia

Esthonia was occupied on June 17, 1940, on the same day of the Soviet occupation of Latvia.

The task of realizing the plan of sovietization, already prepared as has been seen for Latvia and Lithuania, had been entrusted to a personage of the highest level of Soviet politics, namely, A. Zhdanov, member of the Politburo and secretary of the Russian Communist Party.

It was he who directly upon the occupation of Esthonia, in contrast to what had been done in the other two Baltic Republics where at least for a time there was an attempt to preserve outward appearances, ordered the arrest and deportation of all the members of the Government led by the President of the Republic, K. Pats, all the Ministers and along with them all other political figures who in the past had held some government post, that is, all the intellectuals and party leaders.

Immediately thereafter began the religious persecution which indiscriminately struck at all religious confessions.

We shall limit ourselves to the Catholic Church.

Although the number of the faithful was limited, still 29 of its priests and members of religious orders were massacred, and another 17 were deported or disappeared. It has been estimated that about 3000 Catholics were the victims of the Soviet persecution in Esthonia from 1940 to 1941.

THE CHURCH AFTER THE SECOND OCCUPATION (1944)

In August 1944, after three years of German occupation which was also marked by the terror of the Gestapo which had deported more than 200 priests to Germany and submitted Bishops and the faithful to the most brutal vexations, the Baltic States again fell under Soviet domination. A second regime of terror was installed, characterized by mass deportations of the inhabitants of those three countries and by their substitution with communists imported from Russia.

Here are the most salient facts about the single countries:

a) Lithuania

Two "documents" of a shattering probatory value, because they were written by eye witnesses, can better than any other exposition give an idea of what happened in Lithuania from 1944 on, under the second Soviet occupation.

The first is the "Act of Accusation," issued in 1948 by the Prosecutor of Tauras, Mr. Budris, and countersigned by two witnesses, about the Communist persecutions against the Catholic Church in Lithuania.

The second is a "Letter of the Catholics of Lithuania addressed to His Holiness, Pius XII in September 1947 and which was received by him toward the end of 1948.

Here are the integral texts of the two documents:

DOCUMENT No. 1:

Lithuania, 20 January 1948

I, Budris, general prosecutor of the district of Tauras, designated to confirm the actions and the crimes of the Soviets in Lithuania, after hearing witnesses and after taking into consideration other sources of information, hereby formulate this act of accusation concerning the persecution of the faithful and of Catholic priests undertaken in Lithuania by the Soviet Government and the Communist Party.

1) Although the Soviet Constitution theoretically recognizes the freedom of conscience this freedom is in practice criminally and continually suppressed.

2) In 1944 when the second occupation took place on the part of the Red Army, all organizations having a religious character were prohibited in Lithuania. There was also prohibited the publication of new religious books and Catholic books confiscated in printing plants and in libraries were destroyed. The Communists prohibited the teaching of religion and abolished the Cross in the schools and all Christian symbols. They even prohibited prayers before and after lessons.

3) Before the Soviet occupation there were four seminaries in Lithuania, at Kaunas, Wilno, Vilkaviskis and Telsiai. The Russians closed the seminaries of Vilno and Wilkavisikis immediately. The one in Telsiai was closed in 1945. The Seminary of Kaunas absorbed some of the students of the seminaries which had been closed. There were about 300 seminarists but in the month of December 1946, the directors of the seminary of Kaunas were expelled and the number of students reduced to 190.

4) From the first days of the occupation the Soviets began to arrest priests. Many of these in order to avoid imprisonment have had to abandon their posts and hide themselves. The number of persecuted priests is considerable.

In the Diocese of Vilkavisk 25 out of 80 members of religious orders were arrested. There is not yet any exact information about the other Dioceses but, according to reliable sources, it can be stated that a third of the Catholic priests in Lithuania has been imprisoned. Only some Jesuits and Franciscans remain free.

The Bishop of Telsiai, Mons. Borisevicus, was arrested at the beginning of 1946 and on January 3, 1947 he was condemned to death in Vilno by the tribunal of the NKVD.

In the autumn of 1946, the new Bishop of Telsiai, Mons. Ramonauskas, was also arrested and immediately thereafter the Bishop of Kaisadorys, Mons. Matulionis, suffered the same fate.

Mons. Reynis and Mons. Poltarokas have already been summoned by the NKVD to be interrogated.

5) The arrested Bishops and priests are accused of "banditism."

6) The convents are closed. The Salesian School in the district of Raselniai has been destroyed, its properties confiscated and a great number of the personnel and students arrested.

7) Before the war, Lithuania had one thousand priests. The Soviet persecution has decimated them and now there are only 350 left and this number is reduced daily. The faithful can now no longer receive not even the comforts of religion. Many parishes have been left without priests, for example, the important parish of the Very Holy Trinity at Kaunas with more than 30,000 faithful has but a single priest.

8) The Soviets launch numerous attacks against Catholic priests in the press. See the first number of "Tiesa" of January 1, 1947: Reactionary clericals, used to living and waxing fat on the labor of the people have banded together in an attempt to obstacle our efforts for progress with terrorism. This *canaille* of heros of history will be destroyed by the majestic march of millions of men. The Soviets have realized these threats!

9) The properties of the Church have been confiscated.

The Soviets have apportioned only 3 hectares of land to the parishes and for this land they demand taxes of a nature which amount to 1500–2000 kilograms of bread flour. Moreover priests must pay very high personal taxes.

10) On December 24, 1946, electricity was removed from the churches in many localities and from the dwellings of priests. And this order has not been revoked.

11) The functionaries of the NKVD and of the NKGB by means of threats attempt to compel clergymen to inform on the faithful or to furnish information about their political conduct.

12) Officially it is not prohibited to go to Church, but in effect those who do must expect punishments. It is known that during a secret meeting it was decided to confiscate the property of a peasant because he went to Church too often. Teachers are under accusation not only if they go to Church, but even if their pupils go. The Ministry of Instruction has announced that these professors who studied at the Catholic Faculty of Kaunas will be dismissed.

13) The Soviets have committed sacrileges in several churches. In Kybartai Russian soldiers fired against statues on the altar. In the same place, in the autumn of 1946, the secretary of the Communist Party, wielding a revolver, chased out women who were attending Mass. In other localities communists have destroyed crosses and statues erected alongside roads. In the church of Sumskiai the faithful were arrested during Mass. And similar occurrences have been confirmed on many occasions.

14) The Soviets affirm that the Communist Party is anti-religious and then they expect the clergy, nonetheless, to become Communist. Thus the clergy finds itself in the face of this alternative: either to become the accomplice of atheism or undergo its persecutions. Since the clergy remains faithful to the Church, the Bolsheviks systematically and pitilessly try to destroy it.

15) The Soviets fight not only against the Catholic

clergy but also against Christian morality. They try to develop the most base instincts, hatred and revenge. They try to degrade man. The Bolshevik doctrine has created a new type of man. It is for this reason that today in Lithuania homicide, cruelties, banditry, the spread of venereal diseases, have become events of a routine nature.

The Communists through their organizations, press and schools try to lodge hatred of religion, morality, of all that is noble and human in people's hearts. In the youth newspaper "Jaunino Gretos," in an article entitled "Morality and Religion" it says, ". . . in what sense do we reject the morality and the customs issuing from the divine law, as the bourgeois conceive them? The basis of communist morality is the struggle to realize Communism. The dictatorship of the proletariat which conducts a struggle without pity, bloody or peaceful, military or economic, pedagogical or administrative, against the forces of tradition of the old society has the following for a motto, '. . . the hypocritical and so-called divine morality of religion, puts intelligence and the will in chains . . .'" (Lenin, op. 25). Such ideas are found everywhere in the Communist press and they are repeated at all meetings and congresses. The Communists exert themselves to educate Lithuanian youth in this vein.

The persecution of the Catholic clergy and of the faithful, the homicides, the imprisonments, the deportations and the other crimes are carried out by the Communist Party, the government, the NKVD and the NKGB on orders of Moscow. For these crimes we hold responsible all those persons who work in the organizations which we have named.

The documents of this act of accusation are preserved as a "corpus delicti." We witnesses have read this act and with our signatures we confirm the exactness of the facts exposed above.

The General Prosecutor of the
District of Tauras: BUDRIS

Witnesses: TRANAS-SERNAS

DOCUMENT No. 2:

Letter of Lithuanian Catholics to His Holiness Pius XII

HOLY FATHER:

We Catholic Lithuanians, persecuted, terrorized, decimated, plagued with hunger and cold, isolated from the entire world by an iron curtain, deprived of the most elementary natural rights of man, invoke Your help and Your protection.

We have been living for more than 8 years under the terror of a foreign occupation. At the risk of our life we are determined to let you know the truth about the martyrdom of our people, for the purpose of unmasking before the eyes of all the lies of the Communists about the alleged freedom of religion in the USSR.

For centuries Russia has tried to destroy our faith, our language and all that which is peculiar to our small people . . .

Since 1939, that is since the beginning of the second world war, our country has been invaded by Soviet Russia. The Russians have destroyed our cities and our villages; they have taken from us not only our lands, our houses, but also our liberty, the liberty of thought and action. For us the slavery of the spirit is the worst of all. They want to force us to believe and to repeat that the Russia of the Soviets is the paradise of the earth, that outside its confines there is only misery and deceit, and meanwhile our children no longer know what sugar, meat and butter are.

They have made us elect a national assembly—the "Seimas"—and they have made us vote under the threat of bayonets and without any international supervision, for the "free" annexation of Lithuania to the Soviet Republics.

In the month of June 1941, in three days, the Soviets arrested 40,000 Lithuanians: men, women, children, aged persons and deported them on cattle cars to Siberia. We have seen with our own eyes the corpses thrown alongside the roads. The first year of occupation cost our people 100,000 human lives.

1) *The National Church:* Since 1944 the Russians have tried all means of creating a "National Lithuanian Church" as they have done in the Polish Ukraine. By intrigue, flattery and arrests, they have tried to enroll young and active elements in the ranks of this National Church. They have sought among priests for groups of activists to make propaganda against the ecclesiastical hierarchy and thereby form the first nucleus. At the same time they have intensified propaganda against the Pope in the press, obliging the people to read and to listen to the litany of their lies.

2) *Arrests of Priests:* Since the first days of the occupation the police has devoted itself to the search for political "crimes" committed by priests. In order to arrest a priest it is enough to show that he participated in Catholic Action. Immediately a policeman presents himself at his house who, at first tries to draw him into his service with promises, and if he does not consent he threatens him with arrest. Those who do not let themselves be intimidated vanish immediately . . . The police agents go so far as to go to confession in order to provoke the priests and draw some secret from them.

3) *Surveillance of Priests:* Every priest is the object of a close surveillance. The houses near parishes are occupied by spies who watch those who come and who go. Inside the houses to which priests are accustomed to go they seek for informers who might report the conversations held to the police. Sermons in church are copied down by two or three agents . . . It is not even possible to talk to a priest in the street without becoming suspect.

4) *Taxes and Fiscal Burdens on Priests:* Priests are taxed with taxes which are higher than for any other functionary. A parish priest must pay 100,000 rubles, a vicar about 50,000 rubles, per year. It not being possible for priests to pay such high taxes, they are forced to sell their own and the church's properties, because the law provides for the penalty of forced labor for persons who have not paid their taxes.

5) *State Subscriptions:* Each year every citizen is obliged

to subscribe "freely" to the "State Loans." While for every functionary the obligatory amount is a month's salary, for priests the sum is raised often to 50,000 rubles. Whoever refuses is considered a "criminal" and as such deported to Siberia.

6) *Taxes on Sacred Buildings:* The taxes on sacred buildings go as high as 50,000 rubles. Since it is impossible in many cases to collect such a considerable sum from the offerings of the faithful, it follows that the churches are closed and the adjoining buildings confiscated.

7) *Restrictions Imposed on Priests:* Officially a priest has the same rights as other citizens, but it is not so in practice. In fact he must pay ten times as much as others for electricity, rent, etc., and often even his ration card is taken away.

8) *Associations:* All religious and welfare associations are prohibited. Those who cannot work, according to the law, should be supported by the Church, but in reality beggars are numerous.

9) *Isolation of Priests:* It is forbidden to priests to bring the solace of religion to hospitals, or to go even as private persons to a school, to exercise any profession. He is completely isolated from public life. The very houses in which he enters become suspect.

10) *The Religious Press:* Despite all the efforts made, it was not possible to obtain a newspaper organ. Even missals are prohibited. No newspaper, no review, no book with a Christian tendency has been able to be printed since the Soviet occupation. A religious book costs a fortune on the black market.

11) *Religious Art:* Religious art is prohibited in all the schools. Only the art of the Soviet Union has the right to exist. In this sense all the museums have been purged.

12) *Schools:* Anti-religious propoganda is carried out even in kindergartens. Catholic professors are tolerated only when there is a shortage of personnel. Several minutes of every lesson must be dedicated to anti-religious propaganda.

It is necessary to teach that which the State of Moscow prescribes. Thus the history and the events of Lithuania are falsified. Finally children are taught to denounce their parents as a patriotic duty.

13) *Seminaries:* At the present time there is only one seminary at Kaunas with 80 seminarists. It seems that even this number may be reduced to 60, so that there would be only 8 new priests a year in all Lithuania, while the mortality of priests alone rises from 25 to 30 a year, not counting the arrests.

14) *The Restoration of Churches:* In the course of this war hundreds of churches were destroyed or damaged. It is impossible to think of their reconstruction; the priest would not receive the materials necessary from the State. Thus the faithful are obliged to assemble in garages.

15) *The Parochial Councils of State:* The Communists try to suppress the parochial councils established by canon law and wish to substitute them with "Councils of State." The State Commissar of religious cults, M. Gallevicius, has given orders that in each department, a part of the members of the councils be designated by the State. Thus they try to take away the administration of the churches from the Bishops and the parish priests.

16) *The Fate of the Arrested:* It takes several years to understand the mechanism of Soviet life. There exist written and official laws which give the citizen every right, but there exist also non-official and unwritten laws. The first are applied only to members of the Communist Party, all the other citizens must be under the unwritten laws . . . A man is judged only by his political opinions. Woe to him who lets himself be arrested. He has no means of defense, it matters little whether he be guilty or less. The tortures will lead him to confess any crime whatsoever. The only way of escape is that of accepting to work with the police as an informer.

Persons arrested are interned for months in cells where there is no room even to sleep. Often they are left with no food in order to force them to break down. They are submitted to every kind of torture. Many of them succumb or lose their sanity. During their trial they have no means of defense. The most common verdict, and the kindest one, is that of ten years of forced labor in Siberia. The journey takes at least a month. They are loaded on cattle cars, often without food and water. Those who arrive in Siberia do not resist more than 5 years.

17) *The Situation of Catholics:* The Catholic, be he a worker or a functionary, is always persecuted. He can never aspire to a higher post, and he is tolerated for the moment only because he cannot be replaced. The persecution of peasants is even more persistent. In 1947 the Communists tried to establish collective farms but they ran into the solid resistance of the peasants and since then the Communists have accused them of collaboration with the Germans, of rebellion, etc. and thousands of them have been arrested and deported.

18) *The Communist Party and the Catholics:* Catholics refuse to join the Communist Party, which, despite all its promises and threats, remains a small minority in Lithuania.

19) *Propaganda:* The foreign press sometimes praises the freedom of the Soviet Union. It is a lie pure and simple. Inside the Soviet Union there exists no freedom of thought or action. The State tells you what you must think, what you must say, when you must applaud, praise or condemn . . . The State is all-powerful, the individual is but a pure automaton.

HOLY FATHER:

1) We pray you to proclaim throughout the world a day of prayer for Lithuania as was done by His Holiness Benedict XV in 1917.

2) We pray you to pronounce to us, Catholics of Lithuania, publicly, a word of consolation.

3) We pray you to transmit our Appeal to all the free and united Nations.

4) We desire to have a one hour radio program to give news of our country and our sufferings.

HOLY FATHER:

We are hopeful of our prayers being granted. We suffer cruelly for our Faith and for our fidelity to the Holy See. We accept death for our Faith but dying we would first listen to Your voice. It will give us courage and consolation. We would be assured that our children will no longer suffer the slavery of the spirit. We have faith that your voice will be heard by the heads of States. When this message of our sufferings will have arrived to Your Holiness, perhaps we shall no longer be in this world.

THE CATHOLICS OF LITHUANIA

Vilno, Occupied Lithuania, September 20, 1947

From 1948 to today the religious situation already so grave, as described by the two documents reported above, has continued to worsen.

The two Bishops, Mons. Rejniys and Mons. Karosas, who at the moment of the preparation of these two documents were still in Lithuania, are no longer there. The first, Mons. Rejniys, was arrested in June 1947, immediately following an interview given to the Tass Agency, and since then nothing more has been known about him. The second, Mons. Karosas, an old man of 90, died in 1947 under unknown circumstances.

Actually of the nine Bishops who were in Lithuania in 1944 there remains only one, Mons. Kazys Paltarokas, the Bishop of Panevezys. Of the others, one was condemned to death, three deported and four sent into exile.

Even the Seminary of Kaunas which in 1948 was still open has been closed and the staff entirely substituted by "progressive" elements who educate the students in their own manner. The vice-Rector, the Canon Rauda and his successor, Father Kuzmitskas were arrested together with several professors.

There remain only one hundred priests out of the more than 1,600 in 1940, and even these in impossible conditions.

Of members of religious orders there have remained only some Jesuits and Franciscans. All the rest were expelled or imprisoned.

b) Latvia and Esthonia

What has been said about Lithuania also goes for the Catholic communities of Latvia and Esthonia.

Of the four Archbishops and Bishops who were in these countries in 1944 there remains but one, the Archbishop, Mons. Springovics. Of the other three, two are living in exile, and the other, the Archbishop Mons. Profittlich, Apostolic Administrator of all Esthonia, was arrested as early as 1945 and deported to an unknown locality. It appears for certain by now that he was killed.

It is thought that only ten or so Catholic priests remain out of almost 200. No member of a religious order or a religious house is to be found in the country. Of the almost 200 churches, few are still open.

It is difficult to say how many of the 600,000 and more Catholics in Latvia and Esthonia have remained after the deportations which continued at a faster and faster rate from 1944 on. It is estimated that more than 200,000 Latvians and Esthonians have been deported to Siberia. Their place has been taken by an equal number of persons imported from Asiatic regions. It is a question of the so-called "scientific transplanting" which within a few years will succeed in totally changing the face and the configuration of these three unfortunate countries whose millenial civilization, and whose traditions of faith and Christian piety, are about to be submerged under one of the most terrible persecutions recorded in human history.

D. THE FOURTH PERIOD:
SUPPRESSION OF THE GREEK-CATHOLIC CHURCH
IN ANNEXED AREAS

With the name "Sub-Carpathian Greek-Catholic Church" it was customary, up to 1944, to designate the Diocese of eastern

Catholic rite which included the entire region situated immediately to the south of the Carpathian mountains and which had
as its center the city of Munkacs or Mukacevo.

Politically it belonged to Hungary until the first World War
when it was transferred to Czechoslovakia, following the treaty
of Trianon of June 4, 1920. Later, at the time of the Vienna arbi-
tration of November 2, 1938, it was divided in two: the southern
part with the cities of Berehevo, Makacevo and Uzhorad was
restored to Hungary, while the northern part, with the center of
Hust, left to Czechoslovakia declared itself independent. On
March 16 of the following year 1939, immediately after the occupation of Prague by the Germans, the Hungarians crossed the
border and put the entire sub-Carpathian region under Hungarian rule. In October 1944 the entire territory was occupied by
the Russians who, making use of Communists who were brought
to power, made a self-styled "Popular Council," elected in Mukacevo on November 26, 1944, request Stalin by telegram for the
"gift" of being received into the Soviet Union. Formal annexation
by Soviet Russia was carried out on June 29, 1945, but already
for a long time the Russians had been acting like the absolute
lords of the country.

At the time of annexation to Russia the population of the
entire territory numbered 851,889 inhabitants, of which 461,555
were Greek Catholics, 81,412 Roman Catholics, 108,907 Orthodox,
77,833 Protestants, 112,653 Jews, and 9,529 belonging to other
confessions.

The Greek-Catholic Diocese had 459 churches, 281 parishes,
374 priests, and about ten religious houses. Flourishing Catholic
Action groups, Marian Congregations, youth Confraternities and
Associations prospered within it, and during the war it was possible to establish nine more parishes, besides a refugee asylum
in Mukacevo and an orphanage in Chust.

For a time at first the Russian occupation troops displayed
a certain benevolence towards the Greek-Catholic Church, in the
vain presumption of being able to Sovietize it in the same way
as the Orthodox Church in Russia. But they met with a courageous opposition on the part of the young Apostolic adminis-

trator, Mons. Theodore Romza, a student of the Russian College
in Rome, who refused to sign the manifesto of "spontaneous"
annexation to Russia. He declared that he did not want to co-
involve the Church in a political act which would not be looked
upon favorably by everybody.

It was this refusal which changed the ostentatious benevolence of the Soviets into an open persecution of the Greek Catholic Church. Within a few months the provisions against this
Church increased with an ever accelerating rhythm. Many priests
were arrested, the Catholic press was annihilated, and all Catholic schools, organizations, and welfare institutions were dissolved.

In the month of July 1947 the mournful balance sheet of these
first months of struggle showed 73 churches taken away from
the Catholics and given to the Orthodox, 15 priests deported, 3
sentenced to death, and 36 forced to flee to escape imminent
arrest.

On November 1 the mortal blow was struck with the murder
of the Bishop, Mons. Romza, by the Bolsheviks which was followed shortly after by the arrest and the mass deportation of
more than one hundred priests and many faithful.

After thus clearing the terrain of the main opposition the
Communists summoned from Moscow an orthodox Bishop named
Nestor who, with the help of Orthodox priests of the area, tried
to induce Catholic priests and faithful to become apostates. When
it was seen that efforts at persuasion were useless, threats were
made and every Orthodox priest would go into the houses of the
Catholic priests and faithful accompanied by agents of the secret
police. Those who did not join were deported.

Even there a "Judas" was found who put himself at the head
of an apostate movement. This was, Ireneus Micahel Kontrato-
vich who, after having been brutally tortured by the Soviets,
had ended up by giving in to their pressures and taking an oath
of allegiance to the Orthodox Patriarch of Moscow. He was immediately named Vicar general of the Diocese and installed in
the Bishopric palace of Uzhorod which had remained vacant
after the assassination of the Apostolic Administrator, Mons.
Romza.

But the real storm for the Greek Catholic Church began in February 1949. On the 22nd day of this month the Cathedral of Uzhorod was taken over and entrusted to the Orthodox. On the 27th a service was celebrated there by Bishop Macario who, in the meanwhile, had been appointed Bishop of Uzhorod by the Patriarch Alexis.

In the same month all the Greek-Catholic Churches were closed and priests were forbidden to exercise their sacred functions therein on the pretext that the Greek-Catholic Church was not officially registered as required by law.

In March the police expelled all the Greek-Catholic parish priests and their families from the canons; five were imprisoned, one, Demetrius Popovich, was sentenced to twenty-five years of forced labor.

The Seminary had ceased functioning already in the early part of 1940, after having changed its residence several times, because the Government confiscated its buildings as fast as they were occupied.

Many priests were interned in a hospital in Uzhorad and forced to attend the so-called re-education courses. Those who would not bend themselves to the new line were deported to Siberia.

Finally on August 28, 1940 (corresponding to the 15th day according to the old calendar, i.e., the feast of the Assumption of Most Blessed Virgin), during a liturgical service celebrated in the monastery of Mukacevo by the new Orthodox Bishop of Ushorad, Macario, the apostate, Kontratovitch read a declaration of the formal passage of the Greek-Catholic Church of lower Carpathia to the Russian Orthodox Church, in which it was affirmed that since August 28, 1949, the union with Rome had ceased to exist.

With this final act the Greek-Catholic Church was definitively liquidated. The few Catholic priests remaining free, because they have escaped arrest, do what they can to help the faithful secretly, but with each passing day their situation becomes more difficult. Many work in the factories to earn their wretched bread.

The only survivor has been the Latin Church which had, as

has been said, 81,000 faithful. But even many of its churches have been seized and few of its priests are left.

Of the 354 priests who existed in 1944, only 35 have supposedly gone over to the new schismatic church. This is an insignificant number and it reveals how the Communist attempt failed completely. Even those who allegedly converted did so only after innumerable tortures, and they were released from jails only on condition that they recognize the Patriarch of Moscow.

The balance sheet of the Communist persecution closed then, at the end of 1950, with one Bishop killed, 12 priests sentenced to death, 111 deported, 93 condemned to forced labor and more than 50,000 Catholics deported and interned.

At the end of 1951 "silence" fell tragically even over this Church.

CHAPTER II

Poland, 1945–1952

In 1945, following the vast territorial changes undergone by Poland, by the ceding in 1939 of all its eastern territories to Russia (about 180,000 sq. Km. with almost 12,000,000 inhabitants) and the absorption of parts of the western territories formerly belonging to Germany (about 103,000 sq. Km.) the entire situation of the Catholic Church in Poland changed notably as compared to 1939.

In fact with the ceding to Russia of eastern Polish territories, carried out by the Germans in September 1939 after the Ribbentrop-Molotov agreement, the Catholic Church had lost 9 of its 24 Dioceses which it had at that time, and more than 8 million (about 33%) of the 23,971,000 faithful which it numbered then.

It had suffered other losses during the German occupation from 1939 to 1945, in the course of which more than 3,000,000 Polish Catholics were deported, its Bishops were decimated (it is enough to consider that out of 46 Bishops who were on Polish territory in September 1939, three years later, in 1942, there were no more than 7), 584 priests killed on the spot and 1,263 died in concentration camps.

Still within the new borders, included between the Curzon-Ribbentrop-Molotov line on the east and the Oder-Neisse line on the west, the situation of the Catholic Church had improved from the new ethnic-religious point of view. For after losing its Orthodox minorities in the eastern territories to Russia (about 4,000,000) and the German-Protestant minorities (more than 2,000,000) which were transferred to Germany, and losing many of its Jews who in 1938 comprised 15% of the population, the new Poland found itself to be an entirely Catholic country (95%), with only some Protestant (280,000), Orthodox (500,000) and Jewish (80,000) minorities.

From an administrative-geographic point of view the new organization of the Catholic Church hierarchy in Poland was composed as follows:

a) 4 Archdioceses: Warsaw, Gniezno, Poznam and Cracow.

b) 14 Dioceses: Gdansk (Danzig), Chelmno (Culma), Katowice, Czestochowa, Kielsce, Lodz, Lomza, Lublin, Plock Przemysl, Sandomierz, Siedlce, Tarnow (Tarnovia), Wloclawek (Vladislavia).

c) 3 Provisional Residences of Dioceses which remained only partly on Polish territory: Vilno (with residence in Bielistok), Leopoli of the Latins (with residence in Lubaczow), Przemysl of the Ruthenians.

This, then, made a total of 25 ecclesiastical districts.

THE BEGINNINGS OF THE STRUGGLE

During the first phase of its relations with the Church (from June to September 1945) the provisional Government of National Unity, established on June 23, 1945, maintained a highly proper and even respectful attitude. This may have been due to a previously prepared tactical plan, or to the presence of non-Communists in the Government who were formerly with the Polish Government in exile in London.

Every official ceremony began with a solemn Mass which was attended by all the members of the Government, headed by the Communist leader Bierut.

From a statistical point of view the scope and structure of the Catholic Church in Poland in 1945 could be summarized in the following data:

	Priests	Parishes	Faithful
Warsaw	507	268	1,570,000
Gniezno	294	272	675,000
Poznam	501	385	1,250,000
Cracow	320	560	1,200,000
Chelmno	447	340	986,000
Czestochowa	354	215	1,000,000
Katowice	403	226	1,200,000
Kielce	240	310	840,000
Lodz	270	140	900,000
Lomza	235	135	550,000
Lublin	400	250	1,110,000
Plock	230	280	800,000
Przemysl (Latin)	645	440	1,100,000
Sandomiers	440	255	950,000
Siedlce	330	246	780,000
Tarnow	600	300	970,000
Vladislavia	310	250	900,000
Danzig	60	70	265,000
Administrative Apostolic Zone (inc. ex-German)	1,500	1,000	4,500,000
Remnants of Eastern Polish Dioceses	400	250	1,000,000
Total	8,516	6,192	22,546,000

The Army continued the tradition of publicly reciting morning and evening prayers, and the Crucifix continued to hang on the walls of schoolrooms. The properties of the Church were left intact, and it also happened that lands which had been confiscated were restored.

Everything seemed to be going along in the best possible

manner, but it was also evident that this entire attitude was not sincere and that it could not last long.

In fact, as soon as the Communists felt themselves to be better entrenched in power and better buttressed by the Russians who occupied the country militarily, they did not waste a day in throwing aside their mask. As the first act of their religious intolerance they began, on September 14, 1945, unilaterally to denounce the Concordat with the Holy See, concluded on February 10, 1925, alleging as a pretext that: "During the German occupation the Holy See had interfered with juridical provisions which were contrary to the conventions stipulated in the Concordat."

The Holy See hastened quickly to reply with a *Note* which appeared in the "Osservatore Romano" of September 25, 1945, in which it declared that it was necessary to deny the accusation of the Polish Government according to which it was supposed to have committed acts contrary to the conventions stipulated in the Concordat. This the Holy See did by demonstrating how the provisions which concerned the appointment of several Prelates during the German occupation were of a purely temporary character due to the necessity of not keeping the Bishopric seats vacant for long and proven by the fact that these Prelates were given only the tasks of "Apostolic Administrators" and not of resident Bishops. It could not understand, therefore, how the Polish Government from such provisions could find cause to declare the Concordat between the Holy See and the Polish Republic unilaterally broken.

The *Note* not only was not answered, but on the very day in which it appeared in the "Osservatore Romano," the Polish Government, in continuance of the activity it had undertaken, promulgated a law which established the non-obligatoriness of religious marriage for Catholics and introduced even the right to divorce for them.

This was a new act which openly revealed the beginning of an anti-religious policy by the Government. The Polish Catholic Episcopate, therefore, on October 21, 1945, was compelled to publish a joint declaration, drawn up in the course of a meeting held in the monastery of Jasna-Gora from October 3–4, in which Catholics were put on guard against the resurgent materialism and yet invited to work loyally for the state, to help the country rise from its ruins. But at the same time they were exhorted to oppose those in Poland who were attempting to unleash a war against the Church, a war which without a doubt would be harmful to the State and to national unity.

A few days after this declaration, the Primate of Poland, Cardinal Hlond, speaking at Liberty Square in Poznam, reminded his audience of that which had happened since the war and afterwards to the detriment of the Catholic Church in Poland on the part of the Nazi regime: profanation of the churches, destruction of monuments, occupation of religious houses, suppression of the Catholic press and publications, imprisonment of Bishops, massacres of the clergy and the faithful, extermination of people, the struggle against the Vatican, etc. And the Cardinal asked if the lesson of such an experience based on materialism had been understood or whether, on the contrary, the struggle between two different conceptions of the world was about to begin anew.

On December 7, 1945 the Episcopate was again compelled to take even a more determined position in the face of the ever more hostile attitude of the Government, and it issued a second Letter in order to protest against the abuses generated by the new law on marriage:

> The Decree concerning civil marriage imposed on Catholic citizens, contrary to the religious ideas of the nation, has no basis whatsoever in any real need of the State. It was necessary therefore to leave to the citizens of Catholic Poland the free choice of the nuptial ceremony according to its ritual form.
>
> The Episcopate must also condemn the fact that with the articles of the new law the door is open to divorce.
>
> The Bishops especially condemn these articles, according to which, in the course of the first three months of the law's establishment, every marriage can be legally annulled

without cause, if the conjoined, who are married for no
longer than three years, request it mutually.

(Tygodnik Warsawski 6-1-1946)

On January 17, 1946, the Holy Father himself, in a noble
letter to Polish Catholics dealing with this marriage law, wrote
as follows:

> Our fear is now justified and founded on fact: there is
> being promulgated in your country a new law which imperils
> the sanctity and the stability of marriage. In conformity with
> the duties of your charge, you have done everything to assure
> the continued inviolability of the family which, as the basis
> of all human society and the seed of civilization, constitutes
> in itself, and naturally, the hearth where the human person
> grows and develops as it should. Despite this your voice has
> not been heeded.

And unheeded from then on were all the voices of protest
which the Catholic Bishops repeated and multiplied without
pause.

On May 24, 1946, the Catholic Episcopate, after a two-day
meeting in the sanctuary of Czestochowa, alarmed by the re-
crudesence of terrorist acts which kept the country in a state of
agitation, was compelled to denounce the gravity of the situation
even more openly:

> One of the problems which must be examined with at-
> tention is that of the agitation which reigns in the country
> and the scant personal security for the citizenry which results
> therefrom.
> The Polish Episcopate, together with the entire popula-
> tion, profoundly deplores these incidents and appeals to those
> responsible for this state of affairs, regardless of the motives
> to which they make obeisance, that they remember the
> commandments of God and cease these acts of violence, and
> that, so as not to inflict new harms on their country already
> sorely tried.
> Among the many abuses which exist in public life, we

point out the demands made on the clergy to participate in hybrid religious ceremonies during holidays or civil solemnities. These requests are neither in conformity with the sacred character of religious functions, nor with the liturgical laws of the Church. The Church authorities cannot permit them, because they are contrary to the way in which divine offices must be celebrated.

Even the care to be taken for the religious education of youth has been equally subjected to profound discussion. And since, under present conditions the youth is more than ever before exposed to moral dangers, the Church has the obligation of surrounding this youth with its maternal protection to prevent its perversion.

The Polish Bishops have often protested with letters against the suppression of babies still in the maternal womb. Now the information which the Episcopate receives regarding abortions is still more frightful from the point of view of morality. And this abuse is so harmful for the future of our race, that we, guardians of the Christian faith and morality, implore all mothers, doctors, midwives and whosoever has any influence in this important matter, to combat this crime. The continuation of these practices would have consequences, for our life and country, more terrible than the hecatombs of the last war.

This time the censorship intervened and the publication of the above Declaration was forbidden in the Polish press. There took place, indeed, a diplomatic incident which provoked a protest by the Warsaw Government to the British Government because Radio London had broadcast in Polish several excerpts of the Declaration. On July 31, 1946 the Foreign Office replied with an expression of regrets for certain inaccuracies in the broadcast which the Polish government had hastened to point out, but it refused the protest insofar as it concerned the act of broadcasting itself, basing itself on the freedom of information and pointing out that the periodicals, "Soviet News" and "Soviet Monitor," circulated freely in Great Britain, often giving Russian opinions and interpretations of events which transpired in England, without anyone making objection.

The temporizing tactic adopted by the Communists in regard to the Catholic Church in Poland, during the first two years of the regime from 1945 to 1947, began to change immediately following the general elections of January 19, 1947.

Having obtained the governing majority, with those methods used by totalitarian regimes, the new regime began to attack the Catholic Church more directly.

The first objective the Communist Government set itself was that of eliminating every Christian influence, progressively but methodically, from Polish public life, substituting for it the dogmatic influence and practice of the Marxist ideology in all possible sectors.

In Poland the Catholic Church was not only the religious institution which embraced almost the totality of its citizens (95%), but it had also so permeated the entire public and national life through the centuries, that an enterprise such as that which the communists had undertaken was not at all an easy one and it was necessary to proceed step by step.

So at first they began by boycotting all public religious manifestations (feasts, processions, etc.) and by making ceremonies of a civic nature fall on the very same days, to which all those dependent upon the State were obliged to attend—and in a totalitarian State this means the entire mass of citizens—under the threat of special punishments, such as the withdrawal of bread ration books, identity cards, etc.

From this they went on to organizing an entire series of public entertainments and spectacles so as to reduce as much as possible the flow of the faithful to the churches. A special Commission for "Popular Entertainments and Recreational Activity" was established as part of the "Propaganda Section of the Central Committee of the Party," (C.K.P.Z.P.R.) with the task of convincing the working classes that the Party was interested in gratifying their cultural and recreational needs with the slogan given to the party organizers: "Your entertainments are better than those of the parishes. Enjoy yourselves with more pleasure than in the old 'functions.'"

They went so far, finally, as to prohibit with a decree dated November 23, 1949, the following public religious manifestations:

a) The organization of public and joint pilgrimages.
b) Processions in the public streets.
c) The solemn benediction of fields. (Rogation Day prayers.)
d) The placing and public benediction of crosses and statues on public roads.
e) The organization of public manifestations and religious cortéges.
f) The convocation of meetings, conferences, Christmas recitations and representations.
g) Open-air parish meetings.

But this was not enough. Even the private activities of single Catholics were made objects of special punishments. If the police noticed that an employee who occupied an important post went to church he was immediately warned, and if despite the warning, he continued, he was removed from his job.

In a Pastoral letter published on March 10, 1947, on occasion of the 950th anniversary of the martyrdom of St. Adalbert, Apostle and patron of Poland, Card. Hlond, the Primate of Poland, rose to protest publicly against the entire maneuver of the Polish Communist Government which was definitively trying to limit every activity of the Church to the precincts of the Temples, eliminating all of its influence in the public life of the country:

At the present time [said the Cardinal] the shadow of Paganism is born again and it spreads over the entire world: a paganism which has nothing in common with the idolatry of our forefathers. It is a modern paganism, with all the characteristics of a militant atheism. Not only does it not recognize any God, but it is hostile to every divine ideal against which it declares war. Its adherents want to substitute matter for the glory of the Creator. In all fields of life and of culture itself they try to wipe out even the traces of religious thought.

These atheists above all want to abolish any principle whatsoever which stems from the Church in the education of youth. They act by trying to drive religion from the masses and by de-Christianizing them. Their tactic is not the same in all countries, nor are the reactions to which they give rise the same everywhere.

This form of neo-paganism has not succeeded in infecting Poland, nor in subverting the soul of the People. The most perspicacious men have immediately understood that it is a question of a struggle undertaken against Catholicism, and that not only is the Church being fought in the factories and in the laboratories, but also in the humblest houses in the countryside.

Each one must understand the urgent necessity of opposing such an invasion. Each one must understand that the time of indifference and neutrality is over. It is not possible passively to witness this attempt to disseminate in profoundly Catholic Poland the theories of neo-paganism. It is necessary to save our Christian heritage. We cannot surrender anything to neo-paganism. A war without quarter has been declared between us and the neo-pagans. Every possibility of compromise is excluded. There can be no agreement between Christ and Belial.

In the course of its tormented history Poland has overcome tremendous crises, ever preserving unaltered its spiritual tradition which was that of Saint Adalbert. The Church has not undergone attacks comparable to the ones of which it is the target today since the time of the persecutions of Nero.

After the defeat of Hitler, the situation of the Church in Poland, internally, appears to be strong, but from without there are noticeable the symptoms of an organized struggle against the Church and its institutions. The independent mission of the Church and its moral influence on men irritate the followers of totalitarian regimes who rear because the Church refuses to close itself within the walls of its churches, or because it refuses to put itself at the service of any party, wishing to remain as it is in a modern state . . .

The situation of Poland, in this relationship, is not yet the most serious one but, alas, even among us the evil has increased beyond measure. It is not necessary to go into details. We observe all that with great preoccupation and we conclude that along this road Poland cannot resurrect itself spiritually.

A few months later, September 8, 1947, this Letter of the Primate was followed by a joint Letter of the entire Polish Episcopate in which, with new exhortations, Catholics were put on guard against atheist propaganda:

There is no lack, alas, of painful symptoms which strike us sorrowfully because of the dissonance which they introduce in the so firm and vigorous activity of our Catholics. Deeds take place which are in flagrant contradiction with the dignity of Catholic morality. They are so numerous that one cannot but think that there exists a secret and consciously directed struggle against God and against the Church . . ."

The Letter encountered the liveliest opposition on the part of the Government organs. Prime Minister, Cyrankiewicz, himself, addressing the Diet on October 29, 1947, denounced it before Parliament as an act of open opposition to the regime. An entire press campaign was organized to accuse the clergy and the Catholic Episcopate of conducting an activity destructive to the realization of the postulates of the so-called "Peoples Democracy," as expressed by "Glos Ludu" (Voice of the People) on October 16, 1947 and "Robotnik" (The Worker), organ of the Polish Socialist-fusionists, of October 17, 1947.

THE CAMPAIGN AGAINST THE HIERARCHY AND THE CLERGY

Frustrated once again in its efforts to eliminate the influence of the Catholic Church in the schools and in the civil life of the country, by the strong resistance offered by the hierarchy and the clergy, the Polish Communist Government, as early as 1948, began a violent press and propaganda campaign against the Bishops and Catholic priests, accusing them of opposing the program of the Communist regime.

At first it began with accusations of "clandestine activity" and "immorality" against the clergy. Every day there were headlines in the newspapers of this kind: "Warsaw priest sentenced to 10 years for raping a child"; "Cracow priest arrested for trafficking in black market"; "Bishop, ex-Nazi collaborator, jailed."

These generic accusations were then followed by an ever increasing toll of arrests and trials against the most prominent members of the clergy and the Catholic hierarchy.

In the month of May, 1948, Mons. Carol Niemira, formerly Auxiliary Bishop of Pinsk, was condemned to six months in prison on the most absurd charges. In the same week, Father Buchala, a priest of the Diocese of Cracow, was sentenced to three years in jail "for having—according to the sentence—ridiculed the people's democracy." Among the principal priests who were arrested the following names are remembered: Father Leon Pawlina, formerly head of the Catholic welfare organization, "Caritas"; Rev. Grzechnik, Monsignor Marchewka, the Canon, Poloska, Rev. Jarkiewicz, sentenced to prison because he was accused of "moral complicity in the assassination of three democratic agitators"; Rev. Boleslaw Stefanski, sentenced to death, because he was accused of "enlisting his students into a secret band;" Rev. Krzeminsk, sentenced to 6 years after charges of being in touch with the underground movement; Mons. Sigmund Kacynski, formerly a member of the Polish Government as Minister of Instruction in London, arrested under the charge of having "carried out activities harmful to the State"; Father Gaetano Raczynski, for many years Procurator General of the Fathers Paolini in Rome, etc.

It has been estimated that towards the end of September 1948 more than 400 priests were interned in prisons or deported to German concentration camps where they had languished for years under the Nazi domination.

This violent campaign against the hierarchy and the Catholic clergy could not exclude the very Primate of Poland, the venerable Cardinal August Hlond who, hardly upon his return in February 1948 from his visit to Rome, was accused by the Communist press of having supported the "Vatican thesis," according to which the Pope would support the German claim to the Oder-Niesse territories assigned to the Poles.

"Spontaneous" meetings were held throughout the country against Cardinal Hlond and against the Vatican. Numerous protests were deposited at the door of Chancellery of the Primate by trade union and political associations and organizations. Even the Professors of the University of Warsaw sent the protest of the Academic Senate, dated June 9, 1948, to the Cardinal.

Cardinal Hlond was forced to fight back against this Communist campaign. On July 3, 1948, he addressed a message to the population of the restored territories, in which with great energy and in the name of the entire Catholic Polish Episcopate, he branded as false the charges made against the Holy Father and the Church of Poland, citing with ample documentation, proofs of the paternal attitude of the Pope towards the Polish nation: ". . . Insofar as regards the Pope and the Church"—declared the Cardinal Primate—"you may rest assured about the fate of your houses . . ."

Unfortunately, this message was to be the last by Cardinal Hlond for a few months later, on October 22, 1948, he died at the age of 67, more the victim of the bitter struggle in defense of the Catholic Church in Poland than of age or illness.

The struggle of the Communist government against the Catholic hierarchy in Poland, after the death of Cardinal Hlond, assumed an even more bitter tone, sparing not even the new Archbishop-Primate, Mons. Stephen Wyszynski, who had made his entry into the Polish capital on February 6, 1949.

In fact on March 14, 1949, the Polish Communist Government

delivered a "Note" to Mons. Choromanski, Secretary of the
Episcopal Commission and Auxiliary Bishop of Warsaw, in which
it was said, that—

> For sometime it has been possible to observe a growing
> anti-government propaganda on the part of the clergy by
> means of pastoral letters and confidential instructions, de-
> signed to incite restlessness and agitation in minds, and
> having the purpose of giving the impression that religion is
> menaced in Poland.

The Polish Episcopate replied to this note on April 24, 1949,
with a joint letter signed by 24 Archbishops and Bishops, in
which it was said textually:

> At a moment in which the situation of the Church be-
> comes ever more serious, the fullfillment of our apostolic
> mission ever more difficult, and when the responsibility of
> such a situation is attributed to the episcopal hierarchy,
> we consider it indispensable to re-establish the truth.
>
> The Church has its own organization fixed by Canon
> Law and moreover it has its own principles of teaching . . .
> It has never used its influence to harm Poland . . . or is there
> really someone who believes that the Church is a political
> power and which as such constitutes a threat to Poland?
> We think that it would be quite difficult to find someone in
> Poland who is convinced that the clergy represents a foreign
> power, hostile to Poland.
>
> Too many priests have died for the fatherland for us to
> doubt their love of the country. We ask you for whom did
> the holy Bishop Michael Kozal, the venerable Archbishop
> Nowawiekski, and his co-adjudicator, the Bishop Wetmanski
> and the Bishop of Lublin, Goral, for whom did they die?
> Why did several thousands of priests die at the hands of the
> enemy during the war? In truth this clergy is at the same
> time Roman-Catholic and Polish.
>
> At a time when nuns are being expelled from hospitals
> and when religious organizations are being dissolved, justice
> and right will end by prevailing.

We share then your sorrow for the fact that so many priests are kept away from the altars. The number of the accused and those sentenced preoccupies us the while we cannot come to their aid, not having the possibility of knowing of what they are accused, nor the power of listening to the accused.

Do your duty towards Poland in such a way as not to neglect your duty towards God. Convince yourselves that it is certainly not by showing yourselves traitors to God, that you will build a better Poland.

As a reaction against this joint Letter of the Episcopate, the Polish Communist Government intensified its campaign of denigration against the clergy, accusing, on July 1949, three Bishops of collaboration with the Nazis: Mons. Adamski of Katowice, Mons. Kaczmarec of Kielce and Mons. Lorek of Sandomir. Over the radio violent attacks were made even against Mons. Czayka, auxiliary Bishop of Czestochowa. Many priests were also arrested for the sole fact of having dared to read the entire contents of the Letter of the Bishops to the faithful. And sensational was the arrest of the Jesuit Father, Wladyslaw Gurgacs, which took place on July 6, 1949, on the charge of "co-guilt in the organization of political *attentats* and assaults on State banks."

The Episcopate once again had to intervene with another joint Letter, published on July 18, 1949, in which new abuses were listed committed by the Government against the Catholic Church in Poland, such as the suppression of the two Catholic weeklies, the "Typodnik Powszechny" of Cracow and the "Typodnik Watszawski," with the simultaneous arrest of its two editors and many other members of the staff, charged with defeatism; the nationalization of all the Catholic printing plants which numbered about fifteen; the secularization of all the hospitals with the consequent dismissal of many nuns and almost all Chaplains; the suppression of many Catholic associations, etc.

This Letter of the Episcopate was followed on September 1, 1949, by a Letter of the Holy Father to the Polish Episcopate, in which the religious situation in Poland was summarized thus:

Although the war has been over for four years, the Catholic Church in Poland has yet to find the freedom which is due to it, not only as a sacrosanct right, but also for all the sufferings and bitter tribulations it has suffered for the common welfare.

Unhappily, its sufferings have not ceased. The Catholic Associations have been almost entirely destroyed, religious instruction in the schools has been extremely reduced; obstacles have been put in the way even of institutions supervised by the clergy or by nuns; the Catholic religion is odiously calumniated. *We ourselves,* the Bishops and the Priests have been insulted; Catholic writings destined for the press submitted to one of the most injust censorships; correspondence and relations between the Holy See and Bishops impeded; the outer manifestations of the Catholic cult made more difficult each day.

The Polish Communist Government replied to the two Letters with a series of restrictive decrees and provisions regarding the Catholic Church which embittered still more the tense relations between State and Church.

Already on August 5, 1949, came the promulgation of the decree for the "Defense of Conscience and Religious Confessions," which threatened harsh punishment, not excluding the death penalty, for persons exploiting religion to create public disorders. On September 11 of the same year another decree established the transference of baptismal records, until then kept by the Church, to State functionaries. On the 18th a new decree changed the regulations on the rights to hold meetings. And on October 1 a law was published which nationalized all the hospitals held by the Church, and by the 3rd it was already in force. On November 23 a ministerial circular, published by the Director of Offices for Church Affairs, Wolski, placed new obstacles in the way of the right to assembly and to the exercise of public worship.

All these acts and provisions clearly demonstrated that the

Polish Communist Government was applying a carefully mapped out plan of intimidations and restrictions in order to induce the Church to come to terms with the State.

The beginning of 1950 was in fact immediately disturbed by a furious campaign against "Caritas."

The Polish "Caritas" was a vast welfare organization, established through the work of the Church and presided by Cardinal Adam Sapieha, which had brought immense benefits to the population sorely tried during the war and the occupation, and which enjoyed a great popularity. In fact the organization at the beginning of 1950 was veritably colossal. It had 665 charitable establishments divided as follows: 334 orphanages with 16,676 children, 258 homes for the aged, 38 infirmaries for sick children, 17 institutions for poor girls, 18 hostelries for women workers; and 346 popular kitchens which furnished about 100,000 meals a day. In a large measure funds came from American welfare associations, primarily from the "War Relief Service," the "National Catholic Welfare Conference," and from Poles in the United States. These funds came to about several million *zlotis* a year.

On January 23, 1950, the Government issued a decree against this worthy organization, in contempt of the very negotiations it was then carrying on with the Episcopate, with which it arbitrarily removed the Bishops from its direction and installed in their stead a new administrative council composed of "patriotic priests" and progressive Catholics, while the press covered the violent maneuver with defamatory articles breathing hatred and calumny against the Church.

The Episcopate could not remain silent and on January 24, Card. Sapieha, the President of "Caritas," sent the President of the Republic the following telegram:

EXCELLENCY PRESIDENT BIERUT, WARSAW:
PROFOUNDLY SHAKEN BY THE METHODS OF CONTROL, AND BY
THE NEWSPAPER ARTICLES FULL OF HATE, I PROTEST TO YOU AND
PRAY YOU TO HAVE THESE PROCEDURES CEASE.

ADM. CARD. SAPIEHA, PRESIDENT, "CARITAS"

Since this telegram received no reply all the Bishops raised their voices in a joint protest and on January 30, 1950 sent to the same President Bierut the following Memorandum:

. . . The Catholic Episcopate, assembled in plenary conference in Cracow, has felt it was duty bound to make known to you, Mr. President, the following:

The Government, in order to justify at the juridical level its last dispositions, directed towards the annihilation of the activities of the ecclesiastical institution "Caritas," has had recourse to the decree of the President of the Republic of April 22, 1927, regarding the inspection and the control of the activities of welfare organizations (see Dz. U.R.P. 1927, n. 40, p. 354).

Now this decree does not authorize the Government to control "Caritas" and much less does it consent that a governmental administration be imposed on the same institution. "Caritas" in fact is not a society, or corporation or an institution which falls under that law, but it is an integral part of the institutions of the Church . . . Therefore the control of "Caritas" ordered by the Government is contrary to the laws of Poland now in force.   .

But in imposing a governmental administration even other laws of the State have been violated. Article 11, in fact, of the decree of April 22, 1937 requires that, when the societies subject to control do not follow the injunctions of the authorities which control them they must be warned in writing, and after repeated warnings with no results, the directors in charge may be substituted . . . Now contrary to these regulations, the Governing authorities, without any previous warning, have instituted a governmental administration of "Caritas" and only afterwards did they proceed to the control of the single institutions. The Church authorities, the only competent persons in this matter, were not even advised.

From the methods of control which followed and by the acts which accompanied it, it is easy to see how the inspection does not aim to review what was accomplished, nor the common good, but it aims only to destroy that church institution and to denigrate and calumniate the Catholic Faith for the purpose of destroying the Church in Poland . . . This is evident from the spectacular campaign unleashed in the press and over the radio, as well as in conferences and meetings. . . .

The Episcopate meanwhile protests not only against this campaign, carried out to harm of Catholics and the Church, but also against the activity of the Governing authorities which mobilize the Catholic clergy, members of religious orders and the faithful, against Catholic welfare, thereby violating the freedom of their consciences.

Priests, members of religious orders and faithful, are summoned to conferences and meetings with different tactics: sometimes terror is used besides the deceit of making them appear as conferences or meetings in line with their duties. Orders are often accompanied by strong moral pressures, exercised personally by heads of Districts or Paltinates, by the prefects of cities, by directors of the Party and by agents of the public security. There is no lack of cases wherein veritable hunts of priests have been organized; some have been awakened at night by armed police who often have not permitted them to celebrate Mass or they have compelled them to interrupt their services; hence certain of them have found themselves present at the afore-mentioned conferences in their liturgical vestments. Many have had to hide themselves. In order to induce those gatherings to make pronouncements against the welfare activity of the Church, the authorities have staged sumptuous receptions in which alcohol flowed freely.

Those priests who were aware of the purposes of the

gatherings and who refused to participate were punished
with fines. In the published lists of priests who were supposed to have taken part in such gatherings there were
inserted the names of persons who have been dead for a
long time. Certain priests have been compelled to accept
posts in the governmental administration of "Caritas" and
they have been registered there without their knowledge and
despite their protests.

The Episcopate of Poland presents to the President its
solemn protest against all these dispositions.

The Episcopate has the right to expect that these deliberations as well as the governmental administrations imposed illegally on "Caritas" be revoked.

CARD. ADAM STEFAN SAPIEHA,
Archbishop of Cracow
STEFAN WYSZYNSKI,
Primate of Poland, Archbishop of Warsaw
ROUALDUS JALBRZYKOWSKI,
Archbishop of Bielistok
EUGENIUS BAZIAK, *Archbishop of Lubaczow*
WALENTY DYMEK, *Archbishop of Poznania*
TEODOR KUBINA, *Bishop of Czestochowa*
KAROL RADONSKI,
Bishop of Wloklawek (Wladislavia)
STANISLAW ADAMSKI, *Bishop of Katowice*
FRANCISZEK BARDA, *Bishop of Przemysl*
JAN LOREK, *Bishop of Sandmierz*
CZESLAW KACZMAREK, *Bishop of Kielce*
TEDEUSZ ZAKRAEWSKI, *Bishop of Plock*
JAN STEPA, *Bishop of Tarnow*
KASIMIRZ JOSEPH KOWALSKI, *Bishop of Pelpin*
IGNACY SWIRSKI, *Bishop of Siedlce*
MICHAL KLEPACZ, *Bishop of Lodz*
CZESLAW FALKOWSKI, *Bishop of Lomza*
PIOTR KALWA, *Bishop of Lublin*
KAROL MILIK, *Apostolic Adm. of Gdansk*
EDMUND NOWICKI, *Apost. Adm. of Gorzow*

BOLESLAW KOMINEK, *Apost. Adm. of Olstyzn*
ZYGMUND CHOROMANSKI,
Bishop, Episcopate Secretary
Cracow, January 30, 1950

On the same day, January 30, 1950, the Bishops sent a circular to the clergy in order to explain the reasons which had compelled them to dissolve the "Caritas" organization and to warn them not to accept posts in the new governmental administration.

Here are the essential parts of the text of the Circular:

. . . The events of the last days, regarding the intervention of State authorities in the question of "Caritas" induce us to communicate to you, most beloved brothers, our thoughts and our observations . . .

The circumstances, indeed, which have accompanied the aggression (it must be thus called) against "Caritas" sufficiently reveal the intentions behind such maneuvers. In this entire affair there comes into play and into discussion not only the manner in which charitable activities were conducted, but it concerns something infinitely more important, and that is that the organization and the unity of the Church in Poland is in danger of its life.

We note the following facts:

a) The civil authorities have interfered in questions concerning the Church authority and have publicly manifested their lack of faith towards the President of "Caritas," the Eminent Cardinal, Sapieha, and the most Excellent Bishops.

b) The civil authorities have seized the Bishopric welfare offices and the properties of the Church earmarked for charitable purposes. They have arbitrarily appointed administrative commissions in the Dioceses, offering posts in such administrations to priests and installing therein persons little known or totally unknown to Catholic circles.

c) They dispose of priests in an arbitrary manner, transporting them as things from one meeting to another. They organized heated discussions during meetings on problems concerning the religious life. Finally, what is most humiliating for a man, they practice corruption by means of costly and sumptuous banquets, free rides on trains and busses, and by adulation of certain priests, exercised even by high functionaries of the State—something which is passing strange given the present condition of priests.

Such are the facts except that they are only a small part of what could be said.

Does not all this, perhaps, give rise to suspicions? Is it really just a question of concern for the ill and the poor? The condemnation of the alleged abuses of the Bishops in the administration of "Caritas," pronounced by priests, does it not prove, perhaps that it is a question of something more serious? . . . The actual forms of this struggle are nothing new or unexpected for us.

Be not surprised, therefore, dearest Brothers, if we are compelled to address you a firm and paternal warning. For this reason:

a) Priests must remember that they are not allowed to participate in meetings having a political character or flavor; more so they must not participate in meetings against the institutions and organizations of the Church so as not to oppose the priests to the Bishops, to weaken the internal unity of the clergy, to detach it from its bond with the hierarchy, or rather the true Church of Christ.

b) All priests must know that the Polish Episcopate has done much, and is disposed to do all that is necessary in the future, to preserve the internal peace of the Country and an opportune collaboration with the secular authorities. With almost superhuman efforts we are trying to keep distant from you the difficulties and the preoccupations deriving from the present state of things. There are, however, certain limits beyond which we Bishops cannot go, if we wish to remain faithful to the Commandments of God and of the Church, and to keep our names as good Shepherds . . .

c) Without condemning those who because of lapse of conscience or deceit have let themselves be dragged into the unworthy enterprises of persons without a Catholic conscience, we invite them, nonetheless, to group themselves spontaneously and with firmness in defense of the honesty of the priesthood and of its inner discipline. . . .

On the same day, January 30, 1950, the Bishops believed it was opportune to inform even the Faithful of the state of affairs with a Declaration which was to be read on February 12 following in all the churches of Poland. In order to prevent it the authorities resorted to intimidations, threats, repressions and imprisonments, subjecting the clergy to a persecution so widespread, as has never been before, perhaps, in the history of Poland. Here is the complete text of the Declaration:

. . . The Polish Episcopate shares its sorrow, provoked by the recent Government dispositions regarding "Caritas," with the entire Catholic community.

The Bishops of all Poland, gathered in assembly in Cracow on January 30, have addressed, in reference to this, a protest to President Bierut, amply documented.

In the face of the lying information now circulating in order to discredit this association, the Episcopate feels it is its duty to render justice to it.

Following the principles of the Gospel, "Caritas" has tried to help all the needy regardless of political tendency. It must also be borne in mind that it received considerable funds from American Bishops and Polish Catholics in the United States and that in distributing the aid coming from there it had to conform to the will of the donors. This was the reason why it had to help materially convents, seminaries and religious institutions.

The Polish Episcopate, under the direction of Cardinal Sapieha, certifies that the conduct of "Caritas" was guided by principles of honesty and justice. And to demonstrate how much we are convinced of that, we proclaim that from the moment when the civil powers furnish "Caritas" with a new organization, from that instant on such an association ceases to be the expression of the charitable activity of the Church. It is for this reason that the Bishops find themselves in the unpleasant necessity of dissolving the religious Association called "Caritas."

To the priests then and to the faithful who have up to now helped "Caritas" to grow, the Episcopate recommends to them that they ever continue their charitable activities, animated by the Christian spirit and from love of their neighbor.

This declaration drawn up in Cracow, on January 30, by all the assembled Bishops, will be read in every Church and at every Mass on February 12. . . .

In his turn, Mons. Stephan Wyszynski, the Primate of Poland, wished to explain to the people of his Archdiocese of Warsaw, the history of the suppression of "Caritas" with a Letter, dated February 3, 1950, which constitutes one of the most categoric documents on the present religious situation of the Catholic Church in Poland.

Here are the most important points of the letter:

. . . You await from me, from your Pastor, some words of explanation regarding the sorrowful question of the suppression of the church welfare association "Caritas."

You should have received this explanation from your parish priests, in the name of the entire Polish Episcopate. For extremely sad reasons, I have exempted my clergy from carrying out this charge. I cannot, however, exempt myself, because I am under obligation to tell the truth first in my own name, as Archbishop of Gniesm and Warsaw, and then in the name of the Episcopate, as the Primate of Poland. In fulfilling this duty, I take all responsibility on myself, deriving from the office of Primate, before God, the Church and the Polish people.

I am convinced that my duty corresponds to right, because I belong to the attacked and the accused. In every civil state the man who is attacked has the right to defense and to help. Moreover, such a right is possessed by the Episcopate, the lofty mission and lofty authority of which it enjoys among the people, will not permit it to leave unanswered the accusations which are hurled against it. Since it is not given to us to defend ourselves in the press and on the radio, we are compelled to use the pulpit in our defense.

THE AGREEMENT OF APRIL 14, 1950

Unexpectedly and just when the negotiations for an agreement between the Catholic Church and the State in Poland seemed to have arrived at a dead end, and the publication of the law for the nationalization of all church properties in the March 23, 1950 issue of "Dziennik Ustaw Rzeczypospolite Polskiej," indicated that a fight to the end against the Catholic Church seemed to be in full swing, on April 16, 1950, the Polish Agency, PAP, officially announced that an "Agreement" had been signed two days before, April 14, 1950, between the Government and the Catholic Polish Episcopate, the contents of which were as follows:

a) Agreement Decided Upon Between the Representatives of the Government of the Republic and the Polish Episcopate

In order to assure to People's Poland and its citizens the best conditions of development, as well as the possibility for common and tranquil work, the Government of the Republic which accepts the principle of religious liberty, and the Polish Episcopate, which takes into account the good of the Church and the present day right of the Polish State, regulate their relations in the following manner:

ARTICLE 1. The Episcopate will make efforts to the end that the clergy, within the limits of its pastoral activities, teach the faithful to respect the laws and the state authorities.

ARTICLE 2. The Episcopate will make efforts to the end that the clergy, within the limits of its pastoral activities, urge the faithful to increase their labor for the reconstruction of the Country, and to increase the welfare of the Nation.

ARTICLE 3. The Polish Episcopate makes it known that economic, historic, cultural and religious rights require that the re-occupied territories belong now and forever to Poland. Starting from the principle that such territories form an integral part of the Republic, the Episcopate will forward to the Holy See a request that the ecclesiastical administrations which enjoy residential archbishopric rights be changed into definitive regulating Bishoprics.

ARTICLE 4. The Episcopate, within the limits of its power, will oppose every hostile activity against Poland and in particular the anti-Polish and revisionist actions of a part of the German clergy.

ARTICLE 5. The principle that the Pope is the supreme and decisive authority of the Church regarding questions of faith, and morals, as well as those of ecclesiastical jurisdiction. In all others, instead, the Episcopate will regulate itself in accordance with the rights of the Polish State.

ARTICLE 6. Admitting that the mission of the Church can be carried out in agreement with the various economic and social regimes established by civil authorities, the Episcopate will instruct the clergy that it not oppose the development of agricultural cooperatives since, in essence, they have an ethical basis in human nature which tends to voluntary social solidarity whose aim is the good of the community.

ARTICLE 7. The Catholic Church which, in conformity with its principles, condemns every crime, will also combat the criminal activity of secret bands, and will stigmatize and punish with canonic punishments members of the clergy guilty of participating in any secret movement whatsoever against the State.

ARTICLE 8. The Catholic Church which, in conformity with its principles, condemns every anti-state attitude, will especially oppose the abuse of religious sentiments to the detriment of the State.

ARTICLE 9. The Episcopate, in conformity with the doctrine of the Church, will approve every effort which aims to strengthen peace and it will oppose, according to its capacities, every tendency designed to provoke war.

ARTICLE 10. Religious instruction in the schools:

a) The Government does not intend to limit the present state of religious instruction in the schools. The programs will be elaborated by church authorities, in agreement with representatives of the clergy; the schools will be provided with convenient text books; teachers of religion, lay or clerical, will be accorded the same treatment accorded to those who teach other subjects. The inspectors of religious teaching will be appointed by the school authorities, in agreement with the Episcopate.

b) The school authorities will place no obstacles in the path of students who wish to take part in religious practices outside the school.

c) The Catholic schools now in existence will be maintained. The Government, however, will keep watch over them to see that dispositions and programs established by the State authorities are carried out and followed.

d) The schools directed by the Catholic Church will be able to enjoy the rights enjoyed by state schools, in accordance with the general principles specified in express laws and in the dispositions of the school authorities.

e) In the case of the institution or the transformation of a public school into a school without religious instruction, Catholic parents who so desire will have the right and the possibility of sending their children to schools which are so provided.

ARTICLE 11. The Catholic University of Lublin may continue its activities within the present limits.

ARTICLE 12. Catholic associations will enjoy the rights had up to now when they have satisfied the dispositions contained in the decree on associations. The same dispositions hold for the Marian congregations.

ARTICLE 13. The Church will have the right and the possibility of directing, within the framework of laws now in force, charitable and welfare activities, and Catechismal instruction.

ARTICLE 14. The Catholic press and publications will enjoy, like others, the rights specified in express laws and dispositions of the authorities.

ARTICLE 15. Public worship, pilgrimages and traditional processions will not be prevented. Such manifestations, however, for purposes of order, will be arranged and regulated by the ecclesiastical authorities in agreement with administrative authorities.

ARTICLE 16. Religious assistance to the army shall be regulated by a special statute worked out by the military authorities in accordance with the representatives of the Episcopate.

ARTICLE 17. In penal institutions religious assistance will be assured by chaplains appointed by the competent authorities on the proposal of the Ordinant.

ARTICLE 18. In State hospitals and in those which are autonomous religious assistance for sick persons who desire it will be assured by hospital chaplains who will be remunerated according to special regulations.

ARTICLE 19. Religious orders and congregations, within the framework of their vocation and laws now in effect, will enjoy full liberty of action.

b) Added Protocol

ARTICLE 1. Following the agreement between the representatives of the government of the Polish Republic and of the Episcopate regarding the activity of "Caritas," and with the aim of rendering the relations between State and Church normal, the ecclesiastical organization "Caritas" changes itself into a Catholic Association with the aim of helping the poor and the indigent. The Association will carry out its activity in zones corresponding to the administrative and territorial divisions of the Country. The Episcopate, in accordance with the charitable aims of the Association, as well as in accordance with the principles and practice of the Catholic Church, will make it possible for priests to be requested to work in this Association.

ARTICLE 2. The Government of the Polish Republic, carrying out the law "of the transference of properties and mortmain" in the framework of art. 2, p. 3 and art. 7, p. 1, of the law, will study the needs of Bishops and religious institutions in order to provide them with assistance.

ARTICLE 3. The ecclesiastical fund will put counterpart sums at the disposition of Diocesan Ordinants.

ARTICLE 4. Carrying out the law of military service, the military authorities will consider the deferment of students of Church seminaries in order to permit them to finish their studies. Priests after ordination and religious brothers after vows will not be called to active military service, but will be put in the reserve and in grade will be attached to the auxiliary service.

> (*signed*) WLADYSLAW WOLSKI, *Minister of Public Instruction*
>
> EDWARD OCHARB, *Vice Minister of National Defense*
>
> ZYGMUNT CHIROMANSKI, *Secretary of the Episcopate*
>
> TADEUSZ ZARKEWSKY, *Bishop of Plock*
>
> MICHAL KLEPACZ, *Bishop of Lodz for the Polish Episcopate*

Warsaw, April 14, 1950

THE COMMUNICATION OF THE EPISCOPATE AND THE MEANING OF THE AGREEMENT

On April 22, 1950, a few days after the signing of the Agreement on the part of the representatives of the Episcopate and of the Government, the entire Episcopate, assembled at Gniezno, believed it was opportune to specify by means of a "Communication" to the faithful the meaning and the circumstances which had induced the Bishops to sign the above-mentioned "Agreement."

Here is the text of the "Communication":

On the 14th of last April, in the name of the entire Polish Episcopate, three bishops signed a document which makes specific certain conditions of the life and the activity of the Catholic Church in the new State of Poland.

The tasks of the Commission were not easy, it having been necessary to carry them out amidst ever greater and sometimes insoluble difficulties, as a result of the divergencies often fundamental of the different points of view. The necessity of regulating things in some way did lead to the finding of solutions at least for those questions which are the most urgent and essential.

If all the questions were not resolved, that is due to the fact that a *declaration* is not a concordat and because, on the other hand, many questions cannot be resolved without the intervention of the Holy See.

The points which make up the Agreement are specified in three documents, recently undersigned. (*a*) a common Declaration; (*b*) an added Protocol; (*c*) several annexes.

What are these points? The most important question for the Church and for a Catholic country is the guarantee given by the State for the preservation of religious instruction in the schools, of religious practices for youth in the schools, of the recognition of the rights of the existing Catholic schools, of spiritual assistance in the army, hospitals, and prisons. The Catholic University of Lublin has been guaranteed its rights to continue its work. The right of the Church to organize charitable activities, to direct the teaching of the Cathechism, to have an independent Catholic press, has been recognized. The youth in the seminaries have been assured the possibility of carrying on theological studies without interruption. Religious Orders and their houses can work in full freedom and they have the right to modest means of assistance.

We consider of great value the fact that the Pope is recognized as the highest authority competent in the matters of faith, morality and jurisdiction of the Church, a recognition which corresponds to the most profound Catholic sentiments of the country insofar as regards the Holy See.

The Church, then, on its side, basing itself on the principles of Catholic morality, strengthens among the faithful the Christian sense of respect for law and authority and encourages them to persevere in their labor for the reconstruction of the country.

By proclaiming the principles of Catholic social morality, it is fully in agreement with the reawakening of the Christian sense of the community and of justice with the common good in view.

With the education that it imparts, the Church reinforces in human consciences the respect for human life, for obedience and public order.

The Church then unites with the entire nation in the effort to see that the historic rights of the Country to the integrity of its territory are respected.

The Polish Bishops, however, following the example of the Holy Father, desire to impregnate the faithful with sentiments of brotherly charity and love of peace, fully persuaded that the riches of the universe must serve peace and the common welfare and not a destructive war. All the prayers that we recite each day at Holy Mass are offered to the King of Peace in order to obtain from Heaven the just peace so necessary to the Polish land.

The Polish Episcopate confides, however, that interior peace, the fruit of justice, is the best safeguard and the best preparation for the elaboration of world peace.
Gniezno, April 22, 1950.

THE GOVERNMENT VIOLATES THE AGREEMENT FIRST

Already on May 1, 1950, hardly more than eight days after the Declaration of the Episcopate, Gen. Ochab, one of the signatories of the Agreement and recently become the Secretary of the Party, referred to the above-mentioned declaration of the Bishops. In a speech full of spite against the Holy See he warned that the Church had to change its conduct, because, he said textually: ". . . half-measures and evasive insinuations would be useless and harmful . . . because we Marxists will continue to intensify our vigilance in conformity with the realism propounded by Marx, Engels, Lenin and Stalin. . . ."

And a few days later, on May 8, 1950, President Bierut himself, in a speech to the Central Committee of the Communist Party said: ". . . We will scrupulously follow the agreement concluded, but we will not permit that in violation of it there are actuated ancient and reactionary political machinations. . . ."

Just what these political and reactionary machinations were to which he alluded were explained later by President Bierut. This explanation took place about a day after the Party organ, "Tribuna Ludu," in an article which was also carried by other newspapers, accused the two Bishops, Mons. Swirski of Siedlce and Mons. Stepa of Tarnow, of having prohibited their priests from taking part in the so-called "Committees for Peace" (Communist) and from signing the Stockholm Appeal, adducing that "the adhesion of the clergy to the cause of peace had been made sufficiently clear in Article 9 of the Agreement." This unreasonable accusation against two of its members was extended to the entire Episcopate which was charged by the entire press with "supporting secretly the criminal plans of the American imperialists." And this because in the view of the regime the ninth article of the Agreement was equivalent to a pledge on the part of the Episcopate to sign the Stockholm Appeal. At a distance of only one month from the signing, there was already at hand proof that one single article could have a different interpretation on the part of the two interested parties.

At the same time there was developing a campaign against religious instruction, imparted in the schools by "priests enemies of peace." For this purpose committees of parents and even of students were set up in order to demand their removal. Thus scores of priests were driven from the schools while others were arrested under charges of favoring propaganda in favor of war.

On June 16, 1950, Mons. Choromanski, in the name of the Episcopate, sought to counter this struggle, which had as its aim the separation of the greatest possible number of priests from the teaching of religion in the schools. He published a declaration in which by recalling the eternal mission of the Church in favor of peace among peoples, he affirmed that the Episcopate and the clergy were ceaselessly committed to peace. But the Government demanded a more binding declaration in favor of the Stockholm Appeal.

It was thus that some Bishops, in order to avoid greater evils, gave in to the pressure and then the Government, immediately upon obtaining the signatures of these few, hastened to publish an official communication, drawn up in a note of triumph over the defeated, and of moral persuasion for the stubborn, against whom it used also the usual weapon of threatened reprisals. Victims, for example, were the Sisters of Saint Maddalena of Plock who were expelled from the convent in the space of an hour for having refused to sign the Stockholm Appeal. A similar incident occurred at the convent of the Sacred Heart in Cracow.

The pressures went so far that even the other Bishops, believing that by so doing they were assuring peace to the Church, also signed the petition.

But when the last signature was affixed the "Tribyna Ludu," on July 15, 1950, published an article declaring itself unsatisfied with the attitude of the Bishops, expressing itself as follows:

. . . Polish public opinion has the right to ask that the attitude assumed by the Polish Episcopate with the signing of the Appeal be logically continued by taking further part in the struggle against acts of aggression and incitement to war and in the struggle for the consolidation of peace. Still more is it necessary to regulate daily conduct in a consistent manner based on the fundamental principle of the "right of the State" expressed in the Agreement. . . .

A few days later, on June 28, 1950, a Major Dziemiduk, in a press conference held in the office of the President of the Council of State, denounced to public opinion, with a heap of charges and insinuations, the lack of observance of Article 8 on the part of the Catholic hierarchy. He spoke of convents which were working for foreign espionage services, of religious institutions which supported clandestine Fascist organizations, without the ecclesiastical authorities having done anything to prevent such crimes.

As a consequence of this denunciation there was a new wave of arrests, and of closings of schools and religious houses, which lasted throughout the summer of 1950.

THE EPISCOPATE'S COURAGEOUS MEMORANDUM TO THE PRESIDENT OF THE REPUBLIC

On September 12, 1950, the Polish Episcopate, after having made a thorough study of the situation of the Catholic Church during the five years of the Communist regime and after drawing a balance sheet of the five months of "agreement," sent a courageous "Memorandum" to the Head of the State from Czestochowa, where it had gathered in special session. It felt obliged to do so more because of its pastoral duty than its legal right. This "Memorandum" listed all the abuses suffered in the tragic five year period between 1945-1950 and then went on to unmask the now cunning and now violent activity of atheist communism against the Catholic Church which frustrated any and every attempt at agreement.

This is a document of exceptional value parts of which are worth quoting because they offer a highly authoritative view of the current situation of the Catholic Church in Poland:

To the President of the People's Republic of Poland,
MR. BIERUT:

The Polish Episcopate, after having, during its plenary conference held in Czestochowa on September 12 and 13 last, examined the situation of the Catholic Church during the last five years, considers it as its duty to bring to your attention, Mr. President, the following observations:

The Losses of the Church from 1945 to 1950

The last five years, alas, are marked in the annals of the Catholic Church in Poland by unprecedented losses:

1) The unilateral breaking of the Concordat, undertaken by the Polish State.

2) The refusal on the part of the Government of the Polish Republic to recognize the ecclesiastical organization in the re-occupied territories.

3) The prohibition of the re-establishment of Catholic Associations and organizations.

4) The progressive and continual liquidation of Catholic schools and institutions.

5) The severe restrictions imposed by the political censorship on the Catholic press and publishing houses, up to their present extinction.

6) The taking away from the Church of all printing plants belonging to Dioceses and Catholic publishing houses.

7) The transformation of Church properties into hostelries as a consequence of nationalization.

8) Attempts on the part of administrative authorities to interfere in the life of Church confraternities and associations, going as far as the compulsory registration of convents and religious Congregations.

9) The restriction of the freedom of public worship to a point where religious functions and pious practices (missions, public processions, meetings, and religious congresses) are impeded.

10) The liquidation of "Caritas," the ecclesiastical welfare organization.

11) The complete nationalization of all the goods and properties of the Church.

12) The alternating violent and inspired campaigns in the press against the Holy See and the Episcopate.

13) The restriction of the rights of religion in the schools.

14) The expulsion and the exclusion from the schools of many hundreds af Catechismal priests.

15) The creation of youth organizations of anti-Christian inspiration and ideology.

16) The support given to publications which insulted the teaching and the life of the Church.

17) The anti-religious propaganda made through the press, books, lectures, instructions and training programs.

18) The restrictions brought to bear on the freedom of conscience of members of party associations and professional organizations.

19) The anti-religious propaganda in pre-school institutions and in the schools, in summer resorts and during the hiking tours of youths of both sexes.

20) The administrative brutalities exercised by the magistratures, the police and the tax-collectors to exert pressure on citizens, including priests and Bishops.

In the face of all these facts, the Episcopate has on various occasions presented its reservations and observations either to the President or to the Prime Minister, and to the other Ministers, but, alas, always without any result.

This year in particular, following the signing of the Agreement, it has been noted most seriously that there has been an acceleration in the liquidation of the social institutions and organizations of the Church.

From the beginning of the re-birth of Poland the Church has continually proposed to take account of the new situation. It, therefore, began by providing for the ecclesiastical organization of the re-occupied territories and it rendered valuable services for the consolidation of social conditions in those areas. The Church set in operation its great religious and moral influence in order to hasten the pacification of spirits, excited by the injustices suffered during the critical period. The Church with its teaching developed the apprehension of those moral values, without which, the reconstruction of the country would have been impossible.

The Campaign Against the Holy See

The Polish Episcopate must also formulate new reservations regarding the methods which wound the feelings of Catholics.

Official circles protest that they are not fighting against the Holy See, but against the State of Vatican City. Now it is clear that this manner of speaking cannot be taken seriously.

Admitting that there is an opposition between the materialist ideas and the Catholic ideas, there must also be admitted the right of the Church to defend itself and to proclaim the principles of the Catholic Church, just as you admit to yourselves the right to proclaim materialist ideas. Consequently when the Holy See defends the threatened principles of the Church, for this alone, it cannot be considered as an enemy of Poland. Even the Episcopate defends the rights of the Church and of Christian morality, but for this it is not an enemy of Poland, even if it is averse to the materialist ideas imposed on Catholics.

The Episcopate expresses its hope that in the new Poland this entire campaign directed against the Holy See will end once and for all and that the strange and hardly serious publications published by "Books and Science" will cease to appear. The Episcopate nourishes this hope even because a certain reciprocity should be admitted in this request. Until now, in fact, although attacked, no publication of the Vatican has ever offended the head of the Polish State, nor any of its ministers.

The System of Reprisals Against the Clergy

One of the most painful aspects of the condition of the Church in Poland is that many priests are under surveillance, that many have been arrested and sentenced to jail without a previous trial. The clergy and the Episcopate feel painfully the vexing system of continuous control, the repeated summonings to the offices of the police or the local authorities. Many have been arrested in churches, in confessionals, in the presence of boys who were awaiting confession. All this gives rise to a deep disquiet among the faithful and it is some-

thing new for us, because up to now priests have never been
treated as transgressors of the penal code. The surveillance
extends even to Bishops who, during their journeys to assemblies or their visits to the Dioceses, are accompanied by
many police.

Many priests have been forcibly obliged to commit espionage. Neither the functionaries of Bishoprics nor those
of ecclesiastical courts have been spared in this regard.

Particularly painful have been the trials staged in connection with the activity of the ancient "Caritas" and they
are still more so for the fact that the Government had assured the Episcopate that all questions connected with "Caritas" would be considered as liquidated. Instead, contrarywise
to these assurances, sentences have been pronounced and
numerous priests condemned to many years imprisonment.
The Episcopate considers all this as a violation of the given
gurantees.

The entire Polish population has resented, in a particularly painful manner, the arrests carried out in the convent
of Mont-Clair in Czestochowa, and the vexing investigations
carried on there for several weeks. Czestochowa represents
so important a role in the life of the nation that every action
of this kind undertaken by the present authorities is considered as a personal offense by Poles. All this creates a most
ugly impression in the Polish nation, before which it cannot
be hidden that veritable persecutions were ordered against
the persons to whom the convent of Mont-Clair was entrusted.

The Fate of the Convents and the Members of
Religious Orders

The state in which the religious houses find themselves is
another most disquieting problem for the Church. Deprived
of the possibility of continuing welfare work, persecuted,
vexed with numerous arrests and continuous investigations,
Polish religious houses find themselves in a most difficult
condition. Dragged for fear of reprisals into the field of

politics (the campaign for peace) the convents defend themselves and desire to stay outside this field. Consequently,
the convents have abstained from signing the so-called peace
appeal.

For this reason the Sisters of Saint Maddalena of Plock
have been driven from their house. They had to leave within
the space of an hour only for the reason that they had refused to sign the appeal in question. The injustice which
was done them has not yet been repaired, notwithstanding
the repeated interventions of the Episcopate.

The penalties which are inflicted on members of religious
orders are not to be found in the penal code and they constitute an open violation of every right. If it be permitted to
express our deep regret on the grounds of the most elementary humanity, this is a case in which to do so.

The Sisters of Charity of the Hospital of the Infant Jesus
in Warsaw, where they have worked for more than 200 years
with the greatest spirit of sacrifice, were in a single day
compelled to leave the hospital and obliged to cease full-
filling their vocation of assistance to the sick.

The Application of the Agreement

The Polish Episcopate has given evidence of good will
by signing the Agreement even if this contained only a few
guarantees on the part of the Government, and even these
on very complicated questions. The Episcopate, as a result,
also maintained a highly favorable attitude towards it and
did everything possible to conform with it and to submit
the still unresolved questions to the Holy See. It also ordered
the clergy to make the contents known to the faithful.

The Episcopate, however, has not seen any comparable
will on the part of the Government to conform to the terms
of the treaty. In fact, since the signing the state of things in
the schools, in these religious houses, and in "Caritas" has
ever worsened. The Minister of Public Instruction openly
refused to recognize the rights of the Church confirmed in
it. A conference of Bishops with the participation of repre-

sentatives of the Government, arranged with great difficulty, was openly ignored by him.

The execution of the Agreement was made to depend upon the signing of the peace appeal by the Bishops. But after they had signed nought else was done. We are face to face with a paradox: from the Episcopate new concessions are ever demanded, while the Government, through the Minister, Bida, continues for months on end just to make new promises.

The Episcopate turns to you, Mr. President, to ask how the present state of things is to be interpreted. Is it possible to make promises, in execution of the agreement now in effect, about the incontestable rights of the Churches by making them always depend on new and unexpected demands?

Conclusion

We limit ourselves to these problems, knowing full well that we are far from having exposed them all. May this letter of ours be a document for history and free us from the reproach of having kept silent about the truth. The responsibility of the conditions of the Church in Poland does not fall on us. It is necessary to declare it, because free Poland has never persecuted the Church or religion.

All that which the Church has experienced in the new Poland in the course of the past five years is so alien to the history of our Country that it gives rise to a justifiable bewilderment and a question: is it, perhaps, necessary that after so many years of suffering caused by the war to prolong the martyrdom of the nation with a struggle against the Church? The Catholic public suffers from it and is justly disturbed. The entire Nation, desirous of unity and peaceful labor, has been shaken in its religious feelings. It can with good reason be feared that this struggle against religion will do very serious harm to national unity and to the State.

We see no other way to the indispensable pacification of souls and to national unity save that of stopping the struggle against religion. The fact that it has been unleashed

just when a new social order is being built is most painful
because it will impede the devoutly desired social progress
in the spirit of Christianity.

Despite the martyrdom to which the Church in Poland
is submitted, the Episcopate does not renounce its belief that
a sound reason may prevail over the system of old atheist
ideas. The Episcopate will not cease working to spread the
gospel of Christ so that peoples may be liberated from social
injustices and the fundamentals of a true peace be deepened.

(*signed*) ADAM CARD. SAPIEHA, *Archbishop of Cracow*
STEFAN WYSZYNSKY, *Archbishop of Gniezno*
and Warsaw, Primate of Poland
Mont-Clair in Czestochowa, September 12, 1950

RECENT EVENTS

As was to be expected the letter of the Episcopate received
no reply and the situation, already so tense, seemed to become
even more bitter.

In fact it was in this period (October 1950–February 1951)
that the arrests of priests and members of religious orders multiplied without let-up, without justifications, or under various
pretexts.

It was in this period that "sensational discoveries" were made
in the monasteries of deposits of arms, espionage centers, etc.
In fact the press and other propaganda denounced the discovery
of arms deposits in the monasteries of the Salvatoriani of Miko-
low, the Franciscans of Radecznica, and the Jesuits of Cracow.

Finally in January 1951, with a decree dated the 26th, the
Government ordered the "deposition" and the expulsion of the
Apostolic Administrators of the dioceses of Gdansk, Gorzow,
Opole, Olsztyn and Wroclaw, belonging to the former German
territory which was ceded to Poland, and with another decree
dated the 29th of the same month, it replaced them with an
equal number of "Capitular Vicars."

The act of the Government was serious indeed and it might
have led to the beginnings of a schismatic movement had not

the Primate of Poland, Mons. Wyszynski, who glimpsed the danger, with an act of veritable genius and inspiration, instead of opposing it, quickly intervened and immediately recognized the newly-elected, passing the sponge of his immense charity over the illegality of the elections.

It was necessary, however, to clarify once and for all the ecclesiastical situation of these former German territories, now become Polish, and for this reason the Primate, Mons. Wyszynski, requested and obtained permission to go to Rome to discuss the problem with the Holy See, with which the final decision rested.

The Primate reported on the results of this visit to Rome in a letter to the clergy and the faithful of his Archdiocese, on May 23, 1951:

> . . . It is my duty as pastor to make you share with me the joy which was conceded to me of seeing Peter in the person of the Holy Father . . .
>
> In the course of my stay in Rome, I was received twice in audience by the Holy Father; the first time on April 9, the second, April 27.
>
> We brought him the testimony of our respect towards him, a respect which no attack, even the most rabid, will ever be able to weaken.
>
> By our presence in Rome we also testified before the entire world that Poland is Catholic, that she is with the Holy Father and that Catholic she can and must remain. Our conscience tells us that with this we have rendered the greatest service to our Fatherland and the Church.

Even "Pravda" in its issue of July 17, 1951, concerned itself with this journey to Rome of the Primate, Mons. Wyszynski, and in a violent article under the title, "The enemies of Democratic Poland," it expressed itself thus:

> Polish public opinion in the last few days has become aware, with the utmost indignation, of new facts which prove and confirm the anti-Polish activity of the high dignitaries of the Catholic Church, an activity aimed at undermining the very base of democratic and people's Poland.

Recently, Stefan Wyszynski, primate of the Polish Catholic Church, with his entourage undertook a journey to the Vatican. . . .

At the Vatican, Stefan Wyszynski, was received twice with benevolence by the Pope and he re-entered Warsaw with his morale high . . . Pius XII has approved and blessed the anti-people activities of the high Catholic clergy in Poland; he gave the Primate, Wyszynski, even wider powers and promised to make him a cardinal. . . .

The journey to Rome of the Primate, Wyszynski has brought no changes . . . Millions of Polish workers are now more clearly aware than ever before that the Vatican is the enemy of peace and of democracy. . . .

The change which the organ of the Communist press invoked was that of seeing the Episcopate make an act of ideological and practical adhesion to the new regime, thereby signing its death-warrant.

The Primate, instead, hardly two weeks after his return, assembled the entire Catholic Polish Episcopate and signed a "Pro Memoria" addressed to the clergy in which the following directives were given:

. . . We have always admonished our clergy to adhere strictly to its priestly mission. It is only in this manner that we will render the greatest service to the faithful, be it in their duties towards God, be it in the moulding of the temporal life in the conscientious fulfillment of their duties towards the family, their profession, their Nation, and towards the State.

We desire, however, that priests do not involve themselves in political activities nor in questions of parties . . . On us there is incumbent a single duty, that of announcing the truth revealed to us by God and to help everybody to go towards God.

It is forbidden, then, to priests to take part in underground or subversive movements or in other political, economic and social movements. Nobody has called upon us to be the dispensors of the things of this world.

But as regarded the problem of the ecclesiastical systemization of the former German territories, the Primate himself explained what the thought and the position of the Holy See were in an interview granted to the Catholic weekly "Tygodnik Powszechy" of Cracow which was published in the 59th number on December 16, 1951.

... After the conclusion of the "Agreement," a Memorandum was sent to the Holy Father in which the situation which had been created in those apostolic administrations was described ... We ourselves during our last sojourn in Rome did not fail to make known the importance of this problem. The Holy Father listened to us with deep interest and at the Secretariat of the State our espousal was followed with the greatest attention and with the best disposition.

Now even if the Holy See has not expressed its thought with verbal declarations, there are still facts which are worth more than words.

It is a fact that the Holy See has taken note of the ecclesiastical organization which was established in the territory of the west by the defunct Cardinal Hlond.

But there is still more: The Holy See has permitted the re-establishment of diocesan curiae, of ecclesiastical tribunals, of Seminaries, etc., all well-defined organisms which belong canonically to the autonomous life of a Diocese. Step by step as ecclesiastical life continues to develop and to stabilize itself even its external ecclesiastical organization will not be lacking in assuming better defined forms.

The Communist press attacked the Primate precisely for this declaration. The newspaper "Trybuna Ludu" attacked him for having assumed, in this field, a defense of the policy of the Holy See and it countered the declaration of the Primate by hailing: ". . . The courageous decisions taken at the Congress of Breslau on December 12, 1951, in which 1,800 Polish Catholics, priests and laymen had, instead, supported the claims of the government. . . ."

And as an example it adduced the deliberations of the clergy of Danzig which had signed the following declaration: ". . . We condemn the German clergy which under the leadership of Card. Frings and Card. Faulhaber, and under the influence of the Vatican, goes about stirring up a spirit of hate. . . ."

The result of this new campaign against the hierarchy was a cruel renewal of the persecution against the Catholic Church which led to the arrest of many priests and faithful.

It is difficult to say just how many priests are presently in prison, but it would not be far from the truth to state that they are more than 700, averaging about 35 from each Diocese.

Higher, instead, is the number of members of religious orders who were deported or who "disappeared." It is believed that these may total twelve hundred.

As regards so-called "progressive" priests they are believed to be about 50 in all. Grouped, with a certain number of Catholic laymen, around the two weekly newspapers, "Dzis Ijutro" (Today and Tomorrow), and "Slowo Powszechne" (Universal Words) they believe that they can collaborate with the Communist regime, from which they receive every help, in the hope of being able to save the salvageable. But with each passing day they become aware that they are being confined to a blind alley, amid contradictions without number, veritable "inoffensive marionettes" who act according to the will of those who make them "march."

What has actually occurred in Poland is the *asphyxia* of the Catholic Church in Poland. The difference from other countries is that it still enjoys some freedom of religion. Its churches are still overflowing with people who come to them, but slowly and progressively the absence of air is being felt. The noose which the authorities have placed around the necks of its Bishops, of its clergy and of its most worthy sons, grows ever tighter. It is marked for death and all that is awaited is the most propitious moment to give the noose the final twist.

But the resistance is still strong and it seems, instead, that the more it is attempted to hasten its death, the signs of life become more vigorous everywhere.

CONCLUSION

As of January 31, 1953, the balance sheet of losses undergone by the Catholic Church in Poland because of the Communist persecution was as follows:

	1945	1953	
Archbishops and Bishops	33	23	(1 died in prison; 7 at present in prison; 1 impeded in his duties)
Priests	8,624	6,377	(37 killed; 261 dead or disappeared; 350 deported; 700 in jail, 900 exiled)
Members of Religious Orders	3,106	2,382	(54 killed or dead; 200 deported; 170 in jail; 300 exiled)
Churches or Chapels	8,273	6,130	(30% lost)
Male Religious Houses	370	220	(40% lost)
Female Religious Houses	1,658	960	(45% lost)
Catholic Schools	135	50	(70% lost)
Welfare Agencies	3,900	0	(100% lost)
Printing Plants and Bookstores	150	0	(100% lost)
Press and Catholic Publications	300	10	(97% lost)
Properties, etc.	0	0	(80% confiscated)

CHAPTER III

Roumania

A. SUPPRESSION OF THE CATHOLIC CHURCH OF THE BYZANTINE RITE

THE SITUATION OF THE ROUMANIAN (UNIATE) CATHOLIC CHURCH BEFORE 1948

Until 1948 the Catholics in Roumania totalled in all about 2,743,000, of whom 1,561,000 were of the Byzantine rite and 1,182,000 were of the Latin rite. They constituted, therefore, the most numerous religious group, after that of the Orthodox (12,250,000). They formed about 15% of the total population of Roumania (15,872,624), the rest being constituted as follows: 1,200,000 Protestants (6%); 500,000 Jews (3%) and 189,000 Moslems (1%).

By virtue of the Concordat concluded on May 10, 1927 between the Holy See and the Roumanian Government, the Catholics in Roumania hierarchically had 11 Dioceses, of which 5 were for the faithful of the Byzantine rite and 6 for the faithful of the Latin rite.

The Dioceses of the Latin rite were the following:

  a) The Archdiocese of Bucharest
  b) The Diocese of Alba Julia
  c) The Diocese of Jassi
  d) The Diocese of Timisoara
  e) The Diocese of Satumare
  f) The Diocese of Oradea Mare (suppressed on
       April 9, 1948, and merged with Satumare)

The Dioceses of the Byzantine rite, according to the last definition fixed by the Apostolic Constitution "Solemni Conventione" held on June 5, 1930, included:

  a) The Archdioceses of Fagarus and Alba-Julia (seat, Blaj)
  b) The Dioceses of Gherla and Cluj (seat, Cluj)
  c) The Diocese of Oradea Mare
  d) The Diocese of Lugoj
  e) The Diocese of Maramures (res., Baja Mare)

The most recent statistics reported the following data:

	Catholics	Parishes	Priests
a) Dioceses of the Byzantine rite:			
Fagarus (Blaj)	481,000	633	694
Gherla (Cluj)	421,000	463	417
Oradea Mare	200,000	212	261
Lugoj	119,000	235	288
Marmures (Blajia)	350,000	264	306
Total	1,561,000	1,807	1,906
b) Dioceses of the Latin rite:			
Bucharest	60,000	34	66
Alba-Julia	400,000	266	411
Jassi	140,000	109	98
Timisoara	380,000	164	270
Satumare	202,000	121	242
Total	1,182,000	683	1,107

In addition, there were complexively:

a) 52 male religious houses with 318 members
b) 91 female religious houses with 1,826 nuns
c) 224 male educational institutes with 28,000 students
d) 152 female educational institutes with 23,000 students
e) 111 aid and welfare institutions (orphanages, shelters, asylums, etc.) with about 10,000 recipients of aid

PRECURSORS OF THE PERSECUTION OF RELIGION

Of the two groups of Catholics, the first to be chosen as a target by the Roumanian Communist regime, was the group of Catholics of the Byzantine rite whose adherence to Rome was considered as "anti-national and anti-history," because it had been imposed with force, it was said, at the time of the Hapsburg imperialists, and in opposition to Roumanian customs and traditions which, it was declared, they wanted to maintain.

In reality the union with Rome had been freely concluded at a plenary synod held in Transylvania on October 24, 1693 and freely undersigned by the Bishops, and by 50 Delegates, who in turn were the representative delegates of 1,582 priests. Since then it had been continuously strengthened and affirmed to the extent that on April 4, 1928, N. Jorga, the country's greatest writer, could make the following declaration to a full session of the Chamber of Deputies: ". . . The 'uniate' Church, which some would break into pieces, is of an absolute necessity to the Roumanian nation. First of all because in it there throbs a truly national soul, and then because for us it constitutes a precious instrument which links us with the West . . ."

Nevertheless the Communists, against the very evidence of history and the force of this authoritative affirmation, staged their struggle against the "uniate" Church precisely on this plane, with the aim of liquidating it and integrating it with the "orthodox" Church which it had already succeeded in making a servant of the regime.

In fact it was the "Union of Democratic Orthodox Priests" which was the first to launch its alleged "Appeal to the Uniate

Church," on March 28, 1948, which was undoubtedly government-inspired and which said:

> . . . Because some representatives and heads of a certain
> cult in Roumania put themselves at the service of foreign
> interests, enemies of the people, thereby removing their
> church far from the people and God and making of them-
> selves unworthy tools of the enemies of peace, the Ministers
> of the Orthodox Church resolutely condemn this attitude
> and array themselves along side the regime of our people's
> democracy in its struggle for peace, freedom and national
> independence.
>
> We have faith in the people and in the regime which
> they themselves have given to themselves. . . .

The Appeal was echoed a few days later by the Minister of
State, G. Gheorghiu-Dej who, on the occasion of the annual
meeting of his party, also launched his own first warning:

> There is in our country a part of the faithful which be-
> longs to the Catholic Church. This being so we must say
> that the circles of the Catholic clergy do not have an attitude
> which conforms with the democratic regime of Roumania,
> with the interests of the country and of the people. Every-
> where in the world the Catholic clergy listens to the orders
> of the Vatican, about whose fanatical reactionary and pro-
> imperialist activity everybody knows. It is inadmissable that
> these Catholic circles abuse the possibilities which are theirs
> of influencing the faithful in such a manner as to utilize the
> Church, in accordance with the orders of the Vatican, as a
> means of propaganda directed against the achievements of
> democracy, and of such a nature as to slacken the will of the
> people to defend its independence against foreign imperial-
> ists. . . .

And on May 15, 1948, in Alba Julia, on the occasion of the
holidays proclaimed to celebrate the centenary of the proclamation of national rights on "the field of liberty," the Orthodox
metropolitan of Sibiu, Nicholas Balan, made the following speech,

which was extensively commented upon by the Roumanian press and radio, before the highest authorities of the regime assembled there:

... There is still something lacking to our national unity to make it perfect, we must still realize the unity of the Church of our forefathers, in the church and in the ancestral faith of the race. The Hapsburgs split our nation in order to weaken us and to subjugate us more easily. Today they no longer have any power over us and we can, therefore, re-unite ourselves anew. In my capacity of successor of the ancient metroplitans of Belgrade, to which the entire Roumanian nation of Ardeal was subordinate, I appeal to you who, deceived by foreign interests have strayed far from your good Mother (the Orthodox Church) and I appeal to you most fervidly to come back home. ...

On the following March 24 there was the speech of the new orthodox Patriarch, Justinian Marina, elected on that very day by the Chamber of Deputies. Replying to an invitation addressed to him by the Minister of Religions, Stanciu Stoian, to collaborate with the Government for the installation of a peoples' democratic regime and to struggle with it against reactionaries and above all against the Catholic church, he said the following: ". . . The first thing that I shall have to realize in the framework of ecclesiastical traditions is the conservation of the faith . . . removing the painful schism provoked by enemies 250 years ago. . . ."

On June 6, on the occasion of his taking possession of Saint Spiridone, the neo-patriarch Justinian Marina pronounced an allocution, directed almost exclusively against the "uniate" Church, repeating phrases and arguments which had already become familiar in the propaganda organized by the Government at that time. They were, in fact, repeated in an article published on June 21 by the Orthodox Bishop of Suaceva, Emilian Antal in the "Semnalul" and by the Archimandrite, Valerian Zaharia in the official Bulletin of the Orthodox Roumanian Church.

This entire campaign, conducted on behalf of the Government by the heads of the Roumanian Orthodox Church, was answered by the Catholic Episcopate of the "uniate" church on June 29 with a noble joint letter in which the faithful were invited not to be intimidated by threats and to remain compact in their union with Rome:

> . . . They tell us to cut ourselves off from the Pope in order to be with the people and united, they tell us that the Pope is the enemy of Roumanian democracy, that the people is a stranger to the Pope. . . . Laws will be made which will be a burden for the Church, and dioceses will be reduced. . . . What must our position be? . . . We will be conquered in advance if we think we can fight with lies, with human calculations and compromises. Our answer to those who will solicit us to betray our faith will be this: "I have no power against the truth." Be firm in your faith; the mission of the Church in the world, far from being fulfilled, imposes new duties on us. The missionary duties, which Providence entrusts to us in these crucial hours, are not those of signing a compromise peace with the world, but to establish for the world a peace worthy of God and men. The eyes of history are upon us.

Aware of the futility of its attempt to dismember the "uniate" Catholic Church by means of the "Orthodox" Church, the Government changed tactics and began to issue a series of restrictive decrees designed to bring about the capitulation of the "uniate" Church in "legal ways."

On July 17, 1948, with the aim of removing the legal base of existence of the Catholic Church in Roumania, especially that of the Byzantine rite, the Government, in a unilateral action, denounced the Concordat stipulated in 1927 between the Holy See and Roumania, and which was ratified in 1929.

The relevant Decree, which bears the number 151, was published two days later in the "Official Monitor," number 164, and reads as follows:

Article One

The Concordat concluded between Roumania and the

Holy See on March 10, 1927, as well as the agreements and the conventions approved in application of the same Concordat, must be considered as denounced as of the date of publication of the present Law.

On this date the application of the Concordat, its agreements and later conventions, ceases.

The Law of June 12, 1929, for the ratification of the Concordat is abrogated, including also the laws of ratification of the conventions and the later agreements.

After the denunciation of the Concordat, the Communist regime felt free enough to be able to organize by itself, and to its advantage, the new statute on Catholic religions.

On August 2, the Government began its "legal" persecution of the Catholic Church, by issuing the law on the "Nationalization of the Schools" which deprived the Catholic Church of all of its many educational institutions, and which decreed the transfer to the State of all school buildings with all their properties, real and immobile, including the dwellings of the teachers.

The Catholic Episcopate protested energetically against this act of violence by sending the following letter, dated August 26, to the Minister of Public Instruction:

N. 2014/1948

MR. MINISTER:

The Bishops of the Catholic Church, of all rites, of the Roumanian People's Republic believed it to be their duty, some time ago, to dispatch a Memorial to you. Almost at the same time the Bishops of the uniate Roumanian Church on their part presented another, containing a pressing and justified request to respect the right of the Church to open and to maintain confessional schools.

With sorrow we must say that we have seen no reply; and that, instead, by virtue of the decrees, numbers 175 and 176, of August 2, 1948, the confessional schools have been nationalized and all their properties, real and mobile, which served for their operation and maintenance, have been made into State property. Thus, without hesitation, a cultural and

physical patrimony has been suppressed which, in the course
of centuries, has served and formed the soul of the people,
thanks to the immense sacrifices of the Church.

In this situation of force, we insist upon declaring, Mr.
Minister, that the Church cannot renounce a right which is
accorded to it by natural law, and to a mission from which
it cannot disengage itself.

Since the entry into force of the above-mentioned decrees
has led to the alienation from our cult of a certain number
of real and immobile properties, necessary for the training
of its personnel and those of other institutions guaranteed
by the Constitution, we have the honor to urge you, Mr.
Minister, to order the restitution of these properties, for
otherwise religious freedom so solemnly guaranteed by the
Constitution (Art. 27) and regulated by Decree, number
177, remains paralyzed in its essence.

When the Episcopate of the Catholic Church makes this
complaint, it bases itself on the law guaranteed by the Constitution (Art. 8) which guarantees property, while the dispositions included in decree number 176, far from appearing
as originating or justified in natural law or in the Constitution, clearly contradict the letter and the spirit of the Constitution itself.

There are many reasons in favor of the restitution by the
State of the properties of the Church and religious Congregations. But the first one of all is that these properties were
not accumulated through the exploitation of workers or by
the sacrifice of the people, but by the sacrifice of Bishops,
priests and by the religious congregations for the benefit of
the people whom the old regime kept in darkness and ignorance. In addition to being an act of strict justice and
constitutional legality, the restitution of properties will also
constitute an act of homage to this institution which has
sacrificed itself only for the people at a moment when the
State did not yet exist, and which in the stone of the schools
has perpetuated its feelings of love and immolation for the
people.

Nor will it be superfluous to note, Mr. Minister, that those authorized by the Ministry of Public Instruction to carry out the confiscation of the properties have gone beyond the mandate given them, by including in their inventories real and mobile properties which in no wise were stipulated in decree 107, since they did not serve either for the operation, the maintenance, or the support of institutions mentioned in the articles of the Decree. Such an act constitutes a veritable illegality in regard to the new legislation itself and it demands a prompt restitution which removes them from the inventory and returns them.

This is the situation in which, among others, the Theological Academy of Cluj, the Monastery and Novitiate of the Sisters of the Congregation of the Mother of God (The Institute of Gratitude) located in Blaj, and the monastery and the Sabaoni parish in the department of Roman, presently find themselves.

With the certainty that Your Excellency, with his lofty understanding, will attend to this just request, we sign below with the expression of our distinguished consideration.

ALEXANDER TH. CISAR, *Latin Metroplitan of Bucharest*

DR. JULIUS HOSSU, *Bishop of Cluj-Cherla*

DR. ALEXANDER RUSSU, *Bishop of Maramures*

ANTON MARTON, *Bishop of Alba-Julia*

JOAN SUCIU, *Apostolic Administrator of the Archdioceses of Alba-Julia and Fagara*

VALERIO TRAIANO FRENTIU, *Bishop of Oradea*

AUGUSTINE PACHA, *Bishop of Timisoara*

JOHN BALAN, *Bishop of Lugoj*

JOHN SCHEFFLER, *Bishop of Satumare*

ANTHONY DURKOVIC, *Bishop of Gassi*

Oradea, Conference of Bishops of August 26, 1948

THE DECREE OF AUGUST 4: THE NEW REGULATION OF RELIGIONS

The most serious blow against the Catholic Church in Roumania, however, was delivered by the new Law on religions which was approved on August 4, 1948.

This revolutionary document was designed to disorganize the hierarchy by throwing it into the greatest confusion. Through it, in fact, administrative cadres were shaken up and the Dioceses reduced from ten to four (two for the "Latin" Catholics and two for the "uniate"), in such a way that each Diocese was composed of about 750,000 faithful.

The document specified, moreover, that no foreign spiritual authority would be able to exercise any jurisdiction whatsoever inside the Country (Art. 41) and that even the relations of a spiritual nature which the diverse religious confessions wished to maintain abroad would of necessity be put under the control of the Ministry of Religions.

The Catholic Episcopate made another attempt to counter this new and more serious blow by sending, on August 27, 1948, a Memorandum to the Ministry of Religions.

N. 2011/1948

MR. MINISTER:

The Bishops of the Catholic religion of the two rites of the People's Roumanian Republic, assembled in conference to discuss the obligation imposed on them by Articles 4 and 56 of the decree on the new regulation of religions which require that within a period of three months, namely, up to the 4th of November of the current year, they present their organic and executive statutes, permit themselves to make you aware that they will do everything which is possible so that this document, which is destined to substitute the Concordat which up to now regulated their situation in fact and in law, may be presented in due time.

But since the decree in question requires (Art. 56) that this statute be in harmony with its directives, we feel it as our duty to present you at this time, in the form of a "Memorandum" addressed to the entire Government, several considerations which we request you to submit to it, because they are considerations based on a special situation peculiar to the Catholic religion, in differentiation from other religions.

1) The first question to make clear, in our view, is that of assuring that the "examination and approval" of the Statute in question insofar as regards its composition in the form provided by the law, will be made exclusively as follows: (*a*) according to the regulations of the constitutional principle, according to which the State guarantees the greatest freedom of conscience and religion on all the territory of the People's Republic of Roumania; (*b*) and according to the fundamental dispositions that guarantee the freedom of organization and operation to every religion whose practices and ritual are not opposed to the Constitution, to security or public order or to good morals.

This "examination and approval" of the State regarding the organization and the functioning of our religion of Divine establishment, which is essentially the same all over the world, is not we trust a camouflage for the idea, certainly somewhat strange and absolutely unacceptable to us, according to which we would have to request today, after almost 2,000 years of existence, authorization to propagandize the Christian faith which we believe authentic, and whose organization in the course of centuries has been condensed in the Code of canon law, as if all this could depend on the approval or less of any secular authority whatsoever.

The reason which authorizes us to think that this is truly the intention of the law and justifies our apprehensions about the real meaning of the phrase "examination and approval" is furnished us also by article 7 of the Decree in which it is categorically stated, without any qualifications of any sort, that religious cults will be organized according to their rules and in conformity with the teachings, canons and traditions peculiar to them, and with the possibility of instituting, in accordance with these rules, Institutes, Associations, Orders and Congregations.

2) Now in direct opposition to this article of law, which admits the possibility of every religious cult to organize itself

to its full extent, in accordance with its regulations, canons, etc., there is item 2 of Article 40 by virtue of which it is not permitted to have relations with "foreign religious cults," except with the approval of the Ministry of Religions and through the intermediary of the Ministry of Foreign Affairs. This strikes directly at the relations of our religion with the Holy See of Rome . . . To cut off these relations, according to the dispositions of the above-mentioned Article 40, would mean breaking off the vine-branch of our Catholic cult from the vines which has given it life and trampling upon the "teaching," the "canons," and the "traditions" which in Article 7, it is solemnly stated, will be guaranteed to all religions.

3) Passing on to another order of ideas, we cannot help not pointing out, Mr. Minister, an entire series of other dispositions of the new law on religions, which in no wise are in accord with the "freedom" of organization and not even with "religious freedom" and the "freedom of conscience," guaranteed in the afore-mentioned articles.

a) One of these dispositions, enunciated in Article 22, disposes that religions organized, like our Catholic religion, by Dioceses, may have a number of Dioceses proportionate to the number of faithful and then without more ado it is established that for a Diocese to exist and function it must have a minimum of approximately 750,000 faithful. Now since our religion numbers approximately one million and a half faithful for each of its two metropolitans, it follows that it is imposed on us either to accept this decision voluntarily or to resign ourselves to the knowledge that 60% of our Diocesan organizations (3 for each metropolitan seat) will no longer be able to function legally throughout the territory of the Roumanian People's Republic.

This act of self-mutilation of several Diocesan districts cannot be accepted by us because these districts are imperiously required for the good and solid administration of the Church and for the proper functioning of our religion, and even because the reform imposed on the districts by the new law is not within their competence since the creation and the suppression of new Catholic dioceses is, as everybody knows, a sovereign and exclusive right of the Holy See.

b) Another of these dispositions, less grave to be sure, but of an extreme importance because of the consequences it could have, is that with which Article 28 of the new Law is concerned. It is concerned with, in relation to the heritage of religious cults, with the juridical personality of the latter and it disposes that only parishes and Dioceses may continue to be considered as juridical persons in public law, but that Institutions, Associations, Orders and religious Congregations be excluded . . . All this constitutes a serious curtailment of the traditional situation of religions and it seriously injures their freedom to organize in conformity with the assurances given by Article 7.

c) Other dispositions which reduce the free exercise of our cult, and which we do not know how to reconcile with religious freedom and the freedom to organize, are the following:

1) Those of Article 24 which require everywhere (and not only during a state of siege which might have in some way justified them) a preliminary authorization from civil authorities for all religious meetings and, more particularly, for meetings which might not have a strictly religious character.

2) Those of Article 25 and Article 26 which recapitulate the articles referring to the "attributions" of the decree relative to the functioning of the Ministry of Religion. They confer upon this ministry the right of interference in and direction of the internal affairs of religions in an absolutely obsolete measure. And it is then applied with an absolute lack of knowledge, as happened recently when several of our pastoral letters were censured which contravened neither security, nor public order, or good morals. Now all this can lead to a complete paralysis of all diocesan activity, which certainly does not correspond to the intentions of the

legislature and which in every way would not be in accord with the fundamental principle of the law by which the State guarantees the freedoms which are the base of every organization and every religious life.

d) Nor can we fail to point out the dispositions of Article 37 of the law which again puts into effect a dictatorial law of the Antonescu regime of sad memory, formerly abolished and now re-introduced with retroactive power. It is concerned with the transfer from one religion to another . . . and we cannot refrain from expressing our disquiet in this regard and proclaiming that measures of such a nature can only compromise security and public order, a danger it is expressly sought to combat by so much insistence on the new law of religions.

e) To conclude we must also include herein, as a kind of a corollary to what has been said heretofore, even the question of the formula of the oath to be sworn by representatives of religions, such as is prescribed in Article 21 of the law. Now, just as we expressed ourselves verbally last spring to the President of the Council, then interim minister of religions, on the occasion of a disposition of the law on religions then in force which prescribed the obligatoriness of the oath, now too we wish to repeat quite clearly here that such an oath can only have reference to laws and dispositions which are not in contradiction with the law of God and the salvation of souls. To do otherwise would be equal to forcing the conscience of persons and especially religious persons for whom the sanctity of an oath is much more effectual and constructive in contributing to the promotion of the interests of the country than all these measures of a quasi-police character of which this new law on religions is so full, and uselessly so, according to our way of seeing things.

Here then are sketched, in the terms expressed above, our observations in relation to the new decree for the general regulation of religious cults, elaborated and published, without anyone having asked our prior opinion as was the custom before and as has been done now in order to oppress us with the orthodox cult. (See Articles 54 and 48.)

This letter of ours, Mr. Minister, was written with the aim of making known to you the difficulties which we are about to encounter in our effort to conform with this law, and to urge you to be willing to help us either personally, or by intervening with the Council of Ministers in such a wise as to be able to obtain some modifications of the dispositions noted by us and that they permit us to present in good time a Statute which will not mark the beginning of animosity, or worse, of conflicts.

We wish, on the contrary, with the deepest sincerity, that it may mark a new milestone on the road which assures peace and cordial agreements among the religions of the country. This will be the best guarantee for the promotion of its greatest religious interests which stand highest in the thoughts of all of our clergy and all of our faithful.

Convinced that we shall be understood both in the letter and in the spirit of our espousal and that our rights will be respected, we urge you to accept, Mr. Minister, the assurance of our most respectful consideration.

Issued at Oradea, at the conference of Bishops of the seats of Alba Julia and Fagora of the Roumanian United Church, attended also by representatives of the Latin metroplitan seat of Bucharest, August 27, 1948.

THE PROTEST OF THE APOSTOLIC NUNCIATURE

The Apostolic Nunciature could do naught else except to raise its voice against this entire campaign of intimidations and threats, and, in fact, on October 2 it sent the following "Verbal Note" to the Ministry of Foreign Affairs:

The Apostolic Nunciature presents its homages to the Minister of Foreign Affairs of the Roumanian People's Republic and has the honor to bring the following to his attention.

According to the peace treaty signed by the Roumanian

State in Paris on February 10, 1947, Roumania pledged itself
"to take all necessary measures to secure the freedom of
religion for all persons under its jurisdiction" (Article 3,
Par. 1). Likewise in the constitution of the PRR it is confirmed (Article 18) that "the freedom of conscience and
religious freedom are guaranteed by the State." Moreover,
the new law concerning religions of August 4, 1948 (Articles
1 and 2) provides for the full religious freedom of citizens,
stipulating that "no person may be persecuted because of
his religious profession."

Now all these solemn commitments have been violated
by an entire series of deeds, meticulously prepared and ably
coordinated, perpetrated in recent days in the various provinces of Transylvania against the Catholic Church of the
Greek rite.

The Apostolic Nunciature refers in particular to the
action, undertaken not by irresponsible elements, but by the
civil authorities themselves to force the Greek-Catholic
clergy to abandon its faith.

These authorities have circulated a "Delegation" in the
various provinces of Transylvania which the Greek-Catholic
clergy had to sign on behalf of two ecclesiastics from each
province who, though remaining unknown to the signatories
nonetheless had to represent them at a meeting organized
by the Government in the city of Cluj on October 1 current,
whose aim was that which the above-mentioned document
calls: "the return of the Greek-Catholic church to the Orthodox Church."

This undertaking of the civil power, which in itself is in
evident contradiction with the principle of freedom and
equality of all the religions in Roumania, has clearly revealed, primarily because of the methods used in extorting
signatures, its character of religious persecution. Priests, in
fact, have been conducted, often by force, to the offices of
the police and there intimidated, and threatened with imprisonment, separation from the families, deportation and

death. Those who resisted these initial violences were thrown into subterranean cells, mistreated, submitted to prolonged interrogations and released only if, faint because of the inhuman procedures of their jailors, they agreed to sign.

These crimes, news of which has not failed to spread throughout the country and which, inevitably, will very soon alarm world public opinion, have been confirmed by the functionaries of the Patriarchate of Bucharest and by the members of the so-called congress for union with the Orthodox Church of Cluj, some of whom still bore on their persons visible signs of the violence undergone.

In the face of this position of the Roumanian Government which on several occasions has repeated and continues to repeat that it wishes to respect, and let be respected, the rights of religious freedom in Roumania, the Apostolic Nunciature, in the name of the Holy See and in the name of the entire Christian world, protests with all the might which the circumstances require, against procedures of this kind, unworthy of a civilized State.

> MONS. GERARD PATRICK O'HARA
> *Archbishop of Savannah*

The Apostolic Nuntio,
Bucharest, October 2, 1948

Two days later the Roumanian Government replied to the protest of the Apostolic Nunciature with a "Note" which categorically rejected it, denouncing it as calumny and fantasy:

1) The Roumanian Government categorically rejects the protest of the Apostolic Nunciature against the return of the Greek-Catholic population of Ardeal to the Orthodox rite, a protest which signifies interference in the internal affairs of the Roumanian People's Republic and an attempt to attack the freedom of faith. The sovereign state of Roumania does not accept any outrage against its national independence and it cannot as a consequence permit foreign interventions, tending to limit a right which the Constitution

of the country accords it, as is the case with the freedom of religious cults.

2) The Roumanian Government rejects the gross calumnies contained in the above-mentioned Note relative to the alleged interference of Roumanian authorities in the movement for uniting the faithful of the Greek-Catholic rite to the Orthodox Church. These defamatory affirmations are a new proof of the hostile attitude which the Apostolic Nunciature systematically adopts towards the Roumanian Peoples Government, its reforms and its democratic achievements.

3) The absurd fabrications and calumnies exploited in this note cannot distract the attention of public opinion from the real and deep reasons for the return of the Greek-Catholic population to its ancient belief.

And it is therefore natural that now, in the condition of full liberty accorded by the Peoples Democratic regime, the descendants of those who for two and a half centuries have had to suffer on account of the Catholic Church and its allies return to their ancient faith.

4) The Apostolic Nunciature, being only the diplomatic representative of Vatican City, cannot arrogate to itself the right of speaking "in the name of the entire Christian world," as it does in the above-mentioned note.

5) The Roumanian Government further denounces the attempt at blackmail, which is contained in the alleged threat that a violation of religious freedom on the part of the Roumanian Government would soon alarm world public opinion. This attempt is akin in method to the campaigns conducted by imperialist circles and their agents against the democratic achievements of the Roumanian Peoples Republic.

6) In conclusion, the Government of the Roumanian Peoples Democracy, in the most curt and decisive manner, rejects the note of the Apostolic Nunciature both in form and content and it considers it as an act of provocation against the State and the Roumanian people.

THE DECISIONS OF THE ASSEMBLY OF CLUJ

While the Nunciature and the Government were exchanging the notes reported above the comedy continued its course and on October 1 there convened in Cluj the 38 Delegates of the Greek-Catholic clergy, nominated by the Government, for the purpose of underwriting, in the name of the entire Greek Catholic Church, its incorporation into the Orthodox Church.

The meeting was held in an auditorium of the "Baritiu" Lyceum of Cluj, under the presidency of the archpriest, Aurol Drumboia, who submitted the following declaration to the Delegates for signing:

We the undersigned, priests of the Greek-Catholic Church of the Roumanian People's Republic, met at Cluj in ecclesiastical assembly today October 1, 1948, in the auditorium of the "George Baritiu" Lyceum, induced by our conscience and by a limitless love for the Roumanian people which today unites all its forces in the struggle for peace, freedom and progress, and convinced that the moment has come to re-make the spiritual unity of our people, hereby decide:

1) To return to the bosom of the Roumanian Orthodox Church, from which two and a half centuries ago our forefathers, because of the bitterness of the times, separated themselves.

2) To make all efforts in our power to illuminate the conscience of our faithful so that they in all faith may also follow our example, so that they may be as one with our orthodox brothers.

The reasons which suggested the act of union of 1700 no longer exist today. The Constitution and the Laws of the RPR assure in an equal manner political, cultural, economic and religious rights to all citizens of the country.

Today the Roumanian Orthodox Church does not find itself in the situation of 1700 *vis-à-vis* the State. On the contrary since it encompasses the majority of the faithful in the country, it finds itself in a most particular situation which points the way to roseate hopes of an ever better future.

In this happy situation, the breaking of relations with the Church of Rome, alien to the interests of our people, the restoration of the spiritual unity of the country and the application of all our efforts to the struggle for peace, democracy and progress, are a sacred duty for our entire people.

In the light of these facts, we proclaim our return to the bosom of the Roumanian Orthodox Church, in our name and in that of those who have delegated us to this assembly and *we decide to break off relations with the Vatican.*

As of today we shall pay heed only to the heads appointed by the Office of the Holy Roumanian Orthodox Church.

Two days later, on October 3rd, the orthodox Patriarch of Bucharest, Justinian Marina, solemnly received the delegates of the Assembly of Cluj who had been accompanied to the Patriarchate by an imposing squad of police. And after listening to the decisions taken at Cluj, he officially registered their break with Rome and drew up the following Synodical Act:

Today, Sunday October 3, in the year of Redemption 1948, we members of the permanent Synod of the Roumanian Orthodox Church . . . have assembled in the synodical chamber of the Patriarchal Palace to receive in solemn session the delegation of 36 archpriests and priests of the united Greek-Catholic Church come to Bucharest.

First a reading was made of the proclamation made on October 1, 1948 at Cluj, by this same delegation in the name of 430 Greek-Catholic canons, archpriests and priests of Ardeal, Banato, Crosan and Maramures, a proclamation by which it was decided to return to the bosom of the Roumanian Orthodox Church and to break all relations with the Church of Rome.

Then a *Te Deum* was sung in the Church of Saint Piridion, by the Metropolitan of Ardeal, Nicolas, surrounded by the group of Orthodox and Greek-Catholic archpriests.

It is with an unutterable happiness that we take note of the realization of this return and we order that at the same time all others be received who shall express the desire to return to the bosom of the Orthodox Church and to break their ties with the Church of Rome.

We decide, moreover, that in confirmation of the above this Act be transcribed together with the proclamation entered in the holy Synodical registries and that it be authenticated by our seal and our signatures together with those of the 36 archpriests and priests of the Greek-Catholic Church.

> JUSTINIAN, *Patriarch*
> NICOLAS, *Metropolitan of Ardeal*
> BASILIUS, *Metropolitan of Banato*
> FIRMILIAN, *Archbishop of Crajova*
> SEBASTIAN, *Archbishop of Suceava and Maramures*
> [*the signatures of the 36 Greek-Catholic
>   Delegates follow*]

All these acts and abuses, carried out not without the open collusion of the Government and according to its directives, could not remain without an open and vibrant protest on the part of the uniate Catholic Episcopate which on October 7 sent the following joint letter to the President of the Presidium, Groza:

N. 3516/1948

MR. PRESIDENT:

We undersigned Bishops of the uniate Roumanian Church have the honor to bring to your attention that which follows:

For about a month the administrative and security organs of the State have begun an investigation of the uniate Church of Roumania in order to determine the opinion of the clergy about the union of their Church with the Orthodox Church. At the same time the political organizations, in an illegal and outrageous manner, have attempted to substitute the personnel of Parish Councils with members of governmental political parties, with the aim of eliminating priests from the administration of the properties of the parish Churches.

Contemporaneously an ever increasing amount of pub-

licity was given to the appeals for a return to orthodoxy,
launched by the Patriarch and the orthodox Metropolitan of
Ardeal, without the hierarchy of the uniate Church being
able, not only to reply to these appeals because the means
for doing so were denied to it, but even to inform the faithful about its thought on the matter. In fact a joint letter of
ours to the faithful was confiscated even though it contained
nothing of a political or polemical character, and the Bishop,
John Suciu, was taken away by security police on a public
street while he was making his regular visits to his faithful.

Mr. President, the agents of this campaign, which has
provoked the indignation of the entire population of the
faithful, have declared quite openly that this is an action
which has as its aim the suppression of the uniate Church
in Roumania. The idea would have appeared absolutely incredible if police deputies and inspectors had not confirmed,
be it with the coercive measures employed by them or by
their illegal acts committed with impunity, the truth of our
assertions the proofs of which are in our hands.

During this campaign which lasted bitterly from September 26 to October 4, 1948, the Bishop of Cluj, Mons. Julius
Hossu, was under house arrest in his residence so that he
could make no contact with the clergy and leave undis-
turbed the action conducted against the Church. All the
priests and about 28 or 30 faithful were arrested in Ardeal
who, in ignorance of this disposition, had occasion to enter
or to leave his residence.

On the morning of September 27 the Bishop, Mons.
Susciu, as he was visiting the parish of Copacel (department
of Fagars), was picked up by the police, conducted to an
unknown place and kept under surveillance for two days,
so that he could have no contact with priests or with the
faithful. If Bishops were treated in such a wise, it can be
imagined how priests were handled! . . .

For reasons of prudence we do not think it opportune
to enumerate the abuses and the violences committed on the
persons of archpriests and priests in order to obtain their
signature. . . . Here we shall limit ourselves only to bringing

these facts to the attention of Your Excellency, to expressing all of our indignation in the face of a veritable persecution directed and organized against the uniate Roumanian Church. . . . At the same time, Mr. President, we express the desire to see you interfere decisively in order to halt this campaign.

Lastly we would declare solemnly and firmly that the uniate Roumanian Church has never made itself guilty, neither in the past nor in the present, of acts hostile to the nation, the country or to the political order . . . and that all of us, pastors and faithful, are determined to remain in the bosom of the Catholic Church, in the service of which we want to remain through life and death, convinced that by so doing we are in the service of the people and the country as we have been up to now without ever falling short.

We urge you to receive, Mr. President, the assurance of our distinguished consideration.

VALERIUS TRAIANO FRENTIU, *Bishop of Oradea*
ALEXANDER RUSSU, *Bishop of Maramures*
JULIUS HOSSU, *Bishop of Cluj-Gherla*
JOHN BALAN, *Bishop of Lugoj*
JOHN SUCIU, *Apostolic Administrator of Blaj*

Bucharest, October 7, 1948

Another letter of protest, drawn up in still more energetic terms and also signed by Latin Catholic Bishops, headed by the Archbishop Metropolitan of Bucharest, was sent on the same day to the President of the Council of Ministers.

After listing therein an entire series of acts and illegalities committed against the Catholic Church and bringing to the attention of the Government the ever growing number of priests who were maltreated, imprisoned or held in jail without any legal procedure whatsoever; the ever more frequent limitations imposed on the Catholic press, so that it could be said to have been completely eliminated; and the total suppression of confessional and religious teaching, the body of Bishops concluded thus:

. ·. . Almost three million citizens of the RPR, children of
the Catholic Church, see themselves treated by the laws and
the authorities as enemies of the country and guilty of who
knows what crimes against the people, these children of this
earth which they have bedewed with their sweat for centuries. They are persecuted by the very authorities of the
State who instead of bringing to the people conditions of a
just and tranquil life, as would be their duty, have sowed,
on the contrary, disorders, agitations, lack of security and
faith among the people with no respect for its religious con-
victions. . . .

But protests and declarations, unfortunately, went without
reply and the struggle unleased by the Government for the complete liquidation of the uniate Roumanian Church continued ever
more determinedly and ever more violently.

THE MOTION OF THE ASSEMBLY OF ALBA-JULIA (OCTOBER 21, 1948)

Throughout the month of October armed policemen went
in search of every Catholic priest in order to violate his conscience. Those who joined were immediately released, the others
were taken out of the country with the same suddenness, and
during their absence the parish Council would be called into
urgent session and in the name of the entire Parish it had to
declare the transfer of the inhabitants to Orthodoxy.

The 21st of October had been selected as the date of a large
congress to be held in Alba-Julia, the metropolis of the Greek-
Catholics, so as to sanction with an accomplished fact in the
very center of Transylvania the passing over of the Catholics of
Ardeal, Banato, Crisan and Maramures to the Roumanian Orthodox Church.

The Orthodox Patriarch, with about twenty Bishops and representatives of the Government, Parliament and the Regime,
were brought to the scene, before whom was read the following
motion, as approved and voted by the Assembly of the Greek-
Catholic delegates gathered in Alba-Julia:

Today, October 21, at a moment just two centuries and half distant from the day in which, precisely here, in this Roumanian Belgrade, a party of our forefathers, deceived by false promises broke the religious unity of Ardeal and united with the Pope of Rome, *we,* people and clergy representing all the Greek-Catholic Roumanians of Ardeal, Banato, Crisan and Miramares, assembled in this primatial residence of the metropolitan of Transylvania in order to celebrate solemnly the spiritual restoration of our people . . . with a clear conscience of our responsibilities, before history, before our people and before God hereby declare:

a) To break for ever our ties, whatever be their nature, with the Vatican and with the Rome of the Popes.

b) To unite ourselves with all our soul to the Roumanian Orthodox Church whose teachings on faith and canonic dispositions we intend to follow.

c) To submit with complete filial devotion to all the decisions of our Roumanian Orthodox Church.

As of today all Roumanians are united for ever in the faith, united in the constant service of our people, united in faithful obedience towards the precepts of the new life of our beloved Roumanian People's Republic.

To the members of the Presidium of the RPR and of the Government of the Country, the homage of our gratitude for the liberties assured to all the sons of the people, a liberty thanks to which it has been possible to restore the integrity of the Roumanian Church."

Immediately thereafter the Patriarch, Justinian Marina, proceeded to the occupation of the Catholic cathedral on the part of the Orthodox, and together with the Bishops present he signed a synodical act which declared that: "In order to conserve the memory of these grandiose days lived by the Roumanian people, the Church of the Most Holy Trinity of Alba Julia, was declared to be from then on, 'The Cathedral of the Unification of the Roumanian Church of Transylvania.' . . ."

On the following days the same fate was undergone by the other five cathedrals of the uniate Catholics of Oradea Mare, Cluj, Lugoj, and Maramures, which were occupied by the Orthodox, while the parish churches one by one were taken over by the exponents of the Orthodox hierarchy who passed them on either to schismatic priests who had joined the union with the Orthodox, or directly to Orthodox priests.

Then there was started a wave of persecution against all the religious Congregations, with the methodical occupation of all their convents, their houses, their properties, while monks and nuns were loaded on trucks and by night transported to unknown destinations. Particularly tragic were the occupations of the Institute of Our Lady of Blaj, of the Assumptionist Fathers of Blaj, and the Basilians of Bixad.

The Congregations affected were the following:

a) *Basilians:* The monasteries of Bixad, Nicula, Moiseiu, Prislop and Obreja.
b) *Conventuals:* The Convents of Dragesti, Decanesti, Gruiulung, Oradea Mare, Sanislau and Bucharest.
c) *Assumptionists:* In Blaj, Bejus and Bucharest.
d) *Brothers of the Christian Schools:* In Oradea Mare.
e) *Sisters of the Mother of God:* In Blaj, Cluj, Juc, Sovata, Sibiu and Aiud.

ARREST AND INTERNMENT OF ALL BISHOPS

Towards the end of October, almost on the same day and the same hour, the six Catholic Bishops of the Byzantine rite were picked up by the police, arrested and after a brief sojourn in Dragoslavale and in Calderusan, they were deported to unknown destinations.

Nothing more has been known about them, the Government has given no further information about them and their fate is unknown to this day.

DEFINITIVE SUPPRESSION BY DECREE
OF THE PRESIDIUM OF THE RPR

On December 1, 1948, a government decree legally suppressed the existence of the United Church and of all of its institutions, and its real and moveable properties were confiscated and taken over by the State. This was the final act with which the Government closed its campaign of persecution. The tragedy had lasted a little more than sixty days.

Here is the text of the Governmental Decree:

N. 1998   Decree N. 358

THE PRESIDIUM OF THE GRAND NATIONAL ASSEMBLY
OF THE ROUMANIAN PEOPLE'S REPUBLIC

basing itself on Art. 44, par. 2, and Art. 45 of the Constitution of the Roumanian People's Republic,

in view of the decision of the Council of Ministers n. 1614 of 1948,

issues the following Decree:

DECREE N. 358: Definition of the situation in law of the ancient Greek-Catholic religion.

ARTICLE 1.—As a result of the return to the Roumanian Orthodox Religion of the parishes of the Greek-Catholic religion and in conformity with Art. 13 of Decree n. 177 of 1948, the central organizations of this religion (Metropolitans, Dioceses, Capitols, Orders, Congregations, Deaconate, Monasteries, Foundations, Associations, as well as all other institutions and organizations), whatever be their nature or their name, cease to exist.

ARTICLE 2.—The real and moveable properties belonging to the organizations and institutions mentioned in Art. 1 of the present decree, excepting the properties of the ancient parishes, return to the Roumanian State which will take immediate possession of them.

An inter-ministerial commission, composed of the Delegates of the Ministries of Religions, Finances, Internal

Affairs, Agriculture, Forestry and of Public Instruction, will decide as to the allocation of these properties. It may return a part thereof to the Roumanian Orthodox Church or to the diverse parts which compose it.

STANCIU STOIAN
Minister of Religions
AVRAM BUNACIU
Minister of Religions

Bucharest, December 1, 1948

B. SUPPRESSION OF THE CATHOLIC CHURCH OF THE LATIN RITE

Since its suppression, in 1948, of the Roumanian Catholic Church of the Byzantine rite, and its incorporation, by a governmental act, with the Roumanian Orthodox Church, the Roumanian Communist Government has for some time been active on a grand scale with plans to transform the still-existing Catholic Church of the Latin rite into a "National Schismatic Church."

The stages of this criminal activity are as follows:

REDUCTION OF DIOCESES FROM SIX TO TWO

The Latin Church in Roumania (or Roman-Catholic as it is commonly called there) numbers about 1,200,000 faithful, the majority of whom are of German or Hungarian origin and who are primarily settled in Transylvania and in Banato.

The Concordat concluded between Roumania and the Holy See on May 10, 1927 had established six Dioceses of Latin rite: (1) The Archbishopric of Bucharest; (2) The Bishopric of Alba Julia; (3) The Bishopric of Jassy; (4) The Bishopric of Oradea Mare (Gran Varadino); (5) The Bishopric of Satumare; (6) The Bishopric of Timisoara.

The Communist Government with its Decree of August 3, 1948, "On the General Administration of Religions" (only a few days after its denunciation of the Concordat with the Holy See with its Decree no. 151, July 19, 1948) reduced the Dioceses of

Latin rite to only two: (1) The Archdiocese of Bucharest; (2) The Diocese of Alba-Julia, adducing as a pretext that at least 750,000 faithful were required in order to have a Diocese in accordance with the new disposition of the Decree on Religions.

During the carrying out of this Decree, in the month of November of the same year, the Communist Government discarded three of the five Latin Bishops left and put them on a "for disposal" list. Thus were the following Bishops deprived of their seats: Mons. Alexander Cisar, Archbishop of Bucharest; Mons. Aaron Marton, Bishop of Alba-Julia and Mons. John Scheffler, Bishop of Satumare.

There remained only two Bishops: Mons. Anthony Durkovici, who was transferred to Bucharest from his Diocese at Jassi, and Mons. Augustine Pacha, who from his Diocese at Timisoara was transferred to Alba Julia. To their care were entrusted all the Roumanian Catholics of Latin rite, about 1,200,000, with 683 parishes and about 800 priests of the secular clergy and more than 250 of the regular clergy.

ARREST AND INTERNMENT OF ALL BISHOPS

In June 1949, the Communist Government ordered the arrest of Mons. Durkovici who administered the Archdiocese of Bucharest and Mons. Marton, formerly the Bishop of Alba Julia and who since November 1948 had been placed on the list "for disposal."

A few months later Mons. Cisar, formerly Archbishop of Bucharest and Mons. Scheffler, Bishop of Satumare, also were arrested. Both had been on the "disposal" list since November 1948. The former was interned in the city of Orastie in Transylvania, and the latter in Baja-Decris, under the strict surveillance of the police.

Only the venerable Mons. Pacha remained in office, an old man of more than eighty who had been spared when the other Bishops were arrested because he was seriously ill. But as soon as he was in somewhat better health and refused to collaborate with the underhanded dealings of the Government which wanted to use him to form a "national" Roumanian Catholic Church, he too was arrested and submitted to a clamorous trial which took place in Bucharest in September 1951, and condemned to 18 years in jail.

Thus, within the space of two years, even the Latin Episcopate was completely suppressed, just as had happened to that of the Greek-Catholic rite in 1948, and no Catholic Bishop at all, either of the Latin rite or the Greek rite, existed in Roumania.

All had been arrested, deposed and interned.

SUPPRESSION OF ALL RELIGIOUS ORDERS

(DECREE 29, JULY 29, 1949)

After eliminating all the Bishops, the Communist Government, with the aim of weakening still further the resistance of the Catholic Church, concentrated its struggle against the Latin Religious Orders and Congregations which were very numerous in Roumania.

Having already taken all their schools from them and deprived members of religious orders of the right to teach with the Decree of Education of August 3, 1948, the Council of Ministers, on July 29, 1949, went on to approve the Decree known as the "Regrouping of Religious Orders" which in effect was equivalent to a decree of suppression.

Here is the full text:

The Council of Ministers in its session of July 29, 1949,

In view of the report of the Minister of Cults bearing the Number 21535 of 1949,

And in consideration of the fact that the tasks of public instruction, sanitation and welfare, in conformity with the laws now in force, belong fully and exclusively to the State,

And in view of the fact that there still exist on the territory of the Roumanian People's Republic formations and organizations of several Roman-Catholic Orders and Congregations, whose sole purpose is to dedicate themselves to teaching or to caring for the ill, or to extending social aid,

And in view of the dispositions of Art. 9, par. 2, letter B

of Law no. 11 of 1944, on the control of non-profit juridical persons,

On the basis of Article 66 of the Constitution of the People's Republic decrees:

ARTICLE 1. The following Roman Catholic Orders and Congregations, with all the institutions which are dependent on them in any manner whatsoever, whether they function as juridical persons or associations in fact, will no longer function throughout the entire territory of the Roumanian People's Republic:

a) The Congregation of the Brothers of Christian Schools.

b) The Order of the Piarists.

c) The Congregation of Our Lady of Zion.

d) The Congregation of Holy Mary (Pitar Mos).

e) The Order of Saint Orsola.

f) The Order of Saint Orsola of the Roumanian Union.

g) The Congregation of the Sisters of Our Lady.

h) The Order of the Merciful Brothers.

i) The Congregation of the Sisters of Charity of St. Vincent de Paul.

j) The Congregation of the Poor Franciscan Sisters of the Holy Family.

k) The Congregation of the Sisters of Charity.

l) The Congregation of the Daughters of Charity of St. Frances of Assisi.

m) The Congregation of Social Sisters.

n) The Congregation of the Franciscan Sisters of the Lily.

o) The Congregation of the Benedictine Sisters of Saint Lioba.

Likewise formations and organizations of several Roman Catholic Orders and Congregations, which are not enumerated in this Article but which carry on activities in the fields of education, care of the sick and social aid, will no longer be able to function.

ARTICLE 2. The members, men or women, belonging to one or another of the Orders and Congregations listed in Article 1, are free to continue their religious life, by joining within 15 days after the publication of the present Decree one of the following religious communities:

a) The men to the quarters of the ancient Roman-Catholic archbishopric of Bucharest Number 19 Al. Popov street, or to the quarters of the Roman-Catholic Bishopric curia of Alba-Julia.

b) The women to the Roman-Catholic monastery of the commune of Radna, in the department of Arad; or to the quarters of the convent of Ploesti Leordeni (Agnes) department of Ilfov; or to the quarters of the convent of the commune of Timisul de Sus, in the department of Brasov.

ARTICLE 3. Those men or women who do not wish to continue their religious life may request:

a) acceptance by some public asylum, if they are aged persons or persons unable to work;

b) to be listed by the Labor Exchange Bureau if they know a trade, or desire to train themselves in some profession.

ARTICLE 4. Members belonging to one or the other Religious Orders and Congregations indicated in Article 1, who do not enjoy Roumanian "citizenship," must present themselves within 10 days after the publication of this Decree to the local police headquarters so that they may conform with the dispositions of the law regarding visiting permits.

ARTICLE 5. Members belonging to one or the other formations and organizations indicated in Article 1, are obliged, within 20 days after the publication of the present Decree, personally to make known to the Ministry of Religions, via a registered letter, the decision they intend to take and the place where they intend to establish themselves.

ARTICLE 6. The Minister of Cults and the Minister of the Interior, by agreement, will be empowered to take all measures necessary to resolve all the questions which may rise from the present Decree.

ARTICLE 7. The Minister of Cults and the Minister of the Interior are charged with the application of the dispositions of the present Decree.

ARREST AND TRIAL OF THE BISHOP MONS. PACHA

(SEPTEMBER 1951)

In August 1951 the tempo of the arrests of priests and lay men faithful to Rome became ever more intense and culminated with the arrest of the venerable Bishop of Timisoara, Mons. Augustine Pacha. Despite his age, he was over eighty, and the precarious condition of his health he was interned in the jails of Aiud and subjected to a clamorous trial which took place in Bucharest in September 1951.

Co-accused with Bishop Pacha were the two vicar generals of Bucharest and Timisoara: Mons. Joseph Schubert and Adelbert Boros, arrested as far back February 17; the priest, John Heber, secretary to Mons. Pacha, arrested on March 10; Father Clemente Gatti, rector of the Italian church, arrested on March 8; and the laymen, Peter Topa, George Sandulescu, Lazarus Stefanescu, in addition to a functionary of the Italian Legation in Bucharest, Eraldo Pintori.

All were accused of having carried out espionage activity in favor of the Vatican and America, and of having attempted to establish a secret Christian social party with the aim of overthrowing the existing regime by means of promised aid from America.

The court proceedings were held in a theatre for the purpose of giving them greater publicity and they were presided over by the infamous Petrescu, who under the Antonescu regime had won an evil reputation of being an executioner of innocents and who now, having changed banners, had put himself at the service of the new masters. The trial lasted six days during which the ten accused, as in other cases staged by the communists, seemed to compete among themselves in self-accusation, foretelling even the questions as if they were reciting a lesson learned by heart. This is so true that on September 17, when sentence was pronounced, it was possible to read the confessions of the accused even though no measures had been taken to record them stenographically during the course of the trial.

The twenty-three witnesses, all brought forward only by the Public Ministry and none by the defense, confirmed the self-accusations of the accused, while the official defense counsel could do nothing else except to admit the crimes of their clients, without adducing any other attenuating circumstance except that of having acted "under instigation and according to higher orders."

The sentence was pronounced on September 17 and it prescribed imprisonment for Mons. Schubert, Mons. Boros, and the Messrs. Eraldo Pintori, George Sandulescu and Lazarus Stefanescu; 18 years for Mons. Pacha; 15 years for Father Clement Gatti and Joseph Waltner; 12 years for John Heber and ten years for Signor Pietro Topa.

Adding the final touch to this farce Radio Bucharest took pains to organize 30 minute serial broadcasts of the trial so that all the accused could derive the sadistic pleasure of themselves repeating and confirming the various charges, point by point, for their invisible listeners. Not satisfied even with this, Father Gatti and Signor Pintori felt the extreme duty of thanking the Roumanian authorities for the "high civility" with which they had been treated.

In addition, before the curtain fell on this macabre show, an assembly of so-called representatives of all the religions which gathered in Brasow (Stalino) who were impressed by the trial against those whom they described as a group of spies, traitors and conspirators in the service of the Vatican and of the centre of Italian espionage, namely, American imperialism, felt it was their duty to denounce:

> . . . the infamous action of the Vatican which by means of its cowardly servants secretly works against the sublime ideals of humanity and against the security of our dear fatherland; an infamous action which has roused the indignation of all honest persons. We representatives of all the religions of Stalingrad and in the region of Stalino, without distinction of confessions, denounce the criminal intrigues which threaten peace in general and the security of our State in particular. . . .

This entire *mise-en-scène,* as appears from the long-winded commentaries which were published in the press at that time under giant headlines, could have only one aim: by slander, to discredit in the eyes of the faithful and the clergy those members of the true hierarchy who were attempting to hold themselves firm and solid against the sacrilegious usurpations of the State; and to predispose men and minds to the acceptance of that famous "Statute" on the practice of religion, which would "integrate the Catholic Church in the framework of the laws."

> The trial [as one newspaper put it] has once more justified the efforts of churchmen and laymen desirous of integrating the Church in the framework of the laws, in the deeply rooted conviction that it is possible to be good citizens and good Catholics . . . It is the fault of the hierarchy if this is not understood; not that of the churchmen who are lovers of peace and who draw lessons from this trial, and the comfort to persevere in their labors. . . .

C. CONCLUSION

As of January 31, 1953, the balance sheet of the losses suffered by the Catholic Church in Roumania because of Communist persecution was as follows:

	1945	1953
Apostolic Nuntio	1	0 (expelled)
Archbishops and Bishops	12	0 (all imprisoned, sentenced or deported; 3 already dead in jail)
Priests and Members of Religious Orders	2,331	1,405 (55 killed; 250 dead or vanished; 200 to forced labor; 200 in jail)
Churches or Chapels	3,795	700 (all Byzantine-rite churches given to Orthodox /2,734/; more than 300 Latin churches requisitioned)
Parishes	2,490	683 (all Byzantine parishes transferred to Orthodox 1,807)
Religious Houses	160	25 (85% lost)
Catholic Schools (Male)	224 (28,000 students)	0 (all suppressed)
Catholic Schools (Female)	152 (23,000 students)	0 (all suppressed)
Welfare Agencies	160	0 (all suppressed)
Newspapers and Catholic Publications	30	0 (all suppressed)

CHAPTER IV

Hungary, 1945–1953

A. PERSECUTION OF THE CHURCH

THE SITUATION IN 1945

In order to obtain an exact picture of the Communist persecution of the Catholic Church in Hungary, and to understand the significance of the destructions carried out by communism, it is necessary to remember the eminent position of the Catholic Church in the life of the country before April 1945.

a) Rich with a millenial history, the Catholic Church in Hungary links its origins to the very origins of the Magyar nation and people. By the will of its first Founder and organizer the King, Saint Stephen, who in the year 1000 had received the royal crown and function from Pope Sylvester II, it had been endowed with particular prerogatives. The Primate was the first public dignitary of the country. Constitutionally no major decisions concerning the life of the country could be taken without his intervention. The Bishops were members by right of the Upper Chamber, and the Primate, moreover, was a member of the Council which, in the absence of the highest authority, directed the affairs of the nation. Hence the importance and the role of the Catholic Church in Hungary cannot be compared to the role reserved to it in other countries. And it is in relation to this special position of the Catholic Church in Hungary that the events which took place in 1945 and thereafter must be considered.

b) In addition to those constitutional prerogatives, it is also necessary to make note of the power it enjoyed through its *vast land holdings*. It is true that the vast patrimony with which Saint Stephan had endowed it had undergone some diminution through the centuries. The Church itself during the so-called second republic of 1919, when Michael Karoly initiated land reform, had given up 71,000 hectars, i.e. 30% of the arable land in its possession.

Nonetheless as late as 1945 the Church owned 877,294 hectares of land. Now this entire patrimonial wealth had furnished the Church with the means of maintaining an immense number of schools, institutions, asylums, orphanages, hospitals, etc. so that it was able to occupy an important position in the cultural life of the country. Statistical data published in 1945 disclosed, as of that date, the following: out of 2,650 popular schools, 1,347 were in the hands of the Church; out of 4,847 general schools, the Church administered 2,095; out of 368 civic schools the Church had 158, and out of 179 gymnasia-lycées, a total of 64 were directed by the Church. Out of a total of 67 teachers' schools, *lyceès* and institutions for the training of kindergarten teachers, 41 were in the hands of the Church and of 11,992 future teachers of both sexes, 10,712 (almost 80%) were being educated by the Church. And out of a total of 1,155,216 pupils in the lower and intermediate schools, 666,836 were instructed by the Church. Moreover, it administered 10 hospitals which it owned directly, and supervised 90 which belonged to the State or to private persons. It had built and maintained, at its own expense, about 120 orphanages, homes for the aged, refectories, etc., in addition to an undetermined number of nurseries for children, and summer camps.

c) In addition to the constitutional prerogatives and to its immense patrimonial and cultural wealth, it must also be borne in mind that it impressed itself on the nation because of its numerical strength. Out of a population of almost 10,000,000 inhabitants, the Catholic Church alone in 1945 numbered more than 7,000,000 faithful (about 70%), while the other 3,000,000 were divided as follows: *(a)* Protestants: 2,450,000 (24.5%); *(b)* Jews: 440,000 (4.4%); *(c)* Orthodox: 60,000 (0.6%).

From the hierarchic point of view the Catholic Church included:

a) Three Archdioceses: Esztergom; Galocsa; Eger

b) Eight Dioceses: Gyor; Szombathely; Pecs; Vestprem; Szekesfehervar; Vas; Csanad; Haydudorog (of eastern Byzantine rite)

c) Two Apostolic Administrators: Szatmar; Rozsnyo

d) Two Apostolic Vicarates: Nagyvarad; Kassa

e) One Nullius Abbacy: Pannonhalma (Benedictine)

On the whole the parishes numbered 2,265, but the number of secular priests was 4,012.

There were 18 male Religious Orders and Congregations, with 187 houses and monasteries, and 2,459 members of whom 1,422 were priests.

Female Religious Orders and Congregations totalled 39, with 456 houses and 7,525 members.

There were more than 5,000 organizations of Catholic Action, male and female, with about 1,000,000 enrolled members.

There were about 2,000 Confraternities, Marian Congregations, etc., with 700,000 members.

The "Kalot" and the "Kalasz" (movements of young peasants) numbered 700 organizations with about 100,000 members. They had 20 popular schools attended by 35,000 young people.

The "Kolping" (an association of business youth) and the "Kioe" (an association of working-class youth) had 40,000 members, with about 100 houses and 6 special institutions.

FIRST COMMUNIST CONTACTS WITH THE CHURCH
(OCTOBER 1944–DECEMBER 1945)

In the face of this impressive organization of the Catholic Church which had, moreover, barely emerged victorious from the struggle waged against it by the Nazi-Fascist government of

Szalassi, the Communists did not dare to unleash an immediate frontal attack. In fact the prestige of the Catholic Church at the moment of "liberation" was very high. It had prevented, through its Bishops, the deportation of 200,000 Jews in Budapest, it had opposed the evacuation of the civil population of Transdanubia with its famous "Memorandum" of October 15, 1944, which had led to the arrest of Bishop Mindszenty by the Germans. And it had remained solid during the difficult days of sieges and battles, assisting the needy and the persecuted. All this was recognized by the Russians themselves and their attitude toward the Church —at least in the first months—had been sufficiently proper.

General Cernissow, the military commander of Budapest, had declared in the first days of the occupation, in the presence of representatives of the various churches, that the Russian Government desired to respect religious freedom and desired that the churches re-open their doors and resume religious life as soon as possible. If difficulties were encountered, he said, all could bring them to the attention of the Russian commander who would take the necessary action. And in reality, in those days, ecclesiastical dress or the cassocks of monks not only did not present danger, but on the contrary assured immunity. The activities of the Bishops, parish priests and monks were in no wise impeded, even though bishoprics and presbyteries were not spared from looting on the part of Russian soldiers which here and there led to acts of violence which cost the lives of some members of the clergy. Among these victims are remembered a priest, Cornelius Hummel, killed while he was trying to save a girl from a Russian soldier, and the Bishop of Gyor, Baron William Apor, killed on the night of Good Friday, in 1945, while he was trying to save several women from the violence of Russian soldiers by hiding them in the cellar of the episcopal residence.

Even the Hungarian Communist Party tried to bring itself in line with the directives of the commander of the Russian troops, and in this first period it concerned itself with avoiding the slightest shadow of suspicion that it was anti-religious. It proclaimed that there would be no difficulties even for priests to become members of the party. It sought to assist the Church

even materially. Members of the local sections of the Party
would present themselves to parish priests, offering their services
to reconstruct the church, the school or the very dwelling of the
parish priest. They wished no payment for the work performed,
and requested only a written recognition that they had worked
disinterestedly. If they could obtain such a declaration, it was
published most prominently in the newspapers on the next day.
Party leaders sought every opportunity to appear in public with
ecclesiastical personages. Naturally an official photographer was
always present. The photographs were to be testimony of a
cordial encounter and later would serve the purposes of Communist propaganda. With the pretext of aiding charitable activities they tried to penetrate Catholic associations. Members of
the Party received orders to take part in the parish life, getting
themselves elected to Parish Councils. The Church enjoyed special
privileges even at the time of land reform; while all land holdings
more than one thousand hectares in extension were simply confiscated, church land holdings, on the contrary, in every case
were left 100 hectares in extension. In fact, needy churches and
parishes obtained new assignations.

Matyas Rakosi, the Communist Party leader, had the bells
restored to the churches from which they had been removed
during the war.

So ostentatious was the attention of the Party that the Church
was seriously worried about how it could avoid the apparent
magnanimity of the regime because it knew that all this was
being done to serve propaganda ends.

Naturally, knowing the inexorable logic of Communist policy
towards religion, it was understood that this attitude could not
long endure. Therefore the Communist tactic of favoritism towards the Church, employed in this first period the better to
conquer it, could already be said to have completely failed.

THE GOVERNMENT BRINGS THE STRUGGLE OUT INTO THE OPEN
(JANUARY–AUGUST 1946)

In January 1946, immediately after the proclamation of the
new "Hungarian People's Republic," the Communists suddenly
discarded their mask of apparent respect shown until then to the

Catholic Church and they gave themselves to a campaign of denigration of the Catholic Church and all its institutions throughout the country.

It had so happened that their game had been exposed and Cardinal Primate Mindszenty, in a public letter on October 18, 1945, had been compelled to denounce to the country at large the bad faith with which they had acted. After detailing, in fact, how the body of the Hungarian episcopate had from the beginning given testimony of the widest understanding of the nascent Hungarian democracy to the point where it had incited the people, in its joint letter of May 24, 1945, to have faith in and respect towards it, the Letter continued:

. . . Our waiting was long and patient: More than once did we think of raising our voice, but we did not wish to disturb the development of the situation. Above all we did not wish to obstacle the diligent and faithful work of men of good will, with our overt attitude . . .

But now . . . we can no longer keep silent. We must declare that there are many phenomena to deplore in Hungarian public life which are in conflict with the principles of true democracy. We must declare that this tendency will drag our country, already so impoverished and ruined, into new dangerous adventures . . .

And the more so must we grow frightened if we consider that a certain sectarian spirit is afoot which *tends to create a regime of arbitrariness and violence.* Everywhere, but principally in several regions there is a delight in arresting men on unfounded suspicion, for personal resentment, *for secret party machinations,* and these men can not even imagine the reason for their incarceration. A priest, who for many years was an inmate of a sanitorium, now aged and still ill, was condemned to forced labor only because he had protested against the dissolution of a religious organization of his parish. Other priests have been brought before the police because of the sermons preached on the day of St. Stephen and they were threatened by the very chief of police *with deportation to Siberia* if they continued their hostile attitude against Communism. . . . We repudiate these tendencies and desire that an end be put to such a state of affairs. We invite you, therefore, to reflect upon our words. We are not frightened by the threats of the sons of iniquity. It is better to bear the threats now rather than favor the coming to power of inconsiderate and loveless men who wish to lead the Hungarian people to its ruin!

The effect of this joint letter was extraordinary and the people, with a sense of relief, welcomed this really free voice, the only one which had had the courage to voice everybody's feelings out loud. The elections which followed, shortly thereafter, marked the open defeat of the Communists, who obtained only 17% of the votes.

On August 1, 1946, the Government, in the name of the Soviet Military Command, sent the clergy a Proclamation in which it observed that:

In recent times in Hungary, attacks against the soldiers of the Soviet Army had become more frequent, and considering that those organs and those associations, and above all the Catholic clergy, which should have an influence on the people in such matters, do not at all contribute to the promotion of a peaceable co-existence between the Hungarian people and the Red Army, the Hungarian Government turns to the ministers of the various religions, and above all to the Catholic clergy, to request that they assume the task of carrying out a mission of persuasion among those elements who are factiously opposing the results of great transformations and who seek, because of some residual defect which may still exist here and there, to rouse antipathy towards the Red Army and towards democracy.

Democracy is not hostile to the Church, nor will it be in the future. The Democratic Republic and the Church must fight side by side for the healthy development of the Nation and the help which the Church will give to the State in its difficult efforts will be reciprocated by the State itself. We do not call upon the Hungarian clergy to enter the field of political parties; we call upon it to help only in its own sphere to assure the good and desirable, indeed the indispensable relations with the Soviet Union, and to strengthen in our people its faith in democratic institutions.

The Government of the Republic declares itself ready to assure even for the future the rights of the Church, and to aid it in the fulfilment of its religious task.

The Government does not doubt that the Clergy will not only listen to this appeal, but will also be ready to follow it.

This appeal was answered by the Cardinal Primate with the following letter to Mr. Ferenc Nagy, President of the Council:

MR. PRESIDENT OF THE COUNCIL,

In recent days the Hungarian Government addressed itself to the clergy with an appeal broadcast over the radio and published also in the Hungarian press.

The appeal had its origin in certain declarations contained in a letter of the Soviet High Command, addressed to the Government, according to which certain organizations and certain elements, and in the first place the Catholic clergy, have not given the necessary help for the purpose of creating a peaceful collaboration between the army of occupation and the Hungarian people.

We have been surprised, above all, by the manner of the appeal. Up to now Hungarian Governments have always respected the church constitution and they have always sent their requests, regarding the behaviour and the activities of the clergy, through the Bishops. The wretched totalitarian regime of Szalasi, it is true, had made certain attempts to establish direct contacts with the Clergy, but my predecessor of blessed memory not only protested against this fact, but imparted instructions to the Clergy to make no reply whatsoever, so that it could be understood that this was not the legal way. If the Government had observed the legal and usual way, even now, the recognized authority which directs the episcopate would have consented to present a more favorable picture of the postulates of the Appeal to the clergy, providing, of course, that they were found to be well-founded.

Moreover, we are greatly offended and surprised because of the public and generic nature of the accusation which is an attempt to hold us up to public scorn.

We thank you for those reassuring declarations of the appeal, according to which "democracy is not hostile to the Church, and will not be in the future" and that "Church can count upon the support of the State" in the same measure in which it would give its support to the democratic State. The declaration of the appeal that "the democratic republican State and the Church should struggle for the unitarian evolution of the nation" has had a particular echo. This collaboration is a desire existing within the Hungarian Episcopate, with its Primate in the forefront, and in all Magyar society. We shall be happy if this collaboration should be perfectly realized, and we shall be very sad if there should be certain imperfections. We have always been and still are ready to avoid these imperfections, and it has not been, nor will it be our fault certainly, if this collaboration should not eventually realize itself in full measure and with full commitment.

We take note of the democratic form of the government and consequently we continue to be sincerely ready for collaboration, but naturally we maintain our vigilance in order that the validity of the rights of the Church be preserved.

But the appeal of the Government accuses us.

The accusations and the unjustified elaborations are the following: We have not helped in the creation of a peaceful understanding between the occupying army and the Hungarian people, we should have expelled from our ranks those who, because of misdeeds which here and there still take place, wish to rouse antipathy towards the Red Army and democracy. Assuming that there be such persons among us, we would have to propagate the ideological elevation of democracy and stimulate gratitude towards the Red Army which has defeated the enemies and the usurpers of the Country and whose presence has assured the peaceful transformation of our national life. The feeling with which the Episcopate received the occupation troops and the triumphant army, is revealed in the pastoral letter of May 24, 1945, which recognized that the news, according to which the Red Army had the intention of eliminating the Church, was false. In fact—the letter reported—many courtesies were extended by the various commands as regards church life. Our churches have remained open, and Holy Mass is celebrated without any impediments. Here then is the official opinion of Hungarian Catholicism on the occupation and the occupying troops. Permeated with this opinion, Hungarian Catholicism has exercised a great self-control, bearing in mind the inconveniences which took place because of the occupation and which, according to the actual affirmation of the Government, still take place here and there.

I certainly believe that nobody has expected or expects from us the denial or the concealment of defects well known to everybody. We have tolerated these defects and we have done nothing to offend the occupying army and the democratic State, nothing except having asked for remedial action against such inconveniences on several occasions. We have never prepared the people for any offensive demonstration, nor have we influenced its attitude.

The appeal of the Government, however, does not content itself with this deportment but requests and expects us to concern ourselves with disposing the people towards a peaceful co-existence and gratitude, and indicates that we are the best qualified to achieve this result. But can all this be expected of us, precisely when we are the targets of a daily and personal offense?

Our written protests are before you, Mr. President of the Council, that is, before the Government, and therefore the series of these offenses is well known to all.

a) Diplomatic relations with the Holy See, although

there had been prior agreement on the procedure and the person, have not yet been established to date.

b) Attacks against our schools and institutions are every day incidents. Repudiations of these attacks are never published in the press; and our queries regarding them are rejected. We have contented ourselves with the faith shown by parents towards our schools and their respectful deportment has furnished us with a genuine consolation.

c) The attacks also extended to our Associations, regarding the circumstances surrounding an absolutely obscure crime which, without any proof whatsoever, has been attributed to us, and without the procedural records being made available to me. I am continuing my negotiations with the President of the Council regarding this question, but public opinion is restive because the authorities are reticent in stating the truth which I am soliciting.

d) There are furthermore prohibitions against our processions, activities of a purely religious character, arrests of priests and long delays and postponements of trials, the absence of a daily Catholic press and a Catholic party, etc.

e) I have not yet fully examined the repeated attacks of the various newspapers, among which that of the Red Army.

f) When I have solicited a retraction of these offenses from the Government, it transmitted the same reply to me several times: the retraction does not depend on the Government or on its comprehension but on other factors. Nonetheless the question of competency regarding these factors is regulated by different official agreements, since the Red Army itself has declared repeatedly that it does not wish to interfere in the internal affairs of the country.

g) While we continually are the butt of such attacks, conducted without factual proof, we cannot put into execution the request contained in the appeal of the Government. After we have received reparations for the offenses against us, after we shall have been guaranteed the possibility of freely exercising our religious activities, then shall we be ready to collaborate without reservation.

I urge you, Mr. President of the Council, to take note

of all these above-mentioned reasons and to transmit this letter also to interested parties. In view of the fact that the appeal of the Government has made use of the propaganda organs for its diffusion, I urge you to guarantee the same diffusion even to our appeal, in its full text. This also for the reason that we have only two weeklies and pastoral letters at our disposal.

Please accept my sentiments of high esteem.

JOSEPH MINDSZENTY
Cardinal-Primate, Archbishop

Esztergom, August 10, 1946

The declaration of the Government and the reply made to it have been almost fully reproduced here in order to show that by then the relations between Church and State were about to enter a period of dramatic tension, and that the imminence of the conflict was to be considered as fatal, and the final clash as inevitable.

In fact, as of this moment, the possibility of an agreement was definitely closed and the stages of the Communist struggle to bring down the Church developed at an inexorable pace. Here is a list of these stages:

1) Suppression of all Catholic Associations and Organizations (Decree 7330 1946 M.E.)

2) Suppression of all Catholic schools, colleges and institutions (Decree Law XXXIII, 1948) and the abolition of compulsory religious instruction (Decree, Sept. 5, 1949).

3) Suppression of the Catholic press and the requisitioning of Catholic printing plants and publishing houses.

4) Suppression of all Catholic manifestations; processions, feasts, meetings, etc.

5) Suppression of all male and female Religious Orders and Congregations and the internment of more than 10,000 members thereof.

6) Suppression of all the immunities, prerogatives and privileges of the Catholic Church; the jailing of Bishops, the arbitrary appointments of Vicar Generals, Parish priests, etc.

7) Liquidation of the Catholic Church and support of the establishment of a National Church.

B. SUPPRESSION OF ALL RELIGIOUS ASSOCIATIONS AND ALL CULTURAL, SOCIAL AND WELFARE ORGANIZATIONS OF THE CATHOLIC CHURCH (DECREE 7330 1946 M.E.)

In the course of the centuries the Catholic Church in Hungary had given birth to an impressive number of Associations, Pious Unions, Congregations, religious, cultural, social, recreational, aid and charitable organizations which made a notable contribution not only to the religious life of the country, but also to the development of its social, cultural and civil life.

Among these organizations the principal ones were:

a) The Catholic Chorus which existed in every parish with 3,000 sections and about 150,000 enrolled members.

b) "Kaolot" and "Kalasz," the peasant youth movements. They numbered about 700 organizations with about 100,000 members. They maintained about 200 popular schools, attended by about 35,000 young people. They also had 18 higher popular schools, a printing plant, newspapers, etc.

c) "Kioe," the national association of Catholic workers had about 300 sections, 70 homes and about 30,000 members. Its principal interest was to help young workers in the factories.

d) "Kolping," the national association of youth in industry and commerce with 11,000 members, 32 homes and another 6 special institutions for members.

e) "Emericcana," the union of university youth with 47 groups, 13 provincial sections and more than 10,000 members. It was particularly interested in the poorest students for whom it provided meals, lodgings, etc.

f) "Dolgoso Lanyok," the union of young Catholic women workers which aided and protected young Catholic girls engaged in heavy work. It had about 200 sections and 7,000 members.

g) "Popular Catholic Associations." These were social mutual aid associations among Catholics with 1,000 unions and about 300,000 members.

h) "Academy of St. Stephen and the Society of St. Thomas Aquinas." These were the two national organizations of scientists and Catholic writers. They owned a large Catholic printing plant, "Stephaneum," and a large publishing house which each year published numerous valuable theological and scientific works.

In addition to all these associations and Catholic enterprises, there were in Hungary more than 5,000 parochial organizations of "Catholic Action," based on a national center with its headquarters in Bucharest and many other diocesan centers whose headquarters were with the Ordinants of each of the 11 dioceses. Established officially in 1931 they had achieved an impressive organization with 5 main sections, religious, cultural, press, social-welfare, and organizational.

There were in addition an indefinite number of other expressly religious associations: Marian Congregations, Companies of the Holy Rosary, Associations of the Heart of Jesus, Third Orders, etc., organized in almost all the parishes with thousands and thousands of members. The "Guards of the Sacred Heart," for example, were organized in 800 localities and its entire membership included about 170,000 persons.

THE STRUGGLE BEGINS AGAINST ASSOCIATIONS AND ORGANIZATIONS
(MAY 1946)

In May 1946 the Communist Party launched its first open attack against the Catholic Church, taking Catholic Associations and Organizations as its target.

The struggle was prepared and stirred up by an intense press and propaganda campaign in which the headquarters of Catholic Associations were made to appear as "centers of plots and conspiracy."

Every day the left-wing press carried long stories about police discoveries of arms caches in the headquarters of some of the principal Catholic associations. Their members were accused of possessing leaflets and of distributing Fascist newspapers and propaganda, or Fascist emblems and decorations and crossed arrows.

For example, in Gyongyos, a city in northern Hungary, the corpse of a Russian soldier was found and the killer was identified as an eighteen year old youth who had so acted to revenge his mother who had been dishonored and killed in the first days of the occupation by a Russian soldier. In the course of the interrogation it became known that the youth was a member of the local Marian Congregation, presided by Father Salesio Kiss. This particular was enough to bring about the immediate arrest of Father Kiss and of about twenty youths, from fifteen to eighteen years of age. In the streets of Budapest "students" staged a demonstration, demanding death for Father Kiss and other conspirators and the dissolution of the associations of the Catholic Church.

In the summer of 1946 a similar case was repeated in Budapest, a Russian officer was found dead one night in front of a bar on Tereskorut street. The police blocked off the entire neighborhood. Passers-by had witnessed that the officer had been killed by one of his Russian colleagues with whom he had been quarreling over a woman, but overcome by terror they did not speak up. A "conspiracy" charge was fabricated and a youth belonging to the Catholic peasant organization, "Kalot," was charged with the crime. The murdered officer was made into a martyr and immediately after such a staging, demonstrations were organized demanding the dissolution of "Kalot" and all other Catholic associations.

General Sviridov, commander of the Russian occupation forces in Hungary, wrote a letter to the Hungarian Minister of Justice in which, after enumerating all the *attentats* directed against the Russian army of occupation, he affirmed that such attacks clearly revealed the existence of a veritable conspiracy against the Russian army and that from the evidence it could be proved that the guilty and responsible principals were to be found in the Catholic associations and organizations. The Hungarian Government was invited therefore, in the interests of general security and of democratic freedoms, to proceed immediately with the dissolution of all Hungarian Catholic associations.

The press and Communist propaganda seized upon this demand by General Sviridov in order to transform it into an official demand by them to the Government. Public demonstrations were organized, petitions gathered, incidents and acts against democracy were invented and multiplied, so that toward the end of June and the first days of July 1946 naught else was discussed in the Communist press except the misdeeds of Catholic Associations and organizations.

DISSOLUTION OF ASSOCIATIONS AND ORGANIZATIONS DECREED
(DECREE 7330/46 M.E.)

The Government, then presided by Ferenc Nagy of the Small Proprietors Party, did not have the strength to oppose these unjust demands, either of the Russians or the Communists, and instead of proving the absurdity of their accusations with facts, as the Presidents of the various menaced Catholic associations had justly demanded, he submitted to their pressures and hastily caused the promulgation of Decree No. 7330–46, M.E. with which the Communist Minister of the Interior was given full powers over all associations of whatever character.

Any religious or lay association whatsoever could be dissolved without rendering account to anybody.

Within a very short time historic associations of great merit in scientific and social fields were dissolved; Catholic and Protestant church associations, innocuous social movements and unions which had made the sole mistake of receiving even non-communist elements in their memberships.

The storm spared only the pious unions—the majority of which had no property—and some insignificant confraternities and several parish organizations whose purposes were exclusively religious.

More than 4,000 Catholic associations were dissolved and their funds—more than ten million florins—taken over by the

Ministry, or better, by the Communist Party since the money was passed on to Marxist organizations.

Many church buildings and Catholic houses of culture were assigned to Communist organizations, hastily—even before the decree of dissolution appeared—on the basis of a postwar law, according which real properties abandoned by proprietors and not reclaimed by legitimate heirs, could be assigned to third "private" parties who made a reasonable request for them.

VAIN PROTESTS OF THE EPISCOPATE

Primate Cardinal, Joseph Mindszenty, in the name of the entire Hungarian Episcopate strongly protested against the dissolution of Catholic associations with the following letter which he sent to the President of the Council, Nagy Ferenc:

MR. PRESIDENT OF THE COUNCIL:

As a consequence of the new and serious offense against the freedom of religion, guaranteed not only by the internal laws of the nation and by different and recent international conventions, but which is also a presupposition of the actual democratic regime, the Body of Bishops is compelled to raise its voice, particularly against the arbitrary procedure which menaces the associations having a religious base.

The Hungarian Government with its Decree 2333/1946 M.E., has charged the Ministry of the Interior with the strictest surveillance of such associations. With this the Ministry of the Interior has been made the sole executor of the article of law 1938/XVII, the article relative to the repression of abuses committed through the freedom of association. The Ministry has already taken action on that basis and has already begun the dissolution of associations and among these even of Catholic associations.

An act of force conducted on the basis of organized suspicion and without concrete proofs would be disastrous for a totalitarian government.

In this regard the Catholic Church has always let its voice be heard and we now are compelled to protest solemnly against the suppression of the rights of our associations, based on un-proven suspicions made against individuals who are members thereof.

On this point we cannot remain silent even before the public. But before all else we make known our position to the President of the Council, urging him to organize a just and legal procedure on this question.

Please accept, Mr. President, the expression of our esteem.

JOSEPH MINDSZENTY,
Archbishop of Strigonia and Primate
Budapest, *July 21, 1946*

The protest of the Bishops, unfortunately, went unheeded and their letter never received a reply. One by one the various Catholic associations were inexorably affected and those which were allowed to continue had to limit their activity to a purely religious field.

Many of the directors were also arrested, some even tried and sentenced. One of these was Mons. Sigismund Mihalovics, formerly director general of Catholic Action, who managed to escape abroad but who was condemned in contumacy to ten years in jail. Still in jail are the two secretaries of Catholic Action, Mons. Nagy Miklos and Father Leonard Odon, of the Pious Schools, and with them many laymen who worked with them.

SUPPRESSION OF "CARITAS" AND ALL OTHER AID ORGANIZATIONS

In 1948, after two years of un-interrupted struggle against the Catholic associations, still holding out was "Caritas" the great aid organization founded by the Catholic Church in 1944 to come to the aid of thousands of refugees, hungry and needy, which the war had reduced to extreme wretchedness.

"Caritas" had carried out an immense program of welfare activity in the immediate post-war period. Thanks to the help which Cardinal Mindszenty had succeeded in obtaining from British, Belgian, Dutch, Irish, Swedish and Danish Catholics, from the Vatican and above all from the great American organization, "The National Catholic Conference—War Relief Service,"

the Hungarian "Caritas" had been able to open 126 kitchens and
to distribute daily thousands and thousands of bowls of soup.
And it was also able to organize winter and summer camps for
many thousands of needy children, by sending to Belgium, Holland or Switzerland more than 10,000 children.

This entire activity had been followed with a jaundiced eye
by the Communist Party which feared that by such charitable
activity the Catholic Church might acquire "political" influence
on those whom it helped.

In the spring of 1948 there began the first press attacks against
"Caritas," accusing it of not helping the truly "poor"—that is,
those supported by the Communists—but the men of list B, that
is, those who were licensed in their occupations and classified as
"dangerous" for Hungarian democracy.

On May 6, 1947, an authoritative government organ accused
"Caritas" of conducting illegal political activity under the cover
of its welfare activities and demanded its suppression. Immediately thereafter the Government, convinced that to suppress
"Caritas" it would be enough to prevent it from receiving aid
from abroad, imposed as its first provision that 80% of the merchandise which came to "Caritas" from abroad would have to be
passed on to the Government, and the remaining 20% distributed
under the surveillance of local commissions, naturally Communist.

The director of "Caritas," Mons. Mihalovics who went personally to the Minister of Supplies, Karoly Olt, to persuade him
of the absurdity of his conditions, and to make known to him
that under such conditions foreign donors would not be disposed
to send aid to Hungary. He was told drily that it was not a disposition of the Ministry, but of the Government.

In short, "Caritas" deprived of aid from abroad and being no
longer hopeful of making collections inside the country, since
there were already in effect compulsory deliveries of their total
products to Government warehouses by the peasantry, had to
proceed to the liquidation of its welfare institutions.

The same fate befell the sending of sick and weakened children abroad. At the beginning of March 1948, a transport of

children was ready to leave for Holland. The children were already in the train and were waiting for it to leave, but at the last moment the Government prevented its departure because it demanded that the accompanying personnel be composed exclusively of members of the Communist Party.

By now the intention of the Government was clear and, in fact, a few months later the director of "Caritas," Mons. Mihalovics was summoned by the Minister of the Interior, Lazlo Rajk who officially invited "Caritas" to suspend its charitable activity, saying that, "the condition of the people was now so good, that an activity of this kind could be considered superfluous. The State would take care of cases that might eventually arise."

Thus by a mere ministerial invitation there ceased the activity of a most worthy organization which had done so much good in the four years of its existence, saving thousands and thousands of persons from death. And the Catholic Church was deprived of one of the most necessary means for carrying out its social work for the relief of the needy.

C. SUPPRESSION OF EDUCATIONAL AND SECULAR INSTITUTIONS
(Decree Law XXXIII, 1948)
AND ABOLITION OF COMPULSORY RELIGIOUS INSTRUCTION
(Decree, September 5, 1949)

According to the latest statistics the Catholic Church in Hungary, possessed, up to May 1948, a total of about 3,650 Catholic schools, distributed as follows:

a) *Popular Schools:* 1,347 out of a total of 2,650
b) *General Schools:* 2,095 out of a total of 4,847
c) *Civic Schools:* 158 out of a total of 368
d) *Lycée-Gymnasia:* 64 out of a total of 179
e) *Teachers Schools:* 41 out of a total of 67

Hence, out of a total of 8,150 Hungarian schools, 45% of them belonged to the Catholic Church.

In addition, it had the following specialized schools:

a) a social *lycée*
b) a Nurses Training Institute
c) a school of domestic economy
d) three girls' commercial schools
e) 10 Gymnasia for workers
f) 3 schools for industrial training
g) a boys' commercial school
h) a school of typing and stenography

There was a total of 167 Colleges and educational institutions. Among these there were several of national and historic importance such as, for example, the five University Colleges of the Association of St. Emeric, each of which took care of one hundred students.

In the field of higher schools the Church had the following:

a) a Faculty of Theology at the University of Budapest
b) an Academy of Law
c) four Higher Institutions of Theology
d) 20 Popular Higher Schools

Even university teaching was of Catholic origin. The University of Sciences, "Pazmany Peter" of Budapest had been founded by Cardinal Peter Pazmany, the Archbishop of Esztergom.

The total figure of the expenses borne by the Catholic Church for the maintenance of its schools was about 85.3 million florins a year, or approximately $6,000,000.

The Communist Party did not dare demolish this colossal bulwark of the Catholic Church directly, but employed the lowest methods of slander and lies to weaken and discredit it, and then to destroy it.

The struggle of the State against the Catholic schools began in the spring of 1946. It tried to arouse, by means of propaganda, an aversion against ecclesiastical teaching, and to create a pretext for state intervention.

For months and months the investigative authorities continued to uncover "plots" in the various Catholic schools (in Esztergom,

Baja, Pecs, Keszthaly, Nagykanizsa, Budapest, etc.). In the Communist press these "plots" were seen as directed against the liberating Red Army. In one case they dragged an old and rusty drum-barrelled revolver which was said to have been found in one school and which was declared to be "an atomic bomb."

To pour scorn on such accusations, which later even the Government was compelled to recognize as ridiculous and unfounded, Cardinal Primate Mindszenty raised his voice again in a speech which he give in *Csepel* on October 20, 1946. Courageously, he declared:

> . . . We know of a State, we know of a country in which, during a certain time, no matter if it were in ancient or recent times, where a rusty shell was declared to be an atomic bomb, and innocent and smiling children were accused of being anarchist or nihilist *attentatistes*. In that State it was officially said that it was the fault of the Catholic Church, if a soldier had been killed on the street. The first Prelate of the State urged the Government that he be shown the results of the investigation because he was interested in it, and because he wished the results to be studied by experts in penal law. But that Prelate received not even a syllable in reply. Now four months have gone by, and the proofs of the charges have not yet been brought forth; or better still accusations have resounded to the four winds without any proof to this day. If some one had had these proofs, if such proofs existed, if the fantasy had assumed a body and had no substance, you then be the judge, at the distance of four months. . . .

Since this first charge failed another was immediately spread through the press and by Communist propaganda, namely, that the Catholic schools in regards to equipment and training were inferior to the State schools.

But the Catholic News Agency answered that charge immediately:

> . . . To the charge that Catholic schools are inferior to those of the State, sufficient answer is given by the plebiscitary

adhesion of Catholic parents to the Catholic schools, which in these last years have affirmed themselves so vigorously. But still more is this charge refuted by the reports of State school inspectors all of whom, without exception, testify to the high value of Catholic schools.

Of the 71 schools which in the course of years obtained first honors, 37 were Catholic, i.e. 52%. And in 19 years the first three places among the schools which won awards were always occupied by Catholic schools. Of 19 schools which obtained the absolute national first prize, 14 are Catholic, i.e., 73% of the total, and only 5 State schools, i.e. 27%. . . .

Not long ago the very Minister of Public Instruction expressed himself on the good condition and the perfect equipment of Catholic schools, expressing himself in these very words, "I could call myself fortunate, if our State schools were as well-equipped as the majority of Catholic schools."

A third charge was then set in circulation by Communist propaganda, namely, Catholic schools, especially those of the priests, neglect the children of the people and concern themselves primarily with the children of the rich.

Even this charge was answered immediately and personally by Cardinal Mindszenty, in a speech delivered at Kalocsa on May 30, 1946:

. . . There is an accusing voice, according to which the Catholic schools, especially those of the priests, neglect the children of the people and concern themselves primarily with the children of the rich. Having repeatedly heard such accusations in Budapest, as soon as I arrived here I asked for a list of the students of the local Catholic institutions, whereon would be indicated the occupations of their parents, and I came upon the following data:

a) In the Jesuit Gymnasium only 40% of the students belong to the well-to-do classes, including minor employees, while 60% belong to the category of small proprietors and workers.

b) In professional Catholic training, the percentage is respectively 35% and 65%; in the Catholic *lycées* and teacher school, 17.5% and 82.5%; and in the children's nursery the well-to-do are 233, while the others are 366.

c) In the Catholic female teacher's school, the proportion is 104 against 438, hence exactly opposite to that for which we are reproached.

The first propaganda offensive against the schools having to a large measure failed, the struggle, in 1947, was shifted against the compulsory teaching of religion in the schools. But even here the Government found so great an opposition that it thought it more opportune to pause for a moment with just the approval of a legislative proposal. In order to hide its lack of success from public opinion, the government then stated that it would negotiate the question directly with the Vatican.

But in 1948, the power of the Communist Party having increased, the struggle against the Catholic schools, which had been momentarily suspended, grew with it, aiming to obtain their nationalization. Even this struggle was preceded by a well-geared propagandistic campaign; for several weeks, from January on, nothing could be read in the newspapers except articles on the backward and scandalous conditions of the church schools, on the sad situation among the teaching personnel, on the lack of school books, etc. And nationalization was invoked as the only remedy to heal all these evils. In order to demonstrate that such nationalization was desired by the Hungarian people, there began a gathering of signatures, and a circulation of petitions, among teachers, workers, state employees, invoking the nationalization of Catholic schools in a loud voice. State employees and workers who did not wish to sign were fired; students were expelled from the schools, instructors and teachers suspended or transferred.

Once again the voice, loud and explicit, of Cardinal Mindszenty was raised against such constrictions. On May 29, 1948 he wrote to the Minister of Public Instruction, *Ortutay,* as follows:

MR. MINISTER,

Permit me, Mr. Minister, to call to your attention to newly inflicted injustices, violating natural and divine laws.

The State continues, and is ever strengthening, its struggle against our school and our teachers.

To this very day, May 29, it can be observed that the battle of the State against Catholic schools and the teaching body has grown to an extreme degree of violence.

Our professors and teachers are incessantly spurred, with violence or with deceit, to participate in nationalization, against their oath. Almost parallel with his invitation to negotiate, Mr. Minister, with propagandistic phrases of a general nature, accuses the orators of our pulpits and our teachers of religion of preaching political hate rather than evangelical love. (See the newspaper "Kossuth Nepe" of May 19, 1948, p. 5.) I must accept as true the news published in the press in this regard, because it has never been denied, and besides, Mr. Minister has also said similar things on other different occasions.

Pedagogical assemblies are held in series—as is shown by the example of Esztergom—from which all that can registered is that they are enormous moral failures. But is exact public opinion, as it is expressed therein, ever brought to the attention of the authorities?

So-called inspectors of studies go visiting scholastic institutions and with threats, lies and deceits incite and compel our teachers to disobedience in front of their legitimate ecclesiastical authority.

The attorney Dr. Nicholas Toth, member of the administrative commission of the Religious Association of Catholic Parents, was arrested in his dwelling by the political police and interned for having defended our scholastic rights. . . .

In the shops and offices of the Capital agents charged with collecting data want to know what kind of a school is attended by the son of the employee or the worker. They compel teachers to take a position against the circular letters of the Episcopate. . . .

In a city of the Great Lower Plain, the police, to the sound of slaps, compelled nine congregationists of general schools to "confess," and using all means and methods they procured a declaration from priests in favor of the parish priest in Bakonykut and against the Bishop of Szekesfehervar. . . .

Hatred against the Church rises ever higher in the Parliament, on the radio, in the press, in the offices, in economic life. In violation of the treaty of peace, employees are driven from their jobs, students from the popular colleges, only because of their religious devotion. . . .

The voice of the press grows ever more vulgar and gross, and in the face of the campaign of lies and slander, the Church feels itself to be almost outside the law. These are the systems of the historic "Kulturkampf."

All this signifies moral constriction, permanent violation of the freedom of religion, the misery of slave souls. And in the face of all this we are lacking the defense 'ex officio debita' of Mr. Minister and the Government.

I do not know if all this and many more things, which it would be almost impossible to enumerate, can truly give a favorable impulse to serious negotiations for peace.

Accept, Mr. Minister, the expression of my esteem.

JOSEPH MINDSZENTY
Cardinal-Primate and Archbishop
Budapest, May 29, 1948

And together with the letter of protest of the Cardinal Primate, thousands of other letters and telegrams were sent to the Ministry of Public Instruction, in the name of all the 300 parishes in Hungary, in the name of organizations and institutions representing millions of citizens who declared their opposition to the nationalization of schools. ". . . We protest," said one of these, "that without our being questioned about it our Catholic schools are being nationalized, built by our fathers and our sweated labor" (The Commune of Pere). ". . . We defend Catholic schools with all our might" (Felsodabas) . . . "On the

basis of the fundamental law of democracy, we desire the maintenance of confessional schools" (Furged).

In the meantime popular demonstrations were organized
everywhere to protest against the project to nationalize the
schools. The Government and the police intervened to disperse
the demonstrators. At *Sparon* 19 priests, who had expressed their
opposition to nationalization, were immediately arrested. At
Poespetri (county of Szaboles) because of the riot which broke
out at the news that the school had been occupied by the police,
a guard, watching over the requisitioned rooms, reached for his
rifle to free himself from the pressure of the crowd, and while
he tried to shoot, the gun suddenly went off, killing him.

Immediately after the assassination 28 persons were arrested,
and among them the parish priest, Asztalos Janos, who was considered to be the inciter of the crime and as such, during the
trial held immediately after, was condemned to death, a sentence
which was later commuted to life imprisonment.

The killing at *Pocspetri* was presented by the Government
and the press, as a bloody crime of the Church agitation which
was inciting to open revolution:

> . . . the real guilty ones are the instigators [wrote Joszef
> Revai, one of the Communist big bosses], and they are
> guilty whether they live in Esztergom or in Pocspetri! . . .
> It is Mindszenty who makes impossible an approach be-
> tween the Church and State for peaceful negotiations . . .
> Democracy has been most patient in the face of the provoca-
> tive and subversive clergy, but now our patience is over!

The Minister of Public Instruction, Ortutay, wrote a letter
to Cardinal Mindszenty, inviting him to put an end to the agitation in progress against Hungarian democracy:

> . . . All over the country, wrote the Minister, there is
> going on a shameful agitation against the Hungarian re-
> public, even in the pulpits of the churches. The incident at
> Pocspetri gives the first serious warning to the Church: I
> urge Your Excellency to make every kind of provocation

against Hungarian democracy cease immediately. . . . Whosoever continues such agitations will find himself in front of the pitiless force of the democratic laws. . . .

On the same day, the Cardinal Primate answered with a letter published two days later by the "Magyar Kurir." Here is the text:

. . . In his letter of the 4th current, Mr. Minister asks the Church to take steps in regard to the incidents which took place in the commune of Pocspetri.

Only the letter of Mr. Minister has informed me of this case. I am not in possession of any other information. Therefore I can express nothing about it. That which I do know is that the question of the nationalization of the schools has aroused and continues to arouse a deeply-felt excitement in the country. It can be placated only if, as was suggested in the May 29 letter of the Episcopate, the nationalization which is the sole cause of the ferment be removed from the Government's agenda.

The affirmation of the Minister, according to which as a result of central directives agitations are in course against the Hungarian democracy, is entirely gratuitous. In the name, indeed, of the truth I must decisively reject such an affirmation. The responsibility rests solely with those who, seriously jeopardizing the so-greatly desired peace and tranquillity, put so disturbing a question on the table and who by every means keep it on the agenda. . . .

This is all that I am able to bring to the attention of the Minister, with the addition that I shall not fail to communicate the content of your letter to the Episcopate.

On June 14, 1948, the Ministry of Religion wrote the Cardinal a second letter, in which it placed the responsibility for the delay in starting negotiations, and the consequences which might result, squarely on the shoulders of the Episcopate.

But on June 15 the Cardinal hastened to make the following declaration to the Minister in a letter addressed to him:

. . . Before beginning the negotiations, we asked that three preliminary points be resolved as a basis and as a guarantee of the very negotiations. We have not received a concrete answer to our request, even though we have waited until today. We cannot accept, as a sufficient guarantee the declaration contained in your last letter, that the negotiations will offer us ample opportunities to discuss our protest against the confiscation of our schools, and those on other questions and demands formulated by us. . . .

Our schools and their patrimony have been confiscated; our schools are occupied by police organs who treat our professors and teachers as if they were thieves and not the proprietors of a legitimate property. This is a grave insult, a painful humiliation . . . This entire manner of conduct is not in fullfillment of the conditions set by us, but their most absolute and brutal rejection.

The only admissable and just manner of handling the question would be for the parties concerned to order a truce, at least for the duration of the discussions and until their termination.

Instead the Ministry replied by immediately presenting the legislative project for the nationalization of the schools, invoking its immediate discussion with urgent and absolute precedence over every other proposal presented to Parliament.

On June 16 discussion was immediately begun in Parliament on the law for the nationalization of the schools.

The project was reported by M. Bognar who could not avoid observing that news of the law had caused a great excitement in Hungarian public opinion. And he hastened to calm the apprehensions to which it had given rise by assuring that even in the State schools full religious freedom would be possible. A promise which later was not kept!

In the name of the Parliamentary minority, *Istvan Barankovics,* head of the Popular Democratic Party openly declared his opposition to the proposal, affirming that even if the Parliament accepted the proposed legislation, the great majority of the

Hungarian people would not sanction it with its approval.

The speech made by the woman deputy, Sister *Margaret Schlachta,* raised a veritable storm in Parliament. Before anything else, she objected that the proposed bill had been put up for discussion too hastily without giving the deputies time to study and evaluate it. She also objected that deputies of the parties of the opposition had not received entrance permits to enter the Chamber for the session. And amid the pandemonium raised by the Left, she deposited 3000 telegrams protesting the nationalization on the presidential desk, and then proposed a motion asking that a delegate from the U.N. be sent. Hell broke loose at this proposal; the siren shrieked incessantly for four minutes and voices yelled out: Traitor! American Agent! etc. Her expulsion from the Chamber was demanded.

In vain did the opposition seek to postpone the approval to a more opportune moment. In vain did several deputies ask for a roll call. Everything had been decided in advance. After the conclusion of the debate presented by the Minister of Public Instruction, the law on the nationalization of the schools was approved by the Hungarian Parliament with 230 favorable votes and 63 against.

As a consequence of the law which had been decreed, the Minister of Religion and of Public Instruction, on that same day, June 18, 1948, gave notice of the executive order of law XXXIII-1948 which envisaged State possession of all non-State schools, the confiscation of all inherited funds and properties in connection with these, and the absorption of their personnel in the State service.

Every right of disposition, stemming from the old ecclesiastical authorities supporting the schools, ceased forthwith. The Church could exercise its right of control and supervision only over the teaching of religion in the schools.

The State integrated all the teachers from the former non-State schools into its own teacher apparatus, paying them salaries corresponding to the positions which they had held formerly.

If the teacher, subject to nationalization, did not accept his transfer to the State service and did not declare himself in regard to acceptance by July 10, 1948, he would be considered as having resigned his office with no right to legal redress.

Naturally, along with nationalization, all properties passed over to the State, the entire patrimony of the schools: class-rooms, model machine shops, stadia, gardens, teachers' dwellings, as well as the internal furnishings of the schools themselves and the living quarters of the students, etc.

Approved on June 18, 1948, the law was signed on that very night by the President of the Republic and immediately put into effect.

Through it the Catholic Church lost 3,163 schools with their immense patrimony, and a mass of about 600,000 students was put outside the scope of its teaching—a teaching which it had been imparting for centuries.

VAIN PROTESTS OF THE EPISCOPATE

The bells in all the churches in the country tolled in mourning for a quarter of an hour on the day the law went into effect, and the Hungarian Episcopate echoed the sorrow of the faithful in a collective Pastoral letter:

IN CHRIST, BELOVED PRIESTS AND SONS:

That which We, the Body of the Hungarian Episcopate, had feared for our Country already afflicted with many wounds, is now an accomplished fact: they have taken away our Catholic schools and our educational institutions.

We solemnly protest against this provision of the Government, in the name of the natural right of the parents, the right to teach of the Church, of the right to teach which is proper to religion, and in the name of the freedom of teaching. Faithful to our duties as pastors, we can never renounce our rights, our schools and our educational institutions, nor will we ever cease to reclaim them with all the legal means at our disposal.

And so that you, beloved Priests and Faithful, may take note with what tenacity we have defended our Catholic schools, we present you the text of the letter written by us

on the question which was transmitted on June 10 current
to the Ministry of Religions:

> In fullfillment of our duty as Bishops and citizens,
> we solemnly *protest* in front of the entire country and
> in sight of the entire world, against the denial of the
> natural right of the Church to teach, against the mani-
> fested intention of taking away our Catholic schools
> and against all that which, in the realization of such
> intentions, has been done to date. We declare that we
> cannot renounce the natural right which we have to our
> schools and that we know our fundamental duty to be
> that of reclaiming, with all legal means, the recognition
> and respect of our rights in question.
>
> *We protest* against the procedure of the Government
> which, contrary to numerous and unmistakeable prom-
> ises, to resolve the problems relative to relations be-
> tween Church and State with bi-lateral negotiations, in
> the question of the school, before these negotiations
> simply communicated its intention of giving legal valid-
> ity to its unilateral deliberations. In such a wise the
> Government, in the question of the schools, has simply
> deprived the Church of the possibility of presenting its
> arguments for consideration in bi-lateral negotiations
> before decisions could be reached. In fact, the unilateral
> declaration of the Government has all the aspects of an
> "ultimatum," in the face of which there is only one alter-
> native, either to accept or to reject it. This is not an
> agreement born of bi-lateral negotiations.
>
> *We protest* against the nationalization of the schools,
> because this is not only an offense against the freedom
> of study and teaching, but it's almost a rendering of
> the very life of religion impossible. The State having
> taken all the schools unto itself intimately offends the
> fundamental right of parents, based on natural law, to
> choose freely and without any juridical disadvantage, a
> school which corresponds to their religious conviction.

We protest against the nationalization of the schools, because in it there is manifested that tendency which would leave to religion only the fields of liturgy and asceticism, forgetting that the Catholic Church, and likewise other confessions, because of their essence and because of the intimate nature are called upon to carry out a cultural activity which without schools is made impossible. In such a manner, instead, the scholastic monopoly of the State is irreconciliable with the right to parity, recognized even by civil laws, for the religions professed within the State.

We protest against the scholastic monopoly of the State in the name of democratic principles. In fundamental questions such as the right of parents to choose the proper teaching it is necessary to have an immediate and positive manifestation of the popular will. In the past there has been no occasion for this, because no party before had ever expressly proposed a program such as the nationalization of the schools. Instead responsible political figures have declared that there was nothing to fear from ecclesiastical schools. Nor can it even be said that the voters have given their deputies the authority of bringing the nationalization of the schools to a conclusion.

On the other hand we can not recognize as liberal manifestations of the popular will those demands for nationalization obtained by that technique now in vogue of government of the people. It is a matter of public knowledge how signatures and adhesions for such demands are obtained.

After having made known to you how our protest was transmitted to the Ministry of Religions, we pray you dear Priests and Faithful, to ask of the Lord, by persevering prayer, that he gives us the strength to persevere in the good and to bear the ever new crosses of life. . . .

In addition to all its Catholic schools the Church was deprived, by the same law, of all its colleges and educational institutions also, numbering 167 in all with all their belongings and equipment.

They were simply declared to be property of the State. The Church received no indemnity whatsoever, neither for the schools, or its colleges and religious institutions.

It could not even save the preparatory schools of the Seminars. In fact with its provision of July 9, 1951 the State ordered the closing of all these preparatory schools and liquidated the entire institutional framework of the so-called little seminaries.

Even the Faculty of Theology, "Pazmany Peter," annexed to the University of Budapest was ordered closed by the State on October 13, 1951.

D. SUPPRESSION OF THE PRESS

Before 1945 the Catholic Church in Hungary had the following:

a) 2 daily newspapers
b) 18 weeklies
c) 25 monthly periodicals
d) 3 tri-monthly periodicals
e) 20 publications and reviews dealing with current events
f) an unspecified number of parochial bulletins, etc.

In all the Catholic press of Hungary had a regular *monthly* circulation of about *one million and a half copies.*

By 1945 the situation changed completely. The Inter-Allied Control Commission, in April 1945, authorized the publication of a purely religious Catholic weekly "A Sviz" (Sacred Heart); in May another weekly of a political-social character was authorized, "Uj Ember" (New Man), which came out for the first

time in August 15 and which was the weekly organ of Catholic
Action. "Vigilia," a monthly literary review was authorized in
1946.

Not only was the publication of any other newspaper or
review not permitted to Hungarian Catholics, but of the three
periodicals mentioned above one of them, "A Sviz" has disappeared from the scene as early as 1950, the monthly "Vigilia"
comes out in a reduced format and in the smallest of editions;
the only survivor is the "Uj Ember," even though many of its
issues have been confiscated and its publication suspended for
long periods.

In 1947 Hungarian newspapers were regulated by the following directives:

1) Products of the press, including among these books and
   periodic and non-periodic newspapers, can not be published
   without the permission of the Minister of Information.
2) Such permission is necessary even for the further publication
   of newspapers which are already being published.
3) The circulation of all products of the press is dependent on
   the permission of the Minister of the Interior.

In reporting these three decrees the Catholic weekly, "Uj
Ember" could hardly avoid pointing out that these three provisions were in conflict not only with the relevant paragraphs of
the 1947 peace treaty, but also with the law on the freedom of
the press, sanctioned and approved by the new Hungarian Constitution of 1946 which read as follows:

> Every individual can without restriction publish his own
> works, and he can freely present himself in public. All
> printed matter of a political character, publications, mani-
> festos, and leaflets of the parties organized in the Hungarian
> Independence Front, and works treating of religion, are
> exempt from any preventative control on the part of State
> authorities. The Church, as are the Directing committees of
> the parties, are directly responsible to the Press Control
> Commission.

It is superfluous to report that the issue of "Uj Ember" containing this note was confiscated and the publication of the weekly suspended for two weeks. In November 1947, however, the suspension lasted for four weeks because it had published a letter which Cardinal Mindszenty had written to the Prime Minister.

In February 1948, after the celebrated speech pronounced by the Cardinal at a meeting of the Academy of St. Stephen, the head of the Press Control Commission telephoned the editors of "Uj Ember" inviting them to take a position against the Cardinal's speech and to publish only a few extracts therefrom with some official comments. The editors of "Uj Ember" did not accept the invitation, insisting upon its right as a Catholic newspaper to publish the speech in full. The issue carrying the speech went to the printer, but the police prevented its publication, seizing the few copies which were ready.

Regulation of the press became even more severe in 1948, and another decree of the Press Control Commission extended prior censorship not only to printed matter of any kind, but also to any writing reproduced in more than one copy, even if typewritten or multigraphed. If up to now it had been possible to publish books, notebooks of documents, minutes of meetings, *vade me cums* for pious organizations, etc., the new decree put an end to these possibilities. Manuscripts were uselessly presented for prior censorship—for in the majority of cases they were not even returned.

The decree made an exception for pastoral letters and the circulars of Bishops, but it was an exception only at the level of theory, because in practice the communist commissions located in the printing plants were obliged to show proofs of all printed material to the press control office, without any exceptions, so that the authorities could take measures to sabotage publication or prevent distribution. It was for this reason that the Cardinal was compelled to have his first pastoral letters multigraphed by trustworthy persons and circulated privately.

The Bishops of Hungary did not fail to raise their voices

against such a provision with a collective pastoral letter published on November 11, 1948, in which, *inter alia,* they said:

> The Government has issued a decree on the freedom of the Press, according to which no printed matter or lithography can be presented to the public without prior government consent. Such a decree is anti-constitutional . . . We have let competent courts know that we would not submit to such a decree. . . . Rather will we renounce—though our hearts bleed for the faithful—the by now centuries-old possibility, widespread throughout the world, of communicating through the press, and, forced to retire to the catacombs, we shall speak to you with the methods of 450 years ago, but we shall never betray the freedom and the independence of the Church.

In addition to the publication of Catholic newspapers and reviews the above-mentioned decree also affected the publication of Catholic books, studies and monographs.

State authorization for the publication of 33 religious textbooks, required for the study of cathechism in the schools, was delayed for two years. Finally, only 19 of these books could be published, but in insufficient editions, because the authorities had granted only five tons of paper, a quantity which at best was enough for one book only.

On the other hand there was a veritable flood of Marxist periodicals and publications. The Communist printing-plant, "Skizra" boasted of having put on sale 860 publications totalling five million copies, in the space of three years!

Another big blow against the freedom of the Catholic press was the nationalization of all the Catholic printing plants. These totaled about twenty, including the large printing plant of the "Stephaneum," so-called because it had been established about a century ago by the cultural association of the Academy of St. Stephen. Loads of telegrams of protest were sent to the President of the Republic by all the Bishops, by the directors of Catholic Action, by all Hungarian Catholic communities. But appeals, telegrams, attempts to negotiate an exemption from the law for the "Stephaneum" plant, all were in vain. The "Stephaneum" passed over into the hands of the State, a Communist worker became its director, and it ceased to be an organ of Catholic thought and culture.

But the struggle for the suppression of the Catholic press was not to end here. Using as a pretext, the application of a law of the armistice which obliged the Hungarian Government to requisition all "fascist" books, or those which in any way reflected ideologies of the past, an "Index" was compiled of all books to be requisitioned.

This "index" meant not only that such books had to be withdrawn from circulation, but that not even private libraries could keep them. If one were found, its possessor would be sent to a concentration camp. It is needless to say that such lists were in the main filled with Catholic books which in one way or another were opposed to Marxist ideology. Voluminous scientific works were banned, even if no more than a single chapter, or a single paragraph, or even a single phrase were anti-marxist.

Thus were proscribed and removed from circulation, and destroyed, all the works of Bishop Ottokar Prohaszka, a great sociologist of the past century; the works of Bishop Toth Tihamer, a preacher of world fame whose books have been translated in seventeen languages; the works of Father Bangha Bela, of the Society of Jesus, a great defender of the Faith; the texts on dogmatics by the theologian, Antal Schutz; the works of Mons. Laszlo Mecs, the most popular writer and poet of recent times, some of whose poems had also offended Hitler, and who had barely escaped the prison sentence handed down by a Nazi court by remaining in hiding until the end of the war.

A Communist purge commission inspected all the libraries of the Capital and those of other cities. It entered seminaries, religious convents, and searched everywhere for prohibited books to be removed from circulation.

Not even the celebrated library of the Hungarian Academy of Sciences was spared, nor that of the thousand-year old Benedictine monastery of Pannonhalma, nor those of the Cistercian monastery of Zirc, and the Jesuit monastery of Szeged. Not even the famous and valuable library of the Primate in Esztergon. The warehouse of the Catholic publishing firm of Saint Stephen was almost entirely destroyed.

Thus tens of thousands of the best literary and scientific collections were sacrificed, even those containing no books which had fallen in disgrace, but only suspected of a "reactionary spirit" because they were works of authors who were famous Catholics or Westernizers.

The "Villagossag," a Marxist daily, in large type and on its first page carried news stories such as this: "In the library of the Benedictine Abbacy of Panonhalma, two freight cars of anti-democratic books were collected." In reality they had filled only two trucks, and they had carried away not only books prohibited by the political lists, but many others also. For example, all publications which had appeared between the years 1919 and 1944. And along with the books were confiscated all the Catholic reviews published between these dates, "Katolikus," "Szemle," "Elet" and various others.

Sometimes, according to Nicholas Boer who, because of his position as a functionary of the Ministry of Public Instruction (now in exile) had to witness these "purges," there were almost comic incidents of mental blindness. A Soviet Colonel who boasted of having "extirpated" a million books had the Baedeker guide books carted away because they carried the titles, "Fuehrer durch die Schweize," i.e. Guide through Switzerland, The Colonel thought they were books dedicated to Hitler, the German "Fuehrer." Another ponderous volume entitled, "Index horti botanici" was condemned because, according to this same Colonel, it referred to the Admiral Horthy, the Fascist "regent" of Hungary: A French edition of Boccacio was proscribed because it had been published in Paris in 1942 when the government of the collaborationist Petain was in power . . . I tried to convince the Soviet Colonel that he was wrong, but I did not succeed."

E. SUPPRESSION OF ALL OUTER MANIFESTATIONS OF THE FAITH, INCLUDING RELIGIOUS FEASTS

SUPPRESSION OF RELIGIOUS BROADCASTS

Up to 1945, in accordance with a well-established tradition, the State-operated radio stations had always included the broadcasts of religious services and sermons in their Sunday programs because of the importance of the various Churches.

Even after the "liberation" the Government did not break this custom. On the contrary religious radio broadcasts were extended even to holidays, and possibilities were offered to Catholics as well as Protestants to use the radio daily in order to broadcast important religious services.

It was during the first months of 1948 that the State radio began to boycott religious broadcasts more and more, returning sermons that had already been presented to the government censorship as "unadaptable" for radio transmission because of their "content," without giving specific explanations.

The reason lay in the fact that the Hungarian radio, by exercising its own censorship, not only desired to exclude from the sermons all that which could be even remotely in conflict with the ideologies professed by the Communist government, but, on the contrary, it had also wished that the Church would contribute in a positive manner to support the new regime, spiritually and ideologically.

In such circumstances it was evident that it was becoming more and more impossible for the Church to broadcast its sermons, and in fact the Cardinal Primate, following the announcement of new restrictions in the field of religious broadcasts, had the "Magyar Kurir" publish the following communication on July 10, 1948.

. . . In the scheduling of programs on the Hungarian Radio recently there is above all manifest an ever increasing tendency to limit the freedom of the Church in the promulgation of the word of God. In this regard already, and on many occasions, broadcasts of sermons, sacred music, and the half-hours dedicated to religious subjects have been omitted.

It is deplorable that the Hungarian Catholic society is compelled to give up these broadcasts.

Furthermore we must at the same time take note that these broadcasts of a religious character very often appeared in a program which did not absolutely correspond with the dignity of the numbers of the repertory of a religious character, nor to the truths enunciated in this.

From that day on, July 10, 1948, every broadcast of a religious character of the Catholic Church was completely suppressed in Hungary. The few radio broadcasts of a more or less religious character which were later transmitted were never approved by the official Catholic Church. They were, in fact, broadcast for and by exponents of the "Movement of Priests for Peace" under the direct inspiration of the Communist regime and only for the purpose of "faking" the existence of religious freedom in Hungary.

SUPPRESSION OF EVERY INDIVIDUAL AND COLLECTIVE RIGHT

But the suppression of religious broadcasts over the radio was only one of the many attacks on the religious liberties, individual and collective, of the Hungarian Catholic population.

A protest letter sent to the President of the Council of Ministers, Lajos Dinnyes, on October 24, 1947, by Cardinal Mindszenty, in the name of the entire Hungarian episcopate, was an exceptionally valuable document which courageously denounced the regime of spying and terror which the Communist Party was trying to install in Hungary.

Here is its text in full:

MR. PRESIDENT OF THE COUNCIL:

In the conference held on the 8th current in *Vac*, the Hungarian Episcopate concerned itself with complaints which several of its members have received from the faithful.

a) Persons who are not in agreement with the program of the Communist Party are compelled to join this party, persons, indeed, whose religious conviction is in incompatible conflict with the program of such a party. Citizens can obtain or hold jobs, or accept jobs, only if they join the party. Membership in the Communist Party has exonerated and exonerates such members from penalties and from the purge list B. These are facts, which have been openly acknowledged even by other parties and to which, in the Parliamentary session of October 9, a speaker of a party of the coalition made allusion.

Mr. President of the Council! We trust that this state of affairs which offends the rights of democratic freedom will cease with the constitutional order which we hope will consolidate itself after the elections which have recently been held. It is inadmissable that for the centenary of 1848, when among other things there is also celebrated the abolition of aristocratic privileges, there prevail and are imposed party privileges which mock every equality.

b) The other complaint is caused by the spying system which is to be observed in the defense section of the State police. In fact, individual agents of the above-mentioned section cite, on the basis of fabricated and frivolous charges, against persons and even priests, and with threats try to induce them to become spies in Catholic pious organizations, in Bishopric houses, and to make reports from time to time on what they have seen and heard. There have been cases in which the reports not being satisfactory, the "spies," already morally tortured, were also materially mistreated.

Such procedures can in no wise accord with the Hungarian character, they remind us of the darkest epochs of our history, that of Bach, following the war of Independence. In the face, furthermore, of church circulars such procedures are absolutely superfluous because among us conspiracies are useless things for which we have no disposition because we are used to expressing our opinion openly, as our congress has demonstrated and as shown by our newspapers which, unfortunately, so rarely see the light.

Mr. President of the Council! In the hope that in this matter it has been only a case of an excess zeal by subordinate organs, we urge you to use your influence to the end that the deplored abuses cease and all Hungarians may enjoy the benefits of peace without fear and vexations.

Accept, Mr. President of the Council, the expression of my sincere esteem.

JOSEPH MINDSZENTY
Cardinal—Primate and Archbishop
Esztergom, October 24, 1947

F. DISSOLUTION OF ALL RELIGIOUS ORDERS (DECREE, JUNE 7 AND SEPTEMBER 7, 1950)

THE FIRST SKIRMISHES

Up to 1948 there existed the following in Hungary:

a) 18 male Religious Orders and Congregations, with a total of 187 houses and monasteries and 2,459 members of whom 1,422 were priests.

b) 39 female Religious Orders and Congregations, with 456 houses and monasteries and a total of 7,525 Sisters.

Of all these Religious Orders, only some, such as the Cistercian and the Trappists led a purely contemplative life, but the others were dedicated to an intensely active life.

In fact they maintained 9 hospitals, directed 293 Catholic schools, and served as nurses in 90 state and provincial hospitals, and supervised 120 institutions of a social-welfare character such as orphanages, aid centers for the poor, etc. Moreover, they occupied important posts in the moral and spiritual life of the nation, in the field of letters, the press, and the sciences.

Immediately after the promulgation of the law on the nationalization of the Catholic schools, the Hungarian Communist

Party began its struggle against the members of the religious orders and their works.

Already, on May 1, 1948, the first skirmishes of the coming struggle took the form of an article published in "Nepszava." In this article whose heading read "Do you believe . . ." followed by a minute analysis of the Catholic schools and activities conducted by members of religious orders, the writer concluded with this question, "Do you believe that this can remain this way?" And the answer of the writer was, "No, this I cannot believe."

And, in fact, shortly thereafter, the Communist police began to arrest several members of religious orders under the charge of "crimes against the democratic regime of the State" for having distributed, as they alleged, publications and circulars inciting to revolt.

The first to be arrested was the 37-year old Professor of the Pious Schools, *Edmund Lenard,* who on June 30, 1948, was denounced under these charges. Shortly after there followed the arrests of Father *Kis Salesio* of the Franciscans, and Father *Olofson Placidio* of the Benedictines. Both were deported to localities unknown.

The persecution grew ever more intense and expressed itself in an especially brutal manner against the Sisters. Even though they had been compelled to concentrate themselves in specially reserved areas of the convents, on account of the nationalization of the schools, even there they were not left in peace. In the bitter cold of night, on December 20, 1949, police broke into the convent of *Lovasbereny,* by forcing the doors and windows. They loaded the Sisters on a truck and at three-thirty in the morning deposited them on the public square of a near-by city. This was not just an episode, but it became a system. Convents were evacuated with only 24 or 48 hours warning, often to give the Party buildings which it required for its organizations. Chapels in the hospitals were kept closed sometimes so that the nuns could not hear Mass. Many nuns were forbidden to aid the sick as early as 1949.

Insofar as regards monks, their fate was not less ugly, and

things became so intolerable that on April 15, 1950, the Superiors
of all the religious orders sent a protest to the Government,
quoted here in part:

> . . . We are often reduced to living as if in a ghetto in our
> own houses, built with such sacrifice and self-denial, or we
> are forced to abandon them. Basing itself on the law nation-
> alizing the schools, but going quite beyond its limits, the
> government has taken away monastic buildings which never
> belonged to the schools or colleges, our courtyards, gardens,
> small fruit orchards, furniture, moveable properties and
> objects of domestic use. They strip us in many localities of
> our chapels, of our houses for spiritual exercises, of our
> cultural institutions and of our printing plants.
>
> They impede us in our missions, in our sermons, in our
> pilgrimages. At every step we are impeded from turning to
> our faithful for exclusively pastoral purposes, or from visiting
> the sick. They confiscate our theological schools and our
> novitiates for the training of our novices; the free movement
> of members of religious orders is limited by unfounded sus-
> picions; and we are forbidden activities which are nontheless
> permitted to other civil persons. They dismiss nuns em-
> ployed as nurses from the hospitals *en masse,* against the
> wishes of doctors and patients. And the offer of a post or
> some special privilege is offered those who abandon their
> Orders. . . .

In its turn the Episcopal body was compelled to take a position against this sad situation. Among other things its circular
letter of May 31, 1950 denounced the fact that ". . . Members of
religious orders are without defense and often find themselves
without possibilities of help, completely at the mercy of their
very enemies. The disquieting procedures not only do not cease.
but instead become ever thicker and disconcerting."

The specific reply to such charges was made by Joseph
Revai, the Minister of Popular Culture, at a general meeting of
the leaders of the Hungarian Workers Party, in a speech which
was reported in full in the June 6, 1950 issue of "Szabad Nep."

It textually declared that ". . . In the People's Democracy there is no need for members of Religious Orders, because they do not correspond to their vocation, and in fact they sabotage the aims of democracy. It is necessary, therefore, that they immediately be put in conditions wherein it will be impossible for them to injure further the interests of the popular democracy."

RELIGIOUS ORDERS DISSOLVED BY DECREE

On the following day, June 7, Josef Veres, Director of the IV section of the Ministry of Internal Affairs, currently Secretary of State, signed the following disposition:

MINISTRY OF THE INTERIOR
General Direction IV
Secret Ordinance

TO N.N. _____ RESIDING AT _____

By virtue of Decree 8130/1948, IV 6 B.M., par. 2, I order your expulsion, with the obligation to leave immediately the place of your present residence and to proceed to the place of forced residence.

Reason: Your permanence in the place of your present domicile is dangerous to public order and security.

The present disposition is without appeal. It must be carried out at once by virtue of law 1929, par. 56.

(*signed*) VERES JOSEF
Director General of the Session

Budapest, June 7, 1950

P.S. The place of forced residence can not be left without special permission. In case of violation, administrative procedures will be initiated.

During the night between the 9th and 10th of June such a ministerial decree was delivered by hand to about 320 members of religious orders and to about 600 to 700 nuns in the southern part of Hungary.

Many policemen of the A.V.O. scaled the walls around the

monasteries in order to enter the nuns' quarters; others broke
windows, and in other places they literally smashed doors and
windows to gain entrance.

In general they allowed only one hour for dressing and
packing, but in many localities even this time was curtailed with
various harassments. Only in two or three places was there a
more human and courteous treatment but in general, unfortunately, the police employed a brutal treatment with indes-
cribable expressions, a veritable vocabulary of miscreants. They
did not permit members of religious orders to bring bed linen
with them, stating that in the new forced residences they would
find completely furnished rooms. The aged and the ill were
ridiculed. They could bring only very little of their personal
belongings and only if the bundle did not weigh more than 10
pounds. But even such bundles were confiscated and in accordance with the personal caprice of the A.V.O. police the bundles
were pilfered of their contents. In the majority of cases the
deportees could not even change their shoes or clothing. Many
had to undergo a personal search. All the writings, and even the
personal letters, of the brothers and monks were taken away
from the religious houses, as well as identification cards and
personal notes of all kinds, including prayer books and sacred
images.

Then they were loaded on and crammed into trucks in which
there was little air and even less free movement because of the
number of bundles and sundry objects. During the very long
deportation trip the unhappy travelers, only now and then, were
permitted to sit on the floor. It was absolutely forbidden to
speak during the trip and violators were threatened with the
most severe punishments. There was a halt for personal needs
only every 6 or 8 hours. The deportees had been forbidden to
take food along and during the trip the authorities made no
provisions whatsoever for feeding them. Here and there the
population provided gifts of food and other necessary items but
in general it must be said that the transfer was truly savage and
inhuman.

On the day after the deportation the police summoned

people and workers of the locality and told them that two short wave transmitters had been located in the monastery, and that women's under-garments had been found in the rooms of monks and brothers. Moreover, they claimed that there had been many photographs of women on the walls and that a huge sum of money had been found. In other localities it was announced that large amounts of propaganda literature had been found, inciting to revolution, sabotage, as well as espionage material and immoral books.

After the first wave of deportations of monks and nuns, the heads of the Religious Orders and Congregations held a joint meeting on June 17, 1950. On behalf of their deported colleagues, and in order to halt further persecution, they asked for a firmer and more determined attitude on the part of the Episcopal body.

As a result, Mons. Grosz, the Archbishop of Kalocsa, announced a conference of Bishops to be held on June 20.

When this became known, a second wave of deportation followed on the night between the 18th and the 19th of June. This time about 1,500–2,000 members of Religious Orders, men and women, were taken away from central and western Hungary.

Even then each one received a personal expulsion order, like the one which has been reproduced here, but the reason therefore was changed. The presence of members of Religious Orders in a given place was no longer "dangerous to public order and security," but simply "the transfer from the localities in question and the occupation of new places of residence in the general interest." As can be seen it must have been quite clear even to the authorities just how "dangerous to public order and security" an aged and helpless monk, or a contemplative nun could be, so the people's democracy substituted the ridiculous reason of public danger to that of "general interest!"

Under the pressure of events the Bishops, at their June 20 meeting in which they tried to find a solution for the very serious situation in which thousands of monks and nuns found them-

selves, requested a face to face meeting with the Government
which did take place on June 28, 1950.

Even though talks were in progress between the Government
and the Episcopate, the persecution of the Orders did not stop,
nor did it give signs of diminishing. By now their intention was
quite clear. This was not only to exercise an ever increasing and
continuous pressure on the negotiating ecclesiastical body, but
also to create an opportune situation to obtain the drawing up
of a mutual agreement. *The third wave of deportations took place
between July 10 and 12.*

The deportations always took place at night with different
methods and procedures. But all of them were commonly characterized by a crude violence and a savage terror. After the
deportations meetings of the people were again called, harangued
by Communist activists and tribunes who tried to justify the
necessity and the urgency of the persecution and the deportation
of the monks and nuns labelled as "traitors to the fatherland in
connivance with the imperialists."

These inhuman methods against the members of Religious
Orders gave rise to a unanimous wave of resentment among the
people, and because of this, new techniques were employed later.
The authorities and the Bishops came to an agreement on the
houses which had to be evacuated and the Bishops themselves
were made responsible for the orderly carrying-out of the deportations. The Bishops, alas, were forced to notify officially the
members of the various orders whose houses had been designated for "transfer." Even in such cases the members were taken
away on trucks but without violence and inhuman acts, and they
were permitted to bring elementary items of clothing with them.

This *third deportation* struck principally against the monks
and nuns who had not yet been deported from western and
south-western Hungary.

The agreement between the Government commissions and the
Church was signed on August 30, 1950 after a series of inter-
minable meetings.

The agreement re-established eight religious schools: that of
the *Benedictines* in Pannonhalma and Gyor, the *Piarists* in Buda-

pest and Kecskemet, the *Franciscans* in Esztergom and Szenten-
dre, and the *Sisters of Szeged* in Budapest and Szeged.

It was clear that the intention of the Government was to
re-establish these eight religious schools (six male and two
female) with an "adequate number of men and women teachers,"
so that it could declare all other members of Religious Orders as
superfluous and thus proceed, as quickly as possible, to their
total liquidation.

On September 7, 1950, a few days after the above-mentioned
Agreement, the Presidential Council issued Decree No. 34/1950.
In accordance with it about 57 male and female Religious Orders
and Congregations were declared dissolved and warned to cease
all activity in Hungary. Members thereof were ordered to quit
their monasteries within three months. All were forbidden to
engage in any pastoral activity, excepting for about 400 priests
who were permitted to carry out ecclesiastical tasks in the various
dioceses, but without their religious vestments. All were compelled to remove their clerical garb, nor could they reside where
they had formerly lived as members of Religious Orders, and
not even in their very birth-places, if these happened to be in
the frontier zones bordering on Jugoslavia.

G. THE OPEN STRUGGLE AGAINST THE EPISCOPATE

Already in the spring of 1947 it had been noticed with what
frequency the Communists were attempting to undermine the
unity and the agreement existing in the body of the Catholic
Hungarian Episcopate, by trying to show that there were strong
differences of opinion in their attitude towards communism.

On April 27, 1947, the Budapest daily newspaper, "Friss
Ujsag," for example, carried a story that the Bishop of *Pecs* had
ordered that Church bells be rung on May 1st, in opposition to
the position taken by the Episcopal body. The Bishop of *Pecs*,
however, denied this story, declaring it to be an absolute lie.

Another newspaper, the "Magyar Nap," in its issue of January
22, 1947, had written an article on the very subject of existing

differences in the episcopal body. The statements contained in this article were denied in full by an official communication issued by Mons. Czapik, the Archbishop.

The newspaper campaign trying to prove discord among the Bishops had reached such a point by the autumn of the same year that the Bishops were compelled to interfere officially, by publishing the following joint letter:

. . . The Hungarian Episcopal body in a plenary held September 6, angrily rejects the malicious articles which continually appear in the press, by which it is wished to put the activity of the Cardinal Prince Primate in a bad light before the faithful, and which would have it believed that the Episcopal Body, or a part thereof, or some of its individual members, do not share the Primate's position and that they even oppose it. In order to calm and to inform our faithful we declare that each member of the Episcopal Body not only does not disapprove the manly and courageous comportment of the Cardinal Prince Primate in defense of the Church, the freedom of conscience and of the real interests of the Fatherland, but, instead, adheres to it unconditionally and approves, supports and serves it with all its might. . . . (Circular Letter 6-9, 1947.)

This struggle to break the unity of the Hungarian Episcopate reached its climax in August 1948 when the Government thought it had completely isolated Cardinal Mindszenty. Day in and day out, the Government had been sending delegations to different Bishops, partly to protest against the "warlike policy of Mindszenty," and partly to convince them to detach themselves from the Cardinal.

Public opinion in this period was assailed by statements attributed to the Bishops which they had never made, or which at best had been greatly distorted. The Bishops had no opportunity to make corrections, nor did the newspapers report their denials.

Cardinal Minszenty himself had to intervene against this

state of affairs. And in a letter to the people, dated November 18, 1948, he denounced the open struggle which the regime had unleashed against him. Here is the full text of the letter:

. . . For weeks now, in various localities of mutilated Hungary, "motions," ever the same, are being approved against me. They condemn the *"counter-revolution and anti-democratism promoted and re-kindled by me"* on the occasion of the Marian days organized in the various centers of the country in 1947–48. They deplore the failure to achieve an agreement between Church and State, claiming the *"impediment of my harmful activities."*

The Marian days had the single purpose of deepening the traditional Marian cult and strengthening religious conscience. Insofar as regards the attacks made upon me during these celebrations, the Episcopate has identified itself with me. This solidarity demonstrates to those millions of citizens who constitute public opinion—in the face of whose heroic perseverance the persecutors must employ so many methods humiliating to them, and irreconcilable with the freedom of religion guaranteed by law—the failure of the Government propaganda to divide us.

As regards the legal value of the "motions" it must be declared, that notwithstanding the many official promises formulated since the end of the second world war and later, there have not been any local elections held except in the capital. Therefore the "motions" adopted in the counties, in the cities and in the communes, substantially do not have any juridical base. The approval of such "motions," forcibly obtained from individuals by the threat of the loss of their means of existence and their personal freedom, *while the entire public opinion of the country is condemned to silence,* and it is denied that local autonomy, guaranteed by the Constitution, constitutes a frivolous mockery of public life. The freedom of speech of democracy expresses itself in these motions by the absolute exclusion of any debate, and if, as some significant examples show, there be some one who dare protest, the consequence is the loss of his job or some similar hardship. The suffering of these courageous persons causes me deep sorrow. *All those who have fought against force, have all my compassion.* These noble examples of strength of soul and faithfulness have greatly moved me.

As regards the alleged "offenses" attributed to us, our attackers have once more, as has been the case from the beginning, failed to confute any of our statements. We have repeatedly urged the Government to publish those letters of mine to which it objects and to submit them to the judgment of the country and the world. This has not happened. The Government contents itself with vague and generic accusations.

As regards the lack of an agreement between the Church and the State or better between the Church and the political parties, it is commonly known that the invitation to negotiate and to participate in the conference called for that purpose arrived *after a delay of three months!* Naturally the Church is saddled with the responsibility for the absence of conciliation.

There is something deeply disconcerting in the fact that insofar as regards the Marian days organized in Pelfoldeszentke Rest, Mariaguad, Baja and Celldomolk, complaints were formulated not by the Church, but by those who carried out arbitrary and coercive acts.

Even the inmates of Kohida were forced to sign a declaration of protest against me. I was once held in that very prison by Hungarian Nazis, together with Ende Bajcsy-Szilinsky and twenty-six of my priests. Even those who were arrested by the Nazis would remember all this. But I view with calm this artificially roused tempest. At the post where I stand guard, not on the authority of parties, but by the grace and trust of the Apostolic Holy See, such tempests are not rare in annals and battles of history. Two before me had all their properties confiscated; Johannes

Vitez was imprisoned, Martinuzzi was killed by the hired assassins of those in power, Pazmany, the greatest of all, was exiled . . . But none of my 78 predecessors was attacked as I am, by such a flood of strident lies, deliberately fabricated, a hundred times denied, but stubbornly repeated.

I rest solidly on my positions for God, for the Church and for the Fatherland, because this is the duty which history imposes on me in the service of my people, the most derelict of all peoples in this world. In the face of the sufferings of my nation, my fate is of no importance.

I do not accuse my accusers. If from time to time I am compelled to clarify the situation, this serves only as an act of justice toward my country because of its lacerating sufferings, its flowing tears, and for its invocations of justice. . . .

JOSEPH MINDSZENTY
Cardinal-Primate and Archbishop
Esztergom, November 18, 1948

All these attempts had no other aim except that of preparing the final attack against the hierarchy and the clergy.

And in fact the arrest of one priest after the other began around September 1. The arrests were made for the most different reasons and, without trial, they were sent to concentration camps.

The parish priest of the Cathedral of Gyor, Jankovics Joszef, was arrested and sent to a concentration camp because he had refused a church burial to a Communist who had died suddenly with no signs of repentence, and who had lived in an ambiguous wedded state. He was promised immediate release from jail if he would sign a statement declaring that he had acted in this wise on specific orders of his Bishop. But the parish priest chose to remain in jail. The Ministry of Religions sought an explanation of this incident from the Bishop with the pretext that since the State supported the Church it, therefore, could demand that citizens receive Church burials. The Bishop rejected the demands of the Ministry and in reply the Council of Ministers deprived the Bishop, the Chancellery and the cathedral chapters of Gyor and Sopron, of state support. A similar provision was taken against the cathedral chapters of Kalocsa and Esztergom.

On November 19 the secretary of the Primate, Zakar Andras, was seized on the street by the police. And on the same day the dwelling of the Primate was surrounded by a police cordon.

On November 23 the police prohibited the transfer of the remains of Bishop Apor Vilmos, killed by Russian soldiers in his residence in Gyor, from the crypt of the Church of the Carmelites to a tomb erected in the Cathedral. Fearing a popular demonstration, the Government flooded the city with 200 police agents and called out the fire department so as to block the main thoroughfares of the city. And on December 23 two priests of the Curia of Esztergom were taken into custody, Rev. Boka Imre, an economist, and the Rev. Fabian Janos, an archivist.

ARREST AND TRIAL OF CARDINAL MINDSZENTY

On the evening of December 26, 1948, the second feast day of Christmas, Cardinal Minszenty himself was arrested.

Locked up in the main prisons at number 60 Via Andrassy, after almost 40 days of submission to a combined drug and psychic "treatment," this man of steel was transformed into a "wax puppet" as if he had been in the laboratory of some evil sorcerer.

No one has ever known with certainty just what drugs, tortures and abominations were employed to reduce Cardinal Mindszenty to such a condition, but there are ample documented proofs that "something" of a terrible, inhuman and shameful nature happened to Cardinal Mindszenty.

The Hungarian Government published a notorious "Yellow Book" in which it sought to confirm its own accusations with "confessions" written by the Cardinal himself in his own hand. But it is precisely these "confessions" which constitute the most tremendous act of accusation against the accusers themselves. The shaky handwriting, the errors in spelling (64 were counted in those pages), inconceivable in a man known and almost feared by his closest collaborators as a man of extreme precision and unequalled accuracy, reveal the induced nightmare of a man tortured and broken-down, and robbed of his basic self-hood.

The Government had no witnesses, and precisely because it had no proofs, it had to have recourse to the trick of causing an iron tube containing incriminating documents to be hidden in the cellars of the archbishopric residence at Esztergom, or to compelling the Cardinal to become the *accuser of himself* by sinister and unimaginable means.

But against these underhand tricks of the Government there are the clearly written words which the Cardinal, about one hour before his arrest, had sent to the Archbishops and Bishops of Hungary:

> . . . Since I have not taken part in any plot whatsoever, I will never resign, I will not talk. If, after this, you should learn that I have admitted this or that, that I have resigned my office (even if this be authenticated with my signature) you must know that such a declaration can only be the consequence of human frailty . . . In the same manner do I declare null and void any confession which may be attributed to me as of today and thereafter. . . .

The trial began on the morning of February 3, 1949. And it was to end with the sentencing to prison of the illustrious Cardinal, on charges of treason, espionage, attempt against the security of the State, and illegal currency dealings.

The particulars of the trial, the baselessness of the charges made and the extraordinary echo which the trial produced throughout the world, make it unnecessary to narrate the events anew. By now there exists an entire series of publications, memorials, reports and testimonies on the subject in the public domain that a veritable literature on the case can be said to exist.

We shall report only that his sentencing aroused a vast wave of protest and denunciation on the part of world public opinion, a protest which was directed against that which in the Mindszenty trial had shocked human conscience.

In Rome on February 20, 1949, a crowd of more than 300,000 persons assembled in the Square of St. Peter to hear the Pope, who on February 3 had already protested the arrest of Cardinal Mindszenty in a letter of great nobility addressed to the Catholic Hungarian Episcopate, pronounce the following memorable speech:

ROMANS! BELOVED SONS AND DAUGHTERS!

Once again, in a grave and sorrowful hour, the faithful people of the Eternal City have come running to its Bishop and Father.

Once again, this superb colonnade seems barely able to embrace with its gigantic arms the crowds which, like waves moved by an irresistable force, have poured up to the very threshold of the Vatican basilica, in order to attend the Mass of atonement at the central point of the entire Catholic world and to express the feelings which well up in their souls.

The sentence inflicted, amid the unanimous reprobation of the civilized world, on the banks of the Danube against an eminent Cardinal of the Holy Roman Church, has on the banks of the Tiber aroused a cry of indignation worthy of the *Urbs*.

But the fact that a regime hostile to religion has this time struck at a prince of the Church, venerated by the overwhelming majority of his people, is not an isolated case. It is one of the links in the long chain of persecution which some dictatorial States conduct against Christian life and doctrine.

A notable characteristic common to all persecutors of all times is that, not content to destroy their victims physically, they wish also to render them contemptible and odious to their country and to society.

Who does not remember the Roman protomartyrs about whom Tacitus writes (Annales 15, 44) immolated under Nero and represented as incendiaries, abominable evil-doers, enemies of the human race?

Modern persecutors show themselves to be docile disciples of that inglorious school.

They copy, so to speak, their teachers and models, even if indeed they surpass them in crudeness, able as they are in adapting the most recent advances of science and technique for the purpose of domination and enslavement of the people, as would hardly be conceivable in times past.

Romans! The Church of Christ follows the path marked out for it by the divine Redeemer. She feels herself to be eternal, she knows that she cannot perish, that the most violent storms will not succeed in submerging her. She does not beg for favors; the threats and the disgrace of earthly powers do not frighten her. She does not interfere in merely political or economic questions, nor does she care to argue on the usefulness or the harmfulness of one or another form of government. Ever eager, insofar as it depends on her, to live in peace with all (Romans 12, 18), she gives to Caesar that which is his according to law, but she cannot betray nor abandon that which is of God.

Now it is well-known what the totalitarian and anti-religious State demands and expects from her as a price for its tolerance or for its problematical recognition. It would want, that is:

A Church which is silent, when she should speak;

A Church which weakens the law of God, adapting it to the tastes of human wills, when she should loudly proclaim and defend it;

A Church which detaches herself from the unbroken foundation on which Christ has built her, to adapt herself on the moving sand of the opinions of the day or to abandon herself to the passing current;

A Church which does not resist the oppression of consciences and which does not watch over the legitimate rights and the just liberties of the people;

A Church which with indecorous servility remains amid the four walls of the temple, forgetful of the divine

mandate received from Christ: "Go ye therefore into the
highways" (Matthew 22, 9) and "instruct all nations"
(Matthew 28, 19).

Beloved sons and daughters! Spiritual heirs of an innumerable legion of confessors and martyrs!

Is this the Church that you venerate and love? Do you
in such a Church recognize the lineaments of the coun-
tenance of your Mother? Can you imagine a successor of
the first Peter who should succumb to such demands?

The Pope has divine promises; even in his human weak-
ness he is invincible and unshakeable. As an announcer of
truth and justice, as a principle of the unity of the Church,
his voice denounces errors, idolatries, superstitions, and it
condemns iniquities, and makes charity and the virtues to
be loved.

Can he, therefore, be silent when in a nation, with violence and deceit, Churches are torn from the center of Christianity, from Rome to which they are united, when all
Greek-Catholic Bishops are arrested because they refuse to
separate themselves from their true mother Church?

Can the Pope be silent when the right to educate their
own children is taken away from parents by a minority
regime which wants to take them away from Christ?

Can the Pope be silent, when a State, going beyond the
limits of its competence, arrogates to itself the power to
suppress dioceses, to depose Bishops to disrupt the ecclesiastical organization and to reduce it below the minimum exi-
gencies necessary for an adequate care of souls?

Can the Pope be silent when things reach the point
where a priest is punished with imprisonment because he
is guilty of not wishing to violate the most sacred and invio-
lable of secrets, the secret of the sacramental confession?

Is all this, perhaps, an illegitimate interference in the
political powers of the State? Who could affirm that honestly?
Your acclamations have already given the answer to this
and many other questions.

H. CONCLUSION

A LIST OF PRIESTS AND MONKS ASSASSINATED, JAILED, INTERNED
OR DEPORTED

a) The Assassinated:

1) Mons. Apor Vilmos, Bishop of Gyor
2) Szalai Alajos (Diocese of Gyor)
3) Berger Antal (Tavankut)
4) Dupp Balint (Csurog)
5) Pater Adalbert (Gyor)
6) Hauck Antal (Csonopla)
7) Father Gussmann (Bacszentivan)
8) Meszaros Istvan (Palanka)
9) Novotony Josef (Palona)
10) Klein Tivador (Palmonostor)
11) Plank Ferenc (Szivac)
12) Unterreiner Karoly (Palanka)
13) Werner Mihaly (Martonos)
14) Ruppert Istvan (Budapest)
15) Hummer Kornel (Budapest)
16) Nementh Gabor (Nagyvaszony)
17) Bergendi Janos (Szekesfehervar)
18) Padonyi Sandor (Inke)
19) Martincsevics Pal (Gyekenyes)
20) Zarka Josef (Pakod)
21) Levai Istvan (Balatonfokajar)
22) Laskai Antal S.J. (Budapest)

b) Sentenced to Prison or to Concentration Camps:

1) Mindszenty Josef, Cardinal Primate, imprisoned for life.
2) Grosz, Josef, Archbishop of Kalocsa, to 15 years imprisonment.
3) Meszlenyi Zoltan, Auxiliary Bishop of Esztergom, sentenced to imprisonment without a trial where he died on March 15, 1952.
4) Zadravecz Istvan, Bishop of Castrense, sentenced to two years imprisonment; at present interned.
5) Endredy Vendei, Abbot of Zire, sentenced to 14 years imprisonment.
6) Arday Tibor, S.J.
7) Asztalos Janos, imprisoned for life.

8) Acs Istvan, Pauline Order.
9) Agoston Julian, Order of Cistercians.
10) Bardos Domonkos.
11) Bencsik Joseph, S.J.
12) Baranyay Justin, Order of Cistercians, Prof., University of Budapest.
13) Bodolay Gyula, S.J.
14) Boka Imre, Economist of the Primarzial Curia.
15) Bolyos Akos, Pauline Order.
16) Borbely Karoly, Parish priest, sentenced to 2½ years in jail.
17) Botka Lajos.
18) Bozsik Pal, Parish priest
19) Bejczy Gyula, Chancellery of the Bishopric Curia.
20) Csak Boldizsar, S.J.
21) Csavossy Elemer, S.J. Provincial of the Jesuits.
22) Csellar Jeno, Pauline Order.
23) Csontos Oszkar, O.F.M.
24) Fabian Istvan.
25) Fabian Janos.
26) Fekete Peter, Chaplain.
27) Forgo Mike, Cistercian Order.
28) Fritschi Adam, S.J.
29) Galambos Kalman, Pauline Order.
30) Gigler Karoly, Prot. Apost., sentenced without trial.
31) Gombos, Karoly, Canon.
32) Gusztav Josef.
33) Gyarfas Gyozo, O.F.M.
34) Gyetav Peter, Canonic Chancellor of the Bishopric Curia.
35) Gyeressy Agoston, Pauline Order.
36) Hagyo Kovacs Gyula, Cistercian Order.
37) Horvath Mihaly, S.J.
38) Ispanki Bela.
39) Jankovics Joseph, canon, sentenced without trial.
40) Jakab Beniamin, S.J., died in prison.
41) Justh Istvan, Parish priest, sentenced to 10 years in jail.
42) Kajdi Ferenc, S.J.
43) Karolyi Bernat, O.F.M.

44) Kerkai Jeno, S.J., Director General of the Kalot.
45) Kis Horwath Paskal, Cistercian Order.
46) Kovacs Jeno, S.J.
47) Konyves Tibor, S.J.
48) Kristen Rafael, O.F.M.
49) Krupa Kolumban, O.F.M.
50) Lazar Josef, S.J.
51) Lenner Josef, S.J.
52) Lekay Anyos, Cistercian Order.
53) Lenard Odon, Piarist Order, Secretary of Catholic Action.
54) Majsai Mor, O.F.M.
55) Matyosovicsh Henrik.
56) Mate' Joseph.
57) Merenyi Josef, S.J.
58) Mocs y Imre, S.J., sentenced without trial.
59) Nagy Gyula, Parish priest, Vic. Foraneo, sentenced to 3 years in jail.
60) Nagy Miklos, Secretary of Catholic Action.
61) Nemeth Lajos, sentenced to 5 years in jail.
62) Nemeth Tibor.
63) Pallos Peter, O.F.M.
64) Perenyi Josef, S.J.
65) Pozsgay Janos, Parish priest, sentenced for an undetermined period.
66) Regoczy Istvan, Director of a College.
67) Sass Imre, S.J.
68) Somogyvar Heteny, O.F.M.
69) Strilich Karoly, Secretary to an Archbishop, sentenced for an undetermined period.
70) Szabo Laszlo, Pauline Order.
71) Szentey Ferenc, sentenced to 4½ years in jail.
72) Szokoly Lajos, Parish priest, sentenced for an undetermined period.
73) Takacs Laszlo, Cistercian Order.
74) Tamas Alajos, O.F.M.
75) Toth Erno, Chaplain, sentenced for an undetermined period.
76) Tull Alajos, S.J.

77) Vezer Ferenc, Pauline Order, sentenced to death.
78) Vid Josef, S.J.
79) Weber Janos.
80) Zakar Andras, Secretary to Cardinal Mindszenty.
81) Mons. Nicola Dudas, Bishop of Hajdudorog.
82) Mons. Emerico Kisberg, Auxiliary Bishop of Szekesfehenar.

NOTE: In addition to the 82 priests listed above, 50 other priests were sentenced to imprisonment for terms of varying lengths, long and short, many of whom, having served their terms, have been released under conditional liberty, while others have been interned.

About 300 secular priests have also been through concentration camps for terms of varying lengths, and at the present time about 3,500 members of religious orders, forcibly deported from their convents and monasteries, are interned in special places.

c) Deported to Russia:

1) Dr. Saly Laszlo, Canon, sentenced to 8 years of labor.
2) Father Olofson Placid, O.S.B., sentenced to forced labor.
3) Father Kis Szales, O.F.M., to forced labor.
4) Haranzogo Ferenc, Seminary Econ. Mist., to forced labor.
5) Meszaros Tibor, Secretary to a Bishop, forced labor.
6) Kulley Gyorgy, theologian, to forced labor.
7) Lukacs Pelbart, O.F.M., to forced labor.
8) Vagh Josef, to forced labor for an undetermined period.

BALANCE SHEET OF CHURCH LOSSES, 1945–51

	1945	1951	Per cent lost
a) Schools, Shelters and Education Institutions:			
Shelters	191	0	100%
Popular Schools	1,216	0	100%
Elementary Schools	1,669	0	100%

	1945	1951	Per cent lost
Magistral Schools	86	0	100%
Gymnasia	49	8	84%
Middle Schools (rural, industrial, commercial, etc.)	22	8	67%
Schools for Workers	27	8	70%
Schools for Training Shelter Teachers	3	0	100%
Schools for Training Elementary School Teachers	32	0	100%
Nursing Schools	1	0	100%
Domestic Science Schools	1	0	100%
Commercial High Schools (Girls)	1	0	100%
Industrial Preparatory Schools	3	0	100%
Commercial Preparatory Schools	1	0	100%
Popular High Schools	20	0	100%
Stenographic Schools	1	0	100%
Social Lycée	1	0	100%
Higher Schools for Teacher-training for Middle Schools	4	0	100%
Higher Schools of Theology	22	13	59%
Theological Faculties	1	0	100%
Law Academies	1	0	100%
Small Seminars	8	0	100%
Colleges, etc.	167	8	95%

b) Convents and Religious Houses:

Religious Houses of Male Orders	187	6	96.8%
Religious Houses of Female Orders	456	2	98.2%

c) Catholic Hospitals:

Hospitals Owned Completely by Religious Organizations	9	0	100%
State and Provincial Hospitals Operated by Members of			

	1945	1951	Per cent lost
Religious Orders	90	0	100%

d) Orphanages, Mendicant Centers, Etc.:

	1945	1951	Per cent lost
Orphanages	65	0	100%
Shelters for the Aged	20	0	100%
Mendicant Centers	15	0	100%
Other Social-Welfare Units	20	0	100%

e) Buildings and Offices of Catholic Associations:

	1945	1951	Per cent lost
Urban Buildings	35	0	100%
Rural Offices	165	0	100%

f) Printing Plants, Bookstores, Newspapers:

	1945	1951	Per cent lost
Catholic Printing Plants	20	0	100%
Bookstores and Publishing Houses	20	0	100%
Newspapers and Publications, etc.	50	8	84%

g) Land Holdings:

	1945	1951	Per cent lost
Total Square Hectares	877,294	2,011	96%

h) Libraries, Treasures in Cathedrals, Collections of Cultural and Art Items:

All confiscated November 16, 1949, and in part declared State property

CHAPTER V

Czechoslovakia

A. BEGINNINGS OF COMMUNIST PERSECUTION
(1945–1948)

THE SITUATION IN 1945–1947

Czechslovakia is a country whose population primarily belongs to the Catholic Church. According to statistics published in 1945, out of a population which then numbered about 11,500,000 inhabitants, the figures on the various religious confessions were as follows:

a) Catholics: 8,750,000 (75%)
b) Protestants: 900,000 (8%)
c) Czech Catholic Church: 900,000 (8%)
d) Orthodox: 60,000 (0.6%)
e) Hebrew: 50,000 (0.5%)
f) No Religion: 970,000 (8%)

Insofar as regards its ecclesiastic-administrative organization, the Czechoslovak Catholic Church, immediately following the

war, was divided as follows: excluding, of course, the territories
lost by the Czech State:

a) Bohemia: Archbishopric Seat, Metropolitan of Prague; Auxiliary Bishopric seats in Budejiovice, Hrdaec Kralove, Lit-
   merice.
b) Moravia: Archbishopric Seat, Metropolitan of Olmouc; Auxiliary Bishopric seat of Brno.
c) Slovakia: Bishopric seats of Neosolio (Banska Bystrica), Nitra,
   Scepusio (Spis), Cassovia (Kosice), Roznavia (Roznava)
   Presov (for Ruthenian Catholics).
d) An Apostolic Administrator at Trnava, and an Apostolic Administrator of the parishes of the Diocese of Satumare or
   Szatmar, situated in Slovakia.

In all, then, the Church organization included:

   a) 2 Archbishopric seats
   b) 10 Bishopric seats
   c) 2 Apostolic Administrators

Comprehensively it numbered:

a) 4,149 Parishes.
b) 5,185 Priests.
c) 1,363 Religious Houses and Institutions.
d) 1,750 members of religious orders.
e) 3,500 Nuns.
f) 8,750,000 faithful, of whom 8,600,000 were of the Latin rite,
   and of whom 150,000 were Ruthenians of the Eastern rite.

The relations of the Catholic Church with the new Czechoslovak State, formed after the German defeat in 1945, were at
first quite satisfactory, so much so that the Government itself
took the initiative to resume normal diplomatic relations with
the Holy See.

It is true that during this first encounter there was a minor
dissension of a procedural nature concerning the rank which was
to be given to the representative of the Holy See. This rose

because, by tradition, the Apostolic Nuntius became the dean of the diplomatic corps, and in this case he would have had to occupy the position then held by the Ambassador of the Soviet Union. In order to avoid trouble with Soviet Russia which might have taken offense at seeing its ambassador obliged to cede his post as dean to the representative of the Holy See, and because it was not considered fitting for the Holy See to have only a *Charge d' Affaires* in Czechoslovakia, the Vatican Secretary of State and the Czech Government agreed upon the appointment of an "Internuntius" who, in accordance with tradition, would take his place among the Ministers Plenipotentiaries.

His Excellency, Mons. Saverius Ritter, formerly Apostolic Nuntius in Prague before the Nazi invasion, was appointed to the post of Apostolic Internuntius. At the same time the Czechoslovak Government which had been represented at the Holy See by Prince Johannes of Schwarzenberg, solely as *Chargé de Affaires,* accredited Dr. Arthur Maixner, a Catholic and a career diplomat who had been formerly head of the Division of Church Affairs, as a Minister Plenipotentiary to the Holy See. The speech which he made upon presenting his credentials, and the particularly benevolent reply of the Holy Father encouraged the hope that future relations between the Church and the Czechoslovak State would be cordial.

Instead, difficulties began immediately following the resumption of relations over the question of appointing a successor to Cardinal Kaspar, Archbishop of Prague. He had died in 1941 and there still was no successor to him, because first the Germans, and now the Czechoslovak Government, had vetoed the appointment of Mons. Picha, the Bishop of Hradec Kralove, a man of great sanctity and politically irreproachable, but who was feared by the one and the other because of his flawless integrity.

The difficulty was at last overcome on November 5, 1946, and the Holy See could proceed to the appointment of Mons. Joseph Beran as Archbishop of Prague and metropolitan of Bohemia. He had been rector of the Greater Seminary of the Capitol, and was a man well-known for his courageous past, having been for almost three years, June 6, 1942, to March 1945, a prisoner of the Germans, first in the prisons of Pankrac for a month, and later in the fortress of Terezina for two months, and then in Dachau for two years and a half.

His appointment was accepted throughout Czechoslovakia with genuine enthusiasm. It was announced over Radio Prague, on November 7, 1946, with unmistakable satisfaction, and newspapers, of all tendencies, commented on the significance of the event. By appointing a former inmate of Dachau as the new Archbishop of Prague, it was felt that the Holy See had wished to reward the struggle conducted by the entire Catholic clergy of Czechoslovakia which had had more than 500 ecclesiastics interned in the prisons and concentration camps of the Gestapo, of whom 8 had been shot, 58 died in prison and 7 had perished because of ill-treatment.

On November 14, 1946, the new Archbishop made his first official visit to the President of the Republic, Eduard Benes, who decorated him with the "War Cross" and the "Order of Merit first class." And on December 8, 1946, the Cathedral of Prague was the scene of the ceremony of his consecration and enthronement, performed by the Apostolic Internuntius, Mons. Ritter, in the presence of the representatives of the Czech Government, headed by the President of the Council himself, the Communist, Clement Gottwald.

The presence of President Gottwald at the ceremony and the fact that shortly after the Minister of the Interior, Vaclan Nosek, himself wished to confer the medal, second class, of the Czech resistance, on Mons. Beran, gave rise to the hope that relations between the Catholic Church and the Government, in which the Communists were in the majority, might take a turn towards a mutual understanding.

But instead, on the very night of the ceremony, the newspapers published a new legislative proposal of the Government for the suppression of several traditional Catholic feast-days, with the pretext that they slowed down the realization of the two-year plan, and robbed "the State of precious hours of work."

The Archbishop had to intervene immediately in order to protest against this proposal. On the following day, December 9, 1946, he issued his first pastoral letter in which in a calm tone, he said:

My friends (I think I have the right to call you my friends because we all love our Republic) leave to us the possibility of a legal competition. You say that without work shifts on Sundays and feast-days, it will be impossible to fulfill the two-year plan. . . . See to it that you do not oblige those who, in their souls and in their consciences, hold to the observance of Sundays . . . We will hasten our tempo of work on holidays and thus will we surpass our production. . . .

Unfortunately the invitation of the new Archbishop went unheeded, and a few days later the Government and Parliament approved the law concerning the suppression of several traditional Catholic feast-days.

Shortly after the Communists tried something else. They presented a legislative proposal aiming at the "nationalization" of all schools and the establishment of what they called the "Single School."

Against this attempt the new Archbishop again had to rise in protest. Having just returned from Rome where he had visited the Holy Father on February 7, 1947, and taking advantage of the presence in Prague of more than 80,000 Catholics who had come from all parts of Czechoslovakia to celebrate the 950th anniversary of the death of Saint Adalbert Vojtch, the first Bishop of Prague, he delivered a memorable address on May 13, 1947, during which he said:

. . . I felt it was my duty to make you again hear my words, urged not only by my duty as Archbishop but also in my capacity as an ex-political prisoner who bears perfectly in mind that, if after the appeal of the President, all ex-political prisoners must constitute the living conscience of the nation, an Archbishop who is an ex-political prisoner must give the first example . . . But to be the conscience of a people does not only mean the registering of protests against evil actions . . . And I declare again that the codification and the approval of the law on the schools constitutes an ugly harm done against the people and the State . . . We therefore are determinedly opposed to this forced unification of our schools . . . And if its responsible sponsors think it an opportune time to establish a "Single School," we place all the responsibility upon them. But for our part we shall oppose the nationalization of the schools. . . .

Even this time his protest was in vain, for immediately thereafter measures were taken for the abolition of all teaching which had earmarks of confessional inspiration. The hours of religious instruction, which up to then had been obligatory, were reduced and placed at the bottom of the school program, monk and nun teachers were appointed to posts distant from their convents in such a manner as to make their displacements impossible, and seminarists were obliged to attend public schools where doctrines hostile to religion were taught.

On September 28, 1947, a solemn religious ceremony was celebrated in Prague in honor of the patron of Bohemia, Saint Venceslao, and huge crowds such as had never been seen before packed Araccany Square. This was the last great religious manifestation in Czechoslovakia.

Two days later the Communists, angered by the success of this manifestation, plotted a diabolical plan, organized by the Communist Minister of the Interior himself, Vaclav Nosek, who, with the pretext of punishing members of an alleged plot against Benes and Masaryk, ordered a great purge which affected many members of the clergy and of the Catholic laity.

The Czechoslovak Catholic Episcopate was compelled to protest with a joint letter in November 7, expressing itself in part, as follows:

. . . With the excuse of the law and justice, scandalous wrongs against property and individual rights have been committed . . . The very purge which was to be carried out in order to assure the nation, has sunk to the level of a supreme injustice and it is not even possible to appeal against it to obtain reparation for the wrongs inflicted. The honor of the nation is definitely compromised in the eyes of all. . . .

The letter at that time produced deep repercussions, so much so, that for a time it seemed as though direct attacks against the Church had diminished. In fact, there was an attempt to win it to the Government cause, by praising some of its Bishops and in particular, Archbishop Mons. Beran, of whom it was written:

. . . It is not an Austrian nobleman who today has the dignity of being the Archbishop of Czechoslovakia, but a simple man of the people, a man who has undergone the sufferings of political imprisonment in his noble Body, an enemy of fascism, a personal friend of some of your best comrades, who today hold many important posts in the new and young democratic republic. . . .

EPISCOPAL ATTITUDE TOWARD EVENTS OF FEBRUARY 1948

In the meantime, however, events in Czechoslovakia were crowding one upon the other. On February 25, 1948, three days before the Communist *coup d'etat*, the Archbishop of Prague, Mons. Beran, forseeing the imminent danger but impotent to prevent it, launched this appeal to the people:

. . . Many letters come to me from everywhere. Each one advises me on what I must do and on what I must not do, on that which I should do and on that which I should never do. One writes me, "Be not silent, O Archbishop, you must not be silent!"

I have thought upon it. You must not be silent! . . . You must not let yourself be carried away by the falling avalanche. . . . Perhaps, it would be better to keep silent and leave people in ignorance? But Paul has written: "I entreat you before God and the Christ, say that which you have to say, speak to the point and beside the point, beseech, warn, correct, with the patience and the wisdom of a teacher. . . ."

This is why I cannot be silent. The good Czech people know me. I have never betrayed my fatherland, nor will I ever betray it and I have known how to suffer for it. This is why I have decided to speak to you:

1. I entreat you all, for the blood of our brothers and sisters dear to you which was shed in the concentration camps and prisons, for the tears and the lamentations of women and mothers, remember! I know that you would not want to live in the sad memory of their struggles, but that you will be faithful to them. Reflect upon your responsibilities!

2. Preserve order in legality! Everybody would approve the program of socialization. All would work and would be ready to collaborate, providing reforms, even the most radical follow the path of legality.

3. Do not destroy that which has been left to you by the President-Liberator, Masaryk, and by the work of the President-builder, Benes! You yourselves have called them thus. Their work is approved by the entire nation. They worked and suffered for you and for your posterity. You have always had confidence in them. Ingratitude causes suffering and is doomed to malediction!

I would desire that each one of you could read my heart. I feel myself truly completely united with my people and with the nation. Will my words be truly understood? I wish to hope so. . . .

The appeal fell in a void. On February 28, 1948, the Communists, by a *coup d'état,* seized power and the Archbishop was invited to sign a declaration according to which the Catholic Church declared its approval of the violent *coup* and declared itself favorable to the Communist regime.

The text of this statement had been drawn up by the Minister of Justice, Alexis Cepicka, but the Archbishop, Mons. Beran,

refused to sign it. Instead he convoked an extraordinary session
of the Czechoslovak Catholic Episcopate at Brno, on March 4,
1948, and from there he answered the Minister in the form of a
joint letter in the name of the Episcopate and the Catholic
clergy of Czechoslovakia:

> We have not believed and we do not believe it necessary
> to publish a special declaration or a special pastoral letter
> on the political events of the past few days, because the
> Catholic Church does not link itself to any political or con-
> stitutional form, desiring in its particular mission ever to
> serve the highest interests of the people and the nation.
>
> As Bishops and Catholic Ordinants we shall, even in the
> future, carry out all our duties towards God, towards the
> Church, towards the nation, and towards the State, with
> conscience and fidelity, and we are convinced that our
> Catholic people with its clergy will do likewise. . . .
>
> It is with gratitude that we have accepted your assur-
> ances that there will be nothing to disturb the good relations
> between Church and State. We immediately point out, how-
> ever, to some abuses which we cannot approve and by
> which the rights of the Church have been seriously violated,
> above all when church buildings and institutions were occu-
> pied by violence and their official priests, monks, and nuns
> expelled. The fact that a great number of Catholic periodi-
> cals have been suspended, and that impediments are put in
> the way of Catholic organizations, also gives rise to our
> apprehension. . . .

The words of this declaration were clear, and yet Minister
Cepicka, with the aim of showing the people that even the
Church supported the new regime, had the effrontery to remove
its most displeasing paragraphs and to publish it, on March 9,
in the party newspapers under the caption: "Positive attitude of
the Catholic Bishops towards the new regime."

The falsity of this manipulation was so serious that the Archbishop, Mons. Beran, on March 21, felt obliged once again to
write to Minister Cepicka, in order to explain that the Episcopate

had not taken any positive attitude favorable to the new regime, and *inter allia,* he said:

> . . . Christianity and Communism can never be reconciled. He who would attempt such an enterprise would prove that he did not understand history and that he was trying a trick. . . .
>
> We will never betray neither the State nor the people, but neither will we betray God or the Church. . . .

Even this time the declarations were sufficiently clear, yet the impudence of the Communists went so far as to ignore them and to request the Bishops to publish a special pastoral letter, in occasion of the new elections scheduled for March 30, 1948, in support of their single list.

All the representatives of the various religious confessions in Czechoslovakia adhered to the request, but not the Catholic Bishops despite the promises and the threats with which the request had been accompanied.

In the absence of a declaration from the Catholic Episcopate, the regime, with the aim of deceiving the people and letting them believe that the single list had the consensus of the Church, on May 25, 1948, ordered all newspapers to publish a communication in which it was said that "the conversations, between the representatives of the Catholic Church and the new Government, were continuing with success."

Two days later, May 27, 1948, the same Minister Cepicka, in a speech made in *Litovel,* added his own voice to the deceit of the press, and in an interview which was reported on that very day by the Communist party organ, "Rude Pravo," he repeated the refrain of religious freedom, stating again that "negotiations with the ecclesiastical bodies had been carried on in a friendly atmosphere," and that "the ends which we have in view are in complete harmony with the moral principles of Christianity." And he added:

> . . . For an understanding to be perfect, it is enough that the Church understand its mission in the nation, that it not op-

pose the progress of the people and that its activities in the field of morality and the spirit, with the way which we have taken upon ourselves . . ." (Rude Pravo" May 27, 1948.)

THE "TE DEUM" FOR GOTTWALD'S ELECTION AS
PRESIDENT OF THE REPUBLIC (JUNE 14, 1948)

Meanwhile on June 7, 1948, President Benes handed in his resignation and on June 14 following Clement Gottwald, up to then President of the Council, was elected unanimously as President of the Republic. And thus began a new chapter in the history of the Communist regime of Czechoslovakia.

It was traditional to offer a *Te Deum* upon the election of a new President in Czechoslovakia; therefore when Minister Cepika went personally to Mons. Beran to request him to perform the ceremony in the cathedral of Saint Guy, the Archbishop had no objection, the more so because on that very occasion the Minister had given him assurances that the activity of Catholic schools would not be suppressed.

Immediately after the ceremony an official communication from the Presidency of the Council of the Republic notified that the President:

. . . on entering the holy place, wished to express his respect for the national tradition and at the same time wished to manifest his desire fully to respect the moral and spiritual mission of the Church, in the measure that it is ready to collaborate with the Government of the National Front for the carrying-out of the work of reconstruction in the country. . . .

On the following day, June 15, 1948, Mons. Beran, with Mons. Joseph Matocha, Archbishop of Olomune, and Mons. Andrew Skrabik, Bishop of Banska Bystrica, in the name of the Bohemian, Moravian and Slovak Episcopate respectively, hastened to make a courtesy call on the newly-elected President and to deliver a declaration. To him the purpose of the declaration was to avoid a misinterpretation of the ceremony of the day before and to prevent its exploitation for political purposes. It began thus:

Mr. President, we know and we are often reminded of it that according to the words of Christ: "Give Caesar that which is Caesar's" and that we have serious duties toward the State of which you have been elected President. We assure you that we shall faithfully carry out all such duties, as they are imposed on us by our Faith and conscience.

Let us not forget, however, the words of Christ which continue in the second paragraph: "Give to God that which is of God." Even this precept imposes duties upon us, which we must carry out faithfully and without compromise, we, Catholic Bishops, together with our clergy and our people. . . .

On the following Sunday then, June 19, 1948, in all the Churches of the Archdiocese the following courageous "Communication" was read which made even more clear the position of the Catholic Church in the face of the latest events:

. . . At the moment in which this State has obtained a new head, I feel in conscience my duty clearly to express these principles:

1. The Church is not an institution which has to organize political adhesions or oppositions.

2. The Church can prevent no one from petitioning, if he wishes, the help of the Lord.

3. I must, however, seriously give notice that with that the Church does not accept the ideology of tendencies and movements which are in conflict with its doctrine.

4. When the Church shows good will and a readiness to meet with men in a common effort to resolve temporal problems, she can never betray her mission which obliges her to distinguish between that which is of Christ and that which is not. In the name of such a mission she must condemn evil without distinction of persons.

5. I exhort the believing people to stay firmly with the Holy Father, with his Archbishop, and with his priests. . . .

A few days later, on March 6, 1948, Mons. Beran was again

compelled to intervene with a letter to Minister Cepika, authorized by the Government to negotiate with the Church, in order once more to explain that the participation of the Church at the *Te Deum*, for the nomination of the new President, did not at all signify adhesion to or approval of Communist ideologies. And he hastened to remind him that while the Church had sought to show its good will towards the State, the latter instead had too soon forgotten its promises, especially those made in regard to the existence and activities of Catholic schools.

BEGINNING OF SYSTEMATIC PERSECUTION

Three events, meanwhile, had taken place which aggravated the situation of the Catholic Church in its relations with the State: (*a*) the suppression of the entire Catholic press; (*b*) the nationalization of the Catholic schools; (*c*) the struggle for the suppression of Catholic Action.

a) Suppression of the Catholic Press

Ever since February 26, 1948, that is, immediately after the formation of the new Government, the Ministry of Information forbade the publication of the three greatest Catholic weeklies:

   a) The "Rozsevac" (The Sower) with a circulation of
        180,000
   b) The "Niedle" (Sunday) with 120,000 copies
   c) The "Katolik" of Prague with 30,000 copies

In June 1948 several important Catholic cultural reviews were suppressed such as:

   a) "Vyzchood" of Prague
   b) "Na Hlubrim" (In Profundis), published by the
        Dominicans
   c) "Hostynskerpravy," published by the Jesuits
   d) "Verbum" of Kosice
   e) "Smest" (Orientations), Dominican

In November 1948, a decree of the Minister of Information suppressed all other periodical publications (about fifty), alleging a scarcity of paper. A vain pretext because just when they

were suppressing Catholic publications, communist publications
were multiplied, and because of the approach of the Italian elections of April 1948, the newspapers announced that "Rude Pravo"
had given two freight cars of paper to "L'Unita," and the "Pravo
Lidu," an equal quantity to the "Avanti."

Shortly thereafter even the official Gazette of the Archbishop
and the "Acta Curiae" themselves, which had never ceased publication even during the Nazi occupation, were suppressed and
it was even forbidden to mimeograph leaflets carrying the provisions and acts of Diocesan ordinants to the clergy.

The only publication to survive this total destruction of the
Catholic press was the "Katolicke Noviny" of Bratislavia, but
even this weekly which in the past had a circulation of 250,000
copies, had to cut its circulation down by two-thirds, and to
submit to the severest censorship.

b) Nationalization of Catholic Schools

On April 28, 1948, a law was approved, which the Minister
of Instruction, Nejedly, had tried to have approved several times
even before the Communist *coup d'etat,* and it concerned the
nationalization of all the schools.

"Instruction in the schools," reads the first article of this law,
"is exclusively governmental." The law made no explicit mention
of Catholic schools, but once the law was promulgated its application was gradual.

In the early part of June 1948, a circular of the Ministry of
Instruction, enjoined Catholic educational institutions from accepting enrollments for the new scholastic year. And on the
morning of June 11, 1948, the newspapers announced the nationalization of all the Catholic schools from the first to the second
grades, elementary and middle schools, including also the minor
seminaries and those seminaries conducted by the various religious orders for those aspiring to the priesthood.

By October 1948 the greater part of Catholic schools were
nationalized and the few still open found themselves in serious
difficulties, compelled to accept anti-Catholic curricula, Communist principals and teachers, many of whom did not neglect
to teach atheism and materialism in them.

Then with a decree of September 30, 1948, the dispositions sanctioned by the law of April 21, 1948 were also extended to other private institutions (church schools included) of the first and second grades, middle, lower, and higher schools.

And from November 1948 even the kindergartens, although not encompassed by the law, were nationalized little by little and the nuns, in many cases, expelled. A special decree was about to be promulgated which would make it obligatory for Czech children to attend State-sponsored kindergartens. Nejedly, the Minister of Instruction, gave notice of it as follows: ". . . To assure that the education of children is carried out in the spirit of Communism, it is never too soon to take them from the first years of life. . . . It is necessary to wipe out the last traces of bourgeois morality and to create a new and really Communist man."

Even more explicit in this regard was the statement of the Minister of Information, Kopetky, who said: ". . . We proclaim the right of the State to administer all the schools without exception and to direct every form of extra-curricula education in the spirit of our ideology, in the spirit of scientific truth, and in the spirit of the purest Marxist-Leninist teaching. . . ."

In order to force the Church to renounce its teaching function, the Government had recourse to the confiscation of its land holdings which permitted it to maintain the schools. Thus it was that of the 40,000 hectars of land once owned by the archbishopric seat of Olomoue, it was left with only 250.

It must be noted that the abolition of religious instruction went on hand in hand with the nationalization of the schools. No special law was promulgated for this and it continued to remain on the lists of teaching materials. It was, however, impeded in so many ways that it became impossible.

c) Suppression of Catholic Action

On November 22, 1948 a decree of the Ministry of the Interior dissolved the central Catholic Chancellery of Bratislavia. This was the executive body of the Slovak Episcopate of Catholic Action, whose director was also placed under arrest. This took place even though the organization had scrupulously kept itself clear of any kind of political activity whatsoever.

On December 20, 1948, with another arbitrary and a totally grotesque provision, the authorities decreed the merger of the "Slovak Catholic Union," which was the association of Catholic Women, with the Communist League of Slovak Women, with this given as a reason: ". . . this provision is carried out, in the public interest, which requires the union of all forces, as is desired by the democratic people's order."

In the same month of December 1948 the same provision was taken against the "Catholic Youth of Bohemia," which it was intended to merge with the Communist League of Czech Youth. And Minister Syroky, then Vice-President of the Council, gave this as a reason in a speech made in December of that same year in the name of the Government and the Communist Party:

> . . . To unite the youth and to create a single federation for it is the logical result of the development of the policy of Czechoslovakia. . . . It is universally known that in a people's democracy confessional freedom is guaranteed, but we can not admit that there be youth organizations having a religious base, because they break the unity of youth and restrain its efforts to build a better future. . . .

Everything which has been reported here did not have merely an episodic character but followed a systematic pattern. These were only the first signs of the persecution which the new Communist regime in Czechoslovakia was about to unleash.

Two documents are testimony to the gravity of the situation of the Catholic Church in Czechoslovakia in 1948: a) the "Memorandum" to the Government of the Republic compiled by all the Catholic Bishops of Bohemia, Moravia and Slovakia, during the meeting held at Nitra on August 16, 1949, and, b) a "Pastoral Letter" of the Czech episcopate dated October 13, 1948.

In the "Memorandum" of August 16, 1948, the Czechoslovak Episcopate courageously denounced the behaviour of the Government, affirming that:

. . . Despite the promises of religious freedom and the repeated affirmations of good will, an anti-religious and a silent anti-clerical struggle are being waged, according to a well determined plan, exactly reflecting those which in other countries have been undertaken against religion and the Catholic Church. . . .

In particular it deplored that obstacles were placed in the path of the exercise of religious functions, and that the question of Catholic schools, religious and welfare organizations, the Catholic press, and educational institutions, had not been resolved. It deplored further that the State, after having taken away the Church's properties to nationalize them, had not taken any measures to help priests and members of religious orders, as it had promised, so that since the first of October these had been without resources.

The Document, in addition, vindicated the right of the Church to suspend ecclesiastics who did not do their duty and it protested energetically against the suppression of the entire Catholic press, and in particular, of the weekly "Rozsevac." And finally it deplored that the Communists sought, by unjustified attacks against the Holy See, to create opposition between the Episcopate and the people, between the interests of the Church and those of the nation.

The "Pastoral Letter" of the Czech Episcopate of October 13, 1948 dealt with the same complaints. But it could never be published. It was seized while still at the printers and the plates destroyed, while the newspaper, "Katolicke Noviny" which was to have published it in part, was suppressed on the same day of October 17, 1948.

By December 1948, every hope of an understanding with the State could be said to have completely vanished.

THE MEMORANDUM OF MONS. BERAN (APRIL 4, 1949)

Efforts made by the Episcopate to achieve a loyal understanding with the Government failed during the meeting held on January 19, 1949 with President Gottwald, and on February 17,

1949, with several representatives of the Government. Moreover, it had to suspend a meeting which it held on March 22, 1949, in Dolni Smokovec, because of the discovery of a microphone which had been installed there. Because of this, on April 29, 1949, the entire Czechoslovak Episcopate decided to send to the President of the Republic, Gottwald, a complete "Memorandum" on the entire question of the relations of the Church with the State.

Here are the principal points made in the "Memorandum":

TO THE PRESIDENT OF THE CZECHOSLOVAK REPUBLIC CLEMENT GOTTWALD:

1) The Catholic Bishops and Ordinants of Czechoslovakia assembled in conference on April 29, 1949, have discussed the present state of the negotiations between the Government and the Czechoslovak Episcopate.

These negotiations were opened after an audience which you granted the Czechoslovak Episcopate on January 19, 1949, and February 17, 1949, and negotiations were begun between the representatives of the Government and of the Episcopate in the offices of the Central Action Committee of the National Front in Prague.

But in the course of these negotiations, lasting six hours, the Government requested that the representatives of the Church make a new declaration of loyalty to the State on the part of the Church, as a principal condition for the further progress of the negotiations.

2) Now insofar as regards the loyalty declaration which has been asked of us, we urge you to remember that the Episcopate has already formulated its attitude towards the events of February, at the conference held on May 4, 1948 in Brno, as well as in the declaration which the Archbishop of Prague made to Minister Cepicka on May 4, 1948, in which it is declared that the Episcopate is not tied to any political form or government and that it continues to carry on its duties towards God and towards the State.

And for this reason the Bishops refused to take any part in the campaign for the May 1948 elections and demon-

strated their loyalty in words and deeds when you were
elected President of the Republic.

On February 15 a delegation called on you and assured
you that the Church and Catholics would always faithfully
carry out their duties towards the State and in exchange
asked that their duties towards God be respected by the
State. On Sunday, June 20, a solemn *Te Deum* was sung in
all the Churches and a special ringing of bells was ordered.

This having been made clear, on February 17, 1949, we
were surprised to be asked to make a new declaration of
loyalty at the start of conversations.

Despite this it was decided that the Episcopate would
accept to renew its declaration of loyalty to the State and
that it would do so at the meeting in Dolni Smokovec, on
March 23, 1949, had not the meeting itself been suspended
as a result of the famous incident (the secret microphone
found under the radiator in the main meeting hall), the
presence of which has not yet been explained in a satisfactory manner.

3) In our above-mentioned "Memorandum" we asked for
the cessation of the systematic attacks in the press, over the
radio and in public speeches, against the Church and its
representatives, and especially that an end be put to the
campaign against the Holy Father. We consider it natural
that such attacks cease while negotiations are in course between the Church and the State.

But we must acknowledge, with displeasure, that not
even this request was taken into consideration and that
newspapers like the "Lidove Noviny" have published new
invectives against the Vatican:

> March 13, 1949: "The Vatican, ally of reaction" by Jiar
> Putik
> March 18, 1949: "It is no concern of Religion" by St.
> Budin
> March 25, 1949: "The Philosophy of the Vatican" by J.
> Putik

March 31, 1949: "The Vatican and the Germans" by
St. Budin

April 10, 1949: "In what waters fish the fishermen of
the Vatican"

The same thing has taken place in Slovakia in the newspaper, "Novy Slovo," with an article on "The Politics of the
Vatican in the light of documents" by F. Chrojka.

The very Ministry of Information in Bratislavia published, in 1949, brochures bearing titles such as: "The Vatican in the service of American reaction."

The Czech radio, for which the Minister of Culture and
Information (Vaclav Koppesky) is responsible, broadcast on
the March 15, 20, 23 and 30, bulletins in which the Vatican
was called "the bulwark of imperialism."

4) We request a just modification of the situation of the
Catholic Press, which at the moment of the presentation of
this Memorandum, finds itself practically suppressed, save
for rare exceptions having no importance. Still on the same
subject we must declare that in March 1949, save for rare
exceptions even here, the press was even forbidden to publish Acta and the bulletins of Catholic Action, and now, in
the greater number of the Dioceses even the "Acta Curiae,"
which not even under the Nazi domination, under which the
entire Catholic press was suppressed, were the object of any
special restrictive measures, these, too, have actually been
stopped by the Ministry of Information and Culture.

5) In our Memorandum we demanded the freedom of
association for religious ends, but instead the Central Action
Committee of the National Front has given entirely unconstitutional orders, prohibiting every meeting of youth and
of other associations depending on the Church.

This prohibition is based on an entire series of special
legislative provisions, of which we shall cite:

a) Decis: Knv Gotwaldov 24-2-49 n. 263/00-2

b) Decis: Onv Uherske Hrodiste 31-3-49 n. 370/29 and
349/111

c) Decis: Valnake Klobonty, 28-3-1949 n. 267-28/111-49-B

d) Decis: Kralupy, 12-4-1949 n. 457/49

e) Decis: Rychnov, 28-3-1949 n. 645/49, etc.

6) The Church has been stripped even of that which remained to it in agricultural property following the application of the law on the nationalization of all Church lands (N. 10835/48-A-11-1162). We have not discussed the legality or otherwise of this provision, but we demand that there be compensation for and a regulation of all the problems which weigh down this question of landed property.

All these provisions listed above are a proof of insincerity on the part of the representatives of the Government during the course of negotiations between Church and State.

Today there is further proof, and an irrefutable one, that the Government has launched a campaign against the Church, using all the means in its power, because instructions and precise procedures have been given to provincial and district commands of the police for this purpose.

We know that these orders represent only a preparatory phase of the final and decisive blow.

We protest in our name and that of the entire Catholic people against these unconstitutional measures taken against the Church and its faithful, measures which mean the outlawing of Catholicism, the religion of the majority of the population of the State.

We denounce all the public representatives who systematically insinuate that the break in relations is the fault of the hierarchy.

We are sure, Mr. President, that you will recognize the correctness of our complaints, based on facts, which do not contribute to the unification of the nation, but which rather ruin and destroy the peace and the well-being of the nation which you desire to unite.

In the name of the Catholic Hierarchy

(*signed*) JOSEPH BERAN, *Archbishop*

Prague, April 29, 1949

B. ATTEMPTS TO FORM A NATIONAL CATHOLIC CHURCH (MAY 1949–JANUARY 1950)

ISOLATION OF BISHOPS AND INVITATION TO CLERGY TO CUT ITSELF OFF FROM THE HIERARCHY

Having seen the failure of all their attempts to attract the Catholic Bishops to their side, the Communists, in May 1949, decided to isolate the Bishops from the clergy and the faithful, and to invite the latter to cut themselves off from the hierarchy which was presented to the people as the only cause for the failure of the negotiations for an agreement between the Church and the State, promising that in this wise that the dissidence which up to then had disturbed so many consciences and imperiled the religious life of the country would cease.

In order to prepare for the realization of this plan, which definitely aimed at the formation of a real and genuine "National Church," cut off from the hierarchy and directed by churchmen and laymen loyal to the regime, the Communist Government began by supporting an extremely violent press and propaganda campaign against the high hierarchies of the Catholic Church, and in particular against the Czechoslovak Bishops, presented to the people as capitalists and protectors of capitalism. A typical document of this campaign of lies and accusations is represented by a pamphlet entitled, "Conspiracy against the Republic," published by the Ministry of Information and printed in an edition of 100,000 copies.

The second preparatory act towards the realization of this plan began with the publication, as of May 11, 1949, of a "Bulletin of the Catholic Clergy," published by the Ministry of Public Instruction, with the evident aim of substituting itself for the voice of the legitimate church authorities, which had been silenced with the suppression of the entire Catholic press, for the transmittal of orders and directives to the clergy.

The aims which this publication set itself were already apparent in the first issue issued under the title, "Words of Introduction." And just what this "objective news" was could be discerned by turning to the next pages on which several decrees were published which strongly restricted religious freedom and authority.

The first of these decrees, which harked back no less to a Hapsburg law of 1874, bore this title: "The necessity for prior approval by the Ministry of Instruction for the publication of Pastoral Letters, Circulars, or Instructions to the Clergy."

The second concerned the "Control of associations, public meetings and public collections," and even this based itself on a law of November 15, 1867, n. 134 and n. 135 of the old Imperial Code, merged with paragraph 24 of the Constitution, according to which every meeting of priests and faithful, outside the functions of worship, must be announced three days before to the National Committee of the district, and it can not take place except with the permission of the said Committee.

The third decree, on the other hand, dealt with the "Condemnation of Church sanctions against democratic priests and their inadmissability."

. . . Acts of such kind, declares the Decree, are against the law now in effect and in particular against the constitution of the Czechoslovak Republic and as such are punishable in the eyes of the State.

All sanctions of this order are without effect, thus the priests concerned do not lose their right to exercise their pastoral ministry in public spiritual administrations.

The legality of their position will not be effected; on the contrary the Government will give them its full support. . . .

As can be seen, the interference of temporal power in questions of a spiritual nature could not be more clearly set forth.

BISHOPS' PROTEST LETTER TO THE MINISTRY OF PUBLIC INSTRUCTION
(MAY 17, 1949)

In opposition to this so-called "Bulletin of the Catholic Clergy," published arbitrarily by the Ministry of Public Instruction, the Czechoslovak Catholic Bishops, assembled in episcopal conference in Prague on May 17, 1949, decided to send Minister Nejedly the following letter of protest:

... We learn that your Ministry is about to send members of the Clergy of the Roman Catholic Church a so-called "Bulletin of the Catholic Clergy" which according to what is written in the Introduction is supposed to furnish the Roman Catholic Clergy with "just and objective news."

1) We protest against the use of the title, "Bulletin of the Catholic Clergy." Such a title in fact can mean that either it is published by the Catholic Church, or that it is directed by the Catholic Clergy.

We protest against the first meaning, because from the first to the last page it is expressly declared that it is published by the Ministry of Public Instruction. It is clear that this Ministry can not present itself as "The Catholic Church," especially since we know how the compilation of this Bulletin has been entrusted to apostate or suspended priests, or even to members of other religious confessions.

We protest against the second meaning of the above-mentioned title. In fact it is the task of Bishops to advise their clergy about all the laws and dispositions emanating from the Ministry of Public Instruction, as well as from other Ministries and authorities, whenever these laws touch on religious and church life. It in no wise whatsoever belongs to the jurisdiction of the State and its organs to give instructions or to communicate information to the Catholic Clergy.

If it is wished to refer to the fact that at present the Bishops find it impossible to communicate information on State laws and dispositions to the clergy because they have been deprived of their Church Bulletins by an illegal act, the State organs may transmit this information through their official Bulletins.

We regret, however, to be forced to note that while the Bulletins of the Bishops are suppressed because of the scarcity of paper, there seems to be enough to add to the various bulletins of the respective Ministries, even a "Bulletin of the Catholic Clergy" which furthermore is sent gratis to the entire clergy.

2) We protest again against the obligation put on the clergy to make known the content of the Bulletin to persons dependent on them and to keep a copy in the Official Collection. As the Bulletin is now published it does not bear any person's name and is completely lacking in any sign which would make it recognizable as an official Bulletin. If anything it should carry the title, "Official Bulletin of the Ministry of Instruction for the Clergy."

3) In the article entitled "Subvention" on page 2, the Clergy is not informed of the profits realized by the State as a result of the confiscation of Church properties by virtue of law n. 142/47 and 46/48, profits amounting to several hundred million crowns, of which the Prime Minister of that time, today the President of the Republic, had pledged to give each year at least 300 million crowns to take care of the needs of the Roman Church . . . It should have also declared, among other things, that the clergy had spontaneously refused the proposal of a new law on salaries, just as the non-Catholic clergy had also refused.

4) We protest, finally, against the interpretation of the Decree of the Ministry of the Interior of May 9, 1949, N. 260/20-3-5/1949-VB-3a, reported on page 3 of the above-mentioned Bulletin under the title, "Official Reports" dealing with the right of association:

"It is evident, on the basis of that which has appeared above, that the violation of these orders will be punished as a transgression of law. This is applicable to the different free associations such as the male Congregations, the Associations of St. Albert, the Associations of Evangelical Youth, and the Youth Unions of the Czechoslovak Church, etc. . . ."

We hope that the present protest will be taken into consideration, and that, therefore, the above-mentioned "Bulletin of the Catholic Clergy" will be suspended, and that, instead, we will be given the possibility of publishing the "Letters of

the Bishops" (Actae Curiae) to communicate officially with
our Clergy.

SECRET CIRCULAR OF THE EPISCOPATE TO THE CLERGY
(MAY 17, 1949)

At that same episcopal conference of May 17, 1949, the
Bishops hastened to put the clergy on guard with the following
secret circular which they addressed to it:

1) Take notice that parish offices, as are also individual
priests and laymen, are visited by provocateurs masquerad-
ing as priests, monks and nuns. Be on guard!

2) Again, as at the time of the German occupation,
attempts are being made to close the churches or parish
houses, with the pretext that a secret radio transmitter,
arms, leaflets, etc., have been found in them. Keep in mind
paragraphs 4 and 5 of the Constitution during house
searches.

3) You are not obliged to accept information or public
instructions presented in a non-official form (for example,
the "Bulletin of the Catholic Clergy" recently distributed).

4) Do not forget that even the Devil has quoted Scrip-
ture when he calls Our Lord (Matt. IV, 6). No one who
fights against the Church and against God can make his
the rights which derive from the words of St. Paul to the
Romans, XIII, 1-2. And in the first "Memorandum" presented to the then Minister of Instruction, Dr. Zdenik
Nejedly, November 5, 194,5 we declared that "mindful of
the words of the Divine Teacher 'Man does not live by bread
alone, etc.,' we shall not let ourselves be satisfied with material bribes, but fearlessly and without compromise, we all
keep our eyes fixed on religious and cultural principles as
our historic times require in the interests of our beloved
State and our Holy Church."

5) As you well know there is taking place a radical
separation of the Church from the State. No contrary state-

ment in any bulletin, which proclaims its intention to be
that of informing "well," can change this fact.

6) If someone tells you that the State pays the clergy a
subvention of more than 700 million crowns . . . do not
forget that the State by confiscating Church properties has
gained many thousands of millions and that it was promised
to give an endowment of 300-450 million crowns each year
from the revenues of the confiscated properties. This you
are not told. And it was with this that the debits of the Religious Fund were abolished. As has been already confirmed
in several cases, it is precisely those priests who are most
zealous, and who dedicate themselves exclusively to religious activity, who are deprived of their posts, because it is
said that they do not have a positive attitude towards the
constructive efforts of our State.

7) Note that neither the law of November 15, 1867, n.
134, concerning the right of association, nor the law of the
same date n. 135, refer to religious meetings or to religious
congregations, orders and associations. Therefore if the decree of the Ministry of the Interior of May 9, 1949, declares
that according to paragraphs 173 and 24 of the Constitution
of May 9, 1948 both laws to be abrogated, this does not in
any way concern church institutions which in no wise came
under those two laws (par. 3 of Law n. 134 and par. 5 of
Law n. 135). It is therefore completely mistaken to deduce
from the cited decree the prohibition of "different free
associations in the framework of the Church, as for example,
the Marian congregations."

8) There is the intention of establishing a new "Czechoslovak Catholic Church" or a new "Union of Catholic
Clergy." Those persons who have underwritten the appeal
are known. We hope that you will not accept information
from suspended, apostate and excommunicated priests.

9) In regard to the League of St. Venceslao we inform
you that the service for lectures and films, formerly arranged
through the League itself, have now been assumed by the
Archbishopric Ordinant, Prague IV.

10) Because in many cases, contrary to our will and contrary to the intentions of the organizers, pilgrimages and religious feasts have been abused for non-religious purposes, we recommend great care in organizing such manifestations, both in the selection of preachers and celebrants, and in drawing up the program. The Saviour said: "Beware of false prophets! They come to ye dressed as lambs, inside they are ravenous wolves. By their fruits ye shall know them.' And our people has a saying, 'To catch a bird, sing to him sweetly.' "

Prague, May 17, 1949

CIRCULAR OF THE ARCHBISHOP OF PRAGUE (MAY 28, 1949)

On May 28, 1949, the Archbishop of Prague, Mons. Beran, in the face of the increasing propaganda of false news disseminated by the Government on the relations between State and Church, advised the faithful as follows:

1) We warn you again that any cooperation and collaboration whatsoever with those who limit the rights and liberties of the Church "ipso facto" incurs ex-communication. Therefore even the sending of articles and letters to periodicals which approve such efforts. This also involves the "Bulletin of the Catholic Clergy" (Can. 1386). For priests this means ex-communication, that their priestly functions are sinful and sacrilegious, and since they are deprived of jurisdiction, they become invalid before God and the Church.

2) Signatures are being collected among Catholics for requests addressed to the Ordinance soliciting a resumption of negotiations with the Central Action Committee. Minister Kopecky on Saturday, May 28, 1949, openly declared that the education of the youth and the school monopoly according to Marxist ideology, can only be in the hands of the State. After such a declaration it would be useless and vain to resume an attempt at negotiations. The Church can not renounce its right to educate the youth, just as no other confession could renounce such a right. Given that in many

of these requests—imposed by the Secretaries of the district National Committees—the signature of the parish priest never appears, they are of no value.

3) The reviews and newspapers, "Krestanska Zena," published in Brno, and "Lidove Democrazie" and "Lidova Obroda," are not Catholic reviews and newspapers. And, therefore, it is forbidden to sell them in Church or near Church.

There is being formed a "Catholic Action" without the Bishops. It is forbidden to take part in such a non-Catholic organization. Whoever does participate will be punished with Church penalties.

This new "Catholic" organization is supposed to be propagated by the leadership of the popular party. We remind once again that this party has no right to call itself "Catholic."

4) Do not propagate, do not accept and do not recommend any review, any publication or book, which is not expressly approved by the Ordinance. In doubtful or suspect cases inform yourselves by referring to the Ordinance. Even objects of devotion, sacred images, must have the approval of the Ordinance (can. 1385). For collections on behalf of "Caritas" the existing prescriptions of the Ordinance are still valid. No one save the Ordinance itself has the right to change such dispositions.

5) Certain events demonstrate quite well the so-called "truth" of what is written in n. 2 of the "Bulletin of the Catholic Clergy." All Catholic schools have been nationalized. All Catholic reviews have been suppressed. Those which bear the designation "Christian" or "Catholic" are not Catholic. Pilgrimages are forbidden, church processions not permitted. Our "Memoranda," complaints, protests, and requests are never even answered. A priest who had 40 hectars of land and who was recognized by the agricultural commission as the best agronomist of the town, was labelled by a higher commission as a "bad agronomist" so that his land could be taken away from him.

Peasants who do not wish to accept confiscated parish lands were threatened with harsh penalties and accused of sabotage. You yourselves certainly must know of similar events. Think upon it therefore.

On page 7 there is praise for the development of "Catholic literature" while it is known to everybody that all the publishing houses were confiscated and all Catholic books destroyed. "The number of Catholic books published by the Church ever increases," it is written. What do you say about that?

6) On page 3 the decree of May 20, 1949, n. P-110 83-49 P-6 is cited, which was also sent to the Archbishopric Ordinance in Prague on May 20. It is interesting that in the mentioned decree it is expressly said, "communications . . . will be valid from the viewpoint of the state administration only if published in the "Bulletin of the Catholic Clergy," while in that very Bulletin (which claims to "well" inform!) these very important words are omitted, "from the point of view of the state administration," and the disposition is announced in general terms, "will only be valid." Now since the Bulletin is not published in an official form, we warn that the validity of the publication of decrees and laws in the said Bulletin are juridically contestable.

I hope that in the ranks of the Catholic clergy will not be found a single priest who does not understand the aims set itself by the "Bulletin of the Catholic Clergy," and that the clergy will always and exclusively believe the Ordinance, to which you all have sworn obedience. I am also convinced that for "thirty pieces of silver" you will not sell your sacerdotal honor nor will you betray Christ.

JOSEPH BERAN, *Archbishop*

Prague, May 28, 1949

GOVERNMENT PROCLAIMS NEW "CATHOLIC ACTION"

On June 10, 1949, the Government assembled a small group of priests and laymen, gathered from all parts of the Republic, in the Prague city hall, for the purpose of forming a "Committee for Catholic Action," and launching its proclamation.

First it must be made clear that the majority of the assembled ignored the real purposes of the meeting and many had joined it only because they believed that it constituted an attempt to restore peace between the State and the Church. This was made apparent by the numerous declarations made immediately afterwards by the participants and above all by the fact that almost everybody present energetically refused to sign the proclamation already prepared in advance by the Government, the contents of which had been held in strict secrecy, so much so that when the deception was bared the majority left the room.

Father Joseph Fiala himself, who had induced himself to take part in the meeting and who had opened it with a speech, refused to honor with his signature the proclamation presented by the Government, by openly disavowing its contents.

It must be noted that it was precisely Father Fiala whom the Communists had chosen to head the new Catholic Action. In fact he was widely known in all Czechoslovakia as a partisan fighter and one of the most influential members of the resistance movement against the German occupationists, so much so that he had been honored with the highest decorations of the Republic for his merits. By the Communists he was considered as a "living example of a Catholic priest, Communist and ardent admirer of Stalin." He had been put at the head of the new national administration which had arbitrarily taken the place of the great welfare organization, "Caritas." And he had been so sincere in his adherence to the Communist program that in May 1949, when the relations between the Church and the State had entered a highly critical phase, he wrote an article for the Communist daily in Prague, stating that the Government was seeking a way to compose differences, and asking the ecclesiastical authorities to give the State their cordial collaboration.

Now hardly a month after this declaration, he not only refused to sign his name to the Proclamation for a new "Catholic Action," but he also handed in his resignation as President of "Caritas." And while the Communists nervously sought for him in all the corners of the Republic and openly accused the church authorities of having kidnapped him and interned him in some monastery (Rude Pravo, June 26, 1949), he openly denounced their maneuvers from abroad where he had sought refuge, by writing:

. . . After having sought for months for the possibility of loyally collaborating with the Government of Prague, I must recognize that the Communist leaders are not in good faith and therefore they can not be trusted in any way. I could not permit that my name be used and abused by the present Czechoslovak policy, nor was it proper for me to offer my trust to a Government which did not show itself faithful to its own promises. . . . If there were an agreement, for the Communists it would quickly become a veil behind which to hide their persecution of the Church. There can be no compromise with people of bad faith as are the Communists. Even the Catholics of the Eastern rite will be liquidated and soon even the Protestants will experience the shock of persecution. . . .

The Government, however, found a faithful collaborator in Joseph Plojhar, a priest who had been suspended for having accepted to be a candidate for Parliament and for having participated in the Communist Government as Minister of Sanitation. It is to him, in fact, that the drawing-up of the "Proclamation of Catholic Action" is attributed, which was submitted for signatures to those assembled at the meeting in the Prague City Hall on June 10, 1949, and published on that occasion.

For the purposes of documentation, here are some of the most important passages:

. . . We priests and we Catholic believers, sincerely rejoice over the efficacious social changes which are taking place in the Democratic People's Republic, because we see in them the concrete realization of the teaching of Christ regarding love for one's neighbor.

We had hoped that the negotiations between the Church

and the State, begun in May 1948, would lead to a fruitful
solution of all pending questions . . . Now negotiations are
at a dead end, because, as we have come to know, several
ecclesiastical representatives, did not wish to accept the
fundamental pre-suppositions of the agreement, to wit, an
explicit declaration of loyalty to the Republic, a thing which
is evidently required from us, according to the words of St.
Paul. . . . We believe we are fulfilling our duty, if we seek
for the improvement of the relations between Church and
State . . . We hope to find understanding from our Bishops,
but we also wish to warn whoever might dare in any way to
persecute our priests or Catholic laymen because of their
positive attitude towards the State, that we are fully aware
that the overwhelming majority of the faithful is with
us. . . . We cannot accept any orders of a political character
from abroad. . . .

It is passing strange that Plojhar who had organized the
movement, and directed the constituent meeting of the new
"Catholic Action" and formulated, as has been said, its program,
did not affix his own signature. Perhaps he did not wish to compromise the success of the fraud with his name of a "suspended
priest." The fact is that efforts were made to obtain the names
of real priests who, either had not been asked or who had refused
to join the movement outright.

Names of priests already dead for some time, or who had
never even existed, names of convents or religious congregations
which were sheer invention, flatteries, deceits, tricks, all these
were used by Communist propaganda to enlarge the "list of
lies."

The reality, however, was one and it was this: among the
first seventy signatures which, as Communist propaganda put it,
"included people of all walks of life, from deputies and university
professors to charwomen" there was not a single priest.

The signatures of priests which follow later were obtained
either in bad faith and by deceit, or with an insistence which

was continued to the point of exasperation. It is known for example that a parish priest was approached by seven different communist organizations for his signature, and of another priest whose house was surrounded by 200 men in order to intimidate him.

The establishment of the new "New Catholic Action" therefore was naught but a giant Communist hoax which can be said to have failed from the start.

NEW INTERVENTION OF THE BISHOPS (JUNE 15, 1949)

Against this entire hoax, become more serious and carried out with impunity because of the total absence of a Catholic press which could reply to it and unmask it, rose the Bishops who, assembled once again in Prague on June 15, 1949, addressed to the clergy and the faithful the following circular letter which was to be read in all the Churches on the Sunday of Corpus Domini, on June 19:

. . . In recent days there are being spread false statements, by all means of propaganda, to the effect that negotiations for the solution of the relations between Church and State have been wrecked because of the fault of us Bishops.

Such accusations are false.

We declare that we have remained loyal to the State. Upon taking over our office we swore an oath of loyalty to the Republic and we declare that we have remained faithful to that oath.

We declare, moreover, that we are and we have always been in favor of a just agreement with the State in all political-ecclesiastical questions, because such an accord forms the presupposition for a fruitful cooperation between the Church and the State for their tasks. This collaboration naturally will be possible only on condition that the State does not interfere in ecclesiastical and religious affairs, and the Church does not interfere in political questions.

Notwithstanding all the assurances of good-will on the

part of Government functionaries, hostile proceedings have been undertaken against the religious freedom and against the rights of the Church.

a) We have no possibility whatsoever of keeping you informed through the press or over the radio. You yourselves are witnesses of the fact that after February 1949 the entire Catholic press was progressively suppressed. Remember only the popular weekly reviews, "Rozsevac" and "Nedele." In April 1949 even the Official Diocesan Bulletins "Acta Curiae" were prohibited, and these had not been suppressed even during the German occupation.

b) Paragraph 18 of the new Constitution guarantees us the freedom of expression. But in reality the Ministry of Information with its decree of April 27, 1949, contrary to the law on publications, intervened and prohibited even the dissemination of information made by mimeograph.

c) Things have come to such a pass that there is intervention in internal church affairs, as evidenced by the occupation of church offices. And with the participation of suspended priests and ill-informed laymen there is being formed, against the will of the Bishops, a pseudo "Catholic Action," which has as its aim the sowing of confusion among the faithful and to make the defense of the freedom and the rights of the Church impossible to the Bishops.

From these facts it clearly results that here it is no longer a question of an agreement between Church and State, but of the sub-ordination of the Catholic-Roman Church to an anti-Christian ideology which intends to substitute religion with Marxism, and attributes to the State the right to interfere in things of the conscience, of faith, and of morals, something which no Christian can accept.

Thus, for example, on the occasion of the IX Congress of the Communist Party, the Minister of Information, Vaclav Kopecky, declared: "We must liberate ourselves from all that which is old, surpassed, of all that which has remained of the capitalist ideological superstructure . . . we must build a new progressive world ideology which is based on his-

torical and dialectical materialism, on Marxism and Lenin-
ism, on the system of the doctrines of Marx, Engels, Lenin
and Stalin."

At the same Congress, the Minister of Schools, Dr.
Nejedly, said: ". . . there exists among us still many remnants, even old feudal remnants, of the old church education
. . . we must exert ourselves to uproot them all and to form
a new man, the truly Communist man. . . ."

Every Catholic Czech or Slovak must realize that the
time of trial is upon us, that each one must distinguish the
lambs from the wolf in lamb's clothing, and that in the
question of religious freedom there can be no compromises
and that from each one, from now on, a clear method of
action is demanded, because it concerns the eternal salvation of every immortal soul. . . . Let us thank the priests and
the faithful for their loyalty, we have firm faith in their
perseverance and we exhort them to be strong in the
Faith. . . .

THE POLICE CONFISCATE THE BISHOP'S LETTER AND
OCCUPY THE PRAGUE ARCHBISHOPRIC

On the dawn of Sunday June 19 in which the priests were to
read from the pulpit the letter of the Bishops reported above,
police descended on all the parishes and with the threat of
making arrests, they warned them not to read the letter, presenting a false order bearing the seal of the archbishopric curia of
Prague.

Many opposed this order and were immediately arrested.
In many cases it was the Bishops themselves who went to the
parishes to read their circular in person and to comment upon it.

Meanwhile a serious incident had taken place in Prague.
Early in the morning, a government commissioner, sent by the
Ministry of Instruction, presented himself at the Archbishopric
Curia, and installed himself there while pretending to carry
out a house search.

On the following day about ten policemen searched the

offices of the Curia, removing the mimeograph machine and the circular with which the Archbishop was about to request an oath of loyalty from the clergy on the ground that such an oath was "contrary to the democratic regime." At the same time the Chancellor and another priest working in the office were arrested. And a policeman was left in the ante-room of the archbishopric residence to check on telephone calls.

Ever since June 17 the mail, private or official, was no longer delivered to the Archbishop and later even visitors were no longer permitted to see the Prelate.

The police took away the seal with which the Archbishop validated his acts. The Bishopric's official stationery was also removed and it was with this paper and this seal that the order shown by the police to the parish priests was falsified, to prevent them from reading the circular of the Bishops.

Archbishop Mons. Beran rose up against all these brutalities. On June 17 he protested to the Ministry of Instruction against all the outrages undergone, and on the following day he sent a letter directly to the Minister of the Interior, writing as follows:

> . . . Until I receive a detailed explanation of these provisions, I consider as unconstitutional the restrictions imposed on my personal freedom and on my right to send and receive correspondence, as well as the right to freedom of action necessary to the concistorial office (curia) and the Ordiance. . . .
>
> Insofar as regards the confiscation of my "Declaration," by which the so-called "Catholic Action" was disavowed, it was ordered by me with my full right for the internal administration of the Diocese; and therefore even its reproduction does not constitute a transgression of the law on publication . . . I repeat again that the Declaration was made by me and reproduced under my orders for the internal administration of the Diocese and I cannot understand what is anti-State about its contents.
>
> The so-called "Catholic Action," formed on June 10, is an illegal church institution, even because, as I know in many

cases, the signatures of priests have been affixed there, under compulsion, even with threats and often against wishes publicly expressed.

I have, therefore, as Archbishop the duty of asking my subordinates for a clear and sworn declaration of loyalty. By asking this of my priests, I see nothing of an anti-state nature, nothing which is in opposition to the popular democratic order, because even political organizations have this same right, and, according to articles 41 and 42 of the Constitution, an analogous oath is demanded from every member of Parliament.

I hope that the reasons which have led to the measures which have been taken will be communicated to me as soon as possible, or better still that the same are revoked.

JOSEPH BERAN, *Archbishop*

Prague, June 17, 1949

To this clear position of the Archbishop, the Government replied with slander, and taking advantage of the fact, that the Episcopate, completely bereft of a press, could not defend itself, on June 19, 1949 it had an article published in the Czech Communist paper, "Rude Pravo," entitled, "The Catholic people take the side of the Republic."

Here are its most salient passages:

. . . During the week which is coming to an end the Catholic citizens of our Republic, and among them 1,500 priests, have taken a clear position in the question of the relations between Church and State. The adherence of Catholic priests of all kinds—chaplains, parish priests, assistant parish-priests, deacons, archpriests, professors of theology, prelates, canons, etc.—has a particular value. Priests and faithful unanimously proclaim that they are good citizens of a State which guarantees them complete religious freedom and which authorizes the fulfillment of their religious duties. And they desire to see the question regulated in the best possible way in the interests of the State, of the Church, of the Clergy and of the faithful.

Unfortunately the reactionaries of the higher spheres of the Roman Catholic Church have tried to abuse their high functions by abandoning themselves to hostile acts against the State and the Government of the Republic.

They were supported by circles abroad who have an interest in breaking our work of consolidation of the Republic.

From this moment we can state that such reactionary plans have failed. . . .

The same issue of the same newspaper, "Rude Pravo," carried a letter by the very President of the Republic, Clement Gottwald, addressed to the "Committee of Catholic Action." Here is the text:

. . . I am particularly happy with the assurance that you, Catholic priests and faithful, have given me to collaborate completely with the planned reconstruction of our Republic.

Our State desires a friendly cooperation with the Roman Catholic Church. And proof of this lies in the concrete help which the State furnishes the Church on the economic plane, and not only our official declarations. Evidently everything depends on the Church itself.

For me your Catholic Action is an expression of the very desire of all the clergy and the faithful to arrive at a sincere understanding and at a loyal collaboration with the State. It will have an immense significance for the Catholics of our country if it succeeds in carrying out the task it has set for itself.

CLEMENT GOTTWALD

Prague, June 19, 1949

And Mr. Zapotocky, in a radio broadcast made on that same day, said the following:

. . . The Government will not tolerate that the Catholic hierarchy terrorize patriotic Catholic priests and rob them of the freedom of their political opinions.

The law and justice must act severely against tyrants,

provocateurs and those who seek to incite disorders and agitation.

The greatest responsibility for the present situation must be attributed to Archbishop Beran, who has ordered his priests to take part in his activity directed against the Republic.

A NEW GRAVE JOINT LETTER OF THE EPISCOPATE (JUNE 19, 1949)

On June 19, 1949, the Czechoslovak Catholic Episcopate, assembled again in Prague, underwrote a new letter which was sent to the priests, despite the rigorous surveillance of the police, and it was supposed to be read to the faithful on Sunday June 26, 1949.

Here are its main points:

DEAR FAITHFUL:

In an immensely grave moment of your religious and national life we turn to you with this our letter, having on our side the right of the Mother Church.

All of you, in these recent times, have been witnesses of an extensive and general action whose aim is to compel the Czechoslovak Bishops to conclude an Agreement between the Church and the State.

We share the view of public opinion that the relations between Church and State are really desolate and sorrowful. Such a state is certainly unnatural because both societies should mutually complete themselves and it does not even contribute to the common outer and inner peace of believers.

We understand your evident right to be informed as to the truth even from our side, because we are so beseeched, and continually, by many.

Having no other possibility we are trying to do it, as our conscience commands us, with this Pastoral Letter, praying God that the voice of your Pastors come to your ears and that it be heard with faith and rightly understood.

It is not necessary, dear Catholics, that we present you with special proofs!

Just look around you, follow events and you will easily notice that the Church of the Czechoslovak Republic, in exchange for its services rendered the nation through hundreds of years, for its cultural and charitable activity, for its devotion to its own people, for its firmness and its sufferings endured during the German occupation, has received only the bitterest of recompenses.

Today it is robbed, deprived of the greater part of her rights and of her freedoms, calumnied, slandered, openly and secretly persecuted.

Observe the state, today, of the Church in Czechoslovakia:

a) Over the radio, and in public speeches, a systematic campaign is being conducted against it, particularly against the Pope and the Bishops, who are its superiors established by God.

b) The sacred character of the family and the supreme right of parents to the education of their children, are deliberately undermined.

c) The entire religious press, save some unimportant exception has been abolished. Even the official publications of the Bishops (Acta Curiae) have been prohibited. Instead of these there has been introduced, by the Ministry of Public Instruction, the "Bulletin of the Catholic Clergy" which is not at all Catholic, because it does not have ecclesiastical approval, and is published against the will of the Ordinance. And notwithstanding that it has been instituted for the Catholic clergy, it is directed by non-Catholic persons with an anti-ecclesiastical policy. And through State bodies it exerts itself to administer merely Catholic affairs, eliminating thereby the Bishops from exercising their jurisdiction. Every Catholic book which is to be published, even prayer books, are submitted to the prior censorship of the State; and State commissars are attached to Catholic publishing houses.

d) Under the threat of sanctions, there have been promulgated prohibition of any gatherings for Catholic instruction outside the Church proper; even the fate of the Churches, as can be forseen by the compulsory listing of objects destined for the religious service and of sacred vessels, is, it seems, very uncertain.

e) The Church has been deprived of the last remnants of its properties, even that minimum established by the law is not respected, and in many cases the payment of the "subvention" to the clergy has been withheld.

f) Church schools hardly exist and the fate of those few which remain, is rooted in a sad uncertainty about the future. This is a state of affairs of which the sorrowful effects are felt first by the students and the parents. There has also been pressure exerted on parents to remove their children from church schools, and this was done by direct threats of the consequences to their lives which might follow.

g) Teachers of religion are re-examined from an ideological point of view and they are giving orders on how to teach religion in the spirit of materialism. Every other religious education of the youth in the associations, in the Marian congregations, etc., has been prohibited in many places under the threat of punishment and it is systematically rendered impossible by the fact that the State has appropriated the monopoly of materialist education both in the schools and outside, so that education in a Christian spirit is prevented and considered illegal.

h) Even in the Seminaries and in the theological Faculties lecturers in the so-called "social sciences" have been seated whose task it is to see that our theologians are gradually educated in materialist ideologies.

i) Completely contrary to law, a compilation of all Church properties has been ordered, including collections made in Church, a compilation which is made by direct investigation on the spot and in many cases without any decorum and by means of unconstitutional searches.

j) Continual efforts are made to deprive the Church of buildings still left to it for religious ends, in particular do they want to occupy all the religious houses and educational institutions for the young people who are dedicating themselves to a sacerdotal and religious station. In Slovakia especially they have been evacuated with violence, some nuns and priests having been carried away on trucks. . . .

m) The Ministry of the Interior has sent directives to the regional commands of the police on how to act against the Church and its members. In some places even spiritual exercises have been forbidden, and in many localities religious processions have been prohibited or they have been exploited for anti-religious purposes.

n) The conference of Bishops in Dolni Smokovec, at which they had to establish the line to be followed in the face of State demands, had to be interrupted because a recording device was found in the main meeting hall. The Minister of the Interior has been asked to conduct an investigation of this incident, but up to now no satisfactory answer has been forthcoming.

o) The last conference of Bishops in Prague was disturbed by the police. At that time the Prague Concistory was occupied by State commissioners and the archbishopric seat put under the control of the secret police, so that the freedom of the President of the Meetings of Bishops was limited. Such measures are very grave violations of constitutional liberties and of many other laws still valid at this moment.

p) In general it can be said that every religious activity outside the Church is impeded; many faithful take care not to go publicly to church so as not to be accused of reaction and be threatened with the loss of their means of livelihood.

It is certain that in this manner a situation is being created which is in conflict with divine rights, but even with natural law itself and those rights of man which are commonly recognized.

Judge by yourselves, dear Catholics, after a confirmation of these realities, if the State has been harmed, or if the exact opposite is not the case!

Despite this sorrowful situation, the Czechoslovak Epis-

copate has always been disposed to negotiate and in reality
it has negotiated, through its delegated representatives, driving itself to the most extreme sacrifices just to obtain, for the
most substantial things at least, some regulation of affairs
and to assure for its believers at least the essential conditions
of religious life.

It has, however, convinced itself, with great sorrow, that
despite its good will this could not happen, not only at the
price of substantial concessions, but only on the condition
no less of exploiting the Church against its own divine mission. And during the entire time in which negotiations were
proceeding, hostile measures were being taken against the
Church in many localities and in this manner the faith of the
Bishops in the success of negotiations was systematically
destroyed.

It is useless that we hide from you that in truth there is
a systematic, well-prepared and logically carried-out persecution of the Catholic Church in Czechoslovakia.

This is not in the least changed by the resolution voted,
in accordance with a pre-established plan, at the conference
of the so-called "Catholic Action," held at the "Abecnidum"
of Prague on June 10, even if in it loyalty is professed to the
Catholic Church, and there is recognition of the Holy Father
as its visible head, and submission to Him in questions
relative to faith and morals, ecclesiastical discipline, and the
recognition of the jurisdiction of the Bishops in the questions
of faith and morals.

This secretly prepared meeting was convoked without
the knowledge and against the will of the episcopate. Its
purpose was clear, namely, to lessen the jurisdiction and the
influence of the Bishops even more.

In truth the greater part of the delegates present at this
gathering were sent, and paid by, Committees of Action.
And most of them did not know anything of what was afoot,
nor did they imagine that their signatures on the attendance
list would be abused for the so-called "Catholic Action."

For this reason even the body of Bishops in its meeting of June 15 felt it to be its duty to declare that this so-called "Catholic Action" was not Catholic Action but a dissident movement and that every participation or collaboration with it would be liable to ecclesiastical penalties. . . .

Similarly, as has been mentioned above, there was an abuse of the signatures of many priests, making them appear as declarations of agreement with the so-called "Catholic Action" because they knew nothing about its aim and their signatures were obtained by an artifice, through the use of slogans of an entirely different nature as, for example, "just agreement," "preservation of the rights of the Church," "religious teaching in the schools," "recognition of the Holy Father as visible head of the Church," etc.

Even the so-called "Catholic Gazette," published by the Committee of "Catholic Action," is evidently lacking the authorization of the Bishops, and because of this it can not be considered as Catholic. It is forbidden, therefore, by the Church to be read, received or distributed.

As the responsible representatives of the Catholic Church in the Republic of Czechoslovakia, we vividly feel the serious responsibility for the development of religious events in our fatherland and we do not hide that the decisive moment is come of great trials for our dear faithful and for our clergy.

But if, as it is said, the principle purpose of all this which is now being organized, with every means, against the Czechoslovak Catholic Bishops, is that of inducing them to a just agreement between the Church and the State, we declare that this entire crusade is superfluous.

The Czechoslovak Catholic Ordinants have had, and still have, a great interest in the realization of a sincere and just agreement between the Church and the State and they will never cease to pray for this intention.

We do not desire, however, that the Church become only a handmaiden of the State, because it will thus become a bearer of another ideology under the mantle of the Christian religion. We desire an agreement but not a "Diktat."

CONDEMNATION BY THE HOLY OFFICE AND FAILURE OF THE
COMMUNIST CATHOLIC ACTION

On June 20, 1949, the Holy See intervened directly in the question, by confirming the canonic sanctions threatened by the Bishops, and by promulgating the following Decree through the Holy Office:

In these last days, the adversaries of the Catholic Church in Czechoslovakia have fraudulently instituted a false "Catholic Action," through which they strive to induce the Catholics of this Republic to rebel against the Catholic Church and to separate themselves from obedience to the legitimate pastors of the Church.

This "Action" is the more iniquitous, insofar as its promoters did not shrink from compelling many, by force and deceit, to join it. Indeed they were so bold as to register and publish as members even the names of many priests and laymen who had never belonged and who on the contrary had manifested an opposite will.

Meanwhile the Supreme Sacred Congregation of the Holy Office, authorized to guard over the faith and the integrity of morals in the name and by the authority of His Holiness, Pius XII, reproves and condemns as schismatic the aforementioned action, fraudulently called "Catholic Action," and at the same time declares that all and single, clericals and laymen, who knowingly and spontaneously have joined it or will join it in the future, and its nominative founders and promoters, to be schismatics and apostates of the Catholic Church who have incurred or will incur the excommunication which the Apostolic See especially reserves to itself according to Canon 2314, other sanctions of Canon Law standing, by which they will be effected if—may God not will it—they contumaciously persevere in censure.

This Decree, despite the lively oppositon of the Communists was publicly read in almost all the parish churches, and it served to dissipate the confusion sowed among the clergy and the people, inducing many who had been deceived to make a public retraction of their adherence.

Out of the 33 priests in the Prague diocese who had let themselves be convinced, 25 immediately withdrew their signatures after the reading of the Decree of the Holy Office. And it has been estimated that out of the total of 6000 priests who constitute the Czechoslovak Catholic clergy, only about 170 agreed to join, more or less, the new organization.

C. INTERNMENT OF MONS. BERAN AND ARREST OF OTHERS

ARCHBISHOP MONS. BERAN

On Saturday June 18, 1949, the Archbishop Mons. Beran, after having vainly protested to the Government against the restrictions placed on his personal freedom, and after receiving no reply whatsoever to a letter he had sent on the preceding day to the Ministries of Instruction and Interior, decided to break the police cordon which occupied the Archbishopric residence. So he went to the Church of the monastery of Premostratensi of Strakow in order to denounce his status of internment to the people. He pronounced a spoken memorandum in which *inter alia,* he said the following:

> . . . It may be that not long from now you will hear all sorts of calumny about me over the radio . . . Perhaps you will hear it said that I have made confessions or other declarations, I hope that you will have faith in me. If on one day or another you come to know that an agreement has been reached between the Church and the State, know that I shall never conclude an agreement which could undermine the rights of the Church and those of its Bishops. . . . It is possible that some day you may learn that I have concluded an agreement and that I have given it my consent, perhaps, you will hear it repeated day and night over the radio, but I hereby declare solemnly before God and the nation that I

shall never conclude an agreement which damages the rights of the Church. Nothing and no one can make me do it, because the Catholic Church is only one, and without Bishops, the Church can not exist. . . .

You know that I would like to talk to you about so many other things but I shall not. . . . I do not wish you to be persecuted, I do not know how many more times it will be possible for me to speak from the heights of a pulpit. . . .

At the end of the speech, it took the Archbishop twenty minutes to walk out of the Church so great was the crowd of people who wished to do homage of their devotion to him.

Thousands or more persons had gathered in the square in front of the archbishopric residence to acclaim Mons. Beran, who had to show himself at a window of his apartment: "We will not permit them to take you! Have faith in us!" the crowd shouted up to him and the Archbishop replied, "You have faith in me and I in you!"

At this the police intervened to dispel the crowd and in reprisal they arrested the abbot of the monastery of Strakowv, Don Jerolimek, in whose church the Archbishop had preached.

On the following morning, June 19, there was scheduled to take place in the Cathedral of Prague the outdoor celebration of the feast of "Corpus Domini," which had been postponed until that day because the Government had abolished all feast days which fell on week-days, but the procession, unfortunately, had to be suspended on account of the uproar staged by the Communists. In fact since early morning the Church had literally been occupied by Communists, recruited in the factories and transported there by the authorities, who as soon as the Archbishop began to speak started to heckle so loudly that his words could not be heard. And when he, above the deafening noise, did manage to say that "the newspaper which is being sold at the door of the Church is not a Catholic newspaper . . . The Catholic Action of the Government is not our Catholic Action!" the commotion was such that the ceremony had to be interrupted, while the crowd of the faithful tried to drown out the shouts and whistles of the Communists by singing the national anthem and the patriotic song of St. Venceslas.

The Archbishop was forced to leave the Church, while the police on the square attacked the crowd which shouted "Long live the Archbishop" and which tried to accompany the Archbishop back to his residence, as the square echoed to voices from powerful loudspeakers, previously installed, which continued to blare the shout, "Long live Gottwald!"

This was the last time that Archbishop Mons. Beran was seen by the crowd. As soon as he reached his residence the large doors closed behind him and no one else could approach him.

This is how a correspondent of a British news service describes his visit to the archbishopric on Friday, June 24, 1949, a few days after the transpired internment:

. . . I was received at the door by one of the State commissioners, functioning for the Archbishop, and introduced before one of the secretaries of the Archbishop. . . . The office was very busy. . . . Four men and a young woman were busy sealing envelopes. The seal of the Archbishop could be seen on each of these letters. There was nothing too ecclesiastical about these four persons. They were young men of vulgar bearing, dressed in civilian clothes, two of whom without ties, the other wearing plaited shoes . . . Up to the time when the office was occupied by the Government, on June 13, the personnel was exclusively ecclesiastical. These evidently were the new Government employees. . . . Dr. Houska who, in the name of the Government, directed the office told me that the Archbishop was well, but that he did not wish to leave his residence and did not receive anybody. . . . I asked if I could speak with his secretary, Dr. Jan Boukal, but I was told that he was not in the building. I then said that there was a rumor that Dr. Boukal had been arrested, and then the above-mentioned commissioner gave an order to one of his subordinates to call him to the telephone. Dr. Houska refused to say whether he were a Catholic and when he had assumed his new functions, limiting himself only to saying that . . . all was proceeding normally. . . .

A French journalist describes his attempt to interview the Archbishop in this manner:

. . . At the Ministry of Information where I had gone to request authorization to interview the Archbishop, they sent me from one office to another, they observed me with a strange air and answered me that nobody could give such an authorization.

Then I went directly to the archbishopric residence. . . . All may freely enter its gardens and the courtyards of the edifice, but to enter the personal residence of the Archbishop is something else.

Two men in civilian clothes wearing a gray and red arm-band, asked me what I wanted. "To speak to the Archbishop," I said. They understood and spoke French. They examined my documents and very courteously they accompanied me to the reception room. There a third man examined my papers, then he picked up a telephone receiver and said in Czech, "Monsignor, there is a French journalist here, Jacques Terrier of the 'Paris Match' who has asked me for an interview." The conversation continued in Czech for some time and then putting down the receiver, he said to me: "The Archbishop is very disappointed in foreign journalists and no longer grants interviews. . . . This is all that he has authorized me to say to you." The two civilians with the arm-bands re-accompanied me to the door. . . .

PROTEST TO THE ATTORNEY GENERAL (AUGUST 5, 1949)

Against this situation of a veritable internment, after having vainly protested to the Ministers of Public Instruction and Interior, on August 5, 1949, Mons. Beran decided to appeal to the Attorney-General. Here is the text of his letter:

. . . Having received no replies to my letters addressed to the Ministry of Public Instruction, to the Ministry of the

Interior and to the Government, no other means is left to me
except to turn to the Attorney General of the State.

This letter, perhaps, is not drawn up in conformity with
legal style, but unfortunately I do not have the opportunity
of legal counsel. No person can come to me, and the lawyers
themselves fear to lose their posts if they take on my defense.

Now, being unable to appeal to others, I am permitting
myself to submit the following questions to you?

Is the Catholic Church still recognized by the Czechoslovak State? If, yes, by virtue of what law has it been deprived
of the right to direct its own internal affairs?

a) With the Note P. 12.388 49-P/6 of the President of
the Ministry of Public Instruction, dated June 13, 1949, Dr.
Miroslov Houska was appointed, by the Ministry of Instruction, as Commissioner to exercise control of the Administration of the Archbishopric of Prague, by virtue of paragraph
60 of Law n. 50, dated May 7, 1874.

The Archbishop of Prague was never directly informed
of this provision and immediately he became aware of it, he
decided to protest against this measure, by announcing on
June 15 that the administration of the Archbishopric would
be closed. He informed the representative of the Ministry of
Instruction of his provision who, in turn, informed him that
by June 17 he would receive a reply to the protest he had
filed.

Instead, in the afternoon of June 15, Dr. Houska, assisted
by State police, occupied the offices. I protested again, but
neither my letter of June 17, nor my protest were taken into
consideration.

Instead Dr. Houska who, according to the Note of the
Ministry of Instruction, was supposed to exercise only the
functions of an inspector, in fact took over the very administration of the archbishopric, exercising all its functions,
while the law of 1874, provides only for control.

b) Now I permit myself to ask if the Commissioner, on
the basis of par. 60 of the Law n. 50 of May 7, 1874, has the
right:

1) To exercise all functions in the name of the Archbishop, without having received any mandate whatsoever from the Archbishop?
2) To use the seals and the official stationery of the Archbishopric, without any such delegation from the Archbishop?
3) To take over the treasury of the archbishopric administration and to let it be known, without advising the official treasurer, that he has full powers to dispose of cash funds?
4) To take over as well the central treasury of the Prague diocese which juridically does not belong to the administration of the archbishopric, thereby making it impossible for this treasury to make payments due to the employees of the archbishopric residence?
5) To interfere with the normal functioning of the archbishopric administration, preventing the Archbishop even from receiving official correspondence?

c) Permit me also to point out to the Attorney General of the State the following facts:

1) The archbishopric residence of Bob Brezanay was put under state administration without the Archbishop being informed.
2) When the last 50 hectars of the archbishopric properties of Cervenia Recice (district of Pelhrimov) were nationalized, the Archbishop was never officially informed. His representatives were not authorized to intervene and the Diocese was represented by a Government Commissioner attached to the archbishopric administration.
3) The liquidation of the properties of the Diocese was carried out without the knowledge of the Archbishop who still is the legitimate proprietor.

Are all these acts legal? Do they all stem from the aforementioned decree of 1874?

Since June 19 I have been *interned* in the archbishopric

residence of Prague. Visitors can not be admitted and they are told that the Archbishop does not wish to receive visitors.

All the personal and official correspondence of the Archbishop and of the staff of the archbishopric residence is confiscated and only post cards and periodicals are delivered to them.

I am deprived of every personal freedom and of all my rights as archbishop and all this without any open investigation being initiated or any sentence of a Court of justice, or any other official decision.

The Commissioner attached to the archbishopric administration exercises his functions in the name of the Archbishop and the Archdiocese.

On June 19, 1949, the Cathedral of S. Gyuy, was thrown into disorder by shouts and whistling. Ever since Saturday I knew that there had been an order given to all Prague factories to come *en masse* to the cathedral in order to provoke incidents which would prevent the faithful from entering the Cathedral.

The police had taken security measures around the Cathedral and in the nearby thoroughfares.

Now I ask: Why had all this been prepared? Why was not any disturber of public order arrested when there were so many national security agents in the Cathedral?

Is the law concerning public order which forbids the interruption of religious exercises (art. 122, penal code) still in effect?

Why was not the Archbishop informed before hand? Why were all these police measures taken?

I have asked the Ministry of the Interior to make an investigation regarding these incidents; but I have received no reply.

These then are some of the questions which I urge, and trust, the Attorney General of the State will wish to answer.

JOSEPH BERAN, *Archbishop of Prague*

Prague-Hradkany, August 5, 1949

RECALL OF THE CHARGE D'AFFAIRES OF THE HOLY SEE

The Czechoslovak Government had been asking, since April 1949, the Secretary of State of His Holiness, for the recall of Mons. Gennaro Verolino, Chargé d'Affaires *ad interim* of the Holy See in Prague.

No reason had been attached to the request, but the purpose of the Czechoslovak Government was quite evident. Not wishing to come to a breaking-off of relations with the Holy See because such an open break would have exposed in one fell swoop to the people the asserted desire of the Government to come to an agreement, it nonetheless wished to make use of the diplomatic form of recall to save appearances and to achieve, nonetheless, the effect of removing from the scene a much too qualified witness to its struggle against the Czechoslovak Episcopate, and retarding as much as possible, at the same time, the coming of a new Pontifical representative.

The Holy See, although it protested against this highly incorrect diplomatic procedure, recalled Mons. Verolino and designated Mons. Paolo Bertoli, to become his successor as *Chargé d'Affaires* at the Internuntiature in Prague. It was stipulated that Mons. Verolino would not leave Prague before the arrival of Mons. Bertoli, stationed in Berne, Switzerland as Councillor to the Apostolic Nuntiature there.

Through the Ministry of Foreign Affairs, the Czechoslovak Government hastened to assure Mons. Verolino, in writing, that instructions had already been transmitted to the Czechoslovak Legation in Berne to grant an entry permit without delay to the new *Chargé d'Affaires* of the Holy See.

Meanwhile, with the aim of inducing Mons. Verolino to leave his post immediately, the Government began to create continual difficulties for him. It went so far as to submit him to incredible police measures, during a journey he made in Slovakia, between June 25 and 29, despite his rank of diplomat still in office.

Under the pressure of these difficulties and submitted, as he was constantly, to pitiless attacks in the press and over the radio which lied in the most vulgar manner against the Pontifical representative—portraying him as a professional plotter to the detriment of Hungary first and now of Czechoslovakia—Mons. Verolino was forced to leave Czechoslovakia, on July 13, before the Czechoslovak Legation in Berne had decided to give its visa which had already been promised in writing by an authority none other than the Foreign Minister himself.

On the very evening of his departure, a great uproar was staged against the Holy See, seizing as a pretext upon the publication of the decree condemning Communism on the part of the Holy See which had appeared on that very day, July 13.

Two days later, July 15, Minister Cepicka, at a meeting of the Central Action Committee, pronounced one of his most violent speeches against the Bishops, labelled as "traitors to the fatherland," and against the Vatican, accused of being the principal enemy of the country, and in particular against the Pontifical Representative, Mons. Verolino. Here is a record of the main passages:

> . . . On the evening of the day in which Verolino left our country forever, which he wanted to lead to civil war, a decree was read over the air waves of the Holy See dealing with the excommunication of Catholic Communists and of those who collaborate with them.
>
> . . . All this is an expression of a mad hatred in the face of the successes of the working people in the struggle against the exploiters.
>
> There is no doubt that all those who strive to put in practice the orders of the Vatican, become traitors to the State and to the people.
>
> Whosoever tries to transmit to our country the orders of the greatest enemy of our State, know now that he has no right to call himself a Czech or a Slovak. . . .
>
> ("Rude Pravo," July 17, 1949)

After the departure of Mons. Verolino, it was impossible to obtain a visa, neither for Mons. Bertoli, nor for two other diplomatic functionaries, designated the one after the other for the Internuntiature in Prague.

According to international custom, the Internuntiature was

then entrusted to the secretary, Mons. Octavius De Liva, and before his departure, Mons. Verolino hastened to notify the Ministry of Foreign Affairs in Prague of this measure, in writing.

ANTI-RELIGIOUS LAWS

The struggle of the Communist Government against the Catholic Church in Czechoslovakia in October 1949 moved from the field of tactics and intimidation to the legislative field. And in the space of only four days three laws were approved by the Czechoslovak National Assembly which if fully applied would be enough to destroy, by themselves, the entire organization of the Church, its liberties and its moral mission.

a) The Law on the State Office for Church Affairs

ARTICLE 1. A State Office for Church Affairs is hereby established, directed by a Minister, appointed by the President of the Republic.

ARTICLE 2. This Office is charged with the task of assuring that the church and religious life develop in agreement with the Constitution and the principles of the people's democratic regime, and thereby to assure to every citizen the right to freedom of confession guaranteed by the Constitution, on the basis of religious tolerance and the juridical equality of all confessions.

ARTICLE 3. It arrogates to itself all the analogous competencies of pre-existent central Offices. . . .

ARTICLE 5. In Slovakia there will be established "A Slovak Office for Church Affairs," under the jurisdiction of a Commissioner to be appointed by the Government.

b) The Law on the Economic Treatment of Ecclesiastics (Ref. Law n. 218–49, approved Oct. 14, 1949)

ARTICLE 1. The State assumes the costs of personnel, that is to say the treatment of the Clergy belonging to all the Churches and religious Societies recognized by the State and employed in the public care of souls or in ecclesiastical administration with the approval of the State.

ARTICLE 2. Ecclesiastics who are citizens of the Czechoslovak State, of irreproachable conduct, politically secure and obedient to the general dispositions regarding public functionaries, are entitled to the treatments provided for in the present law. . . .

ARTICLE 9. The task of those engaged in the public cure of souls involves the obligation of giving free religious instruction in the first and second grades of schools in this measure: ten hours a week for cooperating vicars, and eight hours for parish priests. Only ecclesiastics who exercise supervisory functions, such as deacons, rural deans, etc. are exempt.

ARTICLE 10. The prior approval of the State is requested for the appointment or the election of ecclesiastics, paid for the exercise of their functions, by virtue of the present law.

Candidates proposed for nomination to Bishops, Archbishops, auxiliary Bishops, coadjutors with the right to future succession, Apostolic Administrators, Ordinants of the Army, or the Head of a religious society must be approved by the Government beforehand.

The Government can also refuse its approval for reasons of a political character against the person of the candidate.

ARTICLE 11. The State assumes the ordinary material expenses of the Church (expenses for worship and administration). For extraordinary expenses which are adequately explained the State will grant special subventions.

ARTICLE 12. For the purpose of determining income, the bodies which represent the State will make an inventory of all real and moveable property, as well as of all the holdings of organizations within their jurisdiction, including therein single individuals, communities, institutions, foundations, etc. and they will send this inventory to the Ministry of Instruction in the three months following the entry into effect of the present law. Every year thereafter, at the end of he month, they will present the old and the estimated budget, together with a record of any changes which may have taken place in the inventory.

ARTICLE 13. The State has the supreme control of all the

properties of the Church. Each transfer, change, etc. requires the prior approval of the State.

ARTICLE 14. The State assumes the charge of Seminaries and educational institutions for the training of candidates for the priesthood.

ARTICLE 15. Every public and private patronage of the Churches and benefits are transferred to the State. All incomes of ecclesiastics accruing by virtue of a title or custom (gifts, personal regalia, etc.) are suppressed.

ARTICLE 16. The Ministry of Instruction is authorized to emanate a decree for the practical application of the present law.

ARTICLE 17. Every act or omission contrary to the dispositions of the present law will be punished as an administrative crime by the popular regional Commission with a maximum fine of 100,000 crowns, unless it is a question of a crime referrable to a penal court. In case of inability to pay the fine, this will be substituted by a maximum prison sentence of six months. The fines will be paid to the public treasury.

ARTICLE 18. All dispositions which have been in effect up to now concerning the object of the present law are hereby abrogated.

The present law enters into force on the very day of its promulgation.

c) Decree of Execution of the Church Laws (Law n. 219–49 of Oct. 18, 1949)

[The decree of application of the two laws, nn. 217–49 and 218–49, was approved by the National Assembly on the following October 18 (n. 219–49) and brought with it new and even more serious violations of the freedom of the Church. Here are some of its main articles.]

ARTICLE 7. *a)* Activities of a sacred character (preaching and similar functions) peculiar to the Church and religious societies may be conducted only by a person having the consent of the State and who will be sworn. The text of the oath will be established by the Government through the decree.

b) Every office (by election or appointment, entrusted to these persons have the prior consent of the State.

c) Posts which are vacated must be filled within a period of 30 days, after which time the State may take the necessary measures to assure the normal development of spiritual administration, of church administration and of the training of the Clergy.

ARTICLE 8.   *a)* If the ecclesiastic loses the qualifications required for nomination in the meaning of Art. 7, n. 1, the competent government body will negotiate with the competent church body and if the latter does not regulate the case within 14 days, the government will ask that the priest be removed and at the same time it will determine if his stipend is to be suspended.

b) If the church body does not regulate this within 14 days, the post is to be considered as vacant, in effect.

ARTICLE 30.   *a)* Vacant offices will be open to competitive examinations through the publication in the "Bulletin of the Catholic Clergy."

b) Applications of candidates, however, must be addressed to their respective Bishopric Curiae which will forward them to the State Church Office. Curiae are reminded that when indicating candidates who are considered unsuitable they must not claim reasons which conflict with the juridical order of the Czechoslovak People's Republic.

INTERVENTION OF THE HOLY SEE

The most typical example of state interference in the internal affairs of the Catholic Church, in the application of the anti-religious laws of October 1949 despite the repeated protests made against them by the Czechoslovak Episcopate, took place in January 1950 when the death of Mons. Andrew Skrabik, which occurred on January 8 of that year, left the seat of Banska Bystrika vacant.

This is how events developed:

Immediately after the death of Bishop Skrabik, the members of the canonic chapter met in order to elect a Vicar Capitulary, according to Canon law, to serve until the Holy See appointed a new Bishop.

On January 13 the canonic chapter elected Mons. Daniel Briedom to the office. Immediately upon his election, he confidentially informed the state authorities of his election.

Their answer was that they did not recognize such an appointment made without prior government consent. And they demanded, by virtue of law n. 218–49 and its relative decree of application n. 219–49 of October 18, 1949, that, instead of a simple notification, the party concerned should make request for formal consent. The State authorities added that until such formal consent was received and obtained, the appointment would not be considered valid and that, by virtue of the same law, if this was not all provided for within 30 days from the date of vacancy, the State Office for Church Affairs would take steps prescribed by the law.

Meanwhile, since Mons. Briedom had refused to follow this alleged government procedure, the State Office for Church Affairs, on January 20, 1953, ordered the Government Commission, already installed in the Curia, to prevent the newly elected Vicar Capitulary from exercising his functions.

On February 13, 1950, at the end of the stipulated 30-day period, the Government, seeing that its demand for the presentation of a formal request for government approval was not forthcoming from the newly-elected head of the canonic chapter of the Cathedral of Banska, proceeded on its own to appoint an "ecclesiastic administrator" authorized to administer the Diocese of Banska Bystrica, in the place of the "barred" Vicar Capitulary.

The Government appointed the Rev. John Dechet, "a faithful servant of the Republic" to this post. He belonged to that small group of priests in the Apostolic Administration of Trnava who had joined the movement of the schismatic Catholic Action.

On February 17, 1950, the entire Catholic Episcopate of Czechoslovakia, protested against this illegal act of government intervention, by referring to the Code of Canon Law which forbids the acceptance of any church office from a civil authority (Can. 2394, 2395, and 2399).

On the following day, February 18, the Holy See intervened directly. Through the Concistorial Congregation it emanated the following Decree of Excommunication:

> . . . the priest, John Dechet, having dared to accept from laymen, and then exercise, the functions of "administrator" of the vacant Diocese of Banska Bystrica, The Holy Concistorial Congregation inflicts on him the punishment of excommunication reserved "speciali modo" to the Holy See and declares him expressly "scomunicato vitandus."
>
> The Holy Concistorial Congregation, therefore, warns all ecclesiastics and the faithful of the laity to comport themselves towards this priest, in conformity with Canon 2361, par. 3, of the Code of Canon Law.
>
> Issued in Rome from the offices of the Holy Concistorial Congregation, February 18, 1950.
>
> (*signed*) A. G. CARD. PIAZZA, *Bishop of Sabina and Poggio Mirteto*
>
> J. FERRETTO, *Surrogate*
>
> ("Osservatore Romano," February 19, 1950)

Unfortunately, the Government did not retreat from its action, despite this grave procedure by the Holy See, and the Rev. Dechet, supported by the Government, continued to remain at Banska Bystrica, thereby prolonging a situation which had become extremely delicate and intolerable, as will be seen in the continuance of this narrative as further developments are reported.

BREAKING OFF DIPLOMATIC RELATIONS WITH THE HOLY SEE

The intervention of the Holy See in the episode of Banska Bystrica, with the consequent excommunication of Dechet, had greatly annoyed the Communist Government, so much that it was induced to break off, definitively, its diplomatic relations with the Holy See.

In order to prepare public opinion for this act, which up to now had been retarded for tactical reasons, the Government sponsored a violent press and propaganda campaign, making use of all means at its disposal to launch accusations and to denigrate the activities of the Holy See as much as possible.

The opening shell was the publication of a book entitled "Plot Against the Republic," launched in an edition of 100,000 copies, from which are hereby reproduced some of the charges it contained against the Holy See and the Czechoslovak episcopate:

. . . The criminal politics of the Vatican drives Bishops to betray their Government. The aristocracy of the Church, under the guidance of Archbishop Beran, was ready to commit an act of high treason.

Beran is the most guilty, because we had confidence in him, because of his detention in a German concentration camp.

And with Beran, all the Bishops are guilty of treason for having organized a revolutionary plot and launched a campaign against the Republic, giving orders to all their priests to betray and to revolt.

And Verolino, the former Chargé d'Affaires of the Vatican in Prague, who had to leave the country last June and who will never be granted a visa to come back, must be considered as the most able spy of the Vatican, the fellow who has effectively organized the plot against the State.

It was he, in fact, who last June, when Beran was heckled in his own Cathedral, incited the Archbishop to resist and to incite the crowd so that he could get himself arrested, because, he said, "the Church needs a martyr. . . ."

On Christmas Eve of 1949, the very President of the Council, Zapotocky, violently attacked the Holy See and not much later, on February 28, 1950, Gottwald, the President of the Republic, joined the campaign of charges against the Holy See and the Czechoslovak Episcopate, by stating:

> . . . The high clergy of the Catholic Church in Czechoslovakia is the enemy of the regime; it is against any understanding with the Government and it is the center of internal reaction . . . All the Czechoslovak reactionaries, at home and abroad, are in contact with the high Catholic clergy and are preparing a struggle against our democratic Republic . . . ("Rude Pravo," February 29, 1950.)

A few days before the Radio had announced:

> . . . The Czechoslovak people in 1948 definitively broke with the tradition of Rome and the Vatican.
>
> The last hour has sounded for an ancient world founded on Roman and canon law.
>
> Rome and the Vatican will fall and a new world will rise, a socialist world for which millions of men are fighting, who do not fear the columns of the forums of Rome and the deeds of the Popes.
>
> In the east has been born a man, to whom Czechoslovak workers trustfully extend their hand, following his example. The false prophets must be destroyed not only by physical but rather by moral annihilation. . . .
>
> The hour will come in which the world which is represented by Rome and the Vatican will be destroyed. . . .
>
> A resolution adopted by the workers of Skoda in Pilsen says, Rome and the Vatican are our centuries-old enemies, but there will come a day when they will be uprooted and only on that day will the world be free. . . .

This whole campaign of propaganda and hostility against the Holy See had been started, as has been said, for the purpose of preparing public opinion for the expulsion of the Pontifical Representative from Prague and a definite rupturing of relations with the Holy See.

At first the Prague Government had raised no objections to

the appointment of Mons. De Liva, as "Interim Chargé d'Affaires of the Holy See," finding it natural that with the departure of Mons. Verlino the Internuntiature should be entrusted to the only functionary in Prague of the Holy See, in accordance with accepted diplomatic custom. But now, following the afore-mentioned events, the Government began to create difficulties.

In vain did Mons. De Liva try to explain to the Czechoslovak Minister of Foreign Affairs, as did the Vatican Secretary of State to the Czechoslovak *Chargé d'Affaires* attached to the Holy See in Rome, that the Government's position was untenable and its behaviour inexplicable.

On the one hand the Prague Government denied Mons. De Liva the right of administering the Internuntiature until the arrival of a new *Chargé d'Affaires;* and on the other hand it refused to permit the entry into Czechoslovakia, for a period of nine months, of any ecclesiastics designated by the Holy See to occupy this post.

Proceeding towards the realization of its plan, the Government had sought for more ways of obstacling the functioning of the Pontifical Representative, going so far as to make it difficult for the *Chargé d'Affaires* to negotiate with functionaries of the Ministry of Foreign Affairs, sometimes actually barring him entrance to the Ministry.

The Government, of late, had also increased police surveillance of the *Chargé d'Affaires,* and two large automobiles were parked permanently in front of the offices of the Internuntiature to take note of and to photograph the persons going in and out.

On March 16, a radio broadcast announced that the Government had invited Mons. De Liva to leave the territory of the Czechoslovak Republic within three days.

Immediately thereafter the press and radio, for the purpose of explaining this serious measure to public opinion, adduced the pretext that Mons. De Liva had interfered in internal political questions, by spurring the Episcopate and the clergy to resistance against the laws of the State relative to religious matters, and by inciting the faithful to revolt against the Government, and by undertaking illegal activity against the Republic.

The facts recited here prove the baselessness and the falsity of these accusations. On the contrary the opposite can be proved, to wit, that it was not the Holy See and the Catholic Episcopate which interfered in questions of internal politics, but that it was the Government, instead, which invaded the strictly religious field, demanding control of the internal organization of the Church, disrupting its discipline, violating its unity by the establishment of a schismatic Catholic Action, and, finally, by trying to reduce the Church to the role of a mere instrument of the State.

TRIALS OF EXPONENTS OF THE CLERGY

Simultaneously with the expulsion of the Pontifical Representative, there took place a change in the entire tactics which the Communist Government had been following until then in its struggle against the Catholic Church.

Up to then, in fact, the Government had limited itself to attacks against Mons. Beran, against the Episcopate and the clergy only for the purpose of having them swear a loyalty oath to the Communist regime.

But since February 1950, having observed and noted that this struggle had not succeeded in breaking the resistance of the Catholic clergy, the Communists tried to make the clergy bend to its will by the use of force and threats, carrying out arrests on a vast scale, staging trials, submitting the clergy to nerve-wracking interrogations, and by inflicting numerous sentences to jail or forced labor camps.

In two consecutive letters, dated January 21 and February 17, 1950, the Czechoslovak Catholic Bishops denounced the persecutions and the brutalities against the clergy, revealing how a day did not go by without some priest being arrested or sentenced. All district Action Committees ("Okresni Akni Vybor"), they said, invite ecclesiastics to "friendly conversations," but in reality they are confronted with functionaries of the administration and workers from the factories. And, naturally, these conversations were exploited by the Communists against the Catholic Church.

In fact, at the end of these "conversations," the priest was invited to partake of refreshment and he was photographed from all sides. These photographs were then reproduced in news reels, so that the "refreshments" looked like "banquets" offered to the priests by the workers.

All this was part of the premeditated tactics of discrediting the priests in the eyes of the faithful and to oppose them to the Bishops. This is the reason why the Bishops, in the afore-mentioned letter of February 17, 1950, put the clergy on guard, thus:

> ... We consider it our specific duty to remind you that the new church laws have demanded a promise from you in order for you to be able to exercise your ecclesiastic mission. You have given this promise, with our consent.
>
> Following that, any request whatsoever which is made to you to participate in similar activities and "meetings" does not have any basis in law.
>
> In the interests that the conduct of all be uniform in this regard, we forbid you to participate in these "conversations," and above all in those "courses of instructions for the clergy," which are being given in the various districts.
>
> Be conscious of your dignity as priests, of your duties towards the Church and the Nation and pray for all the undecided and the misled. ...

Thanks to the prompt intervention of the Bishops then, even these last "friendly" attempts failed, so the Communists immediately passed on to the second phase of their tactic which was to consist in terrorizing priests, above all the most faithful and courageous, by un-nerving and disgusting them with interrogations without end, and by striking at the rest with sentences and exemplary punishments.

THE FIRST BIG TRIAL AGAINST TEN PRIESTS (APRIL 31, 1950)

On the morning of Friday, March 31, 1950, a big trial was opened before the State Tribunal of Prague against "ten high dignitaries of the Roman Catholic Church." The *mise en scène* was such that it could be clearly understood how, rather than a trial against some priests, it was in reality an attack in grand style against the entire Catholic Church, and in a special way, against the Holy See and the Episcopate.

The charge sheet, in fact, which was read at the first hearing by the Prosecutor, *Cisek,* a Communist fanatic, and signed, on March 27, 1950, by another Communist, Dr. Bohumir Ziegler, in reference to the accused priests, declared the following:

> . . . They are faithful servants of the Vatican, recruited into its espionage service, whose primary purpose is to enlarge and maintain the power of the Vatican.
>
> Following the great October Revolution, the Vatican adopted a hostile attitude towards the USSR. It has united with the interventionists and the White Guardists, and with their support, it has established an Eastern Institute in Rome. This Institute is a school for spies and for agents, who receive special instruction there so that, under the pretext of missionary activity, they can penetrate the USSR and there create chaos and carry-on espionage.

The same tone was employed by the Czechoslovak press. Here, for example, is what "Mlada Fronta," the organ of Communist Youth, wrote on April 1, 1950:

> . . . It remains clearly established that the guilt does not stop only with the accused. By now it appears, undoubtedly, that behind the walls of convents, high treason and espionage have formed a grand alliance, and that all the religious Orders, and not only some of their dependent organizations, have received precise orders from the Vatican to disrupt, destroy and to spy in the Czechoslovak People's Democracy.
>
> It has again been revealed, by these charges, that the high church aristocracy, particularly the Archbishop Beran, has been deceitful and that it has given the Orders directives against the State. . . .

And as reinforcement, the Czechoslovak Information Agency, a few days later declared:

. . . The religious Orders have become instruments in the hands of the enemies of Czechoslovakia. The recent criminal trials have brought to light that their houses were hideouts of enemy emissaries, spies and assassins; they had illegal transmitters, and they had become centers of activity against the State. . . .

Not all the guilty were seated on the bench of the accused.

The testimonies have shown that not only were monks implicated in this plot, but the entire episcopacy, and that all the monasteries and all the religious orders represented elements of the very plot. . . .

For the purposes of documentation here are some of the most important features of the trial:

1) The first to appear before the court was Father Augustine Machalka, Prior of the Monastery of Premonstratensi in Nova Rise, 43 years old.

He had already been arrested once in 1942, by the Gestapo, and sentenced to the concentration camps of Aushwitz and Dachau where he had remained up to the end of the war. That notwithstanding, he was again made to come before a Communist tribunal and to hear its President, Dr. Nosek, put the same questions which the Nazis had done before: "Are you a fervent Catholic?" "Have you ever taken confession?" And after having served a three year prison sentence under the Nazis because of his faith, the Communists now sentenced him to 25 years of forced labor.

2) The second to appear was Father Vit Bohumil Tajvsky, Prior of the Monastery of the Premonstratensi at Zeliv.

He was a man of 38 years of age, who responded courageously to the questions put to him. He did not deny that he was opposed to the present regime and that he had attacked it in his sermons. Asked for the reasons for his aversion, he explained that the Church was diffident towards countries having a people's democracy because such countries restrict religious freedom. Asked to cite an example of such religious

oppression, Father Tajovsky courageously cited the trial of
Cardinal Mindszenty.

Accused of having hidden arms in his monastery, allegedly found by the police on the night of February 1 last
during a search of the premises, Father Tajovsky denied the
charge, declaring he did not know anybody who would have
been interested in hiding the arms in his monastery.

For these courageous answers he was condemned to 20
years of forced labor.

3) The third was Father Adolph Kajpr, former editor of
the "Katolik" of Prague, 48 years of age. He declared that
he did not feel himself to be guilty of anything and explained
that his activity had nothing in common with high treason.
But during the interrogation, the most serious charge made
against him was that he had been in continuous contact
with Archbishop Mons. Beran, and it was for this activity
carried out on behalf of Beran, that he was found guilty of
the crime of high treason and sentenced to 12 years in a
convict prison.

4) The fourth was Father Frantisek Silhan, 45 years of
age. He was the Provincial of the Jesuits in Czechoslovakia.
He was accused of having relations with Mons. De Liva,
the pontifical representative, who forced to leave (as the
President of the Court, Nosek, put it) the territory of our
Republic was saved from appearing at this trial against the
ten traitors and spies only because of his diplomatic pass-
port. Then the President asked Father Silhan, "In the case
of a conflict between a law of the State and a law of the
Church, by which law would you feel yourself bound?" "By
the law of the Church," answered Father Silhand, and for
this he was sentenced to 25 years of forced labor.

5) The sixth was Father Frantisek Mikulasek, 37, who
was accused of having circulated the decree of the Holy
Office on Communism. He declared that he could not understand how this could constitute a crime and he had the
courage to tell the President who was trying to convince
him of his guilt, "Then it is not against me that the trial is

being held but against Catholicism itself!" He was sentenced to nine years of forced labor.

6) The sixth accused, with whom the first day's hearings were concluded, was Father Stanislav Bartak, 35, who was accused of having relations and contacts with his Prior, Father Machalka, co-accused and present at the trial. Father Bartak declared that he did not feel in any way guilty of any blame, but he was likewise sentenced to two years of forced labor.

7) The seventh, with whom the hearings of the following day, April 1, 1950, began, was Father Sylvester Braito, 52, professor at the theological faculty of Olomouc. He was accused of having listened to the Vatican Radio. He declared that he was not against the State and that he was working only for the realization of a Christian state, and that since in a totalitarian State it was forbidden to have an ideal, he could not support the present regime. He was sentenced to 15 years forced labor.

8) Father John Blesik, 40, minister of the monastery of the Redemptorists of Mala-Strana in Prague, was condemned to 10 years forced labor only because he was in contact with Father Prior Jarolimek, with the accused Father Silhan and with Mons. Picha.

9) The Provincial of the Franciscans, Father Joseph Urban, 49, began his deposition by declaring that he was perfectly aware of his activities, but that in no sense did he feel guilty.

The verdict sentencing Father Urban was for 14 years forced labor.

10) The gravest penalty—life imprisonment—was reserved for the last of the accused, Father John Mastilak, 38, and Rector of the Theological Institute in Oboriste. One of the most serious charges was that of having been a student at the Pontifical Oriental Institute in Rome.

To the President who asked him, "What is your attitude towards the Czechoslovak Republic?" Father Mastylak answered precisely, "Christian and Catholic." The President questioned him again, "Do you feel yourself to be a citizen of Czechoslovakia and obliged to obey its laws?" to which Father Mastylak answered, "I am a Czechoslovak citizen who obeys the laws of his republic, but only when these laws are not contrary to the laws of the Church and humanity!"

D. ATTEMPTS TO FORM A "NATIONAL CHURCH" (APRIL 1950–JUNE 1952)

ARREST AND "CONCENTRATION" OF ALL MEMBERS OF RELIGIOUS ORDERS

On the night between April 13–14, 1950, Communist militia occupied all Catholic convents by force and deported all their members to concentration camps.

This measure had not been improvised, nor did it rise from any specific event, but it was, as we shall see, part of a police plan, already methodically prepared, to exterminate the forces of Catholicism.

In fact, already one month before, since the night between March 14–15, two State commissars had been forcibly installed in every religious house; one for education, and the other for economic administration, each one flanked by secret police whose assignment it was to watch persons, make a careful survey of the disposition of the house, and supervise every activity so as to serve as liaison agents for the central police commands.

Therefore, on the night of April 13–14 it was easy for the police to gain entry into these convents, because the commissars themselves opened the door to them, and it was also easy to capture the members because it was the very police, who flanked the commissars, who furnished lists with names, and who stood guard at possible escape points since they had carefully studied the layouts of the houses.

One by one the members were awakened, called out by name, and assembled either in the refectory or in the courtyard. Then, in groups of 30 or 40, they were loaded on trucks to be deported to their new destination.

The Superiors were the most harshly treated. Often they were submitted even to blows and threats in order to induce them to show the police the entire house, to hand over the cash box, the inventory and keys, and then after they were separated from their subordinates, they were led away to a different and an unknown destination.

Once the members were gone, the raids began. Everything was turned topsy-turvy, all corners were searched, floors broken up, and holes dug under the churches in a search for arms, munitions, radio transmitters and anti-revolutionary propaganda material.

But after finding nothing of this nature, the vandals appeased their disappointment by appropriating everything which fell into their hands: linen, food provisions, furniture, etc. They even profaned and sacked the churches, taking away holy vessels and vestments. Eyewitnesses have reported seeing a uniformed policeman, in a store in Prague, exchanging a "holy chalice" for imported merchandise.

The assault against the Catholic convents had been prepared and carried out with an impressive array of police. Each convent had been surrounded by 30 to 60 men, fully armed. In some cases, as in *Valehrad*, and in *Frystak*, in Slovakia, 30 or more military trucks were counted.

Fear of popular uprisings in Slovakia, on that night, caused entire cities such as Zlate, Moravce, Pezinok and Trnava, etc., to be literally occupied.

In Orechow a truck halted in front of the town, soldiers jumped out of it, and secretly they occupied the houses located around the monasteries. Only afterwards did the trucks come which took the monks away.

At Hodonocice, near Frudek, a great number of citizens came to defend the monks. From the crowd there rose shouts: "Shame on you! You are taking away our priests! Is this the way a Czech treats his fellow-citizens! Not even the Gestapo practiced such barbarisms!" From the monastery, the police were heard to reply: "You shout this way because you are in the dark! And immediately a reflector was flashed on the crowd. Those who continued to shout were pointed out, seized and themselves loaded on the trucks and taken away.

In many localities, the people in the morning saw machine guns posted in the windows of the cloisters to prevent indignant citizens from giving vent to any form of protest.

In the face of public opinion which was disturbed and indignant over the suppression of so many monasteries and the arrest of so many of their members (it is thought that on the night between April 13–14 and in the successive nights of April 28 and May 5, 1950, about 7,000 members of religious orders were forcibly removed) the Communist press, at first, tried to minimize the facts, speaking not of "suppression" but of the "reduction" of a certain number of monasteries, and by stating that the monks had not been "concentrated" but "assembled" in more adequate monasteries where "they would be better able to complete their religious training and revive the genuine spirit of monasticism!"

In this regard the most salient passages of an article which appeared in n. 6 of the "Vestnik Katol Duchor," May 20, 1950, are reported here:

> . . . What is actually going on? In our region we have about 20 male monasteries or, better said, buildings almost empty.
>
> As the trial against the 10 monks has shown, who for the most part were ecclesiastical dignitaries, *the monasteries had become in recent times nests of subversive action against the State*. . . . There was the danger that even the other members of these Orders, knowingly or unknowingly, seduced by their Superiors might, even against their will, come into conflict with the law.
>
> Therefore the monks have been concentrated in larger and more suitable monasteries. This concentration has been carried out in such a way that the inner life, required by the rules, be affected as little as possible . . . The greatest possible scope is giving to those so concentrated to fulfill their religious duties and to develop their productive capacities

in circumstances much better than in the monasteries, often badly administered.

In truth the time of monasteries has passed: little by little even their social function has ceased.

We are doing what the spirit of the times, progress and the interest of working people demand. Our Constitution of May 9, 1948, in its Articles 15–17, assures the freedom of religion, the equality of the rights of the various confessions, religious tolerance: all the provisions that we have taken attest that this freedom is assured against any interference by other ecclesiastical bodies existing beyond the frontiers, and who have nothing in common with our country and with our people, and who, in substance, are against the people and enemies of its just aspirations. . . .

HARSH TREATMENT OF MONKS

There are, this regard, many depositions and much testimony from which it emerges clearly:

1) That the few convents selected as places of "concentration" were in reality veritable prisons, with guards at entrances, in the cloisters, in the corridors, everywhere, so as to prevent any communications whatsoever with the outside.

   Such convents at first were established in Zeliv (in eastern Bohemia, for all the Superiors of religious orders; in Bohuso-dow (in northern Bohemia for Jesuits and Franciscans; in Broumov (in northeast Bohemia for Capucins, Dominicans, the Premonstratensi, etc.); in Karliky (in eastern Bohemia where Redemptorists were detained; in Osek and in Hejnice, where the police interned the Salesians, the Piarists, the Agostinians, etc.

   Later the so-called convents were further reduced and their members scattered here and there.

2) That all the monks, dressed like convicts and marked with a number were assigned to the most varied tasks, divided into groups, each one of which was watched over by an armed guard who prevented any contact with civilians.

It also emerges clearly that not a few monks were assigned to work in the Yachymov mines where Czechoslovaks work under Soviet control. Of others it was said that they were seen in sealed trains, crossing eastern Czechoslovakia, bound undoubtedly for Russia.

3) That all the monks were subjected to a "re-education" through the obligation imposed on them of attending classes in Marxism-Leninism, taught by "cultural reporters." It is difficult to say what a torment it must have been for these scholarly men, among whom were many specialists in philosophy, theology and law, to have to attend such classes taught in the main by plain workers. From a moral point of view, this obligation, even more than the work, constituted the greater pain and torment.

4) That the younger monks and the novices were in the main drafted into the army, at the beginning of September 1950, or either they were incorporated in the so-called "voluntary labor brigades," and subjected to all manner of seductions to induce them to leave the religious life.

5) That psysical and moral mistreatment was so prevalent that many had to be taken to Opocno, a convent reserved for the aged and the ill, and more than one died there.

A convent at Zeliv was reserved for the most stubborn and those defined as "dangerous," in which the Superiors of various convents had already been concentrated, and there they were subjected to even harsher treatment.

Equally brutal was the treatment accorded to nuns. Even for them, as for the monks, the stormy invasions of their houses had begun between May and June 1950, climaxing in the following September with the complete closing of all the feminine religious houses, including those dedicated to the works for which they were founded, such as hospitals, clinics, shelters and orphanages.

With a notice of only a few days and sometimes of only a few hours, the nuns were removed from their convents and transported just like the monks to "convents of concentration" and permitted to take only the most necessary things with them.

The deportation drive, concluded about the end of October, effected about 1,500 nuns, sparing temporarily the nuns attached to hospitals, until the lay nurses designated to take their places are ready.

German nuns, who had not yet been able to leave the country and who numbered about one hundred, were expelled from their houses and shipped to Germany.

NEW ATTEMPTS TO FORM A "NATIONAL CATHOLIC CHURCH"

After isolating the Bishops, and eliminating the monks, and interning or imprisoning the principal exponents of the clergy, the Czechoslovak Communist Government believed that now was the easiest time to realize the formation of a "Czechoslovak National Catholic Church" depending directly on the regime.

At the end of June 1950, the government directors of the so-called "Catholic Action" began to send out notices to priests inviting them to participate in "Diocesan conferences" in which new plenipotentiary delegates would be elected for a "National Ecclesiastical Synod," which would have the sanction of the people, and which would convene during the annual pilgrimage to Velehrad, on the occasion of the feast of St. Cyril and St. Metodio.

Minister Plojhar himself, in a speech delivered at Brno on June 30, 1950, made the purposes of the meeting even more specific, by declaring:

. . . It would be well if the ecclesiastic dignitaries were elected from the ranks of priests who are close to the working people and not from the scholars and theologians who are far from practical life. The two next meetings (Luhacovice and Velehrad) will have as their aim the solution of the present ecclesiastic situation in Czechoslovakia. . . .

Others spoke even more openly and said:

. . . If the action undertaken by the Government does not move the Bishops to establish an understanding with the State, we ourselves shall consecrate the Bishops. It is high time that we definitively resolve the religious question once and forever. . . .

Since the true intentions of the Government were thus unveiled, the priests hastened to put the faithful on guard and to urge them not to participate in the afore-mentioned meetings.

Aware that their course of action had been exposed, the Communists, unable to postpone the already scheduled meetings, tried to camouflage them by transforming the heralded "national synod" of Luhacovice into the "Interconfessional Conference for Peace," and the pilgrimage to Velehrad into a "Popular Manifestation for Peace."

At the Luhacovice meeting the Catholics were represented only by excommunicated priests like Plojhar, Horak, Dechet, etc., while the greater part of the ecclesiastics was formed by representatives of the different a-catholic confessions: the Russian metropolitan, Nikolaj, the Dean of Canterbury, Johnson, the Bishop of the "national Czechoslovak church," Novak, and the delegates of Hungary, Bulgaria, Roumania, Australia, etc.

Long speeches were made and at the end a "Resolution" voted by which it was made clear that rather than as a meeting of ecclesiastics, it could have been well-described as "a political meeting in favor of a Russian peace and Communism."

Here, for the purpose of documentation, is the text of the long "Resolution" approved and undersigned at that meeting:

> . . . We, the clergy of all the Christian Churches and religious associations in Czechoslovakia, assembled at the conferences for peace in Luhacovice, unanimously proclaim that we place ourselves fully at the service of peace and on the side of those who in the spirit of socialism are building a new, socially just, world order.
>
> We are Christians, we are bearers of the Christian doctrine of love and peace and therefore we are for peace. Therefore, we give our adherence to the great campaign for peace.
>
> We are convinced that we shall best serve the idea of peace if we help, in conformity with the Divine will, in all

our sacerdotal ministry, the efforts of our working people in the building of socialism the victory of which is also a pledge of an enduring peace among nations.

Christianity and socialism are not mutually exclusive tendencies, but which in their mutual exchange can create ideal conditions of life on earth and the presuppositions for a happy life in eternity for those who will do good in this life and who will realize the standards of justice and love, common to Christianity and to Socialism.

At the meeting in Velehrad, the Government took all measures to see that there was a mass participation of Catholics and that the meeting should assume a plebiscitary character.

Propaganda leaflets were dropped from airplanes, extraordinary reductions, of 70%, were made on railroad tickets, free trips offered to priests and a prize of 80 crowns, threats against those who would not accept, etc.

The Communist press reported that there were about 140,000 faithful and 453 priests present. But the truth is otherwise. No more than 30 to 40,000 persons went to Velehrad and there were 132 priests, of whom 45 were Orthodox, 20 from the Czechoslovak Church, 20 from the Evangelical Church and other confessions. There were just a few "progressives," and very few indeed.

Even at Velehrad, after a long series of speeches among which one by the Minister Fierlinger was particularly important because of its anti-Catholic tone, a "Resolution," similar to the one made at the Luhacovice meeting, was presented for approval to those present.

NATIONALIZATION OF SEMINARIES AND THEOLOGICAL SCHOOLS ABOLISHED

On July 14, 1950, a few days after the progressive manifestation of Velehrad, the Ministry of Instruction emanated a Decree for the re-organization of the Seminary and the study of theology, as a complement to an analogous decree emanated on June 3, 1949 and of another provision of April 25, 1949.

Not only were the minor Seminaries (gymnasia and *lycées*)

already abolished by a prior decree, declared definitively closed by this new decree, but the following as well: (*a*) all Diocesan theological Seminaries, and those conducted by religious Orders; and (*b*) the theological faculty of Olomouc and all Catholic Learned Societies.

Instead the only theological faculties officially recognized were the "nationalized" ones of Prague and Bratislava. (Art. 1.)

At these faculties the education of students, says the decree "will be carried out through the care of the State and the Church in the spirit of popular democracy and of ecclesiastical principles." (Art. 4.)

ARTICLE 5. The deacon and the proto-deacon are to be appointed by the State office for Church Affairs which will also emanate the statutes relative to the organization, administration and direction of the two faculties.

ARTICLE 6. The courses will be for four years and the program of studies will include: a) in the first two years, the study of the ethical-social sciences (Marxism-Leninism) b) in the last two years, the study of a non-reactionary theology, which really helps the interests of the people.

ARTICLE 9. Access to study is not free to all, but subordinated to the needs of the Church; studies, examinations, statutes, will be regulated by the State Office, which will also establish the requirements for the acceptance of candidates.

ARTICLE 11. The State will take care of the students, not only in a social and hygienic sense, but also at a cultural and moral level, so that all will prepare to become patriotic priests. It will be the concern of the State Office also to draw up the prescriptions regarding the rights and the obligations of the students.

ARTICLE 12. The appointment or the removal of professors and instructors is the exclusive competence of the State Office, on which their specific stipends will exclusively depend."

With this act it was clear how the Communist Czechoslovak Government had violated one of the most delicate of religious freedoms, which is that right which every society has to select, to train and to educate those who must be put under its direction.

TRIAL OF BISHOP MONS. ZELA AND EIGHT OTHERS
(NOVEMBER–DECEMBER 1950)

On November 27, 1950, a great trial was staged before the People's Tribunal of Prague against Mons. Stanislas Zela, auxiliary Bishop and vicar general of Olomouc, and against eight other church dignitaries.

The trial lasted seven days and unfolded in accordance with the technique and the stage direction by now become familiar in similar trials. In fact a pamphlet was published entitled, "The Trial against Vatican agents in Czechoslovakia" covering all the phases of the trial, including the stenographically recorded replies of the accused and the charge sheet as prepared by the legal expert, Dr. Hobza.

The charges ranged from espionage to high treason, from illegal activity to political plotting, and from fraud to collaboration with the German Gestapo. The depositions of the accused, as reported in the afore-mentioned pamphlet, far from denying such charges tend, instead, to aggravate them, by adding more details about persons and citing even more damning circumstances. They acknowledge everything, admit all, so much so, that they feel compelled to make public repentance of everything, as if they were happy to be able to atone for their "activity against the people."

That such depositions were made by persons who were not free can be deduced, in addition to other arguments, with certainty from the fact that the accused formulated their own depositions according to communist terminology. It is absolutely impossible that a priest can speak so freely in this manner, without a long training, and especially before a court! Accustomed as he is to use his own terminology, it is hardly possible, that to express himself he use phrases, expressions, and terms, which are used only in especially prepared Communist "agit-prop" material.

Moreover, the accused, as they formulated their depositions, seemed like persons who were reciting special roles by memory. This was even noticed by those who listened to the radio broadcast of the proceedings.

It was also felt that they were persons unsure of themselves, repeating precedent words like ill-prepared school boys, awaiting the cue of the prompter, and frequently stuttering.

Insofar as regards the specific charges made against them, it is easy to observe that although the charges were grave they were also generic. They were the "archtypical accusation" of the Communists who, unwilling to exhibit their direct intention of persecuting the Church and of exterminating the Catholic clergy, camouflaged their activity by charges of treason, espionage, illegal activity, capitalist interests, revolutionary plots, etc.

Even the charge of collaboration with the German Gestapo was entirely baseless; it is enough to remember that such charges were made against Mons. Zela, the Canon Svec, and the priest Mandl, all of whom, during the German occupation, were actually the victims of Nazi barbarism. But there were other reasons. They knew too much about the Communists and the "patriotic" struggle for liberation which had been conducted by them, and they remembered the names of too many true patriots turned over to the Nazi Gestapo by the Communists, only because they did not share their views! It was, therefore, necessary to silence these voices and to accuse them of the very crimes which could be hurled against the accusers.

The trial begun, as has been said, on November 27, 1950, ended on December 2 with very harsh sentences: one to the penitentiary, two to 25 years in jail, two to 20 and the others to 18, 17, 15 and 10 years in jail, without taking into account the astronomical amount of the fines imposed and the deprivation of all civil rights.

TRIALS OF THREE BISHOPS AND MANY PRIESTS AND MONKS
(JANUARY–FEBRUARY 1951)

On January 10, 1951, less than a month after the first trial, another trial took place, this time in Bratislava. It was less important because of the small number of the accused, but much more significant because the accused were all Bishops. They were:

a) Mons. John Vojtassak, an aged man of 73, Bishop of Spis.
b) Mons. Peter Paul Gojdic, 63, Bishop of Preseov.
c) Mons. Michael Buzalka, 65, auxiliary Bishop of Trnava.

They had been arrested in the autumn of 1950, and their trial began, as has been said, on January 10, 1951, with the reading of a very long charge sheet by the State prosecutor.

The stenographic proceedings of this trial were also published in book form and widely circulated in and outside Czechoslovakia, under the title 'Le Procès des trois Evèques Felons: Vojtassak, Buzalka et Gojdic," Prague. Published under the imprint of the Ministry of Information and Popular Culture, this report, issued in 1951, numbered 248 pages.

Here, too, the depositions of the accused were revealed to be of a surprising gravity, the more strange and unheard of when it is borne in mind that they were made by three venerable Bishops. Whatever had been legitimate in their conduct, and that which had been most sublime in their sacerdotal mission, was disowned and denigrated by them. Often they confessed even to their own intentions, presenting them in the most sinister light, and adding the most unfavorable motivations to them. And they not only renounced any self-defense but went so far as to accuse themselves. From their lips there flowed an alternate series of abject self-denunciations, unworthy of men of honor, and the grossest lies, which sometimes were neither suggested by the judge, nor relevant to the context of what they were saying.

There was not a syllable about their great pastoral solicitude, but only a nauseating insistence on the theme that the material interests of the high clergy had been the mainspring of their activity and that of the Holy See. All this demonstrated and revealed the biggest crime committed by the Communists, namely, that of imposing a new soul upon the accused, of imposing words on the lips of their victims with which they boasted of their iniquitous prowess.

Equally painful was the selection of witnesses, all of whom, without exception, were on the side of the prosecution. They had been picked among the most fanatical Communists or rebel priests. Even those priests who had enjoyed the best possible relations with the Bishops, and some who had been helped most generously, took the stand as accusers.

The attitude of the defense counsel was downright nauseating. The counsel assigned to Mons. Vojtassak began by disclosing that the crimes listed in the charge sheet had been fully admitted in the confessions of the Bishop, by the depositions of the Bishops, as accomplices, and by other documents produced in the course of the hearings. Following this the defense counsel discharged his obligations by requesting that extenuating circumstances be taken into account. No less cowardly and summary was the defense of the other two Bishops, Buzalka and Gojdic, whose attorney could find nothing better to say than the following:

> . . . In a trial such as this, in which the prosecutor has been able to amass such a quantity of proofs and where it has been possible to document the guilt of the accused so exhaustively . . . defense is difficult. . . . I can only say that . . . the death penalty would be too severe. . . .

The trial ended on January 15 and the sentences handed down were most severe: for Mons. Vojtassak, 24 years imprisonment, a fine of 500,000 crowns, confiscation of his property, and loss of all civil rights; for Mons. Gojdic and Mons. Buzalka, the penitentiary, a fine of 200,000 crowns, confiscation of their properties, and loss of civil rights.

Two other trials followed soon after in the early part of February 1951; in the one four distinguished ecclesiastics were sentenced respectively to 20, 13, 12 and 11 years in jail; in the other, the second secretary of Mons. Beran to 13 years, and the secretaries of the Bishops of Hradec Kralove and Olomouc, including the prior of a monastery, to 12 years, and other priests from 11 to 3 years.

ATTEMPTS TO ESTABLISH A NEW HIERARCHY

Become aware of the futility of outside attempts to induce the Catholic Church to break off its relations with Rome, the Communist regime—even because of the deep repercussions which the results of the trials of the four Catholic Bishops had had in and outside Czechoslovakia—decided to change its tactics. Now the Church was to be attacked from within, aiming at the systematic substitution of its hierarchical bodies by elements who were more loyal, or at least more accommodating, to the regime.

As the first act in this maneuver it decided to gradually take over the Dioceses, making its first substitutions with the "Vicars General." Having learned from the Code of Canon Law that seats declared to be "Impeded" because of the forced absence of the Bishop (prison, internment, exile or incompetence) are to be administered by Vicars General who, as regards jurisdiction, were to assume the full power of the Bishops, the government immediately proceeded to appoint new titular heads, compelling the old ones to resign, or arresting them if they resisted. This was done through the State Office for Church Affairs even though there had been no deaths among the Vicars General then in charge, and without even waiting for any of them to renounce their posts voluntarily.

The second act of this maneuver went even further. Learning from the same Canon law that when a seat is "vacant," on account of death, transfer or the release of a Bishop, it is to be administered by a "Capitular Vicar" until the appointment of a new titular head, the Communist regime, after having arrogated to itself the right of naming vicars general to the "impeded" seats, wanted to exert its authority even in the appointment of capitular vicars. It removed this privilege from the cathedral chapter head, and delegated it to a "college of diocesan consultants," already chosen by the Government among priests who were more "democratic" and loyal to the regime.

It was thus that the Government, in a short time, was able to have trusted elements in positions of authority in the various

Dioceses. In fact the Bishops who at first had denied their approval to these appointments, later had to suffer them, if only to avoid a jurisdictional dualism which would have seriously harmed the proper administration of the Dioceses. And the new "Vicars General" installed themselves in the *curie,* acting as substitute for, or taking over completely, the authority of the Ordinant of the locale.

Thus there was formed a "new schismatic hierarchy," shorn of an episcopal character and placed under the direct dependency of the State Office for Church Affairs.

On February 15, 1951 the first meeting of this "pseudo-hierarchy" took place in Prague, in the presence of the Minister Fierlinger, successor to Cepicka as head of the State Office for Church Affairs. According to a broadcast over Radio Prague, the assembly was supposed to have asked that "committees" be established in all the Bishopric *curie,* composed of truly "democratic" priests, to which the administration of the Dioceses should be entrusted, thereby bringing into being a kind of Diocesan Soviet.

A few days later, on March 3, 1951, there took place the appointment and the "installation" of the new chapter canons of the Cathedral of Saint Guido in Prague. They were assigned the task of electing a "Capitular Vicar" to the archbishopric seat of Prague as a substitute for Mons. Beran who, on that same date, was declared "suspended" from the "competent administrative bodies," with the following comment broadcast by Radio Prague: ". . . The competent authorities have levied a fine upon Mons. Beran, Archbishop of Prague, because of his negative attitude towards the Church laws; the same authorities have assigned him to a residence located outside the borders of the Diocese of Prague . . ."

On the same date, the same Czech radio station, announced that the canon, A. Stehlik, had been unanimously elected to the post of "Capitular Vicar" of the "vacant" archdiocese. He had been one of the canons installed by Government order a few days before and as his first act he removed the penalty of "suspension" against Mons. Plojhar.

In order to compound the confusion that such government provisions generated within the Catholic Church, Radio Prague two days later, on March 12, 1951, broadcast another communication which announced the "oath of four Bishops," who in contrast to the attitude maintained until then, had allegedly sworn their loyalty to the regime.

Among these four Bishops, according to the information released by Radio Prague, were: Mons. Maurice Picha, Bishop of Hradec Kralove and deacon of the Czechoslovak Episcopate. He was 82 years of age; Mons. Stefan Trochta, Bishop of Litomerice; Mons. Ambrose Lazik, Apostolic Administrator of Trnava, and Mons. Joseph Csarsky, Apostolic Administrator of Kosice.

In addition, according to the announcements of the same radio station, one of these Bishops (Mons. Csarsky) was supposed to have made the following declaration:

> We declare our acceptance of the new Church laws approved by the Assembly in October 1949 and to provide for their publication. . . .
>
> We further declare that we do not recognize the Church sanctions and that we will never proceed to the application of these same sanctions against ecclesiastics or laymen, when they are imposed for merely political reasons.

THE HOLY SEE CONDEMNS THE NEW HIERARCHY

The Holy See intervened at a most opportune time in order to dissipate the confusion engendered over the real situation of the Catholic Church in Czechoslovakia. On May 17, 1951, the Holy Concistoral Congregation issued a decree in which, after a brief summary of the most recent events and acts which had taken place in which the rights of the Church had been seriously violated, it reminded those who had committed such acts of the penalties involved.

Here is the text of the declaration of the Holy See:

> . . . For several months, in the Republic of Czechoslovakia, the rights of the Church have been violated in a continuous

and unheard of manner, and iniquitous attacks have been made against ecclesiastical persons.

In fact local Bishops and Ordinants have often been prevented from carrying out their functions and their pastoral rights have been usurped. The very seats of the Curie and of the Bishopric offices have been distributed to intruders, at the pleasure of laymen who have dared to interfere in the administration of the Dioceses.

Moreover, many priests and many monks have been imprisoned and there has occurred the insolent sacrilege of dragging some Bishops before judges and putting them in chains.

More recently, also, the Archbishop of Prague, Mons. Joseph Beran, who already for a long time had been held as a prisoner in his bishopric residence and completely deprived of the exercise of his jurisdiction, has been unjustly deported outside his seat and his archdiocese.

The authors of these misdeeds are hereby made aware of the various canons which effect all of them with excommunication, reserved simply and in a special way to the Holy See, according to the diversity of the cases:

a) To those who brought a Bishop before a civil judge (Canon 2341).

b) To those who violently threaten the person of an Archbishop or Bishop (Canon 2343, par. 3).

c) To those who directly or indirectly impede the exercise of ecclesiastical jurisdiction, having recourse for this to any civil authority whatsoever (Canon 2334, n. 2).

d) Those who oppose the legitimate church authorities or who seek in any manner to destroy their power (See decree of the Holy Congregation of the Council, June 29, 1950, Acta Apost. Sedis. Vol. XXXII, 1950, p. 601).

e) Those who take over an ecclesiastical office or a benefit or a dignity, without having received investiture or a canonic authorization, according to the rules of the sacred canons, or who allow themselves to be investitured illegally, or who continue to keep such offices, etc. (Ibidem).

As a consequence the Holy Concistorial Congregation declares that all those who have physically or morally participated in the execution of the above-mentioned crimes, or who have been their accomplices (Can. 2209, par. 1-3), are guilty of the above-mentioned excommunications and shall remain so effected until they have received absolution from the Holy See.

Issued in Rome, Offices of the Holy Concistoral Congregation, March 17, 1951.

FR. A. J. CARDINAL PIAZZA, *Secretary*

P. FERRETTO, *Assessor*

As was natural, the publication of this document provoked a very strong reaction on the part of the Communist regime which tried in every way to keep the masses of faithful in ignorance of it. But the Bishops, nonetheless, succeeded in getting it to a great part of the clergy and they took advantage of this situation the better to clarify the situation which had been made more confusing than ever by the contradictory news broadcast over the Communist radio station.

Here are some passages from the secret letter sent on this occasion to the priests:

... Do not be shaken if you hear news of proclamations or of events which are attributed to personalities from you would never expect similar behaviour. In view of the present situation it is never possible to be sure about the truth of statements made in Communist propaganda. But even if the event corresponds to reality, it must be remembered that it can be the consequence of physical or moral constriction, or of another kind, which limit one's responsibility for his own acts. . . .

It is necessary to be alert and not let yourself be deflected from the true path, nor let yourself be deceived, especially if you are forced to listen to the voice of anti-Catholic propaganda.

Such a declaration also explained the attitude of the Bishops who had taken the loyalty oath.

From other sources, in fact, it became known that the oath had been extorted from them, with the threat that if they did not do so, the greater part of the clergy would be interned. It is also known that they were segregated for long periods and submitted to "special treatments."

RECENT DEVELOPMENTS (JUNE 1951–JUNE 1952)

In the period between June 1951 and June 1952 the plan followed by the Communists, of unhinging the joints of the Church from the inside by replacing its organizational structure with a clergy disposed, from conviction or fear, to support the Communist regime, registered new and more serious manifestations.

On June 16, 1951, Minister Fierlinger convoked a meeting of all the Vicar Generals and the new government canons in the State Office for Church Affairs. Present at the meeting were: Mons. Plojher, Mons. Oliva, director of "Caritas," Mons. Eltsckener, auxiliary Bishop of Prague, Mons. Stehlik, Capitular Vicar of Prague, Mons. Onderek, Administrator of the Czechs of the diocese of Breslavia, Mons. Dechet, Capitular Vicar of Banska Bystrica, and Mons. Buchta, Vicar General of Ceske Budejovice.

The main subject discussed at this meeting concerned the recruitment of seminarists for the two government theological seminaries at Prague and Bratislava. The Government, worried by the almost total desertion of the seminarists from the two government seminaries put pressure on the new hierarchy to proceed to a virtual draft. In Prague, out of a total of 700 students who previously were registered with the theological faculty, only 50 had appeared, and in Bratislava, less than 30 had shown up, where formerly 160 seminarists had been registered and in which region there were about 400 theologians. The preoccupation of the Government lay in the fact that it wanted to make use of the two government seminaries in order to prepare "democratic and patriotic" priests, with whom to substitute, without arousing alarm, the more stubborn priests.

In this manner it could achieve the realization of a Church at the service of the regime.

At the same meeting it was made obligatory for all parish offices to subscribe to and to pledge themselves to the distribution, in proportion to the size of the parishes, of the following newspapers:

a) "Vestnik Katolickeko Dukovenstva" (organ of the State Office for Church Affairs).

b) "Katolicke Noviny" (organ of the schismatic Catholic Action).

c) "Zemedelske Noviny" (farm journal to propagandize collective farms).

d) "Mir" (monthly organ of the partisans of peace).

During the summer of 1951 a definitive liquidation of convents, religious houses, schools and other buildings took place which were turned over to government uses.

Here are some examples:

a) The Benedictine abbacy of Prague-Brenov was transformed into a school for the SNB, the State Security Body.

b) The Jesuit college of Litomerice was transformed into an army barracks.

c) In Bratislava, the Jesuit monastery was made into a conservatory of music; the convent of the Daughters of the Saviour was requisitioned for communal and state offices; and the SNB installed itself in the Salesian monastery.

d) In Trnava, the Salesian monastery was occupied by military offices while the Labor Exchange installed itself in that of the Jesuits.

e) In Nitra, the Franciscan monastery is now the administrative headquarters of the nationalized chemical trust, "Chemodroga." The little Seminary has been enlarged to become a hotel for bus drivers, and the Mission House has been altered into a hostelry for Communist youth.

f) In Rusomberok, the Chapel of the Jesuit monastery was transformed into a gymnasium and that of the Franciscans in Kremnice into a movie theatre.

Even all the libraries of the monasteries have been liquidated. In regard to this herewith is an excerpt from a most interesting circular Dr. Suchanek, one of the directors of the nationalized enterprise for the collection of raw materials, sent to his provincial subordinates:

> . . . The State Office for Religious Affairs is in the process of liquidating the monastery libraries through the national district Committees.
>
> We have been informed that in some cases the delegates of the State Office for Religious Affairs consign these books from the liquidated libraries directly to district purchasing agencies. Among the consigned material there is a high percentage of books which we can sell in the foreign market.
>
> We request, therefore, that the district purchasing agencies no longer accept books from monastery libraries and that, through you, such cases be brought to our attention. We ourselves will take the books in order to classify them scientifically.
>
> Further we wish to make known that our intervention has been requested by the delegate for the utilization of books attached to the Ministry of Information and Popular Culture in Prague.
>
> In your communication, indicate the whereabouts of the books, the quantity, and the name of the person charged with the liquidation. . . .
>
> Long live the Five Year Plan!

At the end of September 1951, on the occasion of the feast-day of the national patron, Saint Venceslao, a big state meeting of the Catholic clergy for peace was called in Prague.

The purpose of this meeting was to show to the Government and to public opinion that in Czechoslovakia there really did exist a strong group of "democratic-patriotic" priests. So naturally nothing was neglected in seeing to it that the greatest number of priests participated.

The Vice-President of the Council, Zdenek Fierlinger, head

of the State Office for Church Affairs, and who had been bitterly criticized by the Party leadership because of his failure to date to break the opposition of the clergy and the faithful to the regime, had decided to have this meeting make up for the failures of the past. He had seen to it beforehand that no less than 1500 priests were to participate in this meeting, and each Diocese had been taxed with a specific number of priests who were forced to attend.

In reality, however, the meeting marked another disappointment and Minister Fierlinger had to register another failure which he explained in his inaugural address of September 27 by saying that those present though few, "represented as delegates the entire remaining clergy which could not attend although it had a great desire to do so . . ."

The final act of religious persecution against the Catholic Church in Czechoslovakia was carried out on March 28, 1952, with the deportation of the Bishop of Ceske Budejovice, Mons. Joseph Hlouch.

In making the announcement Radio Prague specified that "a stay outside the Diocese has been fixed for him because of his hostile attitude towards the church laws and the democratic-people's state . . ."

The same Radio, on March 31, 1952, gave out the news that the chapter of Ceske Budejovice had elected Joseph Buchta as Capitular Vicar, whom the Communists had imposed as Vicar General in 1950.

Nor is the persecution over.

A big trial is foreseen for the Archbishop of Prague, Mons. Beran, and perhaps, also for Mons. Hlouch and other courageous Bishops, before the People's Court.

But the strongest persecution is that which the Communists are carrying on within the Church itself. At the present time the greatest number of priests live in isolation. They no longer know just how to recognize who are their superiors, nor can they discern just what may be their authentic dispositions and instructions. They are continually assailed by so-called "religious reporters" who with a tenacious and exasperating insistence are ever on the offensive, alternating threats with promises, in order to break down their resistance little by little.

The disorder naturally has repercussions among the people who no longer know whom to believe, and no longer know whether in the priest who presents himself, they are to see an ex-communicant, a weakling, or a faithful pastor!

And this very disorientation desired by the Communists, constitutes, indeed, the most serious and deleterious persecution against the Church.

CHAPTER VI

Albania, 1944–1952

THE SITUATION BEFORE 1944

The Catholic Church in Albania, even though it had a restricted number of faithful (about 124,000 out of a population of about 1,110,000 inhabitants, of whom 730,000 were Moslems and 220,000 Orthodox) had been making a notable progress during the past fifty years. In fact, before the coming to power of the Communist regime in Albania, in 1944, the Church represented one of the most active and constructive forces in the social and cultural life of the country.

Hierarchically it was divided as follows:

a) Two Archdioceses, in Durazzo and Scutrai.
b) Three Dioceses: Pulati (seat in Koder Shen Gjerg); Sappa (seat in Nenshati); Alessio (seat in Calmeit).
c) One "nullius" Abbacy: St. Alexander of Oroshi (Kashnieti).
d) One Apostolic Administration: Southern Albania.

From a statistical point of view, the ecclesiastical divisions listed above were broken down as follows:

	Catholics	Parishes	Priests	Members of Religious Orders
Durazzo	28,750	21	13	15
Scutari	31,150	31	29	35
Pulati	15,700	16	5	13
Sappa	16,850	20	17	9
Alessio	12,650	15	9	5
St. Alexander of Oroshi	14,500	17	13	2
Southern Albania	4,400	11	7	15
Totals	124,000	131	93	94

These Catholics of the Latin rite had only recently been increased by small groups of Catholics of the Eastern rite, directed by about ten priests and monks of the same rite, who had opened several Churches or chapels at Elbasani, Korcia, Vlora (Valona), Titana, and Argirocastro, and several missions at Lushnja, Berat, Fieri, Dhrimades, Vuno and Pogradec.

There were many Religious Houses and Institutions, both male and female, which dedicated themselves to welfare and educational activity: shelters, schools, hospitals, orphanages, etc.:

a) Male Institutions

1) The Franciscans who over fifty years ago had established a very well-attended elementary School and a reknown Gymnasium-Lycée in Scutari. Next to it was a printing plant where two widely-circulated periodicals were published: "Hylli i drites" (Morning Star), and "Zani i shna ndout" (The Voice of St. Anthony). There were in all 52 Fathers, by now all Albanians, of whom 27 resided in Scutari, while the rest were scattered in the various parishes and religious houses of northern Albania, caring for souls.

2) The Jesuits, who had arrived in Albania in 1848, had opened their house at Scutari. They had assumed the direction of the Pontifical Seminary for the secular clergy, to which was annexed a middle school, a *lycée* and a theological faculty. They had also established a well-equipped printing plant where by 1944 almost 700 publications were printed, of which more than 450 were in the Albanian language, without counting the two monthly reviews, "Laimtari i Zemres se Krishtit" (The Messenger of the Sacred Heart), and "Leka."

In all there were 25 priests of whom nine were Albanians and the rest Italian. In addition to a house in Scutari, they had another one in the capital city of Titana, to which was annexed a Church.

3) The "Sons of Don Orione" who had established a boy's orphanage in Scutari, the first one in Albania, which could accommodate about 50 children. In all they were about 5 priests, assisted by several lay monks.

b) Female Religious Institutions

1) The Stigmate, with 48 nuns, Albanians in the main, who had opened a Lower Magistral School in Scutari with 76 pupils, three elementary schools in Shiroka, Nenshati and Daici, as well as other work schools and shelters.

2) The "Servite," with 27 Nuns, almost all Albanians, who operated various shelters and work schools, in addition to an elementary school in Tirana.

3) The "Salesians," with ten nuns, who operated an orphanage for girls in Scutari with about 40 girls, and who also assisted in the local hospital in Tirana.

4) The "Handmaidens of Charity" of Brescia, with about 71 Italian nuns and 5 Albanians, operated a maternity house in Tirana, an elementary school in Kallmeti, and who also assisted in the hospitals of Scutari, Durazzo and Tirana.

5) The "Daughters of Charity," a Jugoslav congregation, with 6 nuns, who directed two shelters and a work school.

In addition to these Institutions and charities whose activities were carried out in northern Albania, other institutions and charitable organizations had been being established even in southern Albania, in recent times, under the direct supervision of the Apostolic Delegate of that time, Mons. Leone G. B. Nigris, who formed a single Apostolic Administration for that vast territory.

Formerly it included more than 4,000 Catholics, with 6 Albanian secular priests, 7 conventual Fathers, 4 Basilians, and 2 Lazzarists, all Italian.

In addition there were about seventy Sisters, of whom about twenty were Albanians, 13 Basilians of the eastern rite, of Italo-Albanian origin, who assisted in the work of the hospitals of Valona, Argirocastro, Berat, Korcia, or in sanitation or welfare work on behalf of the poor in the shelters and work schools.

This vast complex of institutions and Catholic works was directed by the Albanian Catholic Episcopate, composed exclusively of Bishops of Albanian origin, which supervised the 6 Catholic dioceses of northern Albania, while all of southern Albania was one single ecclessiastical unit, entrusted to the Apostolic Delegate.

The names of the Bishops and Archbishops who were almost all victims of Communist persecution, in 1944 were as follows:

1) *Durazzo:* Mons. Nicholas Vincenzo Prenushi, Archbishop-Metropolitan, born in Scutari, April 9, 1885 (interned).

2) *Scutari:* Mons. Gaspar Thaci, Archbishop-Metropolitan, born in Scutari, January 23, 1889 (died in 1946).

3) *Pulati:* Mons. Berbard Shlaka, Bishop, born in Scutari, June 23, 1875 (interned in his seat).

4) *Sappa:* Mons. George Volaj, Bishop, born in Scutari, September 21, 1904 (shot by Communists on February 3, 1948).

5) *Alessio:* Mons. Francesco Gjini, Bishop of Alessio and Administrator of the Abbocy of St. Alexander, born in Scutari, February 20, 1886 (shot by Communists on March 11, 1948).

6) The Apostolic Delegate and the Apostolic Administrator of northern Albania was His Excellency, Mons. Leone Giovanni Battista Nigris, Titular Archbishop of Filippi.

IMMEDIATE SUPPRESSION OF NEWSPAPERS AND ASSOCIATIONS

The first attacks of the Communist régime against the Catholic Church in Albania only a few days after it took power in November 1944.

This régime had been formed as of May 22, 1944, in Permeti, as "The National Council of Anti-Fascist Liberation," and it had self-declared itself to be invested with legislative and executive powers, by proclaiming the removal of King Ahmed Zogu, and by electing as its head the Communist, Enver Hoxha, and another Communist, Dr. Omer Nishani as his assistant.

On October 22, 1944, this Council assembled in Berat, liberated from the Germans about a week before, and from there it had issued a proclamation guaranteeing to respect all the fundamental rights of man, the freedom of religion, press, and association, etc., and invoking the collaboration of all the other nationalist parties.

It looked as though a new era were about to begin for Albania and even for the Catholic Church, which having suffered much under the Germans and which had also had several priests killed or deported, hoped to be able to resume its activity.

But in November 1944, hardly had the Germans left Tirana and even Scutari a few days later, and Albanian territory become completely free, it was soon seen how the Communists, under the command of Enver Hoxha, had so quickly forgotten their words and the promises made in the proclamation of Berat. In fact no sooner were they installed in Tirana they did not delay in making it quite clear that they would inexorably eliminate whosoever opposed their march.

In the first days of December 1944, the Communists seized the Catholic printing plants in the city of Scutari with the pretext that they were needed for the propaganda of the National Liberation Front. The plants seized belonged to the Jesuits and the Franciscans and the "Scanderbeg" plant, which in the meantime had been compelled to suspend the publication of the two Catholic reviews, "Hylli i Drites" and "Leka," as well as the two popular monthlies, "Zani" and "Laimtari," and the Catholic weekly "Kumbona e se Dielles" (The Sunday Bell). The blow was a serious one because through it the Catholic Church remained suddenly deprived of its entire press, which had cost it so many sacrifices and which constituted the most efficient means of its apostolate.

Having suppressed this voice, a few days later, with equal arbitrariness and swiftness, the Communists trampled upon the right of free association. Without a law, without even a police provision, under the sole charge of being "fascist societies," the various associations of Catholic Action, which had been flowering under the Franciscans, the Jesuits and in the Cathedral of Scutari, were subjected to a violent campaign of intimidations, threats and suspicions. Communist violence was unleashed in a special way against the youth associations, "St. Anthony," St. John Bosco" and "San Prospero," many of whose members were arrested, beaten or deported.

SEARCHES AND ARRESTS IN THE RELIGIOUS HOUSES (DECEMBER 1944–FEBRUARY 1945)

On December 15, 1944, about two hundred partisan Communists blocked the house of the Jesuits in Scutari, and pushing their way inside they began an armed search of the house, looking into every corner and every thing, under the pretext of looking for Germans and fascists, arms and munitions. All they found there was a small amount of material on physics, left there by the Germans, and two cans of kerosene which had been laboriously acquired, quart by quart, for the purpose of domestic illumination. But that was enough to spread rumors that a German General, several officers, a tank, arms of large calibre, munitions and more than thirty cans of gasoline had been found at the Jesuits. The purpose of this grotesque distortion was none other than to direct the hatred of the people against the Jesuits, in order to prepare the atmosphere for their suppression more easily.

At the end of January 1945 General Mehmet Shehu, a former

fighter in Spain, took over the command of Scutari. Following a violent speech against "the reaction" headed by several Catholic exponents, he ordered a new and very strict search of the houses of the Jesuits and Franciscans.

So on February 2, 1945, at eight o'clock in the morning, about seven to eight hundred soldiers, armed with machine guns, again blocked the house of the Jesuits and that of the Franciscans. They tore down the ceilings and walls, ripped up the floors, and even uncovered the tombs of the dead. An aged domestic who had not been able to "reveal the secrets of the Jesuits" was barbarously beaten until he bled, while several other lay brothers were deported or submitted to cruel tortures and interrogations. In order to hide the disgrace of unsuccessful house searches, a violent popular demonstration was staged with a deafening chorus of charges, especially hurled against the Jesuit schools which were described as centers of Fascist propaganda, in which the students were incited to sabotage the work of the Government.

The first arrests of Catholic exponents, among them three priests and two Franciscans, began in the first days of March 1945. By the middle of March, the jails of the city of Scutari, which had less than 30,000 inhabitants, already held about a thousand persons. And at the end of the same month, a people's court began to pronounce the first death sentences, and four priests were executed:

1) D. Lazzaro Shantoja, executed on March 19, 1945, on charges of being pro-Italian.

2) D. Andrea Zadeja, executed on March 12, 1945, on the charge of having favored the "Balli Kombetar." He was judged to be the best Albanian poet of modern times. During the trial, held behind closed doors, he declared that he had committed no poetic crime, but that he could not accept Communist ideology.

3) Father Antonio Sarapi, a Franciscan and former member of the nominating Regency after September 8, 1943, shot on April 7, 1945.

4) Father Giovanni Shllku, Franciscan, shot on April 13, 1945, on the charge of having worked for the establishment of an opposition party to the regime.

PERSECUTION OF INSTITUTIONS AND AGENCIES IN NORTHERN ALBANIA
(MARCH–APRIL 1945)

Immediately after the first signs of Communist persecution of the Catholic Church in northern Albania, there began, in March 1945, a struggle of extermination against all Catholic agencies in southern Albania.

In the space of two months (March and April 1945) one by one shelters, schools, hospitals, orphanages, churches, disappeared, so that nothing which was Catholic survived in southern Albania.

In Korcia the "Stigmate" Sisters (all of whom were Albanian, so there could be no pretext based on nationality) were the first to be dismissed from the Orphanage, and compelled to close their infants' shelter, and finally deprived of the house in which they lived.

In Valona and Argirocastro, the eleven "Handmaidens of Charity" were dismissed from the hospital in which they assisted and compelled to repatriate, because they were Italians.

In Elbasan, the shelter was closed and all the nuns, even though they were all Albanians belonging to the order of the "Servite," were compelled to leave the city.

In Berat, the Church was closed, the house taken away from the missionaries, the shelter closed, and the priests and nuns forced to repatriate.

In Lushnja, the nuns were forbidden every activity, including sanitation, and shortly after compelled to leave the country.

In Fieri, the residence of the nuns was occupied, and the priest who directed the Mission arrested, and without trial held in jail for six months, and then repatriated.

In Dhrimades, Vuno and Pogradec, all the work schools and shelters were closed and the nuns forbidden every activity.

The six secular priests, all Albanians, who carried out their ministry in northern Albania, were sent away from the region. Even D. Isaac Petrqui, who had become well-liked in the area because of his charitable activities and whom the population *en masse* had tried to detain, had to leave in order to avoid greater tribulations.

Even the 7 Conventual Fathers, the 4 Basilians and the 2 Lazzarists, who were in the zone, were interned and shortly after compelled to repatriate.

In the face of these events, the Apostolic Delegate, Mons. Nigris could not maintain silence and in fact, by word and in writing, he had not neglected to call the attention of the head of the Government, Enver Hoxha, to them. But his intervention, in addition to obtaining nothing, served instead as pretext to hasten his own expulsion.

EXPULSION OF APOSTOLIC DELEGATE (MAY 24, 1945)

At the end of March 1945, Mons. Nigris, the Apostolic Delegate to Albania, went to Rome, in order to report on the religious situation of the country, as well as to obtain some help on behalf of the population which wallowed in conditions of absolute misery, lacking food and clothing.

His departure had had the approval of the Albanian Government, which in fact had entrusted him with the task of expressing its desire to have a representative at the Holy See. Premier Hoxha had urged him "to pay homage in his name to the Holy Father and to express to him his admiration for the philanthropic activity he was sponsoring." Everything, therefore, gave rise to expectations that, all notwithstanding, relations with the Holy See would be maintained.

Instead on May 21 when the Delegate returned to Albania, his plane having barely landed at the Tirana airport, he received a warning not to leave the airport and to return to Italy by the next plane, since he was not furnished with a permit of the Albanian military mission in Bari.

It was useless for the Delegate to point out that upon his departure from Tirana, the Secretary General of the Ministry of

Foreign Affairs had assured him that no difficulties would have been placed in the way of his return to Albania, even if he did not have the permission of the military mission in Bari. After six hours of exhausting waiting, he had to leave again for Bari.

On the following May 24, armed with a regular permit from the mission in Bari, the Delegate arrived in Tirana. But hardly a quarter of an hour had gone by since he left the airport, when an officer overtook him, and ordered him to follow him with his baggage to the Chief of the General Staff, by whom he was ordered to leave Albania immediately.

The reason adduced was that since the Vatican was a State, the Albanian Government wished to negotiate with it as State to State in order to reach an agreement on the exchange of diplomatic representatives. Afterwards, the Delegate would be able to return.

The Apostolic Delegate insisted then upon being received by the head of the Government, to whom as a matter of fact he had something to communicate regarding this matter desired by the Albanian Government. But the Chief of the General Staff answered him drily, "Nothing can be done, the Government has already decided!"

The Delegate was then taken again to the airport, segregated in a room with an armed partisan at the door, and prevented from communicating with any other person.

After a wait of seven hours, Mons. Nigris, who had been in Albania since 1938, as the representative of the Holy See, was made to leave for Italy without even the shadow of a farewell, expelled as "undesirable" by order of the Albanian Communist Government.

SUPPRESSION OF SCHOOLS, AND CAMPAIGN AGAINST RELIGIOUS ORDERS
(MAY–DECEMBER 1945)

With the expulsion of the Apostolic Delegate, the Albanian Government appeared to want to rid itself of an inopportune witness and to purchase for itself the complicity of silence, so that it could pass on to the second phase of its program of annihilation of the Catholic Church in Albania with impunity.

A sudden order was issued in May which ordered the closing of all infant shelters operated by nuns, and which compelled all teaching personnel in elementary schools to give up their posts to State personnel. Thus, many Communists took over posts in the Jesuit schools of Scutari, who in addition to regular teaching began to give propaganda lectures on materialism.

In the first days of June, a law was promulgated which declared that elementary schools were the exclusive competency of the State and that therefore schools of this kind operated by private persons could not remain in Albania. Thus, all the pupils, already regimented under new Communist teachers, had to transfer to state buildings.

The provision was exclusively directed against Catholic schools because in Albania there were neither elementary grade nor intermediate grade schools in private hands. The law, hence, was an attempt to exclude the Church from the education of youth by depriving it of a cultural heritage which it had laboriously built up in a country in which, when it appeared on the scene, illiteracy was universal; and by removing from its educational influence, freely imparted and freely chosen by the families, hundreds of children who became prey to Communist teaching.

TWO JESUITS SENTENCED TO DEATH (JANUARY–FEBRUARY 1946)

About a month after the sentencing to forced labor of Father Gardin and Father Vata, two other Jesuits, Father Daniel Dajani, an Albanian, Rector of the Pontifical Seminary of Scutari, and the Italian, Father Giovanni Fausti, vice-provincial of the Jesuits, were arrested on the charge of having distributed leaflets against the regime and of having conducted propaganda hostile to it on the occasion of the political elections of December 2, 1945.

In reality the leaflets had been distributed by some of the seminarists who, having been discovered and arrested, took every responsibility upon themselves. They declared that they had done so without the knowledge of the Fathers, and that they had printed the leaflet themselves with an old mimeograph machine which they had found in the attic where they worked on it at night. Despite the torture to which they were submitted, they continued to deny any cooperation with or instigation from the Fathers. That notwithstanding it was determined to place the blame on the Fathers, and on the day after their arrest which had taken place on December 31, 1945, the newspaper "Bashkimi" (Unity), official organ of the Democratic Front, carried the news under large head-lines which presented the Jesuits as "Organizers and directors of the terrorist fascist organization, Albanian Union" . . . adding also that, "that the entire activity of the band directed by the Jesuits had been discovered . . ."

The trial against the Fathers, the seminarists and others held to be accomplices of the Albanian Union, began on January 31, 1946, before a military court, presided by a former elementary school teacher.

The trial lasted almost a month and terminated on February 22 with the reading of the sentences:

a) *Sentenced to death:* the two Jesuit Fathers, Father Shllaku, a Franciscan, and the two seminarists, one of whom had his sentence commuted to 101 years in jail.

b) *Perpetual prison:* three seminarists.

c) *Ten years of forced labor:* another seminarist.

The execution of the death sentence was carried out on the morning of March 4 and together with the three Fathers, about ten prominent Catholics of Scutari and its environs, were also executed.

The names of Father Fausti, Father Dajani and of Father Shllaku, were only the first of a long list of priests and monks who were to prove with their blood the firmness of their Catholic faith and their opposition to every compromise with communist ideology.

EXPULSION OF ITALIAN MISSIONARIES

On January 19, 1946, all Italian missionary monks and nuns residing in Scutari received an order to present themselves to the Police Command, where they were read an order, come from Tirana, to leave Scutari within 24 hours and to proceed to Durazzo by their own means, bringing only personal items with them.

Present when the order was read were the Jesuits, the sons of Don Orion, the Salesian Sisters, and the Servite, among them one who was more than seventy years of age who had come to Albania fifty years before to found a house of her Congregation in Scutari which she now left to nuns, all of whom were Albanians.

On the following day, escorted by an armed guard, the refugees were conducted to Durazzo where they met with other Italian monks and nuns, come from all the other parts of Albania.

In all there were about 80, that is to say, the entire total of Italian missionaries none of whom had come as was falsely announced on November 14, 1945 by Radio Belgrade, citing the Albanian News Agency . . . "during the Italian occupation to serve the army and the people sent from Italy for the colonization . . ." but instead had been in Albania many years before that. The "Handmaidens of Charity" had come to Albania as early as 1924 in the service of Albanian hospitals; the "Salesian Sisters" had been there for forty years, the "Servite" over fifty, the "Sons of Don Orione since 1928, the "Jesuits" since 1848, and the "Franciscans" for more than seven centuries.

After more than a month's waiting, preceded by a repeated and humiliating search of baggage and persons, on February 26, 1946, they boarded a ship which was to bring them back to Italy forever.

Only a few "Handmaidens of Charity" had remained behind in Albania, kept in a state of quasi-internment, in the hospitals in which they had been serving, while waiting for the Communist personnel who were to replace them. Their definitive expulsion took place two years later in the spring of 1948.

EXTERMINATION OF PRIESTS AND CHURCHES
(MARCH–DECEMBER 1946)

Having expelled the Italian monks and nuns, the entire Communist struggle was directed against the Albanian clergy which remained, with the aim of achieving the complete extermination of the Catholic Church in Albania.

On March 6, 1946, the third phase of the persecution began with the military occupation of the Saverian Institute, which was followed by a similar occupation of the Pontifical Seminary of Scutari, whose students were sent home and compelled to give up their clerical vestment. The Fathers and Brothers of the house who, during the night had hid in the Church, were chased out of there on the next day and forced to scatter.

On April 13 came the turns of the "Stigmate" and the "Servite," whose houses were almost completely occupied, save for two rooms in which the nuns were forced to crowd, after everything had been subjected to an inventory.

The clergy and the monks of Scutari were isolated and forbidden to have any contact with the public. The parish priest of the city, D. Micahel Koloqui, who had already been imprisoned once, and released after serving nine months following his declaration of innocence, was again thrown into jail for no reason at all. He was followed shortly after by Father Marcus Harapi, only because he happened to be the brother of Father Antonio, who had been previously sentenced to death and shot on March 4, the Vicar General of Scutari, Mons. Deda, because he had complained of the tortures inflicted on one of his relatives, Father Peter Meshkalla, for having publicly requested aid for the victims of floods which had taken place in those days, D. Stefan Kurti, parish priest of Tirana for having—it would appear—hidden a bottle containing money destined for the maintenance of the needy clergy, Mons. Thomas Laca, who in May 1946, immediately after the death of the Catholic Archbishop of the city, His Excellency, Mons. Gaspar Thaci, had been elected Capitular Vicar, and finally Mons. Franceso Gjini, himself, the Bishop of Alessio, who since October 18, 1945, had been appointed Regent of the Apostolic Delegation by the Holy See.

Meanwhile, in Titana the residence of the Jesuits was occupied in order to change it into a club for anti-fascist Albanian youth, and the foundling hospital operated by the "Servite" was closed and all the nuns put out with only the clothes they were wearing, and the chapel of the military hospital transformed into a ballroom.

On November 17, 1946, the *coup de grace* was also administered to the old house of the Franciscans, who had been in Albania for seven centuries. With the pretext of a house search which allegedly was supposed to have found a certain quantity of arms and munitions, the house was militarily occupied, and the Father Provincial, Matthew Prennushi, and the Fathers Cyprian Nika, Donato Kurti, Paolo Dodaj, and Vittorio Volaj, were arrested. Meanwhile the great square of Tirana was the scene of giant designs and photographs showing the most sensational montages; bundles of rifles hanging from a crucifix, a Franciscan praying with a Cross in one hand and behind him a machine gun and ammunition. And the press claimed that a "black band" had been caught whose aim it had been to unite all the members of the Catholic clergy to assassinate the men in power, in agreement with foreign reactionaries.

The sad balance of this struggle was that at the end of 1946 there already could be counted 32 priests and monks who had been imprisoned under the most varied and fantastic charges, and about 15 priests and monks killed, almost all young and of the best.

THE TRIAL OF TIRANA (APRIL 1947)

With the aim of justifying, in some manner, the chain of arrests and the misconduct against the Catholic Church in Albania before public opinion in and outside the country, the Communist Government felt it necessary to stage a sensational trial against some of the most important exponents of the Catholic clergy.

It was thus that in April 1947, a trial against the "St. Peter" Catholic Youth Association of Scutari was opened before the Revolutionary Tribunal of Tirana, based on charges that the youth group was a "political organization."

The accused were: Father Petro Mechkala, the Jesuit assistant of the organization, who had already been jailed for several months, D. Stefan Kurti, parish priest of Tirana and his adjutant, Rocco Oboti, and Mons. Bonatti, parish priest of Valona. They

were all accused of being "foreign agents" and "in the service of
the Vatican," and in particular they were accused of using the
pretext of seeking relief for flood victims "to carry out espionage
activity and to sabotage the reconstruction work of the present
government."

The reports of the trial, during which according to Albanian
news agency, quoted by "Tass" and the Jugoslav news service
"Tan-Youg" all the accused had acknowledged their errors, were
carried not only in the local Communist press but over the Radio,
especially during the time devoted to a Sunday program known
as "The Happy Hour." And these news and radio reports were
the base of propaganda meetings held throughout Albania.

The trial ended on April 18 with a sentence of twenty years
for D. Stefan Kurti, 15 years for Father Meshkalla, and five years
each for Mons. Bonatti and Rocco Oboti.

This was the last "official" trial against the Catholic clergy in
Albania. After it the clergy was eliminated without even the
pretense of a trial, for in order to justify incarceration or deportation to a concentration camp, or to forced labor, it was enough to
formulate the generic charge of "agent of the Vatican" against
any member of the clergy.

Thus, shortly thereafter, in November 1947, came the arrest
and the internment of Father John Karma, a secular priest who
had remained in northern Albania, together with three other
Albanian priests following the expulsion of the Italian missionaries, and about whom there has been no more news.

Conclusive proof that the struggle waged by the Communists
against the Catholic Church had no other basis save their inability to make the clergy serve Communist ideology was furnished by an interview granted by Premier Enver Hoxha to
several journalists, reported by the newspaper "Bashkimi," on
January 27, 1946, which quoted the Premier as having declared:

. . . Highly placed elements in the ranks of the Catholic
episcopate of Albania, even today dare to justify their collaboration with the enemy by saying, "We would take part in
a national collaboration, if we had not been disoriented by

a series of ideologies which are in total conflict with our
conscience and our moral prinicples. . . ."

In these words, imprudently quoted by the Head of the
Albanian Government, lie the reasons why on the one hand,
Catholic Albanians could not entirely support the regime in their
country, and on the other hand, why the Government had unleashed its war against them.

IMPRISONMENT OF THE METROPOLITAN OF DURAZZO AND EXECUTION OF THE BISHOPS OF SAPPA AND ALESSUO (FEBRUARY–MARCH 1948)

Having eliminated a great part of the clergy, closed all the
religious institutions and suppressed the schools, the press and
Catholic charities, all that remained to complete the total extermination of the Catholic Church in Albania was to launch the
final blow against the Catholic episcopate. This had been left as
the last target in the program of extermination so that the clamor
of protest abroad would be lessened, thereby making it easier to
have it disappear without any noisy trials.

The first blow was struck against the metropolitan of Durazzo,
Mons. Nicholas Vincent Prennhushi, a Franciscan, native of
Scutari, and who after the death in 1946 of the Archbishop of
Scutari, Mons. Gaspar Thaci, had become the head of the
Catholic Church in Albania.

He was arrested during the first days of January 1948 and,
without the presentation of any specific charge against him, he
was removed from his seat and locked up in jail. According to
the latest information, he was supposed to have died in jail in
August 1952.

The second victim of Communist barbarism was the Bishop
of Sappa, Mons. George Volaj, the youngest Catholic Bishop in
Albania, having been born in Scutari in 1904. He had been
elected Bishop on June 26, 1940, when he was barely 36, and he
had immediately shown himself to be one of the most energetic
and strenuous defenders of the Catholic Church, by alone facing
a group of armed German soldiers and shielding with his person

a group of Albanians who had sought refuge in his residence at Nenshati. He had opposed the same energy to the armed bands of the so-called "National Liberation Movement" which worked for the unification of northern Albanians with Serb-Montenegrans, and which to a large extent was composed of communist elements who received orders from Moscow. And with the same intrepid courage, Mons. Volaj had defended his priests and his faithful from the struggle unleashed against them by the Communist government of Hoxha, by strongly protesting against the measures taken by the government to annihilate the activity of the Catholic Church in Albania, and by going personally to the offices of the so-called "tribunals of the people" to defend many of the accused whether they were Catholics or Orthodox or Moslems against the unjust charges made against them. Such an intrepid attitude could not but draw the attention of the Communist Government which had him arrested towards the end of January 1948. He was shot on the morning of February 3, 1948, without a trial and without any respect for even the outer formalities of justice.

The third victim, among the most capable members of the Catholic Episcopate in Albania, in the struggle against the episcopate waged by the Communist regime was Mons. Francisco Gijni, who administered the two Dioceses of St. Alexander of Oroshi, where he had been appointed Bishop since July 3, 1930, and of Alessio, where he had been transferred in 1943, following the death of Mons. Bumci. Ever since 1945, following the expulsion of Mons. Nigris, the Apostolic Delegate, from Albania, he had been appointed, in addition, as "Pro-Apostolic Delegate" and Regent *ad interim*, of the representation of the Holy See in Albania. It was precisely in this capacity that he had to make such frequent appearances before the Albanian Communist Government, either to protest against the persecution directed against the Catholic Church, or to prevent the sentencing of many innocent victims. His activity could not last long, because hardly a year after his appointment as representative of the Holy See, he was arrested towards the end of 1946 and kept in prison for about a year. Freed in the first days of December 1947, he was again arrested soon thereafter, and on the morning of March 11, 1948, without any trial, shot by one of Hoxha's firing squads.

By March 1948, out of the entire Catholic episcopate, the only one left was the Bishop of Pulati, the venerable Mons. Bernardino Shlaku, a Franciscan, then eighty years old. Nobody dared to put him in prison because of his age and he was confined to his residence in Koder Shen Gjergi, in the mountains in the far north of Albania.

Even the Capitular Vicars, who in the absence of their respective Bishops, had been elected to the Dioceses, such as, Mons. Thomas Laca for the Archdiocese of Scutari, Mons. Gaspar Gurakuqui, for the diocese of Sappa, were all arrested after their election and imprisoned or interned, again leaving the Dioceses without any administrators.

By the end of 1948 it could be said that the aim which the Albanian Communist Government had set for itself, the total elimination of the Catholic hierarchy in Albania, had been completely realized.

ATTEMPTS TO CREATE A NATIONAL CATHOLIC CHURCH
(JUNE–AUGUST 1952)

Having totally destroyed the life and activity of the Catholic Church in Albania, the Communist Government, aping the example which had been set by the other Cominform countries, itself in June 1951 tried to bring to life "Albanian National Catholic Church," independent of Rome.

The order, as was learned later, had come directly from Moscow which had sent the Russian metropolitan, Nikon, the Orthodox Bishop of Odessa, to Albania.

It was he, in fact, who on June 26, 1951 presided over a meeting of several Catholic priests who were made to come to Tirana from all parts of Albania for the purpose of inviting them to sign a "Statute" drawn up by Nikon himself which was then to be presented to the Government of the Albanian People's Republic for approval.

The "Statute" read as follows:

1) The Albanian Catholic Church breaks off every relation, be it organizational, political or administrative, with the Holy See.
2) The relations of the Albanian Church with other Churches abroad shall be limited to religious questions only and submitted for the approval of the State.
3) Said relations exclude any dependency on any agency abroad on the part of the Albanian Church.
4) The Church will be subvened by the State.
5) The dispositions of the Canon Law shall be applied in conformity with the laws of the State.
6) The directors of the Church must foster loyalty to the State and pledge themselves to observe the laws of the State.
7) The Albanian Church may provide for the training of its priests through its own seminaries.

None of the priests present wished to sign the Statute reported above. They claimed that they had no authority to do so since there was no representative of the Albanian Catholic hierarchy present at the meeting.

Invitations and pressures were then applied to the only Catholic Bishop remaining in Albania, Mons. Shlaku. A special commission called on him, giving him even the authority of modifying the "Statute" in those points where he might think changes were desirable. But the venerable Bishop refused every compromise and, instead, exhorted the few surviving Catholic priests not to lend themselves, in any wise, to the maneuver of the Government.

Since its attempt to win over the only person who in some way might have given a legal semblance to its plan to form a National Church had failed, the Government passed on to threats and induced three priests and several laymen to sign the said "Statute," promising them, in exchange, the greatest freedom of religion and worship.

After obtaining their signatures, the "Statute" was presented to the Chamber of Deputies which on August 3, 1951 declared its approval and passed it on for the signature of the Supreme Council of Soviets of the Albanian People's Republic.

Thus was constituted the "Albanian National Catholic Church" depending directly on the Communist Government.

For the purpose of more specifically fixing the relations between the new Albanian National Catholic Church and the Communist Government of the country, a new "Regulation" was approved on March 17, 1952 which determined the features of the new Church to be as follows:

1) The Catholic Church in Albania has a national character.

2) It is a juridical personality and includes all Albanian citizens professing the Catholic faith. It is administered according to the canon law of the universal Church which was founded by Jesus Christ and is directed by the Pope and by the other successors of the Apostles. However, it has no relations, organizational, administrative, or political, with the Pope.

3) The aims which the Albanian Catholic Church wishes to pursue are: a) the glory of God, b) the redemption of souls, c) the well being, even material, of the people.

4) The directors and the members of the Albanian Catholic Church will profess the most absolute loyalty to the State.

5) The Albanian Catholic Church is subject to Divine laws and to the laws of the Albanian People's Republic and it will obey the laws of the Canon Law of the Universal Church, providing these are not in conflict with the laws of the Albanian People's Republic, with the public order, or with its traditions and morals.

6) The highest directive body of the Albanian Catholic Church is the Catholic episcopate. It is liable to submit every appointment for the approval of the Council of Ministers and it must guide the Church according to the laws of the People's Democratic Republic.

7) The Government pledges itself to provide for the maintenance of the Church.

8) The Metropolitan may, in the name of the Bishops, have relations with Religious Orders and Ecclesiastical Institutions

which have their seats outside Albania, but it is not permitted to him to be in any wise dependent upon them.

9) The Parishes, which shall be considered as "state dependencies," have the duty of celebrating Mass, preaching the Gospel and of carrying out all other divine services, in accordance with the obligations of the observance of the Faith, the laws of the Church, and the directives of the Church.

With the approval of this "Regulation," registered, as has been said, on March 17, 1952, the final act of the sorrowful drama which was the Communist Government's campaign against the Catholic Church came to an end. The struggle had begun in November 1944, and after having destroyed almost all of the leaders and many of the members of the Catholic Church, the Government decided to end its campaign with the formation of a "National Church" made up of the remains of the persecuted Church.

But this attempt did not succeed, and save for the few Catholics who lent themselves to the maneuver, the bulk of the survivors has remained firm in its faith.

CONCLUSION: BALANCE SHEET TO DECEMBER 1952

After six years of a dogged persecution, a balance sheet showing the position of the Catholic Church in Albania reveals the following painful losses:

a) *Secular Clergy:* Of the 93 priests who composed the Albanian secular clergy in the various Dioceses in 1944—

  1) 17 have been killed
  2) 39 are in jail or in concentration camps
  3) 3 managed to escape abroad
  4) 11, among the younger ones, were drafted into the army
  5) 10 died of natural causes, or as a result of mistreatments
  6) 13 are still free

b) *Monks:* Of the 94 monks who in 1944 lived in the various male religious houses in Albania, the following facts have emerged.

  1) Jesuits

    (*a*) 17 Fathers and 14 lay Brothers expelled

(b) 3 Fathers shot (the Vice-Provincial, the Rector of the Seminary, and another)

(c) 3 Fathers in prison together with 5 Brothers

(d) 2 Fathers and 11 Brothers, still alive, in hiding to avoid arrest

2) Franciscans

  (a) 13 Fathers killed, 2 by Serbs and 1 by Montenegrans (among the victims were the Provincial and his 3 predecessors

  (b) 27 in jail or sentenced to forced labor

  (c) 6 died of natural causes, the rest vanished or in hiding

3) The "Sons of D. Orion": all expelled because they were Italian; and the orphanage closed

c) *Nuns:* Of the approximately 200 nuns who in 1944 served in various houses, schools and welfare institutions of Albania—

1) 85 were repatriated to Italy as non-Albanians

2) 43 were interned or sentenced to forced labor

3) the rest were stripped of their vestments and compelled to leave their houses

d) *Seminaries, Religious Institutions and Houses:*

1) The Seminary of Scutari was occupied by soldiers. One of the seminarists was killed; 3 are in prison; some were drafted into the army, and the rest expelled from the Seminary and forbidden to wear clerical vestments.

2) The Monastery and the Novitiate of the Franciscans of Scutari underwent the same fate.

3) The Houses, printing plants and the Institutions of the Jesuits in Scutari and Tirana were confiscated.

4) Shelters, schools and female religious houses were completely emptied of Catholic personnel and put to other different uses.

5) The orphanage of the "Sons of D. Orion" in Scutari was closed and confiscated, and the orphans sheltered there were sent to an orphanage entrusted to two Moslem ex-partisans.

CHAPTER VII

Bulgaria, 1945-1952

THE SITUATION IN 1944

As is known, Bulgaria is a country in which the overwhelming majority belongs to the "Orthodox" confession. Of the 6,078,000 inhabitants, listed in the statistics of 1944, 5,128,000 were in fact "Orthodox," 821,000 were Moslems, 20,000 Protestants, etc.

The total number of Catholics was 54,352, of whom 48,352 belonged to the Latin rite and about 6000 to the Byzantine eastern rite.

From the point of view of ecclesiastical organization they were grouped around three principal centers:

a) The Apostolic Vicarate of Sofia and Filippopili, with its seat at Plovdiv, for all Catholics of the Latin rite of southern Bulgaria. It numbered 27,834 faithful, 13 parishes and 65 priests, almost all of whom were monks belonging to the Conventual Franciscans.

b) Diocese of Nicopoli, with the Bishopric residence in Rustciuk or Ruse, for all Catholics of northern and central Bulgaria. It numbered about 20,148 faithful, 20 parishes and about thirty priests, mostly Passionist monks.

c) The Apostolic Exarchate of Bulgaria, with its seat in

Sofia, for all Catholics of the Byzantine eastern rite, spread particularly in Thrace, with nuclei in Burgas and Varna, now called Stalin.

The Apostolic Delegation had its seat in Sofia since 1931. In 1944 it was administered by Mons. Guiseppe Mazzoli, and after his death, which occurred on December 8, 1945, the office was temporarily entrusted to Mons. Francesco Galloni.

In addition, the Catholic Church in Bulgaria possessed numerous religious houses and institutions: 3 in Sofia (belonging to the Brothers of the Christian Schools, the Sisters of St. Joseph, and the Sisters of Charity in Zagabria; 2 in Ruse (Nuns of Zion); 1 in Varna (Stalin) belonging to the Lay-Sisters of the Assumption; and 1 in Burgas, belonging to the Sisters of St. Joseph. All these institutions numbered a total of about 200 monks and nuns, and their schools, which included a Gymnasium and a *lycée,* were attended by more than 5000 pupils of both sexes.

In Sofia, moreover, there was a big university lodging house, operated by the Sisters of St. Maria Annunziata, founded by Mons. Galloni, which in the name of the "Opera pro Oriente," also founded by him, offered hospitality to hundreds of university students of every religious confession. During, and after the war it had ministered to the needs of hundreds of refugees and needy persons.

In addition, there were two large Catholic hospitals, one in Sofia and the other in Plovdiv, administered by the Sisters of Charity of Zagabria; an orphanage in Sofia itself run by Eucharist Nuns, and another named "Narezdu," after the second daughter of Czar Ferdinand, also in Sofia and administered by the Sisters of Charity.

In all, therefore, the Catholic Church in Bulgaria in 1944 included:

        1 Apostolic Delegate
        3 Bishops
      127 Priests
      200 Monks and Nuns
   54,352 Faithful
       18 Religious Houses and Institutions.

THE FIRST THREE YEARS OF THE COMMUNIST REGIME (1944–1947)

Given its small membership, one might have thought that the Church would pass unobserved, the more so because the Orthodox Metropolitan, Cyril of Plovdiv, had told the Pan-Orthodox Congress held in Moscow in 1948, that " the Catholic Church in Bulgaria in no wise represents a political force."

And in fact, for some time, the Catholic Church was untouched by any systematic persecution.

The Government, preoccupied with consolidating its power which it had seized through deceit and also with the support of the Red Armies which had entered Bulgarian territory in late 1944, had taken great care at first not to show itself hostile to any religion. It was concerned, above all, with eliminating the strongest political oppositions. Therefore, its struggle at first was directed against political parties, and against the functionaries of the previous governments. It has been estimated that more than 20,000 persons were executed during this first period, among whom were 22 ex-ministers, 70 ex-deputies, 30 ex-army officers, the three members of the Regency Council, established after the disappearance of King Boris, and Nicholas Petrov, the head of the Agrarian Party. He had been the only one who had openly tried to defend his people against tyranny, and he was hung as a traitor on September 23, 1947.

Having completed this cruel elimination of its more prominent political opponents, the Communist Government, which in the meantime had succeeded in obtaining a strong majority after the October 27, 1946, elections, began another struggle against all the forces of the opposition represented by the various religious confessions.

It subjected the Orthodox Church to its will quite easily through the total enslavement of its leaders to the directives of the Communist leaders. And in a short time it also eliminated the resistance put up by the few Protestant communities (about 20,000 faithful) whose pastors, about thirty, were the first to be arrested and to undergo an ignominious public trial, with the consequent sentencing to punishments ranging from life imprisonment for some (Zypakov, Ivanov, Maumov and Tchernev), to terms of one to fifteen years for the others. So there remained only the Catholic Church which, despite its small numbers, appeared as the most dogged opponent to the ideas of the regime, and as the most compact and militant of them.

First, an attempt was made to get around some priests with flatteries and promises which were incompatible with the character of their religious mission. Even here it was sought to find so-called "progressive" elements who would lend themselves to the formation of a "Bulgarian Catholic National Church." But upon realizing that its efforts in this field were doomed to futility, the Government went from flattery to threats.

It began by withdrawing ration cards from some; others wound up in jail, some were made to disappear mysteriously, and all were caught in an ever tightening net of spying and mistrust.

Two priests, who had just returned to Bulgaria after an absence of eight years during which they had completed their studies in Rome, were immediately arrested, held for a time in jail, and then sent to a concentration camp.

Hand in hand with the realization that the resistance was tougher than expected, attacks against the Catholic Church and the Pope became more menacing and frequent. And towards the end of 1947, no one entertained any illusions about the imminence of the final attack against the Catholic Church in Bulgaria.

SUPPRESSION OF SCHOOLS AND OTHER EDUCATIONAL INSTITUTIONS
(1948)

The first serious blow was struck against the Catholic Church in Bulgaria on August 3, 1948 with the publication of a decree with which the Bulgarian State ordered the closing of foreign schools. In practice this meant the large Catholic schools, which constituted one of the main forms, if not indeed the principal one, of the apostolate to which the various religious congregations especially dedicated themselves.

Such an act had been preceded by an entire press and propaganda campaign, designed to make it understood that in the new progressive climate the existence of private schools, and in particular Catholic ones, was now something intolerable.

In fact, already on November 3, 1947, the newspaper "Novini" had carried a report of the Higher Council of Public Instruction which demanded the prompt approval of a law which would require all students in the country to attend State schools exclusively, and permit only citizens of other countries to attend foreign schools.

The new constitution was approved on December 7, 1947, in which Article 79, dealing with schools, established that:

> . . . All citizens have the right to education. Education will be secular and based on the democratic and progressive State.
> . . . Schools belong to the State. The construction of private schools will not be authorized without a special legal provision. In this case, such schools will be put under State control. . . .

On December 7, 1947, the very director of secondary education attached to the Ministry of Public Instruction hastened to write a commentary on this article of the Constitution which was printed in the same newspaper, "Novini":

> . . . Imperialists send missionaries in order to dominate independent peoples. They open schools, in which is an atmosphere of religious fanaticism, they teach pupils the customs, the tastes, and the ideas of the future conquerors. . . . In these schools the only aim is to deepen superstition and the hatred of that which is new and progressive. . . . It is an entirely retrogade teaching and based on the methods of the Middle Ages. The conceptions of Darwin on the origin and evolution of the world can not penetrate therein. In this very year, a girl student belonging to the Communist Youth somehow managed to explain Darwin's theory in the French women's college in Sofia. It was an atomic bomb against the blissful tranquility of the teaching Sisters. Seized with horror, as if before a sacrilege, a nun stormed into the assembly and forbade the student to read her speech and

dismissed the assembly. Thus the first attempt of science to enter into such schools ended unhappily. . . .

In May 1948 all the directors, men and women, of Catholic colleges in Bulgaria, were convoked by the Ministry of Public Instruction and invited to subscribe to some elementary principles of the new Communist pedagogy which were summarized in the following points:

a) To accept Darwinism as certain science. To the directors who countered with the statement that Darwinism was also taught in their schools, but only as an "hypothesis" and not as a certain science, the vice-minister replied that Westernizers reasoned this way, but that it was not permitted to Frenchmen to come to Bulgaria and dictate laws in Bulgaria where Darwinism is not a hypothesis, but a certain science.

b) Not to speak to pupils about bizarre and un-existing things, such as the super-natural, mysteries, the immortality of the soul, etc.

c) Not to teach natural or super-natural morality. Above all it was forbidden to them to teach the cathechism or to give courses of religion on the premises of schools.

It was natural that the directors would refuse to subscribe to these points and it was then that it was decided to close these schools. It is a fact, however, that such a decision was not shared by all the members of the Government, because it also countervened a Franco-Bulgarian agreement on the functioning of such schools signed on December 17, 1936. Moreover, many could not forget the benefits which these schools had brought in their more than fifty years of existence and what help they had furnished to Bulgarian culture, then just emerging from Turkish domination.

Nonetheless, the counter-proposals in this regard presented by the French Ambassador to Sofia, Jacques Paris, and those of the Apostolic Delegation were in vain. The will of Moscow cruelly prevailed and by the first of September 1948, the schools ceased to exist, being closed forever.

Thus, with an act of political fanaticism, an immense heritage of religious and moral culture was destroyed which effected not only the 200 monks and nuns and the 5,000 students attending these schools, but also the cultural future of the nation.

The second blow struck against the Catholic Church in Bulgaria, immediately after the closing of the Catholic schools, was the closing of the Apostolic Delegation which had its seat at number 11 Ulitza, in Sofia.

The Apostolic Delegation had been established since September 26, 1931, and entrusted to Mons. Roncalli, who had been stationed in Bulgaria since 1925 in the capacity of Apostolic Visitor. After his transfer to the seat of Constantinople, Mons. Guiseppe Mazzoli had been made Delegate on December 15, 1934, and following his death in December 1945, it had been entrusted as a Regency to Mons. Franceso Galloni. He was a highly esteemed priest, founder and director of the "Opera pro Oriente" who, after more than twenty years residence in Bulgaria, had won the veneration, the esteem and the gratitude of persons from all the social strata of the country. Both the people and government officials had always showed a certain deference towards his person, so much so that even the Russians had not dared attack him.

But as early as 1948 the police had begun to spin an espionage web around the seat of the Delegation, bent on finding a pretext or a provocation, sufficient to justify the campaign which it was planned to wage even against the presence of the Apostolic Delegation in Sofia. Its aim was to remove this observant eye from the scene, which might have been able to denounce to the outside world the mis-deeds which the Communist regime was preparing to commit against the Catholic Church.

But since nothing damaging to the Regency could be found, advantage was taken of one of his journeys to Italy, made in response to an emergency call in December 1948 in connection with a fire which had damaged offices of the "Opera pro Oriente" near Vicenza, to warn him never to return to Bulgaria again.

The provision was the fruit of deceit and astuteness. Before leaving Sofia, the pontifical representative took care to make certain that his personal papers were in order, and he had received ample assurances that nothing would hamper his return.

But no sooner had he departed when a veritable campaign, in the press and over the radio, was orchestrated by the Government against the pontifical representative, demanding his expulsion. This campaign of charges and slander against a faultless and worthy man like Mons. Galloni, was officially joined by the Minister of Foreign Affairs, Vassil Kolarov, who in a speech made before the National Assembly on February 23, 1949 pronounced these precise words:

> . . . The closing of the Apostolic Delegation has put an end to an humiliating episode for Bulgaria and its people. The Vatican does not hide its aims. It is an implacable enemy of the Soviet Union, of the people's democracies and of Communism, and it is entirely at the service of those dark forces which today are feeding the fires of a new world war. . . .

THE FINAL PHASE OF THE PERSECUTION

The annihilation of the Catholic Church was progressively realized through a series of provisions, which after having struck, as has been seen, against schools and Catholic welfare activities (hospitals, shelters, orphanages, etc.), proceeded to attack directly the most prominent members of the Catholic clergy, and any manifestation of the Catholic cult.

As early as 1950 every outer form of the apostolate had been suffocated, the celebration of the Mass alone being permitted, with a brief homily, prudently restricted to a few words of purely spiritual exhortation.

In some localities it was impossible to assemble children together to prepare them for their First Communion and Confirmation because of the fear dominating families that they might be punished by having their ration cards taken away, as well as subjected to other punishments.

Then arrests began to take place at an ever accelerating rhythm. Father Damian Ghiulov, the Superior of the Capucin Fathers of Sofia, was arrested on February 17, 1950. A few months later in May 1950 even his successor, Father Robert Prustow was arrested and shortly thereafter even his other successor, Father Fortunato Bakalscki.

The usual trials were staged against these Fathers, one on January 14, 1952, and the other on May 8 of the same year.

In the first trial against Father Damian Chiulov, the entire life of the accused was reviewed. Ever since his childhood, it was said, he had given precocious signs of anti-communism and he had maintained that tendency through all his life, from the time of the Balkan wars when he was a student in Rome until the day of his arrest in May 1950. Those who saw him at the trial attested that after two years of imprisonment he had become unrecognizable. His tall and sturdy figure had become so thin and emaciated that it brought forth fear and compassion at once from the beholder. It was learned later that he had been brought to this state after months and months of torture to which he had been submitted in order to force him to sign his "confessions." He was sentenced to two years in jail for having spoken ill of the Bulgarian government, one year for the same offense against the Soviet government, and two for bad conduct in jail, and the remainder of his 12-year sentence for having been a spy for the Vatican and capitalist powers.

The second trial, with Father Robert Prustow appearing as the chief accused, took place on the following May behind closed doors. He was sentenced to 20 years in jail, which was the maximum penalty the Bulgarian penal code allowed.

The third trial, against Father Fortunato Bakalscki, could not be held because, unfortunately, the priest had died in jail in August of the same year. A communique released after a long time by the authorities attributed the death to pneumonia, but the youthful age of the priest, his vigorous health and other circumstances caused many to blame the death on the tortures inflicted on him by the Communist police.

Meanwhile the Passionist, Mons. Eugene Bossilkov, the

Bishop of Nicopoli was arrested in his residence on July 16, 1952. It was followed soon after by the arrest of tens of priests and nuns in Plovdiv, Russe, Varna and elsewhere. Even two Catholic laymen, formerly editors of the Catholic weekly "Istina," which had been compelled to suspend publication for some time, were also thrown into jail.

On September 21, 1952, the newspapers carried the "Act of accusation and condemnation against the Catholic espionage and terrorist organization in Bulgaria," while the Minister of the Interior, George Zankow, declared publicly:

> . . . Let everybody (the adversaries) know that the Government, through the organs of the Minister of the Interior, is capable of putting anybody whomsoever in his place and that it will deal without mercy with those who think they can hamper it. . . . Neither God nor their imperialist masters will be able to help them. . . .

On September 25, 1952, the Bishop, Mons. Bossilkov, with 26 priests, two nuns and several eminent Catholic laymen, appeared in the palace of justice in Sofia as the accused in a trial against them which had been staged in the grand manner. The defendants were charged with espionage and concealing weapons, or anti-communist propaganda. But it can be definitely said that it was "Catholicism" which was really on trial in Sofia. For the most tragic aspect of this trial was not in the contempt for the most elementary rules of procedure and not even in the execrable cruelty of the sentences but in the fact that the trial aimed to strike an annihilating blow against the Catholic Church in Bulgaria in the persons of its Bishops, its clergy and its most devoted faithful.

Press and radio propagandists took advantage of this trial to discredit the small Catholic community, as if it were a nest of spies and traitors. Wrote one Communist newspaper:

> . . . Abusing the full religious freedom guaranteed them by the Constitution, they had transformed the Churches into meeting places for spies; they used sermons to spread anti-

people propaganda and seminaries as depositories for arms and other material for illegal activity. . . .

During the course of the trial thirty trunks of medicines and other sanitary material was presented as evidence of material for illegal activity. These medicines had been sent to Sofia in 1948 by the Holy Father, and among them were many very expensive drugs, difficult to obtain. And yet everybody knew that these precious medicaments had been distributed to the Bulgarian Red Cross by the Apostolic Delegation, and that various government agencies had anxiously requested them. This was so widely known that Kostov himself, the Foreign Minister, had sent the chief of his office to the apostolic delegation, and later also a letter, to request them, in the name of the country, to thank the Holy Father for the help sent and for the considerable sums put at the disposition of the Maternity agencies which were struggling with a high percentage of infant deaths, particularly in the villages, because of the lack of adequate medicinal care.

On October 3, 1952, after almost eight days of charges of all kinds, the sentences were handed down: Mons. Bossilkov was sentenced to death, and with him three other priests, the Assumptionist monks, Father Kamen Vicev Jonkon, Father Pavel Gigiov, Father Johesephat Sciscov. Two others were sentenced to twenty years in jail, three to fifteen years, two to fourteen years, seven to twelve; further, another seven to ten years, one to six, another to one and a half, while two sisters respectively drew a sentence of five and six years. Among the laymen, the two editors of "Istina" were sentenced to twelve years.

Immediately after the trial, another trial was demanded even for Mons. John Romanov, Bishop, and the apostolic vicar of Sofia and Filippoli. He was accused of having had contact with Mons. Bossilkov, and he was arrested immediately.

For a long time nothing more has been heard of Mons. Cyril Kurteff, the apostolic Exarch for Bulgarian Catholics of the eastern rite, and the third Catholic Bishop resident in Bulgaria. It is feared that even he is in a state of detention.

It is also known that after the trial other Catholic priests were arrested, on the charges that the court hearings had uncovered evidence of guilt against them. And in the meanwhile, all priests, monks and nuns of other nationalities, the majority French, who directed schools, institutions, or hospitals, have been expelled.

At present, therefore, there can at best be about ten priests still in liberty out of the 127 who once formed the small Catholic community of Bulgaria, and perhaps a few monks or nuns out of the 200 who once worked there. No Bishop is left of the three who were there, no religious house or institution is left of the original eighteen which enriched the country. And only a few scattered and frightened faithful of the 57,500 who were listed in the last census.

The destruction of the Catholic Church in Bulgaria by the present Communist Government could not be more complete, more serious, nor more cruel.

CHAPTER VIII

Jugoslavia, 1944-1952

THE CHURCH, ITS GEOGRAPHICAL AND STATISTICAL DISTRIBUTION IN JUGOSLAVIA

From a religious point of view, the situation of the various confessions in Jugoslavia, according to official statistics published in Belgrade in 1938, shortly before the outbreak of the war, appeared as follows:

Orthodox	6,785,501	(47%)
Catholics	5,514,847	(40%)
Moslems	1,561,166	(11%)
Protestants	117,951	(1%)
Jews and others	90,000	(1%)

According to these statistics, the Catholic Church occupied the second place. Hence it was the most important religious community after that of the Orthodox, embracing about 40% of the population of Jugoslavia which at that time (1938) numbered about 14,069,565 persons.

The same statistics gave the following picture of the geographical distribution of the above-mentioned religious confessions within the country:

	Orthodox	Catholic	Moslem	Protestant	Others
Slovenia	2%	96%	0%	2%	0%
Croatia	24%	72%	1%	2%	1%
Serbia	80%	5%	13%	1%	1%
Bosnia	44%	23%	39%	3%	1%
Macedonia	81%	4%	12%	1%	2%

As can be seen, then, the Catholic Church included an overwhelming majority in Slovenia and in Croatia, a goodly percentage in Bosnia and Herzegovina, and small percentages in Serbia and Macedonia.

The same statistics, from an ethnic point of view, gave the State which was formed of Slovenes, Croats and Serbs in 1918 and officially called Jugoslavia in 1929, a most remarkable heterogeneous composition. Here are some data:

Serbs	41 %
Croats	24 %
Slovenes	9 %
Macedonians	5 %
Montenegrans	2.7%
Moslems	5.1%
Albanians	4 %
Hungarians	3 %

Others were Wallachians (.6%), Turks (6.%), Italians (.5%), Slovaks (.5%), Gypsies (.5%), Bulgars (.5%), Germans (.4%), Czechs (.2%), Ukranians (.2%), Russians (.1%), Jews (.04%), Poles (.03%).

From an hierarchic point of view the Catholic Church in Jugoslavia included (a) 4 Archdioceses, (b) 13 Dioceses of the Latin rite, (c) 1 Diocese of the Eastern rite, (d) 2 Apostolic Administrations.

The numerical distribution of the Catholics in the above-mentioned archdioceses and dioceses was as follows:

Diocese	Population	Catholics	Parishes	Priests
Zagabria	2,038,000	1,800,000	366	596
Serajevo	1,225,000	328,000	104	74
Belgrade	2,800,000	60,000	14	1
Antivari	120,000	25,000	20	19
Ljubliana	563,000	521,000	825	551
Lavant	533,000	650,000	239	474
Veglia	35,000	38,000	29	68
Sebenico	305,000	229,000	158	85
Spalato	300,000	283,000	149	168
Lesina	43,000	63,500	45	72
Ragusa	81,000	78,000	57	152
Cattaro	34,000	15,000	29	29
Segna-Modrusa	446,000	439,000	198	210
Sirmio	460,000	460,000	130	311
Banjaluka	620,500	199,000	46	36
Mostar-Margagna	430,000	188,000	61	24
Skopia	1,888,000	30,000	18	30
Crisio		51,000	49	68
Donato (Jugosl.)	585,845	206,000	55	67
Balka	795,000	485,000	92	216

NOTE: These data and figures refer to the situation of the Catholic Church in Jugoslavia from 1940 to 1944. The dioceses of Zara, Fiume and Parenzo-Pola, formerly belonging to Italy, were added in 1945. Comprehensively they contained 345,000 faithful, 120 parishes and 250 priests.

THE BEGINNING OF THE STRUGGLE

The tension between the Communist regime and the Catholic Church immediately showed itself to be overt and incurable. In fact, not many days had passed since the entry of Red troops into Zagrabia (May 5, 1945) when, on May 11, to be specific, an official orator openly attacked the Archbishop and the Primate of the Catholic Church in Jugoslavia, Mons. Stepinac, labelling him a "war criminal."

On the following May 15, the secret police (OZNA) arrested the Archbishop who was interned together with many Catholic priests and laymen.

On May 22, on the occasion of an official visit to that city by Marshal Tito, several priests were convoked by him and invited to study ways of forming a Catholic Church "more national and closer to the soul of Slav peoples." This was the first attempt to create a "Croatian National Church." But the invitation was a failure, because no Croat priest accepted it.

During the following months of June and July 1945, dozens of priests and laymen were arrested on charges of collaboration with the old Ustsachi government. They were hailed before the military court of Zagrabia and, in the majority of cases, sentenced to death.

In the meantime it became clear that it was the intention of the new leaders to introduce a Communist order, with the suppression of all freedoms, as they had already done in the territories of Serbia and Bosnia previously subjected to their power.

According to the news from those areas, the atrocities committed there had been so enormous in nature and extent that an authoritative person declared that "the Turks in 400 years had not sown so much ruin and killed as many priests, as the communists had done in a single year. . . ."

It was then that the Catholic Episcopate could no longer keep silent and with a memorable document, published in Zagabria on September 20, 1945, it denounced the misdeeds of the Communist regime, and declared that collaboration with such a regime was impossible. Here are the principle passages of this important document:

. . . We, Catholic Bishops, assembled in plenary conference in Zagabria, feel it is our duty as pastors to address you some words from this conference, beloved children . . .

a) The Massacre of Priests

In the first place we are pained and preoccupied by the

sorrowful and terrible fate of so many priests. A great many
of them had already fallen during the war, not only in skirmishes and battles, but by sentences imposed by the present
civil and military authorities. When the military operations
ceased, the death sentences against Catholic priests continued.

Their number, according to our data, amounts to 243
dead, 169 held in jails or concentration camps, 89 missing;
a total of 491 victims.

To this must be added the murder of 19 clerics, 3 lay
brothers and 4 nuns.

This is a figure that has not been known for centuries in
the history of the Balkan countries. But what is most painful
is that it was not permitted to them, as with hundreds and
thousands of others, to receive the comforts of religion in
their last moments, as is granted to even the worst criminals
in civilized societies.

The courts which imposed such sentences proceeded
summarily. The accused, in most cases knew nothing of the
charge against them until the hearing. Often they were
denied any defense whatsoever, as required by the very
nature of judicial hearings, namely, the citing of witnesses
and the claiming of legal assistance. Because of this honest
public opinion has the right to deny these sentences that
essential characteristic of a judicial decision, to wit, the
criterion of justice.

Who can prove that the many Catholic priests sentenced
to death were really criminals? Who can prove that all of
them had been assassins?

Thus, for example, in the Franciscan monastery of Siroki-
Brijeg, all the monks present were killed (and they were
38) even if none of them had ever had a rifle in his hand,
and even though none of them had fought against the troops
of the liberating nations, as they were falsely accused. We
can add, on the contrary, that all were known as adversaries
of the fascist ideology.

There have been cases in which thousands of faithful

and considerable masses of people have asked the authorities to free priests, because the faithful themselves guaranteed their innocence. But that notwithstanding, they were sentenced. It is quite evident that such sentences were not inflicted in the name of the people and its Christian rights.

A great number of priests are in concentration camps, sentenced to forced labor for many years. But that is not enough: even the Catholic Bishop of the Greek rite, Mons. Janko Simbak, is still a prisoner and we know nothing of the fate of Bishop Carevic. . . .

There is frequently a lack of sufficient food and even the most wretched of pallets in the concentration camps. Many must perform work which degrades their sacerdotal dignity. . . . Nor were they ever given the opportunity of defending themselves or proving their innocence. Their entire guilt consists in the fact that they had ideas different from those who sentenced them.

We know nothing about the actual whereabouts of many priests who were deported by Government bodies. No inquiry or search is of any avail. Every trace of them has vanished. . . .

b) *Against the Catholic Press*

The lack of a press is the second painful wound in the life of the Catholic Church in Jugoslavia.

Out of the almost hundred newspapers which we had before the war, none are published today. When we asked for permission to publish our newspapers, the most varied arguments were adduced not to grant it to us. Among other things, we were told there was no paper. But many car loads of paper had been taken away from the archbishopric residence of Zagabria which had been ear-marked for the Catholic press.

Most Catholic printing plants are shut or condemned to inactivity. The Zagabria printing plant was hampered in every conceivable way. And because the attempt did not succeed, the director was condemned to the loss of national honor and the printing plant, which was not his property, confiscated . . . The great printing plant of the Catholic Society of Lubiana has been taken away from the Catholics. The same fate befell the Catholic printing plants of Mostar, Sebenico, Maribor and Sarajevo. In this fashion a calculated and systematic campaign against the Catholic press is being carried out.

c) *Against the Catholic School*

A series of blows have been struck against the Church in the field of education, primarily in that sector dealing with religious instruction in the schools. In fact in all schools religious instruction has been declared elective, so that whoever desires it must request it. We are proud to make known that the parents of Catholic children have voted overwhelmingly for religious instruction in all the schools where it was requested . . . 90% in the diocese of Zagabria and Diakova, 80% in the diocese of Split. . . . But in the higher schools of Croatia religious instruction has been completely suppressed.

The Catholic Church had, moreover, a considerable number of private intermediary schools on an equal footing with Government schools. Now newspapers close to the public school authorities announce that these schools will no longer be able to operate.

In addition to the private schools, the Catholic Church had many colleges and institutions for the education of youth. These colleges today are either largely closed, or almost everywhere they have been assigned commissars, male or female.

Religious duties are in many instances hampered by meetings, assemblies or gatherings which take place exactly at the time of sacred functions. . . .

d) *Expropriation of Church Properties*

Even in the purely charitable field the Catholic Church encounters many difficulties. The good works performed by

the archbishopric "Caritas" of Zagabria is well-known. By
its own activity it has saved about 7,000 babies with no regard for religious differences, and it sent scores of freight
cars, loaded with provisions, to our brothers in the devas-
tated areas. But today "Caritas" has a State commissioner
because the State has no confidence in its activity. . . .

Land reform removes and expropriates from the Church
all of its land holdings with all their equipment with no
indemnity whatsoever, as if the Church had acquired them
by theft. The small portion which is left is not sufficient to
maintain seminaries, bishopric offices, etc. This land reform
has rendered the regular life of the Church impossible.

The feminine religious orders, their educational, and
charitable institutions are daily beset with new vexations
and difficulties on account of the spirit of obstructionism
which now surrounds them. Nursing Sisters have to undergo
impediments of all kinds not only in the State hospitals, but
even in their own hospitals.

e) It Is a Virtual Persecution

One other thing afflicts us and it is the materialist and
irreligious spirit which, publicly or secretly, officially or
unofficially, is being spread in our country.

From what has been said up to now it appears clearly
that the Catholic Church in democratic federative Jugoslavia finds itself in unprecedented conditions of great difficulty. The actual conditions of the Catholic Church in Jugoslavia, in our opinion, differ only in name from *an open
persecution against the Church.*

But in making all this known to you, we do not desire
to provoke a struggle with the new authorities of the State.
We have not sought for this struggle. We are for peace and
for harmony. . . .

LOUIS STEPINAC, *Archbishop of Zagabria and*
President of the Episcopal Conferences
NICHOLAS DOBRECIC, *Archbishop of Bar*
JOSEF UJCIC, *Archbishop of Belgrade*

GIRALAMO MILETA, *Bishop of Sebenico*
QUIRINO C. BONEFACIC, *Bishop of Spalato*
JOSEF SREBRNIC, *Bishop of Veglia*
MICHAEL PUSIC, *Bishop of Hvar*
JOHN G. TOMAZIC, *Bishop of Marburg*
VICTOR BURIC, *Bishop of Senj*
SMILJAN CEKADA, *Bishop of Skoplje*
PETER CULE, *Bishop of Mostar*
ANTHONY AKSAMOVIC, *Bishop of Dzakovo*
LAICO BUDANOVIC, *Bishop Vicar General of Subotica*
[*These were followed by the signatures of the Vicar Generals of Serajevo, Baniakuka, Lubiana and Prekmurje, whose Bishops were absent because they had been arrested or exiled.*]
Zagabria, September 20, 1945

The letter of the Episcopate, as was to be expected, provoked a stronger recrudescence of the attacks, and a veritable general offensive against the Church. Tito judged the letter to be an act against the national authorities and for two months there was not a newspaper, or a radio broadcast, which did not attack the letter of the Bishops.

On October 22, 1945, the Holy See, worried over the painful turn of events in Jugoslavia, nominated Mons. Joseph Patrick Hurley as Apostolic Nuntius to Belgrade, in an attempt at pacification. But Jugoslavia made no response to this gesture and its Legation at the Vatican continued to be occupied by an ordinary Secretary of the Embassy, who at that time was, Gabricevic Branimiro.

From November 1945 on, arrests and sentencings assumed a dizzying tempo, affecting hundreds and hundreds of priests, monks, nuns, and lay Catholics, giving rise to the impression that a pre-established plan for the general extermination of the Catholic clergy in Jugoslavia was about to be realized.

The following summary offers, with the eloquence of figures better than any comment, a precise picture of the intensity of the persecution:

a) *Federal Republic of Croatia:*

Priests killed without a trial	91
Sentenced to death and already killed	22
Sentenced to prison	52
Refugees	119

Total 284

b) *Federal Republic of Slovenia*

Priests killed without trial	71
Sentenced to death and already killed	4
Sentenced to prison	19
Refugees	249

Total 343

c) *Federal Republic of Herzegovina*

Priests killed without trial	19
Sentenced to death and already killed	6
Sentenced to prison	12
Refugees	36

Total 73

d) *Federal Republics of Serbia-Macedonia-Motenegro*

Priests killed without trial	5
Sentenced to prison	2
Refugees	5

Total 12

In all, therefore, 712 priests were eliminated, of whom:

a) 186 were killed without a trial
b) 32 sentenced to death and already dead
c) 85 sentenced to prison
d) 409 refugees

This is the sad balance of only the first two years of the Communist persecution of the Catholic clergy in Jugoslavia. It must be noted that these figures are much lower than the realities insofar as concerns the priests who were killed; well-established documents bring this number up to 220. Nor does the statistical table take into account the nuns among the victims; some killed, others vanished without a trace, nor of seminarists who disappeared or were killed.

It is not easy to say in just which one of the Federated Republics of the new Jugoslavia the persecution of the Church showed itself to be most cruel and hostile.

Even here some figures are enlighting:

a) In the Federal Republic of Croatia

- 261 Parishes without priests
- 119 Churches destroyed, confiscated or profaned
- 35 Religious Institutions and houses confiscated
- 70 Catholic shelters, schools and hospitals nationalized

b) In the Federal Republic of Slovenia

- 68 Parishes without priests
- 90 Churches requisitioned or put to other uses
- 27 Religious institutions and houses closed
- 43 Catholic dailies, 8 weeklies, 36 monthly reviews and 5 bi-monthlies suppressed

c) In the Federal Republic of Bosnia and Herzegovina

- 60 Parishes without priests
- 75 Churches confiscated and put to other uses
- 19 Religious houses and institutions closed
- 36 Catholic shelters, schools, and hospitals nationalized.

To get an idea of the destruction carried out in this last-mentioned area, it is enough to remember that the Catholics of the Diocese of Banialuka were reduced from 130,000 to only 40,000. The jails in Mostar had become so full of Catholics that they had lost their usual names and became known as the "Croat House."

In the Diocese of Segna 67 vacant parishes were counted and the Catholic population which was more than 250,000 was reduced by 20%. The number of Catholics said to be killed by partisans is declared to be over 30,000.

Meanwhile in all these regions, the few Catholics remained free, saw themselves unjustly dismissed from jobs and other employment. Prayers were suppressed in all schools, crucifixes removed from the walls, and sermons forbidden in the Churches, etc.

TRIAL OF ARCHBISHOP MONS. STEPINAC AND OF THREE BISHOPS

On the morning of September 18, 1946, just as he was leaving his chapel to climb the steps of the altar, Mons. Louis Stepinac, the Archbishop of Zagrabia, was arrested. This was the culminating act of the tragedy of the Catholic Church in Jugoslavia.

As has been said, Mons. Stepinac had already been arrested once on May 17, 1945, hardly 12 days after the entry of Russian troops into Zagrabia, but since no charges could be made against him he was freed shortly thereafter. He always remained the primary obstacle in the path of the realization of the plan to exterminate the Catholic Church in Jugoslavia, proposed by President Bakaric for Croatia, and by President Kidric for Slovenia. Hence, the action taken against the Archbishop had already been decided upon in advance and this was admitted by Marshal Tito himself at an election meeting, held shortly after his arrest, with these words:

. . . We are accused of having arrested Stepinac in order to free ourselves of him. When Mons. Hurley, the representative of the Pope, came to see me about this I said to him: Take him away and relieve him of his position, or otherwise we will arrest him. . . . And we waited several months before arresting him. . . .

On September 24 the charge sheet was published which listed the reasons which led to his arrest:

1) As member and instigator of a group of Ustachi terrorists he had helped to organize the crimes of this terrorist group.
2) He had collaborated with the occupation forces.
3) He had organized the conversion of Serbs in Croatia, Bosnia and Herzegiovina to the Catholic faith.
4) He had made of the Catholic press, and especially of the "Katoliki List," the official organ of the Archbishopric of Zagabria, an instrument of propaganda in the hands of the occupying powers.
5) In accord with Pavelich he had hidden the archives of the Ustachi Ministry of Foreign Affairs in the Archbishopric.

The substantiality or worth of these five charges can be deduced from the following courageous declarations made by the same Archbishop at the end of the hearings, on September 28, 1946:

. . . My arrest and my detention, as I see it, are designed to prepare, through these hearings, the material which will serve the Court against me, as Archbishop of Zagabria. . . .

Since nowadays throughout the civilized world it is an odious thing to attack the Church and its representatives directly, a political basis must be found for this which for me has assumed this form. . . .

I will tell you what my only crime is. It is that of not falling on my knees before the demands of Communism which alone governs in this country. And here are the reasons why I could not consent to that which was being done.

We are continually being reproached for being "assassins," and I myself have more than once been called "assassin." It would be better to inquire how the cemeteries in our countries have become so large. . . .

And it is in consideration of all this that I hold, and resolve, it to be better that upon being brought before the Court I act as follows: 1) Not to defend myself personally; 2) To refuse every defense; 3) To make no appeal whatsoever against the sentence, it being quite clear that it would be completely useless and that it would have no meaning, when it is known that the Court imposes only those sentences which have already been determined upon by a certain organization. . . .

If the present regime were really concerned about the regulation of the situation in the country, there is a road, and only one, which can lead to it. The State has diplomatic relations with the Holy See. Let it begin clear and sincere negotiations with it as the only competent party. The Holy See, that is to say the Church, does not know Diktats. It knows only sincere and honest agreements. Without that nothing can be successful.

I could also be sentenced, even other Bishops could be sentenced, and even many more priests and laymen could be put to death, but things will not go any better, in fact they will get worse and lead to a complete collapse. . . . Hitler is an example, with all of his trials staged against the Church. . . .

The trial began on September 30, 1946, arranged and conducted according to a pre-established plan. There were many accusing witnesses, but hardly none for the defense as all those who might be able to testify in favor of the Archbishop had been arrested during the days between September 24 and 30. The first of these had been his two closest collaborators, Mons. Francesco Salis Sewis, auxiliary Bishop of Zagabria and Mons. Ante Slamic, who were the directors of the archbishopric chancellery and who therefore knew the value of the documentation to be submitted to the judges.

Mons. Stepinac defended himself vigorously during the course of the proceedings, even though the atmosphere was hostile and diabolically organized against him.

a) In regard to the first charge of collaboration with the "Krusari" and the "Ustachi," Mons. Stepinac answered the charge as follows:

. . . I am charged with having been a military vicar as though it were a great crime, and also that having had relations with the NDH is tantamount to a betrayal of Jugoslavia. I must say that I was military vicar even under the old Jugoslavia and that it was in this capacity, when the German-Jugoslav war was nearing its end, that I found myself obliged to render spiritual help to the remnants of the Catholic forces of the old Jugoslav army and at the same time to the soldiers of the new NDH. If the State was plunging into catastrophe, the soldiers nonetheless remained and it was necessary to take the new situation into account. . . . I was not a *persona grata* either to the Germans, or to the Ustachi. I have never sworn an oath to them, as several of your functionaries present here have done. . . .

b) Mons. Stepinac was even more open in regard to the second charge of collaboration with the enemy:

. . . You accuse me as an enemy of the State and of the people's powers. Will you tell me: who were my civil authorities in 1941? Perhaps, Simovic in Belgrade or the Government of London which you call traitorous, or even that of Palestina, or you yourselves who at that time lived in the middle of the forests? For me you have been the authorities ever since May 8, 1945. Perhaps, I was supposed to obey at one and the same time you who were hidden in the forests and those who were in Zagabria? At that time we could not ignore the authorities established in Zagabria, even though this was an Ustachi power. This was the power which was in command at that time. . . .

c) On the third charge, dealing with the enforced conversion of Orthodox nuclei to Catholicism, Mons. Stepinac pointed out that, on the contrary, ever since December 17, 1941, he had given precise orders to his clergy exhorting them not to carry out enforced conversions, specifying as follows:

It is a fact that I was forced to transfer a Curate because the Orthodox threatened him with death, because he had delayed the acceptance of their conversion. . . .

Besides . . . if we had not agreed to the demands made at that time, it is certain that today we could be called to justice under this charge: "Those men found themselves in difficult conditions. The Catholic Church could have helped them by accepting them, even fictitiously, but it did not wish to do so only for the reason that its adversaries might have been able to exterminate them more easily." So we should have been before the Court, anyway.

d) On the fourth charge which referred to the use of the Catholic press in favor of the Nazis, Mons. Stepinac brought forward the testimony of the editor of the "Katolicki List" himself, the canon Kolarek, who pointed out that many of the articles in question had been arbitrarily inserted by the Nazi authorities. The real thought of the Archbishop must be sought not in these newspaper articles, but in his pastoral letters, in his speeches, in which the Court could find nothing with which to charge him. In fact, Tito himself had used the very words of the Archbishop in a propaganda broadcast of 1943, by transmitting a passage in which he warned the Ustachi government to change its methods if it did wish to alienate completely the soul of the population.

e) The fifth charge, according to which he was supposed to have hidden the archives of the Pavelich Ministry of Foreign Affairs in the archbishopric, could not be supported, because it was proved, that those documents had been spontaneously returned before the prescribed date and therefore it could not be considered a crime.

Despite all the proofs he had adduced to deny the charges, Mons. Stepinac was condemned to 16 years of forced labor and to the loss of all political and civil rights for another five years.

The sentencing provoked protests from the entire Catholic world. On Monday, October 14, 1946, the Holy See published a communication of the Sacred Congregation of the Council, which reminded the judges that since they had placed their hands on the person of Mons. Stepinac, they had fallen into the state of ex-communication in accordance with canons 2341, 2343, and 2334.

The protests were so universal, that Tito, in order to re-
conquer public opinion, was compelled to send Dr. Bakaric,
President of the Croat government, to the Leopglava prison
where Mons. Stepinac was detained to propose that he sign an
appeal for amnesty, already drawn up, to be presented to Tito.
Mons. Stepinac refused to sign it.

The persecutory attitude against the Catholic Church did not
change in the slightest, however, and in fact not long after the
sentencing of Mons. Stepinac, a new trial was staged against
the Bishop of Lubiana, Mons. Rozman. This trial ended with his
sentencing and expulsion from Jugoslav territory, while at the
same time the Bishop of Mostar, Mons. Koule, was arrested. And
shortly thereafter, even the Archbishop of Sarajevo, the venerable
Mons. Saric, an old man of eighty.

COMMUNIST PERSECUTION AFTER STEPINAC'S SENTENCING

After the sentencing of Mons. Stepinac to forced labor and
the arrest of the other three Catholic Bishops, Mons. Rozman of
Lubiana, Mons. Koule of Mostar, and Mons. Saric of Sarajevo,
the persecution of the Catholic Church in Jugoslavia by the
Communist Government seemed for a moment to calm down. It
passed from a virulent phase to a more "normal" phase during
which it was decided, for the purposes of preserving propaganda
"face," to substitute the open and spectacular campaign against
the Church with one which aimed at its systematic destruction
from the inside, without raising too much of a clamor in the
outside world.

And here is the list of the principal "deeds and misdeeds,"
committed by the Communist Government against the Catholic
Church in Jugoslavia in the period between January 1947 and
December 1950, reported in their crude reality:

1) In Lanische in Slovenia in January 1947, Mons. Giacomo
Ukmar was attacked. He was the delegate of the Holy See for
that part of the territory of the Diocese of Trieste which had
been assigned to Jugoslavia. The parish priest, Miro Bulesich,
who had tried to come to his aid was killed on the spot, while

Mons. Ukmar, his skull fractured, had to be taken to the hospital in Fimore as an emergency case. Despite this the Communists still managed to drag him before a people's court which sentenced him to prison.

2) Mons. Lakainer, parish priest of Ruma in the Diocese of Diakovo, was killed in February 1947 in Stara Gradisca, a concentration camp established especially for priests, after he had been subjected to the cruelest tortures.

3) In Uovo Mesto, the Abbot Pavlixh was arrested and sentenced to several years in jail for having refused to violate confessional secrecy, countervening a law which had just then been passed by the Jugoslav Assembly in which it was decreed that "any priest may be interrogated regarding that which he has learned in confession and he is obliged to disclose it before a court."

4) In Buje, in Slovenia, five Benedictine monks were arrested in September 1947 and tried on charges of "crimes against morality." Alleged confessions of women were presented to them and they were forced to sign them.

5) In Maribor the same charge was made against a group of priests. Several laymen were compelled, by force and violence, to sign false declarations. The priests were arrested and brought to police headquarters where they were questioned for entire nights and threatened with death, with the aim of extorting information and declarations against their own Bishops from them.

6) In February 1948, a parish priest was arrested in Slovenka Bistrica under the charge that . . . "the 'gentleman' curate lived lavishly in his residence, amused himself with women and through them spun intrigues against the OF (Popular Front) and against the efforts of the workers." To the parishioners who appealed against his arrest, the police answered, "Solinc has not been imprisoned as the 'curate of Bistrica,' but as an ordinary citizen, a speculator and a saboteur . . ."

7) The expulsion of all nuns from the Catholic hospitals in Jugoslavia was carried out on March 8, 1948. The government order, transmitted to the nuns at 8 o'clock in the morning, had to be carried out before one o'clock in the afternoon. In the space

of four hours, twelve Slovene hospitals were evacuated of their Catholic Sisters, some of whom had served in them for more than forty years. The number of nuns who in the space of a few hours were "thrown on the street" came to more than two hundred.

8) In the same year, 1948, many other houses of nuns, besides those who worked in hospitals, were confiscated and the Sisters compelled to go elsewhere. Here is a brief list for purposes of documentation:

a) In Bielo Pollje, near Mostar, the house and the lands of the teacher nuns who had dedicated themselves to working the land in order to be able to feed their colleagues expelled from the schools, hospitals, and welfare institutions, were confiscated and the nuns dispersed.

b) In Sarajevo, about 90 Sisters of St. Joseph, were expelled from their house which was later occupied.

c) In Livnov, Dovno and Konjic, in the Diocese of Mostar, all the teacher Sisters were compelled to leave their houses and to leave the three towns as well.

d) In Banjaluka, all the Sisters of the Most Precious Blood, who numbered about 100 and who had been carrying out their apostolate in that city for years, were expropriated of their house and their goods, which were assigned to an agricultural institution.

e) In Studelice, near Maribor, more than 300 Sisters of the Congregation of St. Mary Magdalene, were deprived of all their properties and compelled, in the majority of cases, to return to their families.

9) On December 13, 1948, at the closing of the third congress of the Union of Women in Slovenia, the President of the central committee of that union, exhorted women to struggle as follows:

. . . We must never forget that the struggle against clericalism on our soil is the most difficult thing in our development. The traitors of the people abroad base their entire enemy propaganda on the anti-people priests. We women and mothers are responsible before the history of the Slovene people . . . to impede the flow of anti-national priests who poison our youth. . . .

10) In the first months of 1949, fifteen priests were sentenced to jail in a single province, guilty of an "anti-national" attitude. Here are the names of some of these: Torkar, parish priest of Islak, sentenced to ten years in jail; Arch, of the same town, sentenced to eight years; Golob, parish priest of Zaragje, sentenced to two years; Shuhala, sentenced to six years; Planinsek, sentenced to 13 years for "abuse of the confessional."

11) There were also some death sentences passed in the beginning of 1949. It was thus that two priests, Alfonse Jarc and Guglielmo Savelli, were executed on charges of having collaborated with the Italians.

12) In March 1949, 19 nuns of Djakovo were jailed on the same charges.

13) A group of Jesuit Fathers was arrested, tried and sentenced in Lubiana on April 1949. The charge made against them was summarized as follows by the Communist newspaper, "Slovenski Paracevalec" (Slovene Reporter), in its issue of May 4, 1949, under the title, "The Spies of the Vatican under the robes of the Jesuits":

. . . Ever since the time of the occupation the Jesuits of Lubiana have been working under the direction of the high representatives of the Church against national liberation. They then continued their hostile activity even after the liberation, with the intention of destroying by violence the present social order of our country. . . . According to the directives of the Vatican, the Jesuits of Lubiana have helped to hide war criminals and then helped them to escape across the border. As rabid enemies of Socialist Jugoslavia, they have circulated publications hostile to Jugoslavia. In the so-called "Monthly Retreats" for the priests of Lubiana, in their residence where Retreats were attended also by the Vicar General of Lubiana, Anthony Vovk, with the members of the Curia, the Jesuits incited the anti-national priests to a most rabid struggle against the power of the people.

For these "crimes," sentences were inflicted on the five Jesuits, Father Ledehhas, Father Janez Jauh, Father Pape and Father Jonko Koncilija, which together totalled 40 years in jail and 14 years loss of all civil rights.

14) In Lobor, on September 25, 1949, in the Diocese of Zagrabia, the parish priest, Guiseppe Vedrina, was attacked by a group of Communists while he was returning from a funeral. He was killed as a result of the stoning and the caning received, together with his sexton who tried to help him. The assassins were neither punished nor sought.

15) In Fiume on November 1949 the monumental Church of the Redeemer was torn down with picks, while from other places came news of acts of vandalism and profanation committed by Communists against crucifixes, icons, and other religious images which were systematically torn down and destroyed. Hundreds of churches were closed by the authorities and put to other uses.

16) In December 1949 the Government invited the Slovenian clergy to join the "Movement of Slovene Priests of the Liberation Front." Tito himself intervened with a public exhortation, addressed to the Slovene priests of the Association of Saints Cyril and Metodias and published in December of that same year in the review "Nova Pot," the organ of these progressive priests, in which he said: ". . . We have broken with Moscow, why do you not break with Rome?"

17) On April 26, 1950, the Archbishop of Belgrade, Mons. Ujcic, in the name of all the Bishops of Jugoslavia, listed all these "deeds and mis-deeds" in a "Memorandum" addressed to the Bureau of Religions of the Government which replied, on May 19, 1950, that the afore-mentioned "Memorandum" was:

. . . The fruit of an impossible mentality and therefore could not serve as the basis for a discussion or for negotiations between the Government of the Federal Republic of Jugoslavia and the Catholic Episcopate of Jugoslavia. . . .

18) In June 1950, the priest Cedomil Cekada was arrested and sentenced to 20 years in jail for having written articles

against Communism even before the Communists came to power. Another priest was condemned to 14 years in jail for having transported books from one point of the city to the other. It was charged, by the police, that among these books there were some of an anti-communist character.

19) In October 1950, the Bishop, Mons. Frances Cekada, the Bishop of Skoplje and Apostolic Administrator of the diocese of Banjaluka, was expelled without any reasons being given from Bosnia and Herzegivina and warned never to return. In his place the Holy See had to appoint another Apostolic Administrator, Mons. Karl Celik, who underwent many tribulations before he was recognized by the local authorities.

Thus in December 1950 the situation of the Catholic Church in Jugoslavia could be summarized in the following statistics:

a) Out of 22 Dioceses, almost two thirds were without an ordinary Bishop.

b) The number of priests executed or killed by the Communists after 1944 can be fixed at about 348.

c) The number of priests imprisoned and still under arrest is about 200.

d) Of the 18 Seminaries existing before the war, more than two thirds have been closed or requisitioned since 1946, and almost all the rest are partially occupied by government agencies.

e) The Catholic press and publications have been reduced to naught, and 22 Catholic printing plants have been "nationalized."

f) Religious instruction has been almost universally suppressed in the schools.

g) About 300 religious houses, convents, institutions and churches have been confiscated and put to other uses.

h) All the real and moveable properties of the Church have been confiscated.

i) The priestly ministry has been subjected to a government "Placet," which is issued by the Government to each single priest for each specified community, with an absolute prohibition, under pain of fine and even arrest, to set foot in neighboring communities even though they may be without a local priest.

THE LAST STAGES OF THE PERSECUTION (1951–1952)

The surviving Jugoslav Catholic Bishops have themselves prepared a resume of the situation in which the Catholic Church found itself in Jugoslavia during the years 1951 and 1952. This took the form of a *Memorandum* sent to Marshal Tito on September 25, 1952, following a conference held in Zagabria at that time. Here is the full text of the *Memorandum*:

MR. MARSHALL,

During their conference in Zagabria, held from September 23 to 26, 1952, the undersigned Bishops and Apostolic Administrators of the Catholic Church on the territory of the RPF of Jugoslavia, have among other questions concerned themselves with the situation in which the Catholic Church in Jugoslavia finds itself.

They consider it as their essential duty to turn to the Supreme Head of the State in order to outline to him in a *Memorandum* the most burning problems of the religious life of their faithful.

1) *Do Religious Freedoms Exist in Jugoslavia at the Present Moment?*

The Catholic Bishops observe that there is no authentic religious freedom in Jugoslavia. The freedom of conscience and the free exercise of worship about which the constitution of the RPF of Jugoslavia speaks in its Article 25 have been especially reduced to a partial freedom of worship, or as our laws express it, to a freedom of "religious ceremonies."

We say "partial freedom" because the freedom of worship has been reduced to the point where in effect it has ceased to exist.

It is true that the Churches are still open, but many of them, as for example those of the Trappists in Delibassino

Selo near Banjaluka has been for a certain time, in spite of its artistic value, been transformed into a granary and then made into a warehouse for agricultural equipment.

The monumental Church of St. Joseph in Lubiana, a jewel of religious art, has been taken away from Catholics and given to an ancient a-Catholic sect, which has only a few members in Lubiana.

Numerous Crosses and holy images, situated along the roads of the country, have been disfigured and profaned; naturally the perpetrators have not been discovered.

In Slovenia and in other localities in the country, many chapels have been profaned.

The great and beautiful Church of the Saviour in Rjeke (Fiume) was destroyed by a bomb in early November 1949, and it is to be noted that this Church was in the heart of the city.

In the same manner the Church of the Carmelites in Selo, near Lubiana, and the beautiful Chapel at the summit of the "Climb to Calvary," near Rjeka, were destroyed.

According to our information many Catholic Churches of the Banato have been demolished in an analogous manner. Many public Churches belonging to institutions directed by monks have been closed in different parts of the country.

The Church of the Holy Virgin in Ptujska Gora, the largest pilgrimage center of the Diocese of Maribor, against the will of the church authorities, was transformed into a museum.

The civil authorities do not authorize the construction of new churches. Hence, in Osjek, in Bitoliic near Sinj, in Novo Selo, near Rakovica, and in many other places, such authorization has been refused.

Moreover, it is difficult to obtain permission to restore old churches.

The registries of Baptisms, Deaths and Marriages were taken away from the Church in 1946. Government bodies without much ado arrogated to themselves the right of checking the new registers established for use inside the

Church after May 9, 1946. The old registries have never been returned to the Church, despite promises given.

The agencies of the OUDB oblige organists, men and women, and choral directors to abandon their functions.

Processions are prohibited in many regions. Important religious feast-days, during which the faithful of different parishes assembled together, have been frequently molested. In this manner feasts celebrating a "First Mass" are in particular disturbed, and the gifts which the new priest receives from the faithful, in accordance with a most ancient custom, are confiscated by the OUDB.

The freedom of preaching is likewise threatened. The priests are accused of quoting Holy Scriptures. Positive expositions of the truths are considered as activity directed against the security of the State and against the new social order.

In the same manner priests have been forbidden to speak to children against atheist propaganda during catechism.

"Priests," says a circular issued by the local people's authority in Bosnia-Herzegovina, "must not exercise their influence on parents to prevent their children from becoming atheists."

It has come to the point where priests have been asked to urge the faithful not to attend church anymore.

It has been forbidden to priests to impart religious instruction not only in the schools, but even in private homes and in the churches. In many cases it is forbidden to priests to impart religious instruction to youth in the churches.

Even the preparations for First Communion have been prohibited. For having transgressed against such impositions, numerous priests have been sentenced to pay heavy fines and to many days in jail.

The churches and their institutions have been overburdened with taxes which go beyond any measure whatsoever. When priests do not have the means to pay them, their own properties or those of the parish, are confiscated, as can be proved by the occurrences in Trsat, Volar, Destinic, Dragonici, and Novalia.

In the Dioceses of Lubiana and in the localities of pilgrimages dedicated to the Madonna, as in Brezie, Ptujska Gora, even the Mass offerings destined for those officiating were confiscated.

It is forbidden to collect alms in many churches. The Cathedral of Lubiana was condemned to pay a fine of 10,000 dinars, because a sacristan had collected 10 dinars which a member of the church had left as alms.

In Slovenia and other localities religious institutions have been forbidden to accept gifts from abroad.

At the beginning of this year, American Catholics sent powdered eggs and milk to the priests and the seminarists of Rjeka, Senj, Krk and Zadar, as well as bundles of used clothing. These gifts were returned to the sender because the authorities demanded a customs duty amounting to 600,000 dinari, a sum which the diocese could not raise.

In June of this year the same American Catholics sent flour and oil to the dioceses of Senj, Krk, Rjeka and for its "Great Seminary." Even this new shipment was returned to the sender on account of the lack of the necessary money to pay the exhorbitant customs duty.

The arrests of priests continue. The sentences to which they are condemned are more severe than those which are customarily imposed by our courts.

Several days ago a priest of 75 years of age, the beloved parish priest of Zumberex, Karl Nidovec, was sentenced to death for crimes he was alleged to have committed during the war.

At the present time more than two hundred priests languish in Jugoslav prisons.

During the eight years of this regime, a notable part of our Catholic clergy has experienced the humiliations and the discomforts of penitentiaries.

Among these priests, is still to be found, Mons. Peter

Cule, the Bishop of Mostar. The archbishop of Zagabria, Mons. Stepinac, even though he is out of prison, is subject to a close surveillance and can not exercise his functions.

Is it not really surprising that the clergy, which in all countries of the civilized world has never violated the penal codes, should have become so incorrigibly criminal in our country?

Nor are cases rare in which priests are attacked with weapons. During the past seven years about 30 priests have fallen in ambushes or have been barbarously assassinated; naturally the guilty ones have neither been found nor punished.

These barbarities reached their culminating point with the direct attack made against the person of Mons. Anthony Vock, Bishop of Lubiana, who during a pastoral visit to the station of Novo Mesto, made on January 20, 1952, was showered with gasoline and burned. He owes his salvation to his own *personal sang-froid.* The assailants of the Bishop were punished *a forfait* with 9 days in jail!

The same Bishop was forbidden to make his pastoral visit for the purpose of comforting with his presence the parishioners who live along the frontier of the country. The visit of this Bishop to Jeseinc was defined as provocative. He was obliged to return to Lubiana while several thousands of faithful were awaiting his visit in church.

The Bishop of Maribor, Mons. Drzecnik, was likewise forbidden to visit his parishioners along the frontier. Other Bishops have informed us of analogous difficulties during their pastoral visits within their own Dioceses.

The State authorities let no occasion go by to demonstrate their enmity for the church and its institutions.

The Catholic Episcopate since 1945 has sent to the Government of the RPF of Jugoslavia, at least six Memoranda, which have gone unanswered. Only once did the Government commission on worship, on May 19, 1950, reply to the Archbishop of Belgrade that the Memorandum of the Bishops of April 26, 1950, was the fruit ". . . of an impossible mentality and therefore could not serve as a basis for a discussion or for negotiations between the Government of the RPF of Jugoslavia and the Catholic Episcopate of Jugoslavia."

And this is not all! Meanwhile, God knows how many memoranda, requests, prayers, have been sent by the heads of Dioceses to the different branches of the federal government, to the Governments of the Republic and to other subordinate authorities, without ever having received a reply.

It would seem that in Jugoslavia religious authorities are no longer worthy of consideration and that the Church must be humiliated at any cost.

There is also the painful question of atheist instruction in the schools and in the public life of the RPF of Jugoslavia. Atheism is the religion of the regime. Atheism is propagated in all the schools of the State, at meetings, in the press, and it is imposed on civil and military functionaries.

In order to complete the proof of the absolute lack of religious freedom in RPF of Jugoslavia it is necessary to add several facts already exposed in our previous Memoranda.

It is necessary to remember the liquidation of all the Catholic schools throughout the territory of the Republic. Our intermediate, classical and commercial schools, our normal schools which trained our teachers, our schools of arts and trades, our primary schools and even elementary schools and infant shelters have been abolished with the stroke of a pen.

The buildings have been confiscated. The right to maintain Seminaries has been taken away from the Church.

All the printing plants of the Catholic Church have been confiscated without any indemnities. From one day to another the State took over 20 large printing plants and publishing houses and has dissolved the associations to which journalists and writers belonged. It is an incalculable loss.

For this reason the Catholic press has been suppressed, and the few bulletins which are published here and there are so small and limited in the number of pages that one can no longer speak of a Catholic press. There are naught but wretched remnants of a Catholic press which was once so powerful.

Before the war we owned 152 Catholic newspapers. The Church has been over-burdened with taxes and duties even for these small bulletins.

We have been obliged to re-print articles which already have appeared in the State newspapers or the texts of official speeches, and in such detail that no room was left for our religious communications.

The newspaper of Zagabria, "Gore Srca" was recently fined 90,000 dinars for having published without comment an anti-religious speech made by the Minister Vis Krstulorvic in Sl. Brod.

This issue of the same newspaper which published the letter "Sacro Vergente Anno," addressed to the peoples of Russia, was confiscated.

The editor-in-chief Mr. F. Grundler was sentenced to six months in jail for having published an article against atheist schools. Today this newspaper can not be published nor will it be able to resume publication.

All these facts prove that there is no freedom of conscience and religion in the RPF of Jugoslavia and that the Catholic Church is seriously threatened in its essential freedoms and in its vital rights.

We can not give all the details in this Memorandum, but we are ready to present a detailed documentation for all the affirmations made in it.

Permit us to gather all the evidence and to publish it!

2) *Is an Agreement Between the Church and the State Possible?*

Actually an answer to this question is not difficult. If the Church is asked for the love of peace and for a friendly collaboration with the authorities of the State to renounce its essential and fundamental rights, any agreement whatsoever is impossible.

During its history the Church has never accepted an unconditional surrender and it will not accept it even today. To require that our Church recognize the present situation in the RPF of Jugoslavia as legitimate and to confirm it with a Concordat, would be equivalent to asking it "to sign its death warrant."

The Church, however, is ever disposed to negotiate and to make concessions, as long as its moral and juridical status be recognized and all the indispensable rights deriving from its essential nature be granted to it.

This means that, if the State sincerely desires correct relations with the Church, it must abolish all the revolting injustices to which our church institutions are exposed daily. The persecution which began with the present regime of the Federal Republic of Jugoslavia must cease.

Up to now the Episcopate, from day to day, has become convinced that in the RPF of Jugoslavia there is the intent to uproot religion.

This intention proceeds by stages, some of which have already been realized. We probably find ourselves before the penultimate stage. Militant atheism is presently before the doors of our churches and it is preparing to violate the last refuge of religious freedom.

The civil authorities think that, perhaps, the best means of concluding an agreement between the Church and the State lies in the creation of sacerdotal unions. These unions already exist without the permission of the competent Bishops, in Slovenia, in Istria, in Bosnia, and in Herzegivina. We are convinced that they do not correspond to the indispensable conditions for the realization of this grand achievement.

The creation of these unions has been imposed by the regime. Their manner of operation and the directives which they receive from the authorities convince us that the unions of priests, in the intention of their promoters, must progressively weaken church discipline and religious life and not, instead, normalize the relations between Church and State.

If the Episcopate be asked to recognize these unions, their statutes must not injure the rights of the Church and the ecclesiastical authority must be able to control their activities. Only on these conditions can the Episcopate take the creation of unions of priests into consideration.

3) *On What Conditions Can the Episcopate Collaborate?*

The Catholic Episcopate has always acted legally as regards the civil order. We desire to preserve this frank attitude. We are not revolutionaries. On the contrary we loyally love our Fatherland and we ask our priests and our faithful to look favorably on the positive aspects of the present political social order. With our faithful we desire the integrity of our frontiers and we are prepared for any sacrifice for the good and for the prosperity of our country.

But an active participation in political life can not be expected from us. Politics and the responsibility stemming from it we leave to those who intend to assume it.

We shall be concerned with our social life from the religious and spiritual point of view. This is our future and nobody can prevent us from dedicating all our efforts to it.

We do not ask for privileges. We would be content if we were just granted that which derives from Divine law and human law. We do not merely want the freedom of worship, but those liberties, too, inherent in a true liberty of conscience and religion. These are: the freedom of religious education, the freedom of a Catholic press, the freedom of religious organizations, and the right to dispose of the material means indispensable for such purposes.

We do not ask the material means of the State. The people will give us all that we need, because the people believes in its Church, because the people loves its religion.

If the State authorities will recognize these principles, we are certain, we Catholic Bishops, that there will no longer be any tension between the Church and the State in the RPF of Jugoslavia. We are also certain that these relations will be of a great usefulness to the two parties. This is the objective which we pursue and for which it is worthwhile sacrificing something.

This *Memorandum,* Mr. Marshall, we, the Catholic Bishops of the RPF of Jugoslavia, address to you, the Supreme Head of our national community. We have drawn it up during our plenary conference held in Zagabria with the certainty that you would take it into consideration and that it will find the comprehension it merits from you.

Please accept, Mr. Marshall, the expression of our high esteem.

> [*signed by the 20 Bishops present at the Episcopal Conference*]

Zagabria, September 25, 1952

On December 15, 1952 the Holy See followed up this "Memorandum" which the Catholic Jugoslav Bishops had sent to Marshal Tito, with a "Note of the Secretary of State of His Holiness" directed to the Ministry of Foreign Affairs of Jugoslavia. This note was a reply to a "Note" sent by that Ministry on November 1, 1952 to the Apostolic Nuntiature of Belgrade in which it had been affirmed that the most ample freedom of religion existed in Jugoslavia. The note of the Holy See, however, brought forth new evidence that such a freedom did not exist at all, and that, on the contrary, plans for the complete annihilation of the Catholic Church in Jugoslavia had been set in motion.

Here is the full text of the "Note" of the Holy See:

N. 9414/52

TO THE MINISTER OF FOREIGN AFFAIRS
OF THE RPF OF JUGOSLAVIA
BELGRADE

. . . In reply to your Note n. 414835/52 of November 1, the Secretariat of the Holy See has the honor of expounding the following:

1. The Jugoslav Government speaks of a satisfactory bilateral "arrangement" of relations with the Holy See.

The Holy See faithful to its mission and to its program

of contributing, when possible, to the pacification of souls and the spiritual welfare of peoples, is constantly animated by the desire to join in and preserve good relations with the civil Authorities of different countries.

But, on the other hand, the Holy See can not neglect the duty incumbent on it to protect the inalienable rights of religion and of the Catholic Church wherever they may be unrecognized or violated. And such action can not be considered as an unwarranted interference in the internal affairs of a State, because Catholics, besides being citizens in a specific country, are also members of the Church.

2. The Holy See must observe with deep regret that in Jugoslavia, both Government authorities and other persons representative of Communism, with repeated solemn declarations, make an open profession of atheism, and manifest the intention of taking away from the people—and particularly the youth—every religious ideal and feeling, and they conduct a ceaseless struggle against religion and especially against the Catholic Church.

It will be enough to limit ourselves to some examples, selected among the most recent and relative in particular to Croatia and Slovenia, where the Catholics constitute the majority of the population:

a) On February 9, 1952 the "Slovenski Porocevalec" of Ljubljana published a circular sent to the different sections of the Slovene Communist party . . . "During the school year," it said therein, "it is necessary to help the youth to understand, on the basis of scientific reasonings, the negative and reactionary influence of religion and obscurantism. . . ."

This circular bore, among others, the signature of Mr. Edward Kardelji; Vice-President of the Council of Ministers and Minister of Foreign Affairs of the RPF of Jugoslavia, as well as that of Mr. Boris Kidric, President of the Economic Council of the Central Government.

b) The "Vjesnik" of April 20, 1952, reported the following declaration of Dr. Milos Zenko, Minister President of the

Council for Civilization and Culture of the People's Republic of Croatia: "Whoever thinks that, by virtue of the freedom of conscience guaranteed by the Constitution, educational aims contrary to Marxism can be introduced, is not carrying-out his cultural duty, just as if he were teaching that 2 plus 2 equals 7."

c) On June 1, 1952, 'Naprijed," the organ of the Croat Communist Party, quoted some statements made by Mr. Vicko Krstulovic, President of the Assembly of the People's Republic of Croatia, at a meeting of the Communist party held in Osijek: "With the revolution carried out by us, we have broken the ancient bourgeois order, we have destroyed the system on which the bourgeoisie based itself and we have taken everything into our hands. However, we could not destroy the Church as an institution, not because the authorities in our country are weak, but because in the consciousness of a great part of the population, the farming above-all, there still remain strong residues of faith. We are conscious of the fact that the Church has had its day as an institution and we must struggle against it, in the political and cultural life, by raising at one and the same time, the material level of life and the consciousness of the people so that it may understand that the world has not developed according to the holy spirit (sic) but according to the laws of nature. We must mobilize public opinion, in the villages and in the schools, against the harmful work of priests."

d) In Belgrade the "Borba" of November 7, 1952 reported that a Mr. Alexander Ronkovic, Minister of the Interior, addressing the VI Congress of the Jugoslav Communist Party had stressed the necessity of a ". . . resolute, stuborn, ceaseless struggle against bourgeois, clerical and cominformist manifestations and conceptions."

e) The "Vjesnik" of Zagabria of November 9, 1952, explained how this struggle was to be understood with an article by the Academician Marko Kostrencic, a well-known propagator of Communist ideas: . . . "The morality of

Christ," he wrote, "must be rejected, because it is unworthy of man and because it condemns him to a negative life. Christian morality is a stimulus to the committing of cruelties in a grand style. Socialist morality derives from the Marxist conception of the world; it denies the existence of a better world, of a transcendent world in the heavens, with all its super-natural scarecrows and its consolations, from satan, from spirits, from angels, from saints up to god (sic) and to the gods of all sorts. For this conception of the world god (sic) is dead and all the gods are dead. For this conception there exists only this visible, material world."

f) Such affirmations are complemented by other official declarations of the Communist Party. "Nova Makedanija" of Skoplie of March 2, 1952, affirmed: 'Our Party has never been indifferent before religious ideology and the Church, but today it is a question of organizing a systematic, daily ideological struggle, through the press, the mass organizations, the cultural institutions, in order to destroy all religious conceptions of the universe, all the prejudices, all the religious traditions."

g) In the same sense "Borba" of Belgrade on March 1, 1952, reporting the conclusions of the V plenary session of the central committee of the Communist Party of Macedonia wrote: "The ideological work of the Party on our workers must strive to free them from the influence of religion and mysticism."

h) In Sarajevo, the newspaper "Oslobodjenje," on September 13, 1952, reported that during a meeting of the Communist Party held in Foka and Kiseljak, it was deplored that some Party members "consider that the carrying out of religious rites is permitted them, because it is guaranteed by the Constitution of our country and by the law to all citizens, not realizing that the members of the Party must be the bearers of progress, the first in the struggle against superstition, promitivism and all the residues of reaction."

i) In Ljubljana, the "Slovenski Porocevalec," also on November 13, upon giving an account of a Communist

Party meeting held in Notranje Gorice, wrote: "There was talk of the necessity of the struggle against obscurantist religious prejudices, and above-all against the clergy which preserves such prejudices."

j) "Ljudska Pravica," the organ of the Slovene Communist Party, stated clearly on February 16, 1952 that "a Communist is not free to go to church, to attend religious ceremonies, to contract matrimony before a priest, and to have his children baptized. For Communism religion is the opium of the people."

These few quotations, which are only a "specimen" of the multiple and uniform anti-religious declarations in which the press daily abounds, are in accord with the very Statute of the Union of Communists in Jugoslavia which declares: "Membership in the Union of Communists of Jugoslavia is incompatible with the profession of religion and with the exercising of religious rites."

Besides, Marshal Tito himself declared to the representatives of the Congress of the Association of professors, instructors and teachers of Jugoslavia (Borba, April 30, 1952), that: "I know that abroad we are reproached for taking youth away from god (sic) and from the church. But we can not permit that these men practice superstition, because all that is superstitution. We must struggle against superstition."

3) The sad conditions imposed on religion and the Church in Jugoslavia are nothing else, unfortunately, but the application of such declarations and principles.

The legislative dispositions on religion, the provisions taken by the constituted authorities, the initiatives of the Communist Party and the trade unions, the treatment accorded to many faithful and the situation created for the Bishops and a large part of the clergy, seem to tend to a progressive elimination of religion and the Catholic Church in particular.

Even here it is sufficient to cite the more significant facts:

a) Before the installation of the Communist regime in Jugoslavia, there existed 152 Catholic periodicals—dailies, weeklies, reviews, bulletins—in Jugoslavia. There was a proportionate number of publishing houses and printing plants corresponding to this number of publications, 24 of which were particularly important.

At present all the Catholic printing plants and publishing houses are in the hands of the State. The dailies, the weeklies, the reviews, the diocesan and parochial bulletins have, in one way or another, been suppressed.

For a certain time some publications survived such as the "Vierski List" of Maribor, the "Oznanilo" of Ljubljana, the "Gore Srca" of Zagabria. Although all three had already been limited in circulation, they had to cease publication one after the other.

Today the Catholic press is represented only by "Vjesnik," a monthly bulletin for the clergy published in Diakovo, and "Blagovest," a monthly review of Belgrade which nonetheless experiences many difficulties in publishing. And for the past four months a four page monthly in half-format, "Druzina" is published in Vipava by the Apostolic Administration of Nova Gorica.

And these Catholic periodicals would be immediately confiscated should they attempt to answer the slanders and blasphemies systematically diffused by the Communist press against all that which is most venerable and sacred to the faithful. Today in Jugoslavia is no longer practically possible to publish books of a religious character.

b) All the Catholic educational institutions—which were counted in the hundreds with tens of thousands of students —have been closed. In all the schools, in every grade, religious instruction has been abolished and atheist materialism is obligatory.

Many educators who did not teach or did not practice atheism have been removed from the schools, as have also many students, accused of attending Church.

"Viesnik" of Zagabria, on February 22, 1952, reported that

many students had been expelled from the Croatian secondary schools for religious crimes, that is, for having been absent from school on Christmas Day. A total of 32 students were expelled from the normal schools of Maribor, in the first months of 1952, because they attended Church.

c) The arrests of priests charged with non-existent crimes continue and they are invariably sentenced to the maximum penalty prescribed by law. About 200 are still in prison. In these last years about thirty priests have been killed in ambush and the guilty either have not been searched for, or have not been punished, or punished in a derisive way.

The clergy is continually attacked by the press which excites the citizenry to a hatred and a contempt for the clergy.

Churchmen have been reduced to poverty. In the application of land reform the limits established by the law were frequently exceeded, insofar as they were concerned. Now exhorbitant taxes are imposed on church properties and at the same time the faithful are prevented from helping their pastors in a corresponding way. In one city the bishopric curia saw all the money, which had been given as alms for the intentions of Masses, confiscated. In another, the Cathedral had to pay a fine of 10,000 dinars, because the sacristan had collected some dinars from an altar, left there by the faithful.

d) These hostile provisions do not even spare Bishops. While the Archbishop of Zagabria, freed from prison, finds himself in conditional freedom, Mons. Cule, the Bishop of Mostar, is still in prison; Mons. Gargovic, Apostolic Administrator to Zadar is today confined to that city; Mons. Nezic, Administrator of Porec-Pula-Pazin finds himself in Pazin under the same conditions.

The Bishops encounter serious difficulties in the exercise of their ministry, especially during pastoral visits. They are forbidden to go to certain parishes, and in others Communists organize hostile manifestations and violence with impunity.

On January 20, 1952, Mons. Vovk, Apostolic Administrator of Ljubljana was attacked at the station of Novo
Mesto, as he was going to a parish for a religious ceremony,
and the serious injuries he received compelled him to undergo treatment for several months. Only one of the guilty was
sentenced to 9 days in jail with probation.

Mons. Banic, the Apostolic Administrator of Sibenik, was
also the object of various attacks during his pastoral visit.

The Bishops are subjected to frequent interrogations and
intimidations and threats on the part of the police. Mons.
Vovk, the afore-mentioned, in the spring of 1952, was sentenced to pay a very high fine for having explained in circulars addressed to his clergy the Catholic doctrine on abortion
and the profession of faith.

e) The functioning and the very existence of the Seminaries encounter numerous difficulties. Eight seminaries have
been closed; the buildings of some others still open are
partially occupied. Thus, in Zagabria, Ljubljana and Split.
The surviving Seminaries are subject to vexations and floun-
der in serious economic difficulties, not only because of the
confiscation of the properties of the Church, but also because
it is almost impossible to accept the offerings of the faithful
of the country (in money or goods) and to receive the aid
offered by Catholics from abroad.

As a result of provisions of occupation and confiscation
the small Seminaries of Maribor, Ljubljana, Senj, Skopje (in
Prizren), Subotica, Sarajevo (in Travnik) have been closed.

In all Slovenia there is not even one small Seminary
because the house which has been opened in Vipava, in the
apostolic administration of Nova Gorica, does not merit
classification as a seminary.

Likewise no small Seminary exists in Montenegro, in
Bosnia-Herzegivina, in Voivodina, in Macedonia.

As regards Croatia, the Minister President of the Council
for civilization and culture, Dr. Milos Zanko, in a circular
dated January 31, 1952, ordered that all boys under 15 years
must attend State schools, where as has been said above,

Marxism is taught. Therefore it is impossible for the small seminaries to have pupils in the first four gymnasial classes.

f) In Slovenia, Bosnia and Herzegovina, the female religious congregations have been dissolved. Catholic associations have been prohibited almost everywhere on the territory of the RPF in Jugoslavia.

g) The freedom of worship itself is limited and violated. Sacred edifices have been deprived of their function, or even in certain cases, taken away from Catholics to be given to non-Catholics. Thus it happened that the ancient church of the Teutonic Order, in Ljubljana, was given to a sect of old Catholics which has hardly any followers in the city. The great church of the Most Holy Saviour in Rjeka has been destroyed, other churches have been demolished in Banato and elsewhere. The important Marian sanctuary of Ptuiska Gora has been transformed into a museum, etc.

The Civil authorities refuse permission to construct new churches and only with great difficulties do they allow the restoration of certain existing churches.

Processions are prohibited almost everywhere. And there is opposition to the solemnities with which, according to usage, it is customary to celebrate First Masses.

h) Even the teaching of catechism is subject to serious restrictions and limitations.

In Croatia the previously cited circular of January 31, 1952, abolished the teaching of cathechism in State schools— a provision immediately adopted by the other Republics. Moreover, it forbade the assembling of children in order to teach them cathechism in buildings annexed to a church, in parish houses, in private homes.

In Slovenia the priests are obliged (Law of June 20, 1951) to obtain a special permit to teach religion inside churches and the authorization is limited to feast days. Numerous priests have been punished with fines and arrests for having dared to teach without such permission.

In Bosnia-Herzegovina, since 1941, the teaching of catechism has been forbidden in the schools under the specious pretext that the school is separated from the Church. But on the other hand it is not permitted in the Churches because all instruction must be imparted by the schools.

i) Serious obstacles also hamper the administration of sacraments.

Numerous faithful have been attacked in the press, dismissed from their jobs for crimes such as these: for contracting a religious matrimony, for baptizing their children, for having a son in a seminary, for being absent from work on feast days. For example, "Ljudska Pravica" of Ljubljana, on September 13, 1952, threatened to dismiss a mid-wife for having exhorted a citizen to baptize his son.

The Rev. Peter Berisa, parish priest of Djakovica, was condemned to 30 months in jail, on October 24, 1952, for having sought to heal the matrimonial situation of some of his parishioners married only before civil law, or actually bigamists.

The sole fact of going to church represents a grave risk for many. It has been reported above how some teachers have been relieved of teaching licenses and others have been expelled from schools because they attended church. Soldiers are warned against taking part in sacred ceremonies. The carrying-out of religious duties is prohibited to communists, as has also been seen above.

In addition, the civil authorities have suppressed all religious feasts even those which are most solemn (Christmas, for example) imposing the obligation of going to school on that day, or of being present in office or factory.

Even on Sundays students are often obliged to work or to participate in excursions or contests which make it impossible for them to carry-out their religious duties.

The police are present inside the churches, even during the sacred services, to observe and check on priests and faithful.

If, despite all this, the churches in Jugoslavia are still much frequented, the fact, far from attesting to a religious freedom which does not exist in fact, simply demonstrates how alive and deep is the religious feeling of these faithful.

Such a long series of dispositions and hostile acts against religion and the Church has always been accompanied and sustained by violent press campaigns which often distort words, facts and documents, without restraint, and which without pause spread slanders, grave and bloody insults against the institutions and the most venerated personalities of the Catholic Church.

4) The problem of the associations called "Popular Priests" must be considered in the panorama of such a religious situation.

It is known that the civil authorities are the originators of those associations. A great number of priests have been, and still are, compelled to join them by intimidation, threats, or the promise of being enabled to practice their ministry more freely, or with the bait of economic advantages accorded to the priests who join up.

Thus, only because they are not members of such associations, certain priests are seriously hampered in the exercise of their sacred ministry; others have not yet been able to take possession if a parish to which the Bishop has appointed them, or they have not been able to reside there.

Those who exercise a special influence in the above-mentioned associations—under outside directives—are priests who are not in order with divine faith or ecclesiastical discipline, a situation, which has provoked canonic sanctions.

The police attend the meetings, at which political personalities also make frequent appearances. There speeches are made in which the activity of Bishops and even of the Church is openly and publicly condemned. A close collaboration united and unites these associations to the "Popular Front" and through it to the Communist Party, as now it is united with the Union of Communists of Jugoslavia.

A similar state of affairs could do naught but preoccupy the Bishops, primarily because such associations seriously disturbed Church discipline and constituted a danger of splitting the clergy and the hierarchy. These fears of the Bishops are also justified by the fact that the Statutes of these Associations do not sufficiently guarantee the respect and dependency due to the Episcopal Authority.

5) In the face of such sad conditions imposed on the Catholics of Jugoslavia, the Holy See believes it to be its duty to make a precise summary of the fundamental rights of the Catholic Church, rights to which the Holy See can not renounce, and whose non-recognition would deprive any eventual conversations with the Jugoslav Government of any fruitfulness.

a) Catholics must be guaranteed the freedom not only of attending church, but even of manifesting their faith, by attending and participating in rites and sacraments, in pilgrimages and processions. No one must be hampered or prohibited in the practice of his religion.

b) The right of Catholic parents must be recognized not only to have their children baptized and to send them to church, but even to have them instructed and educated in Catholic schools, the existence and administration of which must be respected by the civil authorities. To compel Catholic parents to raise their children according to anti-religious maxims and programs is, in fact, a serious violation of the freedom of conscience.

c) Moreover, Catholics must not be put in a position which deprives them of their press, which explains and illustrates the different points of the freedom of conscience to them.

d) These same Catholics must be given the possibility of establishing associations whose aim would be the assembling of the faithful for religious purposes, according to a program of piety, charity, beneficence and activity, programs always and ever geared to the common good. Likewise Catholics must be free to contribute to the maintenance of the clergy, of worship and the works of charity, and to the restoration of sacred edifices and the construction of new temples.

e) In all these activities, as required by the doctrine and discipline of the Catholic Church, the faithful—without unwarranted interference and obstacles on the part of the civil authorities—must remain in contact and in dependency upon their Bishops.

The Bishops must not be denied the possibility of visiting the parishes, of carrying out sacred functions, of announcing Catholic doctrine and of promulgating documents for the pastoral instruction and direction of their people.

Just as with the Bishops, the clergy must not be hampered in its multiple activities of religious assistance to the faithful and in the preaching of the Christian doctrine.

f) Besides which religious instruction must be allowed in the schools, either parochial or diocesan, and the children must not be hampered from receiving it.

And since the future of the Church is directly tied to the Seminaries (large and small) these must be able to constitute themselves freely and to carry out their irreplaceable task.

The religious congregations, male and female, have a special importance in the life of the Church; religious activity, charity, must be able to be exercised without any obstacles.

The Holy See wishes to hope, on its part, that the Jugoslav Government will not refuse to guarantee the recognition of such freedoms and rights.

The Secretariat of State of the Holy See takes this occasion to extend to the Ministry of Foreign Affairs of the People's Federative Republic of Jugoslavia, the assurance of its high consideration.

From the Vatican, December 15, 1952

THE RUPTURE OF DIPLOMATIC RELATIONS WITH THE HOLY SEE

On December 1, 1952, the Jugoslav under-Secretary of Foreign Affairs, Mr. Ales Bebler, without even studying the afore-mentioned "Note" of the Holy See, whose envelope was returned un-opened to the Apostolic Nuntiature in Belgrade, received Mons. Silvio Oddi, the *ad interim* Charge d'Affaires attached to the Nuntiature, and delivered to him a "Note" in which the decision of the Jugoslav Government to break off relations with the Holy See was communicated. The "Note" ended thus:

. . . The Jugoslav Government at the same time stresses this decision will have no influence in its fundamental attitude insofar as regards the freedom of religion and the freedom of action of the Church in the field of religion within the limits of the Constitution in Jugoslavia. . . .

On the day before, December 16, Tito himself in a speech delivered in Smeberevha Palank, had said textually:

. . . Permit me to tell you something about the propaganda of the Vatican . . . The Vatican is full of resentment against our socialist country, it hates and does everything possible against us. It has also done us the offense of nominating as Cardinal, the war criminal, Stepinac. With this act it has offended our entire country. Are there, perhaps, no other Bishops in Jugoslavia? There are . . . but this is a political Bishop . . . But it will never have the satisfaction of seeing Stepinac, Bishop of Zagabria. I guarantee it!

The final motive which was supposed to have induced the Jugoslav Government to break off its diplomatic relations with the Holy See was, as can be inferred from Tito's remarks cited above, was the appointment as Cardinal of Mons. Stepinac who, previously sentenced to 16 years in jail, had been freed by Tito himself only a month before, and confined to the village of Krasic.

But from the *conclusion* of all the afore-mentioned facts it is easy to see how this rupture is nothing else but a direct consequence of deliberate reasons of principle.

If the Apostolic See were a State like all the others, wrote the "Osservatore Romano" of January 17, 1953, it would have had very good reasons for withdrawing its representative from Belgrade long before. But since its only aim is the welfare of souls, it has shown an infinite forbearance, because the existence of a diplomatic tie would not have rendered a "modus vivendi" impossible, whenever an act of good will or reciprocity might have established the indispensable premises.

This tie was broken on the initiative of the Government of Belgrade and it only remained for the Holy See to take note of it, with deep sadness and with an immense preoccupation over the fate and the future of the Catholic Church in Jugoslavia.

Sources and Bibliography

Here is a list of the principal publications and sources from which the greater part of the information and documents reported in this study were taken.

A. GENERAL VIEW

Dervik, Michael, "Eastern Catholic under Soviet Rule," London, 1946.

Combes, J. "L'assaut contre le Christ au XX siècle: mystiques paiennes de haine et de mort." Paris, 1948.

Roger Latu, "L'Eglise derriére le rideau de fer," Paris, 1949.

"Eglise et Communisme vus d'Europe Centrale" in "Esprit," Sept. 1949.

Gunther John, "Beyond the Curtain" (Italian edition), Milan, 1950.

Nagy Ferenc, "The Struggle behind the Iron Curtain," (Italian edition), Milan, 1950.

J. B. Barron and H. M. Waddans, "Communism and the Churches," a documentation. London, 1950.

Tisserant, Cardinal Eugene, "La situation religeuse derriére le rideau de fer," in "Documentation Catholique," 1951, col. 585-592.

Pisoni, Mons. Ernesto, "Nuovi Martiri Cristiani," Milano, 1951.

Feito François, "Histoire des democraties populaires," Paris, 1952.

Vilnius Conrad "La Croce all'ombra della cortina di ferro," Brescia, 1952.

Rouquette Robert, "Situation de l'Eglise derriére le rideau de fer," in "Etudes," April 1952.

"L'Opposition des Chretiens et des Communistes" in "Ecclesia," May 1952.

"Communisme et Religion" La doctrine—les methodes—les faits, in "Documentation Catholique" 1952, col. 1089-1207.

"Moscou contre Rome" in "Documentation Catholique" 1952, col. 513-572.

"Communistes et Chretiens" in "Chronique Sociale de France," 1952, pps 319-454.

Dufois Francesco "La Stella contro la Croce," Rome, 1953.

B. RUSSIA AND THE BALTIC COUNTRIES

Mac Cullagh Francis, "The Bolshevik Persecution of Christianity," London, 1924.

Harder, B. "Die Religion in Rot-Russland," Harz, 1928.

Emhardt William, "Religion in Soviet Russia Anarch," London, 1929.

D'Herbigny Michael, "Le Front anti-religieux en Russie Sovietique," Paris, 1930.

Idem, "La Guerre anti-religeuse en Russie Sovietique, Paris, 1930.

Kessler, Joseph, "Geschichte der Diozese Tyaspol," Dakota, 1930.

Wasilwewski Joan, "Arcybiskupi i Administratotowski Archdiocesi Mohylowkyij," Pinsk, 1930.

"Les Persecutions Religieuses en Russie": Documents et Faits, Geneva, 1930.

"Anti-Religious Activity in Soviet Russia," Paris, 1930.

Kranjuk S, "Funfjahr Plan und Religion," Moscow, 1931 (Communist).

Elencus cleri et ecclesiarum Archdioceseos Mohilovensis in Russia in die 5 Dec. 1931, Warsaw, 1932.

Martel, Rene, "Le Mouvement anti-religieux en U.R.S.S.," Paris, 1922.

"Le chemin du Golgotha: les confesseurs de la foi en Russie Sovietique," Geneva, 1934.

Madele, Joseph, "Orientem Sovety: Gestopis Katolickeho kneseckommunistickym SSRR," Nove Bydsove, 1936.

Anderson Paul, "People, Church and State in Modern Russia," New York, 1944.

Timosheff, N. S., "Religion of Soviet Russia" (1917-1942), New York, 1942.

Federov, "L'Eglise et le culte en U.R.S.S.," Paris, 1945 (Communist document).

Baumgartner, "La Politique Religeuse en Russia," in "Chronique Social," March-May, 1945.

Anderson, Paul, "L'Eglise et la Nation en U.R.S.S.," Calman-Levy, 1946.

Zernov, Nicolas, "The Russians and Their Church," London, 1945.

Hopko, Vasili, "Greco-Katoliceskaja Cercov v Priusen 2, Presov, 1946.

Von Eckarott Hans, "Russisches Christentum," Munich, 1947.

Paul Antoine, "Greco-Catholiques en U.R.S.S." in "Etudes," Dec. 1945.

Flak Vladymir, "The Martyrdom of the United Greek Catholic Church in occupied Poland" (in Arabic), Beirut, 1947.

"Schematismus dyxovestva Ukrainski Katolickii," Nimicien, 1947.

Briem Ephraim, "Kommunismus und Religion in der Sowjet-Union," Basle, 1948.

Amman, A. M., "Storia della Chiesa Russa," Turin, 1948.

Kosetlnik, Gavril, "Vatican a pravoslavna Cirkev," Prague, 1950 (communist).

Ziegler, Adolph, "Die Religion in der Sovietpolitique," Munich, 1951.

"Il Cristianesimo nella Unione Sovietica," Rome, "Civilta' Cattolica," 1948.

Debray, "Un Temoigne sur le Christianisme dans la cite Comuniste," in "Recontre," Lusanne, 1951.

"La Situation du Catholicisme en Russie," in "Dossier de la Semaine," Paris, May 12, 1952.

"Après la mort de Staline La situation religieuse en U.R.S.S." in "L'actualité religieuse dans le monde," Paris, April 1, 1953.

"Primi Incatenati: Libro bianco sulla persecuzione religiosa in Ucraina," Rome, 1953.

C. POLAND

"L'Eglise et l'Etat en Pologne," in "Documentation Catholique," 1946, col. 1028-1041.

"La situation de l'Eglise Catholique en Pologne," ibidem, 1950, col. 727-2735 and 807-829.

"Sguardo sulle condizioni religiose della Polonia," in "Civilta' Cattolica," December 2, 1950.

"Dopo l'accordo di Varsavia," ibidem, 1951, no. 2, Jan. 20, pp. 182-197.

"La situation religieuse en Pologne," in "La Vie Intellectuelle," Feb. 1951, pp. 143-160.

"La situation de l'Eglise en Pologne," in "Documentation Catholique," 1951, coll. 221-234 and 1195-1202.

A. P. Lentin, "Situation du Catholicisme Polonais," in "Esprit," January 1952.

Luc Retel, "La Situation de l'Eglise en Pologne," in "La Vie Intellectuelle," March 1952, pp. 4-40.

"La Chiesa Cattolica in Polonia," (un-published report), March 1952.

Stomma and Turowicz, "L'experiénce polonaise" (translated from the Polish" in "Terre Humaine," April 1952.

"L'Eglise Catholique en Pologne," in "Dossier de la Semaine," July 7, 1952.

D. ROUMANIA

Reuben H. Markham, "La Roumanie sous le joug sovietique," Paris, 1949.

Hebert Louis, "Le drame de l'Eglise unie de Roumanie," in "La Document Catholique," 1949, col. 833-891 and 923-936.

G.S.J.L. "L'Ora della prova per i cattolici di Roumania," in "Civiltá Cattolica," April 2, 1949, pp. 41-59.

"Persecution of Religion in Rumania," published by the "Roumanian National Committee, Washington, 1949.

Mojoli Giuseppe, "Perseguitata in Romania," in "Ecclesia," 1949.

"Inasprimento della persecuzione religiosa in Romania," in "La Civiltá Cattolica," March 18, 1950.

Janin Raymond, "L'Eglise Catholique en Roumanie," in "La Ducument Catholique," 1951, coll. 423-436.

"L'aneantissment de l'Eglise catholique de rite byzantin," n. 8 of the collection "Verité et documents."

Gerard Stephanescu, "Le calvaire des catholiques en Roumanie," n. 14 of the collection "Verité et Documents."

De Vries Guglielmo, "Persecuzione e vicende religiose nella Romania d'oggi," in "La Civilta' Cattolica, 5 and 19 July, 1952, pp. 20-29 and 139-145.

E. HUNGARY

"Livre Blanc" in "Collection Archives d'Histoires contemprain, Amio-Dumont, Paris, 1949.

Bela Just, "Le forc, at Mindszenty accuse," Paris, 1949.

"Svillupi della persecuzione religiosa in Ungheria e processo al Card. Mindszenty," in "La Civilta Cattolica," 1949, Feb. 19 and March 5.

"La persecution religieuse en Hongrie" in "La Document Cathol lique," 1949, collection 131-161, 209-230, 257-280, and 321-352.

Zsigmond Mihalovics, "Martire non criminale," Rome, 1949.

Gedeone Peterfly, "Il Cardinale Mindszenty," Rome, 1949.

Nicola Boer, "Il Cardinale Mindszenty," Milan, Garzanti, 1950.

Nagy Fernc, "La lotta dietro la cortina di ferro," Milan, 1950.

"L'Eglise et l'Etat en Hongrie," Budapest, 1950 (Communist).

"Recent Events in Hungary" in "Clergy Review," October 1950 (with numerous documents).

"Avec l'Eglise persecutée en Hongrie" in "La Documentation Catholique," 1951, collections 91-102 and 907-930.

Domenach, "Le Procès des éveques hongrois" in "Esprit," Sept. 1951.

Cavalli, Fiorello, "La Chiesa Cattolica nella Repubblica popolare Ungherese," September 15, 1951, pp. 585-599.

"Le persecution religieuse en Hongrie," n. 6 of the collection "Verité et Documents."

"The Case of Archbishop Grosz," in "Clergy Review," August 1951.

F. CZECHOSLOVAKIA

"La persecution religieuse en Tchècoslovaquie," in "La Documentation Catholique," 1948, coll. 991-1019 and 1949, coll. 1451-1469 and 1647-1658.

"The case of Mgr. Beran. An account of the position in Prague and a selection of documents, in "The Tablet," June 25 and July 2, 1949.

J. Cep, "La lutte religieuse en Tchèchoslovaquie," in "Esprit," September 19, 1949, pp. 661-683.

"Documenti sulla Persecuzione Religiosa in Cecoslovakia," in "La Civilta' Cattolica," 1949, July 16 and October 15.

Cep and Boulier, "Tchècoslovaquie," in "Esprit," Nov. 1949.

Craon-Poussy, "L'Eglise catholique et l'etat communiste en Tchècoslovaquie," in "Etudes," December 1949.

Cavalli Fiorello, "Governo Comunista e Chiesa Cattolica in Cecoslovacchia," Rome, 1950.

Cavalli, Fiorello, "Caratteristiche della lotta contro la Chiesa in Cecoslovacchia," in "La Civilta' Cattolica," April 15, 1950, pp. 121-136.

Vida, "Les procès des religieux de Prague," in "Esprit," July 1950.

Cep, j., "Le proces des religieux tchècoslovaques," in "Etudes," 1950, t. 265.

"La persecution religieuse en Tchècoslovaquie," in "La Documentation Catholique," 1950, pp. 369-381 and 1951, pp. 153-168.

Cavalli, F. "Svilluppi della tattica comunista contro la Chiesa Cattolica in Cecoslovakia," in "La Civilta' Cattolica," March 3, 1951.

"Cecoslovacchia: sguardo alla storia politica e religiosa d'un popolo schiavo del communismo," Rome, 1950.

Cep, J., "Le deuxieme procès des religieux de Prague," in "Esprit," March 1951.

Mannoy R., "Comment on bolschevise un pays," Belgium, 1951.

"La condition du clerge catholique tchechoslovaque," in "Etudes," January 1951.

"L'Eglise persecutée en Tchècoslovaquie," n. 7 of the collection "Verité et Documents."

Cavalli, F., "Processo contro tre vescovi slovacchi," in "La Civilta' Cattolica," June 21, 1952.

Laffoucriere, "L'Eglise et l'Etat en Tchècoslovaquie," in "Esprit," June 1952.

"Deux Prisons: Mgr. Joseph Beran," no. 12 of the Coll. "Verité et Documents."

Silvestri Fr., "l'Inferno dei Vivi," Perugia, 1953.

Stranski, J., "Vento dell'Est su Praga," Milan, 1953.

"VERITAS," Information Agency of the Christian Czechoslovak Academy, Rome 1951-52-53.

G. ALBANIA

Cavalli, F., "Persecuzione religiosa nell'Albania comunista," in "La Civilta' Cattolica," 1947, June 7 and July 19.

"FIDES" (International Agency), "Documentazione" (special issue, March 1953).

H. BULGARIA

Cavalli F., "Persecuzione Religiosa nella Repubblica Popolare Bulgaria, in "La Civilta' Cattolica" 1953, January 17, pp. 138-152.

"La loi sur les cultes in Bulgarie" (Feb. 17, 1949) in "La Documentation Catholique," 1949, coll. 1205-1209.

I. JUGOSLAVIA

Migliorati, V., "La Chiesa nella Repubblica Federativa Popolare Jugoslava" in "La Civilta' Cattolica," 1946, July 6, Sept. 7 and October 19, and June 21, 1947.

Cavalli, F., "Il processo dell'Arcivescovo di Zagabria," Rome 1947.

"La persecution religieuse en Yugoslavie et dans l'est Europeen," in "La Documentation Catholique," 1947, coll. 325-328 and 1281-1298.

Indeken, "Le procès de Zagreb" in "Nouvelle Revue Théolo-
gique," March 1947.

"Un anno di persecuzione religiosa" in "La Civiltà Cattolica,"
1950, March 4.

Cavalli, F., "Il Comunismo in Jugoslavia e' antireligiosa come a
Mosca," ibidem, June 7, 1952.